Studies in Philippine
Church History

CONTRIBUTORS

Gerald H. Anderson

J. Gayo Aragón, O.P.

H. Ellsworth Chandlee

Sister Mary Dorita Clifford, B.V.M.

Horacio de la Costa, S.J.

James S. Cummins

Richard L. Deats

Douglas J. Elwood

Peter G. Gowing

León Ma. Guerrero

Eugene A. Hessel

Cesar Adib Majul

Conrad Myrick

Stephen Neill

John Leddy Phelan

Albert J. Sanders

John N. Schumacher, S.J.

William Henry Scott

Studies in Philippine Church History

EDITED BY

GERALD H. ANDERSON

Cornell University Press

ITHACA AND LONDON

First published 1969

Standard Book Number 8014-0485-1

Library of Congress Catalog Card Number 69-18208

PRINTED IN THE UNITED STATES OF AMERICA
BY VAIL-BALLOU PRESS, INC.

Foreword

The history of Christian missions is among the youngest of the disciplines. For a long period the secular historians solved all the problems of the encounter between East and West in the field of religion by the simplest of all methods—they totally ignored it. It has often been remarked that, in the fourteen volumes of the *Cambridge Modern History* in its first form, there is only one reference to Christian missions, and that quite fortuitously in connection with the work of David Livingstone not as missionary but as explorer. To some extent this has been set right in the *New Cambridge Modern History*. Missionaries appear at various points. Yet it is hard to resist the feeling that in the minds of the distinguished authors the missionaries are there as intruders, disturbing the natural course of history, and creating a great many more difficulties than could be compensated for by any supposed value of their work.

Only in the most recent times have the allied fields of history, anthropology, and ethnology been prepared to recognize that in Africa and the South Pacific, to mention only two regions, the Christian mission has been a significantly creative force in the modern age. The missionaries foresaw, albeit dimly, what was coming about, and helped to prepare the people among whom they lived to meet and surmount the grave crises of the Western revolution.

The last few years have seen the appearance of a small number of remarkable works, in which secular historians, with no apparent religious bias, have taken the Christian mission as the starting point of their investigations. It may be hoped that these are the first indications of a change in attitude which will prepare historians to look at the facts as they are and not as predispositions of thought might wish them to be.

If missionary history has for so long been obscure, it has to be admitted that the missionaries and their friends have not been wholly exempt from blame. The published records of missions have on the whole belonged to the realm of hagiography rather than to that of historiography. It seemed wise to show to supporters of missions in the West a favorable picture of what was going on—to emphasize the lights, and to draw little attention to the shadows; the feelings of surviving relatives and friends had to be spared, and in any case the achievements of the missionaries were in many areas so heroic and remarkable as to need no elaboration. Yet the picture was one-sided. And inexcusable in these records is the fact that we are told so much about the missionaries and so little about the converts. For the seventeenth and eighteenth centuries in India we have astonishingly little from the pens of the converts themselves; the darkness in China is broken by the fortunate preservation of the diary of the Roman Catholic priest Andrew Ly, written between 1746 and 1763. This lack of information is probably irreparable; some new documents may come to light, but these are likely to be few. On the missionary side, however, there is still much to be done.

Professor Kenneth Scott Latourette's great work *A History of the Expansion of Christianity* has set the highest possible standard of objectivity and fairness. What can be achieved in one small area is made evident by the work of Professor Arno Lehmann on the archives of the Danish-Halle missionary society in the eighteenth century. In *Alte Briefe aus Indien* we can follow step by step the first tentative beginnings of Protestant missionary work in India. Ziegenbalg wrote immensely long letters; from them we know what the missionaries wore and what they ate, and how they faced the rigors of the climate, and their own inner and outer problems. Much of this is trivial; yet a living picture is built up out of the multiplicity of detail. (Who would ever have guessed, unless the researches of Father H. de la Costa, S.J., had revealed the fact, that the Jesuits in the Philippines were seriously concerned lest the consumption of that dangerously stimulating drink, chocolate, might imperil the frail virtue of the fathers!) Now that years have passed, there is no need for concealment; the story of Christian confrontation with the non-Christian world will only stand out in more splendid colors when the whole is told without extenuation and without false modesty.

The would-be historian of missions will find no perplexity through lack of materials, except, as we have indicated, in certain areas. In earlier days missionaries occupied their leisure in writing enormous letters to their friends and in preparing minutely particularized diaries, of which a great many have survived. Their comments on colleagues and converts in many cases lack nothing in their frankness and are balanced by a sometimes morbid awareness of their own frailties. Government officials, not infrequently infuriated and exasperated, have written at great length to their governments, and these documents have been impeccably preserved. We can see the missionaries also through the eyes of interested and occasionally caustic observers such as Mary Kingsley. Here there is a vast world, of which the exploration has hardly been begun. The problem is to engage the interest and the energies of those who might devote themselves to these rich but neglected fields.

No country in the world offers better possibilities for research into missionary history than the Philippines. Here alone in Asia (except for a small corner of southwest India) is there a continuous Christian history stretching over more than four centuries —and a Christian culture. Independence has brought about a new interest in ancient history and in the local languages, together with a renewal of interest in and appreciation for the less remote Spanish past. But the difference is immediately apparent when Filipino Christians meet Asian Christians from other traditions and backgrounds. Christians from the other nations of Asia are always aware of their minority status, and of the great non-Christian cultures against the background of which they have to live. The Filipinos are content to be frankly and unashamedly Christian. It is, after all, a fact that more Christians live in the Philippines than in the whole of the rest of Asia put together.

How all of this has come about is as yet imperfectly known. We have been inclined to treat the Spanish period as a monolithic unity, during which the Spanish rulers with clear purpose and undeflected aim pursued the Christianization of the archipelago. More recent research, and some of the chapters of this volume, make it plain that the period was much more variegated than had been supposed. The various orders at work were far from seeing eye to eye with one another. All at various times came into conflict with the civil power, and with fellow countrymen who were in the islands for other than Christian purposes. The bishops found themselves in a perplexing position, technically exercising supreme ecclesiastical authority, but at every turn hamstrung by the special privileges on which the orders insisted with illimitable zeal. On one point all students of the period are unhappily agreed—the failure of the Roman Catholic Church to provide an adequate Filipino ministry, and to meet the natural desire of the Filipino Christians to have more than a subordinate position in the church which increasingly was coming to be the center of their being.

Filipino nationalism goes back to a period long before the end of Spanish domination. It was not basically anti-Christian; yet the all-too-close association of the church with Spanish culture and with the Spanish regime inevitably drove the nationalists into opposition, if not to the Christian faith, at least to the church as they had it before their eyes and especially to the friars. Nationalism acquired to itself the halo of martyrdom. It is not surprising that the arrival of the Americans and the disappearance of the Spaniards were accompanied by a number of movements for independence in church as well as in state.

The birth of the Philippine Independent Church and the career of Father Aglipay are still too near to us in time, and still too much associated with the passions of the past, for a totally objective assessment to be made. But the continued existence of this church after sixty-six years, and its renaissance through closer contact with the Protestant Episcopal Church in the United States, suggest that something more than merely negative forces was here at work. The Aglipayan church may be regarded on the whole as not more than the kind of schism within the Christian church of which so many examples are already familiar in Western church history.

In the case of the *Iglesia ni Cristo*, it may be that we are face to face with a genuinely Filipino variety of the Christian faith. At the outset, this fellowship could certainly be condemned by orthodox Christians as being heretical on a number of fundamental points of Christian doctrine; but there is a tendency for heresies gradually to swing back in the direction of the orthodoxy from which they have swerved, and this may prove to be as true in this case as in a number of others that have come under observation.

The arrival of the Americans was accompanied by the proliferation of North American missions and sects—Protestant missionary work in the islands has been almost a monopoly of the North American churches. The Episcopal Church, under the guidance of its first great Canadian-American bishop, Charles Henry Brent, devoted itself to work among the Igorots and other peoples whom the three centuries of Spanish Roman Catholicism had failed to evangelize. Other groups gave themselves without restraint to work among dissatisfied or alienated Roman Catholics, frequently on less than ecumenical principles. The result has been a notable ferment, which has spread beyond the ecclesiastical into the political sphere. The Roman Catholic Church has itself been affected by the torrent of new ideas that has streamed in from the far side of the Pacific, and that church has begun to pay to Filipino national feeling an attention which was undreamed of at the beginning of this century.

Clearly there is here an almost unlimited field for the attention of the historian, the ecclesiastic, and the sociologist. The time has not yet come when the history of the church in the Philippines can be written in more than outline. The book now before us makes a contribution of more than ordinary significance to the theme. Not all the papers are of equal importance—some are devoted to comparatively minor affairs. But all are alike in this— that they manifest a true historical conscience; the writers have gone back to original, or at least to as nearly as possible contemporary, sources. They have eschewed prejudice and *parti pris*, and have tried to see things as they really were. Moreover, the book is international and interconfessional in its conception. Filipinos, Americans, and others, representatives of various churches and confessions, have worked together in the true spirit of ecumenical cooperation. Even twenty years ago the production of such a work would have been regarded as impossible. This is a most promising sign for the future. We need a vast number of such cooperative enterprises, not only in the Philippines but throughout the world. When the time comes that a full history of Christianity in the Philippines can be written, it will be recognized that this book has made its own special contribution, not only for the value of the material contained in it, but as a token and a promise of much that is yet to come.

Inevitably this book will have its strongest appeal to those who live and work in the Philippines, but it is much to be hoped that it may attract the attention of workers interested in church history in other areas. Here they have before their eyes an example of what cooperation can achieve, and of the kind of result that can be arrived at by patient work on sources and on the printed materials of the past. Only one who has attempted, as I have, to survey the whole of Christian history in the world is aware of the extent and the seriousness of the gaps in our knowledge of what has really happened. If others will follow the excellent example set by the Philippines, in thirty years' time my *History of Christian Missions* will need to be entirely rewritten—by some young historian who has been able to profit by the results of researches which I shall not live to see!

STEPHEN NEILL
Bishop

London
July 1968

Editor's Preface

The primary purpose of this volume is to provide students of Philippine church history with a convenient collection of scholarly studies dealing with various episodes, movements, events, documents, and personalities of importance during the period of more than four hundred years of Christianity in the Philippines. It is hoped that these essays will encourage and assist scholars to carry on further research and writing in this field, so that eventually a major account of the history of Christianity in the islands can be written. Hopefully, also, this work may stimulate and contribute to a greater interest and understanding among Christians in other parts of the world concerning the progress and problems of the church in the Philippines.

The ecumenical nature of this project represents a truly pioneering effort. Never before in the Philippines has a study in one of the theological disciplines enlisted such wide participation from the several Christian traditions. There are contributions here from a notable cross section of Roman Catholic, Anglican, and Protestant scholars, both lay and clergy. They do not always agree (neither do those from the same tradition!), but their writing does reflect a remarkably irenic spirit in their common desire to bring some light to bear on the dark corners of the church's history in the Philippines. In many ways the ecumenical situation here is particularly difficult, for reasons that are discussed in these essays. But the very fact that we can now study together the historical circumstances and theological significance of our situation with charity and candor is a sign that the ecumenical era has arrived—at last—and has been embraced with some seriousness by responsible representatives from many sides. This commendable fact calls for thanksgiving and firm resolve to go forward together from this modest beginning.

In the planning of this volume I was greatly assisted by the counsel and encouragement of two friends and fellow church historians in the Philippines, Father Horacio de la Costa, S.J., and Dr. Peter G. Gowing. Editorial decisions, however, were my responsibility alone. Sister Mary Dorita Clifford, B.V.M., Father John N. Schumacher, S.J., and Dr. James S. Cummins rendered special services beyond the normal call of duty, and to all the contributors I am deeply grateful for the generous spirit of cooperation expressed at every point of our work together. Dr. Theodore Friend kindly read the entire manuscript and made a number of perceptive comments and suggestions which benefited the book immensely.

We acknowledge with appreciation the permission received from the editors of *The Americas, Philippine Studies, Silliman Journal, Studia Liturgica,* and *Theological Studies* to use materials that were first published in their journals.

The abbreviation *BRPI* is used for reference to the extensive collection of sources in translation, edited by Emma Helen Blair and James Alexander Robertson, *The Philippine Islands, 1493–1898* (55 vols.; Cleveland, 1903–1909).

A final note that adds to the international and ecumenical dimensions of this work is the generous financial grant that has come from my colleagues in the Deutsche Gesellschaft für Missionswissenschaft to support the preparation of the manuscript and to assist in the distribution of the book in the Philippines.

GERALD H. ANDERSON

Union Theological Seminary
Dasmariñas, Cavite
May 1968

Contents

Part III. Protestantism and Pluralism

PART I

THE SPANISH CHURCH IN
THE PHILIPPINE SETTING

The Controversy over Justification of Spanish Rule in the Philippines

J. GAYO ARAGÓN, O.P.

In preparation for the trip to the Indies proposed by Christopher Columbus, the Catholic kings of Spain "consulted the most eminent jurists and ecclesiastics . . . concerning the most convenient manner of taking possession" of new-found territories.[1] The Portuguese had relied on a number of pontifical documents for their possessions in the Indies, but the Spaniards could only fall back on the provisions of Law 29, Title XXVIII, of Partida III, which gave legal right over any newly discovered land to whoever inhabited it first.[2] On the strength of these provisions Columbus took possession of the lands he discovered for and on behalf of the Spanish monarchs, who, he asserted, could dispose of them just as they would the realms of Castille.[3] Although at the time it was commonly accepted that the lands of infidels would belong to the Christian nation that first discovered and conquered them, this did not satisfy the Spanish desire for clear title [4] since their own legislation provided that only *uninhabited* lands could belong to the discoverer. Clearly this was not the situation in the lands discovered by Columbus. Hence Spain appealed to the Roman pontiff for some more plausible legal title.[5]

[1] Lewis Hanke, *Las Teorías Políticas de Bartolomé de las Casas* (Buenos Aires, 1935), p. 9, note 1.

[2] *Los Códigos Españoles Concordados y Anotados*, III: *Código de las Siete Partidas* (Madrid, 1848), II, 344–45.

[3] "Carta de Cristobal Colón . . . al Escribano . . . Luis de Santangel . . . 15 de febrero de 1493," in Martín Fernández de Navarrete, *Colección de Viajes* (Madrid, 1837), I, 314.

[4] E. Nys, *Les Origines du Droit International* (Brussels, 1894), p. 368.

[5] *Historia General de los Hechos de los Castellanos en las Islas y Tierra Firme del Mar Oceano* (Madrid, 1934), I, *First Decade*, Bk. II, chap. iv, p. 137.

This recourse was in keeping with the prevailing view among jurists and theologians of the time, believing that the pope was universal lord of the world, whose authority extended to the non-Christians and that he could therefore, in a given case, appropriate, transfer, and assign, quite legally, political dominion over their lands to Christian princes.[6] Spain could, therefore, legally acquire sovereignty over an inhabited territory in one of four ways, namely: (1) heredity, (2) voluntary choice of the inhabitants, (3) marriage to an heiress of the realm, or (4) pontifical or imperial grant. Obviously, in the case of the lands discovered by Columbus, provisions one and three did not apply.[7] Of the remaining alternatives, the Spanish monarchs chose to assuage their conscience by the most convenient means possible—an outright pontifical grant. Their royal request was approved with the issuance of the papal bull "Inter caetera," dated May 3–4, 1493. But what was the precise meaning and scope of the grant? Did it really entail political sovereignty or was it simply a special commission to spread the gospel?[8] This was an issue of continuing controversy that occupied the royal attention throughout the sixteenth century.

For those brought up in the English tradition, the considerable attention devoted by the Spaniards to the study of the legal grounds for their rule over the New World might seem excessive, even extraordinary. For Spaniards, however, the legal justification of their king's authority over the Indies remained a burning issue, as indicated, virtually throughout the sixteenth century. This is all the more striking in view of the mood of the times, when blind obedience was accorded absolute rulers, and excessive homage was paid to the so-called superiority of certain races over others. In spite of this, it was the eminently theological culture of Spain, where the principles of Catholicism were an ingredient of everyday life, that caused the king to seek to justify before his people and to his own self the dominion he held over the newly found territories.

[6] Pedro Leturia, S.J., *Las Grandes Bulas Misionales de Alejandro VI, 1493*, in *Bibliotheca Hispana Missionum* (Barcelona, 1930), p. 213.

[7] Partida II, Tit. I, Law 9, in *Los Códigos Españoles, op. cit.*, p. 328.

[8] Juan de Solórzano, *Política Indiana* (Antwerp, 1703), Bk. I, chap. ii, p. 26.

This bizarre attitude of the Spaniards could not have been initiated had there not existed an ample, if regulated, freedom of expression, both oral and written, encouraged by the kings themselves. This explains, for instance, why the Dominican las Casas, for all his open denunciations, was never prosecuted or imprisoned as a traitor to the king.[9]

In this national controversy the views of the Dominican Francisco de Vitoria loom impressive and commanding. The best efforts of the king's counselors, who opposed Vitoria, proved to no avail. The king himself saw the justice of the Vitorian opinion and gave it royal sanction. The pope, said the learned professor of Salamanca, is not the temporal sovereign of the world; hence, he enjoys no authority over the non-Christian peoples and territories, for which reason, whatever the construction to be given to his bull "Inter caetera," it could not entail any grant of political dominion over said discovered lands. This view soon brought forth zealous defenders as well as bitter opponents. But with the years, it gained ground through the sustained efforts of Vitoria's brothers in habit, notably the Dominican Bartolomé de las Casas, bishop of Chiapa. The impact was such that the Spanish emperor, Charles V, was of a mind to forsake the occupied territories of the New World.[10] But Vitoria himself dissuaded the monarch, lest Christianity be lost from among the native converts; for which reason, the emperor pledged to leave these peoples to themselves as soon as they were able to keep themselves within the Catholic religion.[11]

At that stage, therefore, the only legitimate title to justifying Spain's rule in the New World territories would have been that flowing from the consent of the natives deliberately and freely given.[12] Upon royal instructions, attempts to obtain such consent

[9] Lewis Hanke, *Bartolomé de las Casas* (Havana, 1949), p. 48.

[10] *Colección de Libros* . . . *referentes a la Historia del Perú*, IV, 95 ff.; vid., R. Levillier, *D. Francisco de Toledo*, I.

[11] See also: Rubén Vargas Ugarte, S.J., "Fray Francisco de Vitoria," *Boletín del Instituto de Investigaciones Históricas* (Buenos Aires, 1930), no. 45, p. 30, note; and Alfonso García Gallo, "Un antecedente de la Doctrina Española de la Guerra," in *Anuario de Historia del Derecho Español*, II, 15.

[12] *Documentos Inéditos del Siglo XVI para la Historia de México* (México, 1914), p. 176.

were made by the Dominicans in Vera-Paz, Yucatan, and other parts of New Spain.[13] The results were encouraging and fruitful.

The same concerns were to be extended to the Philippines, as seen in the instructions given the *adelantado* Miguel López de Legazpi.[14] That is why as early as 1599 Governor Francisco Tello de Guzmán of the Philippines could write to His Majesty: "When these islands were conquered and subjected, they were placed in obedience to your Majesty with just as many requirements as the other parts of the Indies." [15] Perhaps facts such as these have moved some writers to suggest that, unlike in the Americas, there was in the Philippines during the Spanish rule no need to reiterate the laws protecting the natives, for want of any dispute between the factions that might have been involved, and because there was scarcely a trace of organized opposition on the part of the clergy.[16]

This, however, was not the case. The moment they were in a position to do so, the Augustinian friars, led by Father Andrés de Urdaneta, voiced their opposition to Spanish dominion over the Philippines. They did not even want Legazpi's expedition to sail for the Philippines. Father Urdaneta had already persuaded Velasco, the viceroy of Mexico, and had written to Philip II, that Spain could not legitimately attempt the conquest of the Philippines, if only because the islands were within the zone granted by Charles V to the crown of Portugal.[17] The other Augustinians who had joined the Legazpi expedition—already on the high seas when finally told of their destination, which was not to be the Moluccas as proposed by Father Urdaneta—sided with him in condemning what seemed to them an underhanded ruse. For this reason, when they reached the Philippines, they deliberately re-

[13] Alonso de Zorita, *Historia de la Nueva España* (Madrid, 1909), p. 278.

[14] See "Instructions to Legazpi; Mexico, September 1, 1564," Emma Helen Blair and James Alexander Robertson, eds., *The Philippine Islands, 1493–1898* (55 vols.; Cleveland, 1903–1909), II, 89–99 (hereinafter cited as *BRPI*).

[15] Gov. Francisco Tello de Guzmán, "Letter to the King; Manila, July 12, 1599," *BRPI*, X, 253–55.

[16] Albert Keller, *Colonization* (New York, 1908).

[17] Fr. Andrés de Urdaneta, O.S.A., "Letter to Philip II, May 28, 1560," cited by Fr. Fermín Urcilla, *Urdaneta y la Conquista de Filipinas* (San Sebastián, 1907), p. 188, note 1.

frained from commenting in any way (and Legazpi expressly sought their opinion) on whether or not it seemed right to settle on any of the islands visited.[18] The Augustinians next proceeded to write a series of reports to the king, underlining the unfavorable aspect of events in the Philippines, urging that they be remedied without delay. Upon Legazpi's death on August 20, 1572, and the transfer of command of the islands to Governor Guido de Lavezaris, the accusations made by the religious turned more strident and vitriolic. Moreover, they agreed to send Father Diego de Herrera to discuss with the Spanish monarch the evils and abusive practices in the Philippines. Alarmed by this decision, the government authorities asked the religious to submit a formal account of their opinion on the matter. This was done by the Augustinian provincial, Father Martín de Rada, who took the precaution of sending a copy of his report to the viceroy of Mexico.[19]

Concerning the right of conquest of the Philippines, Father Rada categorically stated, "I have taken the opinion of all the Fathers who were to be found here. They unanimously affirm that none among all these islands have come into the power of the Spaniards with just title." [20]

The opinion of the religious can be outlined in this syllogism: The islands now under Spanish rule are in this state solely by reason of war. This war, from whichever angle it may be considered, was unjust. Therefore, the islands were unjustly conquered.

The major premise can be accepted as being historically correct, in large measure. Thus, on May 28, 1595, royal officials wrote to His Majesty: "From the day we arrived to this moment we have found no ally within this archipelago . . . in no part would they receive us as friends or credit anything that we wished to discuss with them." [21] Of course, proper allowances must be made for such a sweeping statement, considering for in-

[18] Urcilla, *op. cit.*, p. 195, note 1, and p. 222, note 1.

[19] "Augustinian Memoranda," *BRPI*, XXXIV, 273.

[20] "Opinion of Fray Martín de Rada on Tribute from the Indians, June 21, 1574," *BRPI*, III, 254.

[21] Pedro Torres y Lanzas, *Catálogo de los Documentos relativos a las Islas Filipinas existentes en el Archivo de Indias de Sevilla* (Barcelona, 1926–1936), I, cclxxxiii.

stance Humabon's friendly dealings with Magellan in Cebu, which had been preceded by equally amicable relations between Magellan and the natives of Homonhon, Butuan, and Limasawa, particularly Rajahs Kolambu and Siagu,[22] as well as Legazpi's friendship with Leyte's ruler, Malitic, Bohol's Sikatuna, and Dapitan's Pagbuaya, let alone Cebu's Tupas, and later the Manila and Tondo rulers, Matanda and Lakandula and Soliman.[23]

In regard to the minor premise, the conditions for a just war must be considered. These, as defined by Saint Thomas Aquinas, are legal authority, just cause, and right intention. The absence of any one of these would render the war unjust.

Father Rada asserted that no governor or captain could validly engage in war without an express authorization from the king. He added that in none of his dispatches had the Spanish sovereign authorized any declaration of war against the natives. On the contrary, in a letter from El Escorial, the king had expressly declared that any attempt to conquer these islands by force would be unjust, even though there be cause for it.[24] To what degree was Father Rada accurate in his interpretation? In a letter to Legazpi the king had written, "You shall so carry yourself that you may not come to blows with them nor with any other persons unless you should be provoked, and in your own defense." [25] The king, therefore, had not ruled out a war of self-defense, nor could he have done so justly, for such was any man's natural right, whether subject or prince.

The mind of Philip II on this matter is best understood by reading the pertinent injunctions given Miguel López de Legazpi to the effect that once the Spaniards had chosen the most suitable place for their settlement, far from anywhere already occupied by

[22] Antonio Pigafetta, *Primer Viaje Alrededor del Mundo*, trans. by Carlos Amoretti, annotated by Manuel Walls y Merino (Madrid, 1899), pp. 27 ff.; also *Primer Viaje en Torno del Globo*, Austral edition (Mexico, 1954), Bk. II, pp. 61–62, 65–66 ff.

[23] José Montero Vidal, *Historia General de Filipinas* (Madrid, 1897), chap. iii, pp. 31–32; Francisco Combés, S.J., *Historia de Mindanao y Joló* (Madrid, 1667), Retana-Pastells, ed. (Madrid, 1897), I, Bks. I and II, chap. i, col. 78, note 35; col. 662; also chap. ii, cols. 85–87; and chap. x, cols. 34–36. Francisco Colín, S.J., *Labor evangélica*, Pablo Pastells, ed. (2nd ed., 3 vols.; Barcelona, 1900–1902), I, Bk. I, chap. xxii, p. 154.

[24] *BRPI*, III, 254.   [25] *BRPI*, XXXIV, 235.

the natives, they should endeavor to secure their friendship by peaceful means, encourage them to live in communities, defend them against their enemies, teach them a civilized way of life, and convert them to the Catholic faith and the Christian religion.[26] And he added that should the natives continue to resist all attempts by the Spaniards to settle amongst them, it should be pointed out to them three times by a duly authorized representative that the Spaniards intend neither to harm them nor to deprive them of their lands, but only to befriend them and teach them the ways of civilization, bringing them the knowledge of God and the law of Christ by whom they have been redeemed like all other men. If the natives still remained adamant, then the Spaniards could settle, regardless, causing them no harm beyond that necessary in defense of self and settlement. Once this was done, the religious should try to communicate with the natives, to win their friendship and make them understand the Spanish intentions. If there were further opposition to the preaching of the "Word," then a report on the matter, duly documented and endorsed, should be submitted for the royal council to determine appropriate subsequent action.

The question arises, Did the *conquistadores* carry out the instructions from their king? If they did, then any war they might have undertaken would have been supported with valid authorization and just cause. But the religious held that on no occasion were the royal instructions followed. On the contrary, everywhere it was demanded of the natives that they should submit to the Spaniards and pay tribute if they wished to avoid war. No mention was made either of God or of the good purposes of the king. The religious added that many a pretext had been fabricated to seek to justify the subjection of the natives through violence.

In summarizing the views of his confreres, Father Rada alleged, "All the more unjust are these conquests since in none, or almost none, of them has there been any cause." [27]

In September 1581, Msgr. Domingo de Salazar, O.P., the first bishop of the islands, arrived in Manila.[28] It was during his time

---

[26] *Ibid.*, pp. 252–53.   [27] *BRPI*, III, 254.
[28] José de Alcázar, *Historia de los Dominios Españoles en Oceanía: Filipinas* (Madrid, 1897), pp. 64–65.

and on his initiative that an assembly of sorts was convened in 1582, on the lines of a council, "to deal with matters concerning the furthering of the Faith and the justification of past and future conquests by Spain." [29]

In the records of the proceedings of this "Synod," one chapter is devoted to the legal right of Castille over the territory of the Philippines. It begins with the statement that the kings of Castille "do not possess the Philippines by right of inheritance or through a just war." Having dismissed these grounds pertaining to natural law, how did the fathers of the council face the problem from the supernatural angle? They did so through a series of simple syllogisms, such as: "The captains, soldiers, governors and justices have no more right over these lands than that granted them by their king. And the king gave them no more than he, in turn might derive from Christ, which is the power to send those who would preach the gospel throughout the world, not to deprive anyone of what is his." The obvious conclusion was that the sole right enjoyed by these officials was that of preaching the gospel and not dispossessing any man of what was his.

This right, the council believed, entailed that of assigning soldiers to protect the preachers and those recently converted and, in those lands, to undertake whatever might be necessary for the temporal government with a view to this spiritual end. This calls to mind the three legitimate rights upheld by Father Vitoria: freedom to preach the gospel, the right of the new converts to adequate protection, and the right of the pope to depose pagan rulers when necessary for the preservation of the Catholic faith. The religious insisted, however, that the right to preach the gospel did not include that of political and military conquest of the lands being evangelized, since the gospel deprived no one of whatever was his by natural right, nor had the pope or king any right to so dispossess him.

---

[29] *Suma de una Junta que se hizo a manera de Concilio el año de 1582, para dar asiento a las cosas tocantes al aumento de la fe y justificación de las conquistas hechas y que en adelante se hicieren por los españoles,* Bk. I, chap. i; Dominican Archives, Manila, MSS. Vol. CCLXXXII, fols. 123–75, and Vol. LXX, pp. 130–86. Also Archives, University of Santo Tomás, Manila, B. nos. 14 and 15. All quotations of the Synod are taken from this source; translation, ours.

Applying this formula to the case of the Philippines, the fathers of the council came to the conclusion that "if the gospel were preached in places so well governed that there be no question of depriving the natives of their self-rule in order to establish the faith; if the people were so disposed and able to accept the demands of an intrinsically spiritual order; and finally, if the preaching of the gospel were in no way hindered, then they may not be deprived of their lands or of the right to rule themselves." After lengthy deliberation, the fathers of the council finished by advancing this hybrid definition of justification, which combined the right to evangelize and the unsophisticated condition of the natives. This position is not hard to understand because the council fathers had to assuage the troubled conscience of the missionaries. As the religious alleged, in the Philippines there was no real opposition to evangelization, for the known cases of hostility had arisen from the failure of the Spaniards to inform the natives of the real intentions of the king. Hence, the need to resort to a sufficiently all-embracing definition, provisional in character, to ratify the *fait accompli.*

Consequently, native rulers retained their authority, once they had fulfilled the conditions mentioned above. But did that mean that the king of Spain had acquired no right over them? The view of the religious was that the king held certain "quasi-imperial authority" over the natives by reason of the "higher spiritual goal which he had brought to them." Through baptism the natives became subjects of another, independent and sovereign, state, spiritual in character, and consequently came under the authority of the ruler of that state, namely, the pope, without ceasing to be subject to their own native rulers. In certain respects the pope had delegated to kings his spiritual powers over Christians in lands entrusted to the latter by the pontiff himself. By virtue of this delegation, kings could and ought to promulgate the laws necessary for the protection and exercise of the rights of their subjects as Christians. It was the duty of the native rulers to promote and support these laws, in this sense considering themselves subjects of the kings of Spain.

In the Philippines these conditions did not obtain in fact, for nowhere could natives be found who might be entrusted with the political authority that would adequately see to the interests of the faith and of the recent converts. For this reason the King of Spain could be said to have not only that "quasi-imperial authority," but also the right to political governance of the Philippines. Nevertheless, the fathers of the council decreed that "the Viceroy or Governor is in conscience bound to appoint native judges and governors in places that are already peaceably settled. It is equally binding upon the King to see that this is accomplished."

In conclusion, the fathers of the council were of the opinion that no valid claim could be laid to the conquest of the Philippines other than that based on the right to preach the gospel, with the qualifying clauses mentioned above. But for this right to justify possession of territories, it was unnecessary to depend on any direct opposition of the natives to the preaching of the gospel, since the inferior or primitive organization of their government and of their laws as would hinder or thwart their conversion was, in itself, sufficient reason.

This theory of the Council of 1582 was unanimously accepted by the religious of the Philippines, including Bishop Salazar, whose doubts concerning the validity of the Spanish conquests had been dispelled "after consulting learned and God-fearing persons." For this reason the council elected Father Alonso Sánchez, S.J., to expound personally before Philip II the matter of the justification of the conquest of those regions of the islands where peace had not yet been established. This was needed, because, as Bishop Salazar had written, Philip II "was so Catholic and Christian a prince that [he] would undertake nothing unless first convinced of its just and legal execution." [30]

Notwithstanding the generous reception given by the king to the petitions of the council, other problems continued to arise, principally that concerning the collection of tribute. This only served to quicken the doubts of Bishop Salazar, who felt the need for colleagues of similar convictions to support him in his struggle to introduce a state of political life based on solid principles. He found them in the Dominicans who arrived in Manila in 1587.[31]

[30] Msgr. Domingo de Salazar, O.P., "Letter to Philip II, June 18, 1583," in Colín, op. cit., I, 312.
[31] Alcázar, op. cit., p. 81; Colín, op. cit., I, Bk. I, chap. viii, p. 357, note.

They did indeed influence him, but rather in the sense of bringing him back to the Dominican tradition that was unwavering on questions of this nature.

The problem of collecting tribute raised once more the question of the authority of the Spanish king over the natives of the Philippines. This was inevitable, since the solution to the first depended upon that given to the latter.

On this point the opinion of the Jesuits can be summarized thus. The right of the Spanish sovereigns to rule the new territories was based, in the first place, on the natural right to help the needy and protect the innocent. Upon this basis Pope Alexander VI made the King of Spain supreme ruler of these people to advance the spread of the gospel. But what authority did the pope have over pagan lands as far as safeguarding evangelization was concerned? Directly, of course, he had none, but indirectly he could intervene in the affairs of pagan nations when necessary for the exercise of the right to defend the innocent and to preach the gospel. The same indirect authority rested with the king and, by papal concession, was restricted solely to him to avoid friction and confusion in the new lands. Both the pope and the King of Spain could exercise this indirect authority in three cases, namely, should the preaching of the gospel be hindered by these peoples; when there was a probability that the maintenance of Christianity in their lands could not be entrusted to them; and when, in the opinion of learned and virtuous persons, the preaching of the gospel could not be carried out in safety but on the contrary, there was danger that it cease altogether. Consequently, the king might acquire no authority over these peoples without first ascertaining the existence of these conditions. Moreover, once the natives had been converted, the king would acquire added justification to continue his rule over them based on the natural right to be protected in their new faith.[32]

The Augustinians saw in the pontifical grant the justification for Spanish rule over the Philippines. By divine and evangelical law the supreme pontiffs had been entrusted with the proclamation and spread of the gospel throughout the world. Since they were unable to do this personally everywhere, much less in remote

[32] Colín, *op. cit.*, I, 593–98.

places, who could doubt that they might or even ought to entrust this care and task to one who was able to attend to it with less hindrance and greater means. Inasmuch as the discovery of the East and West Indies had been achieved through the intervention and at the expense of Spain and her sovereign, the popes, particularly Alexander VI, had good cause to delegate to the King of Spain the evangelization and conversion of the Indies, and the governance and protection of those converted.[33]

The Franciscans, for their part, were concise in their opinion. They simply assumed the validity of the king's authority over these islands, based on his mission of having the gospel preached, entrusted to him by the popes, so that the king's sovereignty over these islands rested on the spiritual well-being that he dispensed to the people.[34]

The opinion of Bishop Salazar, on the other hand, may be gathered from his brief "Resolution," [35] as well as from his tract on the collection of tribute from the pagans in the Philippines.[36] The Dominican prelate began by distinguishing between two orders or kinds of rule, political or temporal, and spiritual or supernatural. The former, he believed, proceeds from God through the choice made by the subjects and is destined to keep them in peace and justice while the latter, which derives from Christ and was delegated to Saint Peter and his successors, the bishops of Rome, is ordained to the teaching of the true and salutary doctrine that would lead men to eternal salvation.

Only in one of these two ways, he continued, could the King of Spain rule these lands: the political or temporal authority of the king might have originated either when the Spaniards first reached the Philippines, or after they had settled there. In either case, to be valid, he said, it must be founded either on popular

[33] *Parecer de los Padres Agustinos,* Archivo General de Indias (Seville); Expediente: Filipinas, no. 74, 68–I–32.

[34] *Opiniones de las Distintas Religiones de Filipinas acerca de los Tributos* (Manila, February 15 and 23, 1591), Archivo General de Indias (Seville), Sección V, Audiencia de Filipinas, Legajo 74, Ramo 2, cat. 3767.

[35] Msgr. Domingo de Salazar, O.P., *Resolución Breve del Obpo. de las Islas Filipinas* (Manila, January 18, 1591), Archivo General de Indias (Seville), Sección V, Audiencia de Filipinas, Legajo 74, Ramo 2, cat. 3751.

[36] Cf. Lewis Hanke, *Cuerpo de Documentos del Siglo XVI* (Mexico, 1943), pp. 118 ff.

choice or upon a just war. But, in the case of popular choice, the following conditions had to be fulfilled: first, that all the natives, or at least a majority, should have chosen the King of Spain for their ruler—thus becoming his subjects. If originally they had their own rulers, these too should have expressed their consent to the decision. A choice made either by the natives or by their rulers alone would not have sufficed; it had to be a joint action. Moreover, this decision must have been made freely, without the intervention of fear, force, pain, or ignorance. Failure in any one of these conditions would invalidate the king's rule.

Bishop Salazar then broached the existential phase of the question, alleging that all available information failed to show any such deliberate and free choice ever having been made by the Philippine natives and their rulers in favor of the King of Spain and his rule. He went on to say that neither did the Spaniards acquire legal dominion by reason of a just war since two of the essential conditions were lacking: authorization from the king to carry out the war and, secondly, an offense committed by the natives.

Touching on another aspect of the problem, Salazar stated that the Spanish kings could be considered the legal rulers of the Indies by virtue of the concession granted to them by Pope Alexander VI, but this went no further than the right to lead men to their eternal goal through the preaching of the gospel and related activities. Indeed, he maintained, the pope is not the temporal or civil ruler of the world, for Christ had no such dominion nor did He transmit it to the pope, whose rule over the world is therefore of a spiritual nature alone.

Bishop Salazar next dealt with the jurisdiction of the church over pagans. He brought forth the same distinctions established by the Dominican theologian Cayetano. There are those, he said, who are de facto and de jure subject to the church, namely: (1) those residing in the papal estates; the pope may rule them, except in matters relating purely to divine positive law or ecclesiastical law; (2) those who are legally but not de facto subject to the church, such as the pagans living in lands unjustly withheld by them against their lawful Christian rulers; in this case, the latter may validly declare war on such pagans as unjust aggressors; (3)

lastly, those not subject either *de facto* or *de jure* to the church. Those in the third group, he argued, are not hostile to Christians nor do they occupy lands once belonging to the church or to Christian princes; they are the owners and the lawful rulers of their territories, just as the Spaniards are of theirs. The church has authority over them, he said, only to the extent that, through the preaching of the gospel, she attempts to bring them to knowledge of the truth; thus, unless they hinder the preaching of the gospel or are totally opposed to it, or their attitude toward Christians proves destructive and malicious, neither the church nor the Christian princes have any cause for a just war against them. The pagans of the Philippines were to be classified in this third category.

For his part, Father Miguel de Benavides, O.P., later third Archbishop of Manila, also discussed these points, basically agreeing with the views of Bishop Salazar.[37] Commenting in greater detail on the authority of the King of Spain over the natives of the Philippines, he maintained that the Spanish monarch could not deprive the native rulers converted to Christianity of their rule and dominion over their own people, but instead should keep them in their position, just as their followers should remain their subjects. This did not conflict with the supreme quasi-imperial authority of the Spanish king emanating from the papal grant over the Christian native rulers in regard to the defense and promotion of the Catholic faith.

In this vein, Benavides continued, the King of Spain may, by virtue of such authority, release Christian natives from their subjection and allegiance to pagan rulers. Father Benavides, however, true to the orthodox doctrine on the matter, warned against universal and indiscriminate exercise of this right. Rather, following Saint Thomas, he insisted that each case should be carefully studied and weighed, because, he said, the right of the native rulers over their people is obvious in the light of natural law, while the right to overthrow them is not always seen clearly

37 See: J. Gayo Aragón, "Introducción al 'Tratado Segundo de la Predicación evangélica y de el modo de Predicar el Santo Evangelio' del P. Miguel de Benavides, O.P.," *Unitas* (Manila), XXII, 3 (1949), 601–49; XXIII, 1 (1950), 167–95.

under the existing facts; the native rulers are, therefore, to be given the benefit of the doubt, since valid authority is presumed to be in their favor. Father Benavides claimed, however, that this was not the problem in the Philippines where conversion to the faith had always started with the native rulers.

Finally, Benavides categorically denied that the King of Spain had any authority over the pagan natives. His reasoning was concise and convincing: the pope has authority over his own subjects, i.e., Christians; the only way to belong to the society ruled by the supreme pontiff is through baptism; since pagans are still unbaptized they remain beyond the power of the pope—in this respect the King of Spain had no authority other than that granted him by the pope, and, consequently, providing pagans with preachers of the gospel did not give the king any right to rule over them. It is true, Benavides maintained, that all men are in duty bound to profess the religion of Christ and to acknowledge His Vicar, the pope, as the universal sovereign in matters spiritual, but it is also true that no man may be forced to receive the faith and to recognize Christ either by law or through social pressure. Thus, he argued, neither may they be forced to accept the pope as Christ's vicar nor the King of Spain as vicar delegate.

The King of Spain, on the other hand, could not have acquired the Philippines as the result of a just war, said Benavides, since the natives here, in their own lands which had at no time belonged to any Christian prince, had not hindered or prevented the preaching of the gospel. No just cause for war had existed. Nor had the natives' free submission to the king's rule been duly sought.

For Salazar and Benavides the King of Spain had yet to become the political sovereign of the Philippines; his only authority was as an instrument of the spiritual power of the pope, directly so over the Christians and indirectly over the pagans. While Salazar merely rejected the legitimacy of the Spanish dominion over the Philippines, Father Benavides suggested a means of vindicating it. He proposed that the king should send religious and secular clergy to convert the natives in justice and charity, while leaving them to rule themselves. In this way the natives were likely to choose freely to become subjects of the King of

Spain even before becoming Christians. The natives should be attracted to the Spaniards through friendship, so that they might eventually decide, of their own volition, to accept the rule of the Spanish monarch.

From what has been said, it is clear that there was a divergence of opinion among the religious in the Philippines on the temporal or political authority of the Spanish king over the islands. The Augustinians and Jesuits maintained the legitimacy of this dominion, based on the papal concession and the opposition of the natives to the preaching of the gospel. The Dominicans, led by Bishop Salazar, rejected this legitimacy as insufficiently established according to law.

This matter was at length taken up by the royal council of the Indies. Governor Gómez Pérez Dasmariñas sent to this council all the relevant documents supporting the royal claim, and also Father Francisco Ortega, whom he instructed to oppose the view advanced by the Bishop of Manila.[38] Bishop Salazar, then aged 78, also left for Spain to defend in person his opinion before Philip II, taking with him Father Miguel de Benavides.[39]

After lengthy discussions, Philip II issued a decree on June 11, 1594, addressed to the governor-general of the Philippines. All the decisions in it were completely contrary to Bishop Salazar's views concerning the collection of tribute, although—thanks to the efforts of Father Benavides—it was declared that the natives who were rulers before their conversion to the Catholic faith should remain so after their conversion.

Bishop Salazar died on December 14, 1594, at the age of 82. Father Benavides then took the matter into his own hands, determined that the royal decisions should be reversed. He prepared a new study of the whole affair and submitted his views in writing to Philip II, who hastened to convene the Council of the Indies, instructing its members to hold sessions without respite so that a decision might be reached before Benavides left the country. On October 17, 1596, the council signed a declaration, later endorsed

[38] Gov. Gómez Pérez Dasmariñas, "Letter to the King; Manila, October 18, 1591," in Colín, *op. cit.,* I, Bk. II, chap. xxiii, no. vii, p. 180, note.

[39] Antonio de Morga, *Sucesos de las Islas Filipinas,* annotated by José Rizal (Paris, 1890), chap. v, pp. 36–37.

by the king, favorable to the stand of Father Benavides. On February 8, 1597, Philip II issued a decree ordering the governor-general of the Philippines to call together the authorities of the islands to determine ways and means, first, to restore tribute unjustly collected from pagan natives, over whom the king had no legal power, and, second, to obtain, without coercion, ratification of the natives' submission to the Spanish sovereign who, in his own words, had been convinced by Father Benavides that he should cherish submission of his subjects only when voluntarily given.[40]

In 1598, Benavides (by then, bishop-elect of Nueva Segovia) returned to Manila, bringing along with him this unprecedented cedula. In pursuance thereof, on August 4 of the same year, the governor-general convened the council proposed by the king. All the authorities present at the meeting pledged to comply with the royal wish. The next day, the cedula was publicly proclaimed by Francisco Pos, Manila official town crier, before a huge crowd.[41]

Soon thereafter, in the various dioceses of the country, public meetings were held at the town square, with the native residents, led by their chieftains, attending. Once the cedula terms were made known to them in their own dialects, they were asked whether they freely chose to submit to the sovereignty of the King of Spain over them. The results were overwhelmingly favorable, even if in some instances reservations and conditions were attached. On July 12, 1599, Governor Tello de Guzmán could already inform His Majesty, among other things, "that measures have been taken for the execution of the royal decree brought by the Bishop of Nueva Segovia in regard to rendering submission. . . . In the province of Ilocos, in the diocese of the Bishop of Nueva Segovia, this was very well done; and submission was rendered to Your Majesty. Likewise the whole district of Manila, missionary territory of the Augustinian Fathers, has rendered submission. La Laguna, in the care of the Franciscan Fathers, has not so readily yielded, for the natives there have asked for a year in which to reply. . . . Something similar has happened in other

[40] Colín, op. cit., I, Bk. I, chap. xxiii, no. IX, p. 209, note; Francisco Foradada, S.J., La Soberanía de España en Filipinas (Barcelona, 1897), p. 73. A copy of this decree (cedula) is found in Unitas (Manila), XXI, 1 (1948), 157–59; and XXII, 3 (1949), 608–609.

[41] Colín, op. cit.

provinces." [42] Again, in some sectors of Pangasinan, it was agreed that the natives would accept Spanish rule with the understanding that they receive due redress for the abuses committed by the *alcaldes mayores* and *encomenderos* and that the tribute hitherto unlawfully collected from them be returned.[43]

In due time, it can be surmised, nearly all the other regions and provinces of the Philippines gave their free consent to the supreme authority over them of the King of Spain. This can be gathered from the invariable conduct observed by the Spanish government in its rule over the islands. An example is the submission freely given by the natives of the Batanes Islands on June 1, 1782, upon being publicly convened and, through the interpreters, Pedro Paturayan and Marcos Ruiz, told of the message of Governor-General José Basco issued in Manila on February 15 of the same year.[44] There is also the free consent given in 1845 by the different chieftains of Basilan Island in Mindanao, who were contacted by the governor of Zamboanga upon instructions to that effect given him by the then Governor-General Narciso de Clavería. It is noteworthy that, in a later communication to the central government in Spain, Governor Clavería corrected the earlier erroneous information that Dato Usuk and the people of the Maluso region, in the said island had given their consent. Governor Clavería made it clear that such had not been the case, so the government was to refrain from exercising any sovereignty over them.[45] Such was the scrupulousness with which this matter of free consent was regarded by Spain. Even as late as 1881 the same criterion would be followed by the Spanish government. Thus, desirous of incorporating the northern Luzon provinces into the territories under the rule of Spain, Governor-General Primo de Rivera, on January 14, 1881, issued a decree appealing to all the Filipino Igorots to accept the rule of the Spaniards,

[42] Gov. Francisco Tello de Guzmán, "Letter to the King; Manila, July 12, 1599," *BRPI*, X, 253–55; also X, 287.

[43] Original Document, Archivo General de Indias (Seville); Filipinas, 76; 68–I–34. Also Dominican Archives, Manila, MSS. Vol. LXX.

[44] Archives of the Vicariate of Basco, MSS. Vol. I, pp. 29–30.

[45] Gov. Narciso de Clavería, "Letter No. 11; Manila, January 9, 1845," Filipinas (1844–1845), Archives, Foreign Affairs Ministry (Madrid), Legajo 2957.

under pain of being forcibly subdued should they fail to do so within a given time period. Although quite a number of them heeded the call, many more refused to do so, whereupon a punitive expedition was sent against them. The government troops were successful, and the governor-general elatedly informed the home government. But, in reply, Governor-General Primo de Rivera was ordered from Madrid to stop immediately all such expeditions, for they were deemed "in violation of the existing laws that did not allow ill-treatment of the Filipinos nor their forcible submission to Spanish sovereignty." The governor-general faithfully complied with the instructions, and it was left to the missionaries to achieve the government's purposes through persuasion and conversion.[46]

Irrespective of whether such procedure was followed by the Spanish authorities in every instance and in all parts of the Philippines, the overall general picture is undeniably favorable. Certainly it is not true, as some have suggested, that Spain's legal title over the Philippines was based on the so-called right of discovery and conquest of these islands by the Spanish *conquistadores*. Those were the very grounds put to question by the Spaniards themselves, for "discovery" as a legal title could only apply to uninhabited territories, which was not the case with the Philippines, and "conquest" is but a euphemism for the sanctioning of *might* as *right*, contrary to the very ethos of Spain.

In light of all this, it is therefore truly amazing that a king, on whose empire the sun never set, should have evinced such an unswerving determination to seek the free acceptance of his dominion over a people whom he had ruled as subjects for more than thirty years. This, in large measure, was no doubt due to the alert and lively passion for justice and fairness of those early missionaries—men for whom the rights of God and of God's children were more deeply embedded in their hearts and minds than the awe-inspiring majesty of crown and throne.

[46] Gov. Fernando Primo de Rivera, "Memoria; Madrid, March 1, 1883," Archivo Histórico Nacional (Madrid), Legajo 5351, Ultramar-Gobierno-Filipinas, folios 129 31; Overseas Minister, "Letter to Governor-General Primo de Rivera; Madrid, April 20, 1881," Archivo Histórico Nacional (Madrid), Legajo 5246.

Prebaptismal Instruction and the Administration of Baptism in the Philippines during the Sixteenth Century[*]

JOHN LEDDY PHELAN

Magellan's abortive attempts to introduce baptism among the natives of the island of Cebu during the month of April 1521 and the more successful efforts of the Spanish missionaries to preach the gospel following the arrival of the Legazpi-Urdaneta expedition at Cebu on February 13, 1565, occurred during the initial and the culminating chapters respectively of the "spiritual conquest" of those native peoples of America and the Far East who were to enter the orbit of Spanish culture. During April of 1521, as Magellan was transforming himself into a lay missionary, Hernán Cortés was making the final preparations for the siege of Tenochtitlán. Its successful issue on August 13, 1521, laid the foundation not only of the Spanish empire in the New World, but also provided the Spaniards with the base of operations from which eventually they could extend their power to the Philippines. It was Cortés' conquest of the Aztec confederation in 1521 which enabled the Catholic missionaries of Spain to undertake one of the most extensive expansions in the history of the Christian church.[1] In 1565 the Spanish church for its Philippine enterprise was able to draw upon a vast storehouse of missionary experience acquired in both North and South America. Magellan's apostolic labors, ill-starred and brief though they were, exemplify many of

[*] This essay appeared originally in *The Americas* (Washington, D.C.), XII, 1 (July, 1955), 3–23.

[1] For a stimulating evaluation of the Spanish-Portuguese missionary achievement overseas see Kenneth Scott Latourette, *A History of the Expansion of Christianity* (7 vols.; New York and London, 1937–1945), III, 2–10.

the permanent features of the Spanish missionary enterprise. The Magellan episode also illustrates how his successors after 1565 did in fact profit from the circumnavigator's errors of judgment and tactics.

Magellan as Missionary

The principal purpose of Magellan's voyage was commercial. To find a sea route to the Spice Islands was the aim that inspired both Magellan and those who supported his project at the court of Emperor Charles V. It was not until his arrival in Cebu that the religious sentiments of Magellan's nature began to assert themselves with vehemence and ardor. Like most *conquistadores* he obviously regarded the spread of Catholicism as an effective agent of implementing Spanish political control over the natives. But Magellan's newly found religious enthusiasm was not solely the consequence of imperialist motives. Magellan, the navigator and merchant, threw himself fervently into his new role as an apostle of the gospel until he reached a state of spiritual intoxication which undermined his sound judgment of things mundane. The unwise ultimatum to Lapu-Lapu to abandon paganism, the battle of Mactan, and a heroic but unnecessary death followed each other in rapid sequence. Not without some justification in fact did Hernán Cortés offer a gratuitous apology to the "king" of Cebu for Magellan's "lack of caution and foresight." [2] The conqueror of the Aztecs never permitted his own deeply felt missionary zeal to allow him to do too much too quickly with too little.

It was Magellan, not Friar Pedro de Valderrama, who explained to the natives the principal beliefs of the Christian religion. Pigafetta leaves no doubt as to the pleasure that Magellan derived from delivering his sermons to the attentive audience of native notables. They were taught to make the sign of the cross.[3]

[2] The letter dated May 28, 1527, was given by Cortés to his cousin, Alvaro de Saavedra, who commanded an ill-fated expedition to the Philippines. For the text of the letter see Martín Fernández de Navarrete, *Colección de los viajes y descubrimientos que hicieron por mar los Españoles desde fines del siglo XV* (5 vols.; Madrid, 1858), V, 461–62.

[3] Antonio Pigafetta, *Magellan's Voyage Around the World;* the original text of the Ambrosian MS with English translation, notes, etc., by James Alexander Robertson (3 vols.; Cleveland, 1906), I, 153.

The natives' impression of the Christian religion must have been cursory and ambiguous. What information came to them arrived through an imperfect instrument of communication, Enrique, Magellan's slave-interpreter, whose Malay tongue was understood by the natives of Cebu. Magellan's prebaptismal instruction may have been inadequate. It was, however, a good deal more than some of Saint Francis Xavier's converts received, some of whom were baptized without benefit of any preliminary indoctrination whatsoever.[4]

The Spaniards sought to transcend the linguistic barrier. The aim was to capture the imagination of the natives through the splendor of the new religion's ritual.[5]

The proselytizing dream of Magellan came nearer reality when on April 14 Humabon, the local cacique, was baptized amid a Spanish and barbarian display of pomp, protocol, and pageantry. Five hundred followers of Humabon were also received into the church on that same Sunday. Friar Pedro de Valderrama was apparently persuaded not to make an issue of the polygamous habits of the Cebuans.[6] In any event he was spared the indignity of baptizing the men and their plural wives together. The ceremony was performed for the men before Mass in the morning. In the late afternoon Humabon's "queen" and forty of her ladies received the sacrament.[7]

Pigafetta's account suggests that Magellan was the godfather of Humabon, although this is not made explicit. A curious detail of this ceremony, however, was that Magellan was dressed all in white to demonstrate, as he explained to Humabon, his sincere love toward the natives.[8] One ritual of the baptismal liturgy as practiced in the sixteenth century was that the convert, not the sponsor, wore a white garment (*alba*) as a symbol of innocence.[9]

During the week following April 14 a total of about 800 natives

[4] A. Brou, *Saint François Xavier, conditions et méthods de son apostalat* (Bruges, 1925), pp. 36–39.

[5] Pigafetta, *op. cit.*, p. 121.

[6] "They have as many wives as they wish, but one of them is the principal wife" (*ibid.*, p. 169).

[7] *Ibid.*, pp. 153–55.   [8] *Ibid.*

[9] For a sixteenth-century description of the ritual of the sacrament of baptism see Juan Focher, O.F.M., *Itinerarium Catholicum proficiscentium ad infideles convertendos* (Seville, 1574), pp. 94–98.

were baptized. The battle of Mactan and the massacre of Cebu made these baptisms abortive.[10] But the Magellan episode was to exert an indirect but significant influence on the evangelization of the Philippines in the period beginning in 1565. The native chieftains were induced to request a pardon for the responsibility that their fathers and grandfathers had incurred in the massacre of Cebu. A full and general pardon was speedily granted. The Spaniards were being legalistic. They were not being vindictive, however. No punishment was inflicted. No atonement was demanded except that the natives voluntarily "renew" the oath of allegiance to the Spanish crown which their parents had taken in 1521. The Spaniards were acting on the legal fiction that the Cebuans of 1565 were Spanish subjects in revolt.[11]

The Influence of New Spain

The methods employed in administering baptism in the Philippines after 1565 were profoundly influenced by the experience that the monastic orders had acquired during the movement of converting the Indians of New Spain. The content of prebaptismal instruction for adults was defined. The neophytes were expected to repent for the sins of their pagan past and to affirm their belief in the efficacy of the sacrament. A monogamous marriage (a natural and legitimate marriage, according to church doctrine) was another *sine qua non*. Adult converts were supposed to be able to recite by memory the *Pater Noster,* the *Ave Maria,* the *Credo,* and the Ten Commandments. Some idea of the meaning of the other sacraments and an awareness of the principal obligations of a Christian (i.e., attendance at Mass on Sundays and feast days and mandatory annual confessions) were considered as desirable prebaptismal conditions. Each neophyte

[10] For recent accounts of Magellan's missionary activities see: Gregorio Zaide, *Philippine Political and Cultural History* (2 vols.; Manila, 1949), I, 113–19, and Charles McKew Parr, *So Noble a Captain, The Life and Times of Ferdinand Magellan* (New York, 1953), pp. 341–62.

[11] Juan de Grijalva, O.S.A., *Crónica de la orden de N.P.S. Agustín en las provincias de Nueva España* (Mexico, 1624), pp. 120–21. The first Augustinian mission to the Philippines was under the jurisdiction of the Mexican province. Grijalva's text is the most circumstantial and reliable Augustinian source we have for the initial period of the missionary enterprise in the Philippines.

was supposed to be examined by the priest before being granted the sacrament. These standards were not always observed either in Mexico or in the Philippines, but they did provide a yardstick, which was often applied.[12]

The Work of the Augustinians

Three Augustinian friars—Martín de Rada, Diego de Herrera, and Pedro Gamboa—began systematic missionizing in Cebu in 1565. Their first job was to learn Visayan. Friar Martín de Rada is said to have learned to preach fluently in Visayan within five months, much to the astonishment of the Cebuans.[13] In striking contrast to the Magellan period only a few baptisms were administered during the first years of their stay. The friars never allowed themselves to forget the "ease with which the Indians apostatized at the time of Magellan." [14] The Augustinians were determined not to repeat the mistake of the Magellan fiasco—to baptize large groups without a reasonable assurance that the Spaniards would remain permanently in the islands. Both in regard to the ultimate spiritual welfare of the natives and from the viewpoint of the friars' sacerdotal conscience, better for the Cebuans to remain pagans than to become apostates, which is inevitably what would have happened if the Spaniards suddenly withdrew from the Philippines. It was not until 1570 that the struggling colony on Cebu learned of the decision of Philip II's government to remain in the islands.[15] Hence few baptisms were granted before 1570.

[12] For an authoritative account of the Mexican missionary background see Robert Ricard, La "conquête spirituelle" du Mexique, essai sur l'apostolat et les méthodes missionaires des ordres mendiants en Nouvelle Espagne de 1523 á 1572 (Paris, 1933), pp. 103–16.

[13] Grijalva, op. cit., p. 124. Juan de Medina, O.S.A., Historia de los sucesos de la orden de n. gran p. S. Agustín de estas filipinas, published in the Biblioteca histórica filipina (4 vols.; Manila, 1892–1893), IV, 53–54.

[14] Grijalva, op. cit., p. 124.

[15] Letter from Diego de Herrera, O.S.A., to Philip II, Mexico, Jan. 16, 1570, in Emma Helen Blair and James Alexander Robertson, eds., The Philippine Islands, 1493–1898 (55 vols.; Cleveland, 1903–1909), III, 69–72 (hereinafter cited as BRPI). Also Philip II's letters to Legazpi, Escorial, Nov. 8 and Nov. 18, 1568, in ibid., III, 62–66, and XXXIV, 235–38. Father Urdaneta's articulate opposition to the colonization of the Philippines by the

The policy of the Augustinians was cautious, but it was not rigidly inflexible. Baptism was occasionally administered before 1570 but only to those who indicated a fervent desire for it. It was morally impossible to refuse a particular request, especially if it came from someone who was old or sick.[16] It might be impolitic to reject a request coming from a notable of prestige in native society. Such was the case of the widowed niece of Tupas, the local cacique, who was the first convert of the friars. Her ardent and impatient desire for baptism, which was granted late in 1565, may have been sharpened by the realization that her conversion would remove the only obstacle to her marriage with a Greek sailor who was serving as a calker in Legazpi's fleet. Her marriage to Master Andrés took place a few days after her baptism—the first Christian marriage between a European and a Filipino woman. Both the baptism and the marriage of Doña Isabel (her Christian name) were performed with all possible solemnity. The friars' aim in granting these sacraments for the first time to a native was to impress the Cebuans with the beauty of the new religion's ritual.

Grijalva, the Augustinian chronicler, does not conceal the friars' reluctance about granting baptism to natives as early as 1565. Doña Isabel's determination and her bold appeal to the *adelantado* Legazpi (who was her godfather at baptism) did much to remove the doubts of the Augustinians. Furthermore Grijalva implied that Doña Isabel was the most eloquent advocate of her cause. The rapidity with which she learned the prayers astounded

---

Spaniards which sprang from his accurate hypothesis that the archipelago lay on the Portuguese side of the Demarcation Line may also have been a factor which inspired the ultracautious baptismal policy of the Augustinians up to 1570. For Urdaneta's sound hypothesis see *Colección de documentos inéditos de ultramar*, segunda serie, Vol. II, 145–200. Philip II's instructions to Legazpi were not to violate the Demarcation Line, but the king was acting on the incorrect supposition that the Philippines were on the Spanish side (*BRPI*, II, 91–100).

[16] One of the early baptisms, which made a favorable impression on the natives, was the conversion of an aged invalid who recovered his health after being baptized. A trusted friend of the Augustinians, he spent the last years of his life as a porter in their convent in Cebu (Grijalva, *op. cit.*, p. 125).

and delighted the missionaries. Since Doña Isabel and her Greek sailor preferred a Christian marriage to a liaison, the logic of circumstances virtually compelled the friars to baptize her.[17]

Scarcity of Conversions

Not more than a dozen baptisms were administered between 1565 and 1568 when Tupas, the son of Magellan's cacique, and Tupas' son were baptized on the third Sunday of Lent, March 28, 1568—some three years after the arrival of the Spanish expedition. Friar Diego de Herrera performed the ceremony. The *adelantado* Legazpi acted as Tupas' godfather. Legazpi's grandson, Juan de Salzedo, stood as godfather for Tupas' son. Between 1565 and 1570 not more than one hundred baptisms were granted.[18]

Tupas himself was apparently reluctant about committing himself irrevocably to the Spanish cause by requesting baptism until he had convinced himself that the Spaniards were to remain permanently on Cebu. The fact that the Spaniards had brought none of their women with them aroused his suspicions about their intentions. Tupas had no desire to find himself in the predicament of his father when the Magellan expedition was compelled suddenly to withdraw from Cebu.[19] Other circumstances, which delayed the large-scale administration of baptism on Cebu, were the existence of polygamy and the institution of debt slavery. The story of how polygamy was gradually eliminated can best be focused in discussing later the introduction of the sacrament of matrimony. The complex system of debt slavery that they encountered in the Philippines the friars regarded as a way of illegally acquiring property by means of usury. Strenuous efforts were made to coerce the natives into liquidating their holdings in debt slavery before being granted baptism.[20] In the case of

[17] *Col. de doc., op. cit.*, III, 122; Grijalva, *op. cit.*, p. 125; Medina, *op. cit.*, p. 57.

[18] Herrera to Philip II, *op. cit.*, p. 72.

[19] For Tupas' baptism see: Grijalva, *op. cit.*, pp. 133–34; Medina, *op. cit.*, pp. 62–66; Gaspar de San Agustín, O.S.A., *Conquistas de las islas philipinas, etc.* (Madrid, 1698), pp. 200–201.

[20] Grijalva, *op. cit.*, p. 134; Medina, *op. cit.*, pp. 62–64; San Agustín, *op. cit.*, p. 201. For recent accounts of early missionary events on Cebu see

Tupas the Augustinians had to content themselves with the principle of a symbolic restitution. On the whole the friars' labors in this regard had indifferent results. The institution of debt slavery lasted well into the Spanish period, legally recognized and supervised by the *Audiencia* of Manila.

Role of the *Encomendero*

The *encomenderos* played a significant, if obscure, role in the early evangelization of the Philippines. The first contact that most of the natives had with the reality of Spanish sovereignty was their local *encomendero* who visited his *encomienda* at least once a year if only to collect his tribute. If the *encomendero* served no other apostolic purpose, he accustomed the natives, at times a little brutally, to the idea that the Spaniards were there to stay and that they, the natives, had little alternative but to accommodate themselves as best they could to the new state of affairs. As a result of the acute shortage of friars during the early years, the missionaries usually followed the *encomenderos,* and in most cases after a lapse of many years.[21] By the time the friars did arrive in a village any will to active resistance on the part of the Filipinos had been effectively crushed by the local *encomendero.*

The *encomendero* was supposed to be something more than a shock-trooper destroying all organized native resistance in the path of the missionary. According to the theory of the *encomienda* he was visualized as a lay apostle, a coadjutor of the gospel. The *encomienda* system was an exchange of services between the king, the *encomenderos,* and the natives. The king delegated his right to collect an annual tribute from all adult native males (local nobility excepted) to individual Spaniards usually for a period of two lives. The *encomendero* assumed the feudal obligation of rendering military service in times of emergencies. The *encomendero* was obligated to make his wards recognize the sovereignty

---

Zaide, *op. cit.,* I, 147, and Edward J. McCarthy, O.S.A., *Spanish Beginnings in the Philippines, 1564–1572* (Washington, 1943), pp. 95–109.

21 Many natives had been paying tribute for as long as twenty-five years without receiving any religious instruction ("Memorial general de todos estados de las islas filipinas para su Magestad, Manila, June 26, 1586" in Pablo Pastells' edition of Francisco Colín, S.J., *Labor evangélica* [3 vols.; Barcelona, 1900–1902], I, 434).

of the Spanish crown, to defend the life and property of his charges, and to give them a modest amount of religious instruction. The religious-apostolic aspect of the ideology of the *encomienda* was laid down as far back as the Laws of Burgos (December 12, 1512). Article III, for example, provided that in each new village the *encomendero* build a church with an image of Our Lady and equipped with a bell to call the Indians to morning and evening prayer. The *encomendero* was also instructed to teach his Indians how to make the sign of the cross and how to recite the *Pater Noster*, the *Credo*, and the *Ave Maria*. Article XII provided for the baptism of all babies within a week of their birth. If no priest were available, then the *encomendero* himself was to perform the sacrament.[22]

Between the Laws of Burgos and the transfer of the *encomienda* system to the Philippines the spiritual duties of the *encomenderos* had been modified only in detail but not in substance. The Acts of the Ecclesiastical Junta of Manila (1582) state that the *encomendero* must live among his wards to teach them *policías seculares y buenas costumbres*, if there were no priest resident in the area.[23] The *encomenderos* were charged with teaching their natives the three prayers and the Christian virtues in order to prepare their wards for baptism. The *encomenderos* were admonished, however, not to forget their laical status: "All this can be done as best as possible in conversations and not by

[22] Lesley Byrd Simpson, *The Encomienda in New Spain* (Berkeley and Los Angeles, 1950), pp. 32–34. I have encountered no mention of baptisms administered by Philippine *encomenderos*, but some may have been performed. Lay baptism in cases of urgency was a time-honored practice of the church. The Jesuits in their Visayan missions taught their trusted native assistants, the *fiscales*, how to administer the sacrament in case of an emergency (Colín, *op. cit.*, II, 409, 411).

[23] Memoria de una junta que se hizo á manera de concilio el año de 1582 para dar asiento á las cosas tocantes al aumento de la fé y justificación de las conquistas hechas y que adelante se hiciesen por los Españoles" in Valentín Marín y Morales, O.P., *Ensayo de una síntesis de los trabajos realizados por las corporaciones religiosas españolas de Filipinas* (2 vols.; Manila, 1901), I, 326. For rather convincing argument about the date of this document, which has been challenged by Lorenzo Pérez, O.F.M., see Jesús Gayo Aragón, O.P., *Ideas jurídico-teológicas de los religiosos de Filipinas en el siglo XVI sobre la conquista de las islas* (Manila, 1950), pp. 59–60, note 17.

preaching nor meddling in deep [theological] matters which they as seculars are forbidden to do. . . ." [24] According to the ecclesiastics the *encomenderos* were lay missionaries with the accent on the adjective.

The financial obligations of the *encomenderos'* spiritual role were carefully defined. According to Philippine practice the expenses incurred in building churches in native villages were to be shared in equal parts by the crown, the *encomendero,* and the natives. In villages of crown *encomiendas* the crown's share was two-thirds and the natives' one-third.[25] In addition to defraying one-third of the cost for building a church, the *encomendero* was also supposed to build a house for the local friar, supplying the church with ornaments of the cult and providing wine and oil for the Mass. Two reales out of the total tribute of ten reales was supposed to be given by the *encomendero* to the friar as living allowance.[26]

Complaints Against *Encomenderos*

If we can believe two formidable bills of particulars drawn up by Bishop Salazar, one in 1586 and another in 1591, the *encomenderos* were something less than enthusiastic in discharging their quasi-missionary function. The bishop complained that in neither the *encomiendas* of the king nor in the private *encomiendas* had many churches been built. Few churches had been furnished with chalices. The few churches which had been put up were already in a lamentable condition of decay. When churches were built, it was usually the natives who had to bear the full burden. The *encomenderos* were accused of supporting only a minimum number of friars on their *encomiendas.* One friar for every 2,000 natives

[24] "Memoria," *op. cit.*, p. 326.

[25] *Ibid.*, pp. 322–23, 328. See also: "Cedula Regulating the Foundation of Monasteries, Aranjuez, May 13, 1579" in *BRPI*, IV, 141–43; "Memorial del Obispo de las Filipinas, en que se contienen las cosas que el muy R. Padre Alonso Sanchez . . . , que en nombre de toda esta republica va á tratar el remedio de ella con Su Magestad . . . ," in Colín, *op. cit.*, I, 445–51. For Salazar's 1591 indictment of the *encomenderos* see *BRPI*, VII, 268–76.

[26] *Ibid.*

was notoriously inadequate, argued Salazar. One friar to every 450 to 600 natives should be the goal. The bishop also denounced the *encomenderos* for being lax in paying the two reales due the friars. Salazar vainly urged that the Filipinos be allowed to pay the two reales directly to the local priest.[27]

Although he was generously endowed with the Spanish gift for hyberbole, the hard core of Salazar's charges in this case may not be far from the mark. In the face of the rice shortage of the 1570's and the early 1580's and the self-imposed necessity of supporting themselves and their families in the style of a ruling class, many *encomenderos* flexibly interpreted their spiritual and financial duties to the friars and to the natives. That the *encomenderos* often tried to get by with providing as little as possible is illustrated by the fact that as late as November 4, 1606, the king ordered the *encomenderos* to fulfill their duty of providing wine for the Mass and forbade the royal treasury to pay this expense.[28]

Yet there were *encomenderos* who did perform conscientiously what was demanded of them. When Pedro Chirino arrived at Carigara (Leyte) to found a Jesuit *residencia,* the local *encomendero,* Christóval de Truxillo, had not only built a small chapel, but he had also indoctrinated many natives. Some of them were baptized the very afternoon of Chirino's arrival.[29]

The *encomendero* as a lay missionary was at best a stopgap measure. Considered as such it was a moderate success. That the *encomenderos* usually did not fulfil their quasi-missionary duties to the letter, which was the essence of Bishop Salazar's complaint, ought never to obscure the fact that they rendered substantial assistance to the friars in accustoming the natives to the reality of Spanish hegemony and undertook the first faltering steps to give the Filipinos some idea of the new religion.

[27] Colín, *op. cit.,* I, 447–49. As late as 1602 Pedro Chirino, then Jesuit representative at the courts of Madrid and Rome, vainly attempted to arrange that only natives of the royal *encomiendas* be assigned to the Jesuit missions. The royal treasury had a better reputation for meeting its obligations than the private *encomiendas* (Colín, *op. cit.,* II, 329).

[28] *BRPI,* XI, 272–73; XIV, 155, 194; XXIX, 69. Wine for the Mass usually came from Mexico or Goa (Hierónimo de Bañuelos y Carrillo, "Relation of the Philippine Islands" in *BRPI,* XXIX, 68–69).

[29] Colín, *op. cit.,* II, 12.

The Friars' Problem

Thanks to the strong-arm methods of the *encomenderos* the friars had to contend with only passive resistance from the natives. In more cases than not the missionaries had to overcome some kind of sullen hostility whose widespread existence had not always been appreciated. The friar's problem was to arouse the natives' confidence. The initial reaction of the Filipinos was one of distrust and suspicion. It was not uncommon for a friar to wake up one morning to a deathly silence only to discover that his flock had stolen away to the mountains during the night.[30] Governor Francisco de Sande wrote Philip II in 1576, "For these Indians are generally like deer; whenever one wishes to find them, he must employ strategy to catch one of them in order that this one may summon the others who have taken to the hills." [31]

On the island of Panay the inhabitants of the coastal regions refused to be indoctrinated for some time by the Augustinians until the Negritos in the mountains had been converted. That was asking the impossible, and well the coastal natives knew it. The mountain peoples remained fiercely unresponsive to any blandishments from the friars. One of them, Friar Miguel de Sigüenza, lost his head in the attempt.[32] Another Augustinian on Panay, Juan de Alva, not only had his hut burned to the ground by hostile natives, but there were also attempts at poisoning his drinking water.[33] Such were some of the occupational hazards of a Spanish missionary in the Philippines.

Difficulties of the Dominicans

The Dominicans encountered a somewhat different situation in the province of Pangasinan. Little progress had been achieved there except in the capital of Lingayen where the *alcalde-mayor* and a handful of Spaniards lived. In September 1587 five Dominicans led by Friar Bernardo de Santa Catalina arrived. The local

[30] Marcello de Ribadeneyra, O.F.M., *Historia de las islas del archipiélago* . . . (Barcelona, 1601), p. 32. This rare work is perhaps the most illuminating source we have for the history of the early Franciscan missions in the Far East.

[31] Governor Sande to Philip II, in *BRPI*, IV, 84.

[32] San Agustín, *op. cit.*, p. 29.   [33] *Ibid.*, p. 350.

encomendero built them a house, as the law required. The natives refused to supply the Dominicans with wood, water, fish, or rice. After three years of residence the only result was the baptism of a few children. The local opposition seems to have been spearheaded by the pagan priests, the *babaylans*, who spread the rumor that Friar Bernardo was the father of a child by a native woman. Eventually the Dominicans were able to convince the Filipinos of Friar Bernardo's innocence by proving that he was not in the village on or about the time the hapless woman conceived. The question of the innocence or guilt of Friar Bernardo is not to the point. All the available evidence makes him appear blameless. Sacerdotal celibacy was not a manifestation of Philippine pagan religion. The real significance of the charge is that it indicates that the pagan priests were astute enough to perceive that such an accusation would paralyze the efforts of the Dominicans by indicting one of their number for an act which in Christian terms but not by pagan standards was a violation of the moral order. The *babaylans* were able to discredit the missionaries in the eyes of the native community for some time by exposing as an alleged mockery the friars' high claims to monastic virtue. Some Spanish authorities urged that the mission be abandoned. Bishop Salazar knew how to respond to a challenge: "I wish that these Indians who are so difficult should be converted by my [Dominican] friars."[34] Against the sullen hostility of the natives the Dominicans sought to arouse their curiosity and then their respect by practicing what they preached. Eventually the friars' life of monastic asceticism and austerity broke down the passive resistance of the village.[35] Teaching by example was a telling means that the friars often employed to gain the confidence of their new flock.

Envoys from Abulug in the province of Cagayan actually set out for Manila with the intention of bribing the Spanish authorities to relieve them of the Dominican friars. The emissaries never reached the capital.[36]

---

[34] Diego Aduarte, O.P., *Historia de la provincia del sancto Rosario de Filipinas, Iapon y China de la sagrada orden de predicadores* (3 vols.; Zaragoza, 1693), I, 71. The first edition was published in Manila, 1640.

[35] *Ibid.*, pp. 71–72.   [36] *Ibid.*, pp. 149–50.

The missionaries usually sought to gain the good will and the active support of the propertied upper classes of native society, the *datos*. The supposition of the friars, and it was a sound one, was that the lower classes would usually follow the lead of their social superiors.[37] To further this end Father Alonso Sánchez induced Pope Gregory XIV on July 28, 1591, to grant a whole series of generous indulgences to those *datos* who facilitated in any appreciable manner the conversion of their followers to the faith.[38]

Wherever the friars met sullen hostility, they usually contented themselves with asking the leaders of the community to allow a few children to be educated at the convent.[39] The village chiefs might shun for some time the monastery, but out of a combination of curiosity and fear they did not dare refuse the friars' minimum request. Once a mission was established, three buildings went up in rapid sequence—a church, a convent, and a school. The friars realized that the future lay with the children. Primary schools attached to the monasteries enabled the missionaries eventually to train a native elite, which did provide leadership in the new Christian communities.

Number of Converts

As a result of the salient fact that the military conquest of Luzon and the Visayas was relatively bloodless in comparison to the conquests of Mexico and Peru, historians have tended to underestimate the persistence and the effectiveness of passive resistance of many native groups to the first efforts of the missionaries.[40] Between 1565 and 1570 not more than 100 baptisms were

[37] Grijalva, *op. cit.*, p. 130; Medina, *op. cit.*, p. 63; Aduarte, *op. cit.*, I, 71–72; Pedro Chirino, S.J., *Relación de las islas Filipinas* (Manila, 1890), the first edition of which was published in Rome in 1604; Colín, *op. cit.*, II, 394.

[38] Colín, *op. cit.*, I, 481.

[39] Medina, *op. cit.*, p. 54; Ribadeneyra, *op. cit.*, pp. 65–67; Aduarte, *op. cit.*, I, 71–72, 149–50; Colín, *op. cit.*, II, 127; Chirino, *op. cit.*, p. 40.

[40] Zaide's conclusion about the baptism of Tupas creates a somewhat misleading impression. "Following the example of their king and prince, the Cebuans readily discarded their native religion and embraced Christianity." To use Churchillian language, Tupas' conversion was not the beginning of the end of passive opposition of the Cebuans to the friars, but it represents only the end of the beginning of opposition (Zaide, *op. cit.*, I, 147).

administered.[41] Between 1570 and 1578 the number of adult conversions was strikingly unimpressive. In fact the Augustinians, who numbered only 13 friars in 1576, confined most of their baptisms to children. The adults remained suspicious and unresponsive.[42] By 1583 there may have been something less than 100,000 converts.[43] In 1586 there were not more than 250,000 baptized natives, although 200,000 might be a more accurate figure. Of this number the Augustinians administered to around 146,000 souls.[44] In 1594 Friar Francisco de Ortega informed the authorities in Spain that the Augustinians had baptized 244,000 individuals, the Franciscans around 30,000, and the Dominicans about 14,000.[45]

[41] Herrera to Philip II, in *BRPI*, III, 72.

[42] Pablo de Jesús, O.F.M., to Gregory XIII, Manila, July 14, 1580, in *BRPI*, XXXIV, 316–24; Diego de Herrera, O.S.A., "Augustinian Memoranda," *ibid.*, pp. 278–79; Martín de Rada, O.S.A., to Viceroy Enríquez, Manila, June 30, 1574, *ibid.*, p. 291.

[43] Letter of Pablo de Jesús, O.F.M., in *Archivo ibero-americano*, III (July–October, 1916), p. 402. The letter has no date, but it was written while its author was custodian of the Franciscan mission in the islands (1580–1583). I suggest that 1583 is a plausible date in view of the fact that he wrote Pope Gregory in 1590 that not much progress had been accomplished until the arrival of the Franciscans (1578).

[44] The figure of 250,000 baptisms is contained in the report from the Manila community that Alonso Sánchez, S.J., carried to Spain in 1586 (*BRPI*, VI, 185–86). The 250,000 figure may be a somewhat optimistic estimate based on anticipated baptisms for the following years. The Manila colony through its envoy, Sánchez, petitioned for a whole series of concessions from the crown. The bigger the spiritual harvest of which the new colony could boast, the more generous might be Philip II. Sánchez's figure of 250,000 could be reduced to 200,000 without being false to the achievements of the missionaries. Grijalva claims 146,400 natives under the care of the Augustinians as of 1586. This figure may be accurate not only because of the general reliability of its author but also because this figure is demographically plausible and in conformity with the number of friars then in the Philippines (96) and the methods employed in prebaptismal instruction (Grijalva, *op. cit.*, pp. 167, 171, 194, 205). If the Grijalva figure is accepted, then it is highly improbable the Franciscans had baptized 110,000. There is substantial evidence to indicate that the Franciscans had baptized not more than 30,000 by 1586. See the following footnote.

[45] Francisco de Ortega, O.S.A., "Report Concerning the Philippines" *BRPI*, IX, 95–119. Gonzaga's figure of 300,000 baptisms for the Franciscans as of 1586 must be ascribed to a misquotation or a misprint, probably a scribe's error, Gonzaga's Philippine informant meant 30,000, not 300,000 (Francisco Gonzaga, O.F.M., *De origine seraphicae religionis* [Rome, 1587], I, 352). In 1597 the Franciscans reported 60,892 natives under their care

These missionary statistics must be treated as rough estimates, but some conclusions of a general nature, at least, can be drawn from them. The missionary enterprise got off to an exceedingly modest start during the years between 1565 and 1578. The coming of the Franciscans (1578) and the arrival of large contingents of Augustinians and Franciscans after 1578 meant a swift change in the scope and tempo of evangelical operations. The decade of 1576–1586 was, in reality, decisive. The number of missionaries increased from 13 in 1576 to 94 in 1586.[46] By 1594 the number of regular clergy had risen to 267.[47] During the 1590's, the friars came within sight of their ultimate goal, for they had baptized around half of the Filipinos who were destined to enter the orbit of Spanish control.

Curative Powers of Baptism

A substantial aid to the early missionaries in removing the barrier of native distrust was the impression that rapidly gained currency among the Filipinos that baptism not only wiped away the sins of the soul but also often helped to cure the ailments of the body. The first to perform what might be called a "medicinal" baptism was the proto-missionary of the Philippines, Magellan himself. Pigafetta writes:

The captain told them to burn their idols and to believe in Christ, and that if the sick man were baptized, he would quickly recover; and if that did not so happen they could behead him [i.e., the captain] then and there. . . . We made a procession from the square to the house

(Marcos de Alcalá, O.F.M., *Chrónica de la santa provincia de San Joseph de los religiosos descalzos* [Madrid, 1736], pp. 68–74). The first edition was published in Madrid, 1616. An increase from 30,000 in 1586 to around 60,000 in 1597 dovetails with the overall expansion of the missionary enterprise during these years. A decrease in the same period from 300,000 to 60,892 is sheer fantasy divorced from the demographic realities of the time. The archbishop of Manila reported to the king in 1622 that the Franciscans were then administering to 93,400 souls—an increase of about 30,000 between 1597 and 1622 which is about the same ratio that occurred between 1586 and 1597 (Archbishop Miguel García Serrano to the King, *BRPI*, XX, 229–36).

[46] Governor Sande to the King, Manila, June 7, 1576, *BRPI*, IV, 87. For the 1586 figure see *ibid.*, VII, 29–51.

[47] Ortega, *ibid.*, IX, 95–119. For the Jesuits see Colín, *op. cit.*, II, 10.

of the sick man with as much pomp as possible. There we found him
in such condition that he could neither speak nor move. We baptized
him and his two wives and ten girls. Then the captain had asked him
how he felt. He spoke immediately and said that by the grace of God
he felt very well. That was the most manifest miracle [that happened]
in our times.[48]

Pigafetta added, "When the captain heard him speak, he thanked
God fervently." [49] Well might we imagine the intrepid Magellan
wiping his brow in relief. In order to insure a speedy convales-
cence of the warrior, Magellan sent him a daily supply of almond
milk, rose water, sweet preserves, and a few comforts of civilization such as a mattress, a pair of sheets, a bed quilt of yellow
cloth, and a pillow.[50] Magellan, as the first missionary-physician
of the Philippines, tried to make his patient as comfortable as
possible.

The early chroniclers recounted with particular zest many examples of ill people who made miraculous recoveries after receiving baptism and of many other cases of baptized natives who
miraculously avoided catching a local epidemic.[51] The word
miracle was being used figuratively and not literally. The chroniclers knew that only the Congregation of Rites in Rome could
define a miracle. These theological distinctions, however, escaped
the attention of the Filipinos who had come to believe that baptism was efficacious both spiritually as well as corporally.

Whenever possible the friars sought to provide a Christian substitute for a pagan ritual. In order to counteract the pagan ceremonial that the *babaylans* used to perform for those who were ill,
the Jesuits in their Visayan missions developed a Christian ceremony in which the sick person reaffirmed his repudiation of
paganism and made the sign of the cross. The priest blessed the
patient with holy water, and in a short prayer he asked God for a
speedy restoration of the sick person's health.[52]

Another aspect of medicinal baptism was that in case of illness
or an epidemic the local friar was the only person competent to

---

[48] Pigafetta, *op. cit.*, I, 161.   [49] *Ibid.*   [50] *Ibid.*
[51] Grijalva, *op. cit.*, pp. 393–94; Aduarte, *op. cit.*, I, 146; Ribadeneyra,
op. cit., pp. 60–65; Chirino, *op. cit.*, pp. 114–15, 153, 175, 184, 185; Colín,
op. cit., II, 134, 157, 383.
[52] Colín, *op. cit.*, II, 151.

serve as a physician. In some cases the friars were skillful with herbs.[53] The cures that they sometimes performed obviously enhanced the prestige of the new religion. In this regard the nursing activities of the Franciscans were an outstanding achievement. During an epidemic many parents brought their babies to the baptismal font, for the natives generally considered that the sacrament would provide a supernatural immunity against illness.[54]

Social Pressures Favoring Christians

The sacrament of baptism was seldom granted to anyone who expressed strong antipathy to the new religion. Many indifferent natives, however, may have been swept along in the baptismal current, which flowed swiftly during the 1580's and the 1590's. According to Catholic doctrine the efficacy of the sacrament depended upon a sincere act of repentance on the part of the convert, a state of mind which would hardly exist unless the convert wished for baptism. Many missionaries held that the infidels could be compelled to listen to the word of God. No one, however, claimed that the pagans could be compelled to believe. The friars regarded those occasional cases of natives refusing the sacrament as an indication of the inscrutable will of the Almighty who had predestined some for eternal salvation and others for eternal damnation.[55] Although the friars respected the ultimately voluntary nature of baptism, they did exert various forms of individual and social pressure to induce the natives to desire the sacrament. Few Filipinos were able to resist.[56] Magellan once summed up the essence of the missionary viewpoint. Pigafetta wrote:

The captain-general told them that they should not become Christians for fear or to please us, but of their own free wills, and that he should not cause any displeasure to those who wished to live according to their own law, but that the Christians would be better regarded and treated than the others.[57]

[53] Ibid., II, 134.   [54] Chirino, op. cit., p. 184; Colín, op. cit., II, 151.
[55] Colín, op. cit., II, 150, 387–88; Chirino, op. cit., pp. 181–82.
[56] For a few particular examples see Colín, op. cit., II, 125–26, 396–97.
[57] Pigafetta, op. cit., I, 141.

Preferential treatment of Christianized natives was always a standard procedure of Spanish policy.

The most telling form of social pressure was to achieve a Christian majority in a community. Chirino remarked:

It seems to me that the road to the conversion of these natives is now smooth and open with the conversion of the chiefs and the majority of the people, for the excuse which they formerly had saying, "I will become a Christian as soon as the rest do" has now become their incentive towards conversion and they now say, "We desire to become Christians because all the rest are Christians." [58]

When the Christians, on the other hand, were a minority in a community, as was often the case during the early years, the friars zealously defended their right not to be molested by the pagan majority. In May 1578 at the triennial chapter meeting of the Augustinians in Manila the whole issue of Christian minorities living among pagan majorities was thrashed out.[59] In general all the missionary orders demanded that all external and open celebration of the pagan cults be stopped as soon as there was a Christian nucleus in a community. The pagan opposition was compelled to go underground. Any ridicule of the Christians by the pagans should be suppressed whenever possible. In order to avoid the obvious disadvantages of religious diversity inside the bosom of the same family the Jesuits, for example, during the 1590's indoctrinated and baptized by family groups.[60] Baptism should only be granted to natives in neighborhoods where there were priests. It was always recognized that the effectiveness of prebaptismal instruction depended upon subsequent indoctrination in catechism.

The thorny question of "minority rights," either pagan or Christian, was a temporary problem confined to the first generation of missionary effort. After substantial progress had been made in a community, infant baptism was adopted as a uniform practice.

In hardship cases the standards of prebaptismal instruction were lowered. For the seriously ill preliminary instruction was virtually discarded. All that was required was sincere repentance

[58] Chirino, *op. cit.*, p. 233.   [59] San Agustín, *op. cit.*, p. 354.
[60] Chirino, *op. cit.*, p. 187.

and faith in the efficacy of the sacrament. Even deaf and dumb Filipinos were indoctrinated by the sign language.[61]

Faulty Administration

There were many cases of faulty administration of baptism.[62] A dramatic example was what happened in the thirty small hamlets of the Bataan peninsula of World War II fame. The native population was not more than 700 people, occupying an area that was mountainous and isolated. Secular priests, Augustinians and the Franciscans, entered the area. Each order departed discouraged at the difficulties encountered. The natives were baptized, but under conditions that fell short of canonical requirements. In one hamlet, for example, the boys and the girls were lined up and given Christian names. The next day they were baptized. Obviously these Filipinos had the dimmest awareness of the meaning of the ceremony. In September 1587 the Dominicans, who had just arrived in the Philippines, entered the peninsula. Eventually they succeeded in canonically baptizing the inhabitants.[63]

In the Philippines as well as in Mexico there were cases of pseudo-Christians.[64] An old woman in Cavite, for example, requested baptism on her deathbed, although she had lived as a Christian receiving the sacraments of penance and Holy Communion. Born a pagan, she had moved to a Christian village as a child where it was assumed that she had already been baptized.[65] In general the policy of the friars was to deal gently with this form of sacrilege by baptizing in secret the pseudo-Christians. The aim was to avoid scandal to the other converts as well as to make it easier for natives to repent who out of fear and ignorance had acted as Christians without the benefit of baptism.

[61] Colín, op. cit., II, 310, 384; Chirino, op. cit., p. 232.

[62] In 1591 the bishop and the prelates of the missionary orders wrote the governor: "As the inhabitants of many of these islands have received baptism without the aforesaid solicitude [adequate prebaptismal instruction], many sacrileges have been committed; and as a result many and great misfortunes have ensued, which we can now clearly discern and yet poorly remedy" (BRPI, VII, 297).

[63] Aduarte, op. cit., I, 61–70.

[64] For cases of pseudo-Christians in Mexico see Ricard, op. cit., p. 110.

[65] Pedro Murillo Velarde, S.J., Historia de la provincia de Philipinas de la Compañía de Jesús (Manila, 1749), p. 76.

Since the proper administration of baptism was the *sine qua non* for participation in the sacramental life of the church, the friars did make strenuous efforts to meet all the canonical requirements.

Activities of the Jesuits

Although the first Jesuits arrived in Manila with Bishop Salazar in 1581, they did not begin systematic missionary activities among the natives until 1590.[66] Their early missions, most of which were in the Visayas, were models of sound organization. The Jesuits knew how to profit from the mistakes of their predecessors in the other religious orders. Not to be discounted is the generally high level of training and ability that characterized the members of the Jesuit order during this period. The Jesuits chose the sites of their *residencias* with care as to where they could get the greatest result for the effort spent. They seldom abandoned a mission after a few years, a practice of which the other orders were sometimes guilty.[67] The content of prebaptismal instruction that the Jesuits gave their converts did not differ substantially from that of the other orders. It looks as if the Jesuits developed more effective means of instruction. Their system of catechumens was fashioned after the model of the decurial system in Spain, which foreshadowed the Lancastrian system of the nineteenth century. The students were divided into groups of about ten, each unit led by one of the older and more competent students, who in turn would be supervised by the Jesuit.[68] In a period of about ten days each group would learn by heart one after the other the various prayers.[69] The decurial system or a variant of it may have been

[66] Colín, *op. cit.*, I, 503–11.

[67] Archbishop Benavides, a Dominican himself, praised the Franciscans and the Dominicans for their ascetic fervor and their missionary zeal, but he accused those orders of being the worst offenders in abandoning isolated and unrewarding missions after a period of a few years (Archbishop Benavides, O.P., to Philip III: July 6, 1603, *BRPI*, XII, 117–21; see also Chirino, *op. cit.*, pp. 40, 146; Colín, *op. cit.*, II, 127).

[68] The Jesuits were progressive in their teaching methods but not to the point of fostering coeducation; the boys and girls were taught separately (Chirino, *op. cit.*, pp. 184, 185, 231; Colín, *op. cit.*, II, 399, 409, 411).

[69] Chirino and Colín say that it usually took about ten days to complete prebaptismal instruction (Chirino, *op cit.*, p. 185; Colín, *op. cit.*, II, 409, 411). Marcos de Alcalá writes it took the Franciscans about fifteen days to indoctrinate the natives (Marcos de Alcalá, *op. cit.*, pp. 59–60).

used by the other orders, for it did fit the peculiar needs of the Philippine scene.[70] The chroniclers of the other orders, however, are not so precise as those of the Jesuits about the techniques of indoctrination. The Jesuits in contrast with the other orders refused to take on any more natives than they could properly handle—to indoctrinate first the principal village of their *residencia*, then to move on to the outlying villages until the whole area of the *residencia* had been covered.[71] In their catechumenal classes the Jesuits usually graduated between 60 and 100 neophytes at a time.[72] Between 1594 and 1600 the Jesuits baptized in the Visayas some 12,000 natives. An additional 40,000 catechumens were under instruction.[73]

In assessing the introduction of baptism in the Philippines between 1565 and 1600 the contribution of the Augustinians stands out in high relief. Accompanying the *adelantado* Legazpi in 1564, the Augustinians never lost their position during the rest of the sixteenth century as the largest missionary order in the Philippines. The Augustinians led the vanguard of the spiritual conquerors of the Philippines. The Franciscans and the Dominicans were outstanding in setting an example of monastic asceticism, which probably did much to arouse the natives' curiosity, their respect, and eventually their affection for the new religion. The Jesuit achievement lay in their sound pedagogical methods.

The sixteenth century, which saw the dissolution of the religious unity of Christendom with the emergence of the Protestant churches and the conversion to Catholicism of vast numbers of Indians in Spanish and Portuguese America, also witnessed religious events in the Orient whose ultimate consequences are being felt in today's headlines. As the sixteenth century drew to its close, the Spanish missionaries in the Philippines had laid the firm foundation upon which was to rise the only Christian-Oriental nation in the Far East.

[70] Archbishop Benavides had nothing but praise for Jesuit pedagogical methods. He was, however, somewhat less enthusiastic about their alleged habit of acquiring by devious means landed property belonging to the natives. See *BRPI*, XII, 117–21; XIV, 329; XVII, 151–52; XXIX, 183–84. For the indoctrination methods of other orders see: Marcos de Alcalá, *op. cit.*, p. 59; Ribadeneyra, *op. cit.*, pp. 65–67; Aduarte, *op. cit.*, I, 76.

[71] Chirino, *op. cit.*, p. 40; Colín, *op. cit.*, II, 127, 302, 303, 394, 399, 406.

[72] Chirino, *op. cit.*, pp. 146, 153, 180, 184, 187.

[73] *Ibid.*, p. 157; Colín, *op. cit.*, II, 214.

Episcopal Jurisdiction
in the Philippines
during the Spanish Regime*

HORACIO DE LA COSTA, S.J.

The first missionaries in the Philippines were members of the regular clergy. The Augustinians came with Legazpi in 1565. The Franciscans followed in 1577, the Jesuits in 1581, the Dominicans in 1587, and the Augustinian Recollects in 1606. In 1594 Philip II partitioned the islands into missionary districts and gave to each religious order its own separate field of apostolic activity.[1] The Augustinians received the provinces of central and southern Luzon; the Franciscans, the territory around Laguna de Bay and the provinces of the Camarines peninsula; the Dominicans, Bataan, Zambales, and the provinces of northern Luzon; and the Jesuits, the Visayan islands and Mindanao. Northern Mindanao and the western Visayas were later assigned to the Recollects. Each order eventually established a Philippine province under a provincial superior with headquarters in Manila.

The secular clergy were never very numerous and were concentrated in the capital. Most of them occupied the prebends and benefices of the Manila cathedral. They were, for the most part, *criollos*, that is, Spaniards born in the colony, and received their training in one of the two colleges in Manila which had university status, the Dominican Colegio de Santo Tomás and the Jesuit Colegio de Manila.

* This is an expanded version of an article which appeared under the title "Episcopal Jurisdiction in the Philippines in the 17th Century," in *Philippine Studies* (Manila), II, 3 (September, 1954), 197–216.

[1] Cedula to Dasmariñas, Aranjuez, April 27, 1594, in Emma Helen Blair and James Alexander Robertson, eds., *The Philippine Islands, 1493–1898* (55 vols.; Cleveland, 1903–1909), IX, 120 (hereinafter cited as *BRPI*).

The religious orders in the Philippines derived their personnel almost entirely from Spain and Mexico. Missionaries assigned to the Philippines were transported thither at the king's expense. The cost of transportation from Spain in the 1620's averaged 125,000 *maravedis* ($900) per missionary.[2] The voyage from Seville to Vera Cruz and from Acapulco to Manila took at least two years and called for a great deal of courage and self-sacrifice.[3] After his arrival in the Philippines and assignment to a parish or mission station (*doctrina*), the missionary was entitled to receive from the government or the *encomendero* of his territory an annual stipend of 100 pesos and 100 *fanegas* (about 250 bushels) of rice, in addition to the wine and oil required for the altar service.[4]

Judged by any standards, the conversion of the Philippines to Christianity by these missionary religious was a remarkable achievement. The Philippines was not a particularly attractive mission field. When Spanish colonization began, the majority of the native population had not gone beyond a primitive social organization based on kinship. They had, however, a surprisingly complex system of debt-slavery which worked hardship on everyone but the members of the leading families of each clan (*barangay*). Blood feuds and intertribal wars were common. The village economy was based on the cultivation of rice by rudimentary methods, supplemented by hunting and fishing. Worship was mainly animistic with dim recollections of a supreme deity.[5]

All this compared very poorly with the golden legends of Cathay and Cipangu, or even with the less magnificent but still marvelous reality of China and Japan, and one can hardly blame

[2] Pablo Pastells, "Historia general de Filipinas," in *Catálogo de los documentos relativos a las islas Filipinas en el archivo de las Indias* (9 vols.; Barcelona, 1925–1936), VII, 1, ccv–ccvi.

[3] See, for instance, the engaging account of his voyage to the Philippines given by Domingo Fernández Navarrete in his *Tratados . . . de la monarchia de China* (2 vols.; Madrid, 1679), I, 292–99.

[4] Juan de Bolívar to Philip IV, Manila, July 1, 1656, in Francisco Colín, S.J., *Labor evangélica*, Pablo Pastells, ed. (3 vols.; Barcelona, 1900–1902), III, 730.

[5] On Philippine civilization prior to the coming of the Spaniards, see especially two early *relaciones*, that of Miguel de Loarca (1582) in *BRPI*, V, 34–187, and that of Pedro Chirino, *Relación de las islas Filipinas* (Rome, 1604).

the first Spanish missionaries in the Far East for looking on Manila as merely a halfway station to those greener pastures. There was some trouble at first with friars who abandoned their posts in the Philippines to go adventuring across the China Sea, and Philip II had to issue strongly worded instructions on the matter.[6] But the majority faced their unglamorous task among the Filipinos with admirable courage and perseverance. The Franciscans, in particular, distinguished themselves in the basic task of reducing the scattered clan villages into towns and townships, thus making possible systematic government and evangelization. The other religious orders were faced with the same problem in their respective regions and met it with comparable vigor and success.[7]

In addition to their strictly missionary work, the religious took part in the wider life of the colony. In the early years of the settlement, especially, they were often called upon to advise the government on administrative matters. Thus, when a royal cedula arrived in 1578 ordering strict adherence to the existing laws regarding *encomiendas* and the collection of tribute, Governor Sande invited the religious to deliberate on the matter with his military and naval officers, and it was an Augustinian who drew up the regulations to implement the cedula. Again, when there was question of undertaking a punitive expedition against the Zambals in 1592, or declaring war on the Sultan of Ternate in 1593, Governor Dasmariñas requested the religious to determine whether it would be just and expedient to do so. Individual religious were employed by the colonial authorities on political missions of great importance. The outstanding example of this was the Jesuit Alonso Sánchez, whose numerous embassies to China, Madrid, and Rome are copiously documented by Pastells in his edition of Colín.[8]

[6] See his comment on chap. x of the Memorial of the Junta of Manila of 1586 in Pastells, *op. cit.*, III, xlviii–xlxix, and his instructions to Dasmariñas, *ibid.*, cxxix.

[7] On the Franciscan missions, see Lorenzo Pérez, "Origen de las misiones franciscanas en el extremo oriente," *Archivo íbero-americano*, I–VI (Madrid, 1914–1916).

[8] Gaspar de San Agustín, *Conquistas de las islas Filipinas* (Madrid, 1698), p. 356; Colín, *op. cit.*, I, 266 ff. (Sánchez's own accounts of his two journeys to Macao).

Meanwhile, all the characteristic institutions of social service which the church had developed in Spanish America were reproduced in the Philippines. Hospitals, colleges, orphanages, and houses of refuge were founded and endowed. In fact, the relatively rapid and efficient Christianization of the Philippines was due mainly to the fact that it was undertaken by religious who could draw upon the rich and varied missionary experience of their respective orders in the New World. In 1595, the organization of the Philippine church was thought to be sufficiently advanced to permit the creation of an ecclesiastical province with a metropolitan see, Manila, and three suffragan dioceses: Cebu, Nueva Segovia, and Cáceres.[9]

I

The establishment of episcopal sees, however, brought to the Philippines a problem which had already been raised in Spanish America and was to have a long and turbulent history on both sides of the Pacific, that is, the problem of episcopal jurisdiction over the regular clergy. The terms of the problem are briefly these. The hierarchical constitution of the Catholic church demands that its organized activity should normally be under the control and direction of the bishops as successors of the apostles, with the supreme command vested in the Roman pontiff, the successor of Saint Peter. But the work of evangelization in the Philippines, as elsewhere in the Spanish dominions, was, and had to be, carried out by the religious orders before the establishment of an episcopate. And even after a diocesan organization had been established, there remained the frontier missions which were not yet ready for regular parochial administration. It was therefore necessary to commit the direction and control of this pioneering work to the superiors of the religious orders themselves. In order to make their task easier, the Holy See granted to religious missionaries privileges and exemptions from normal rules of procedure, and to their superiors the authority to grant faculties for preaching and the administration of the sacraments

[9] Francisco Javier Montalbán, *El patronato español y la conquista de Filipinas* (Burgos, 1930), p. 121.

which would ordinarily have to be obtained from the diocesan prelates.[10]

Meanwhile, the epochal Council of Trent undertook not merely the precise definition of the theological doctrines challenged by the Protestant reformers, but also a thoroughgoing reform of morals and discipline within the Catholic church. One of the main objectives of the Council's reform program was considerably to strengthen the authority of the diocesan prelate over every phase of religious life and activity within his territory. When the Tridentine decrees were promulgated in Spain and its dominions, it soon became evident that those which defined the jurisdiction of the diocesan prelate would be extremely difficult to reconcile with the existing privileges of the religious orders.

The Council of Trent decreed that the regular clergy engaged in the pastoral care of souls were "immediately subject to the jurisdiction, visitation, and correction of the bishops" in whose diocese they worked, and that no one could be appointed to the parish ministry or be given diocesan faculties, even provisionally, without his approval and consent.[11] But if this was the case, what of the privileges granted by the Holy See to the missionary orders, especially those contained in the bull of Adrian VI, whereby regular superiors in the Spanish Indies and those deputed by them were given "all-embracing (omnimoda) authority . . . in both the internal and external forum, as much as they . . . should judge opportune and expedient for the conversion of the said Indians and their preservation and progress . . . in the Catholic faith and in obedience to the holy Roman Church"? For this authority explicitly included all that bishops are empowered to do, saving only those acts which required episcopal consecration.[12]

To settle the controversy that arose, Philip II obtained a clarification from Pope Pius V. In his brief "Exponi nobis" (March 23,

---

[10] See Pastells, "Historia general," Catálogo, op. cit., VI, ccxcv–cccvi, for a convenient summary of the papal documents which contain the privileges of the religious orders engaged in missionary work.

[11] Sess. XXV, c. 11, in Canones et decreta sacrosancti oecumenici concilii tridentini (Leipzig, 1876), p. 281.

[12] "Exponi nobis" (May 9, 1622), in Francisco Javier Hernáez, ed., Colección de bulas, breves y otros documentos relativos a la iglesia de América y Filipinas (2 vols.; Brussels, 1879), I, 383.

1567), this pontiff authorized missionary religious in the Indies, notwithstanding the dispositions of the Council of Trent, to act as true parish priests with entire independence of the diocesan prelates and without requiring their approval and permission, in accordance with the privileges granted them before the Tridentine decrees.[13] In 1585, however, we find Philip II issuing a cedula to the synod of Mexico enjoining on the diocesan prelates the visitation of the regular clergy engaged in the parish ministry in all matters pertaining to their office, "in accordance with the decrees of the Council of Trent." [14] This was the rather confused state of the question when the Philippine episcopate was created.

In spite of the efforts of all concerned to arrive at a final settlement, the problem was very much a live issue throughout the course of the seventeenth century. One obvious solution would have been to develop a secular clergy in sufficient numbers to be able to take over the parishes from the religious as soon as they were stably organized. The religious would then have been released for the pioneering work which their vocation and their privileges presupposed, while the problem of episcopal visitation would not have arisen, since there was never any question of the subjection of the secular clergy to the diocesan prelate. That excellent statesman, Philip II, saw that this was the ideal answer to the problem. In a cedula to the archbishop of Mexico, December 6, 1583, he stated that according to the ordinances of the Roman church and the established custom of Christendom the administration of the parishes belonged to the secular clergy, the role of the religious orders being to help them in preaching and hearing confessions. Because of the lack of secular priests in the Indies, however, the religious there had taken charge of parishes by special permission of the Holy See.

But since it is proper to bring this matter back to its original state and as far as possible to restore to the common and accepted usage of the Church, in a way that will not cause any difficulty in the Indian parishes, what concerns the said administration of parishes and mis-

[13] Text in *ibid.*, I, 397-98.

[14] Barcelona, June 1, 1585, in Colín, *op. cit.*, III, 683. These orders were extended by Philip III to all the provinces of the empire in 1603 (*ibid.*, III, 692).

sion stations, I beseech and charge you from this time forward, if you have suitable secular priests, to assign them to the said parishes, mission stations and benefices, preferring them to the friars and observing in the said appointments the procedure indicated in the laws concerning our patronage.[15]

It soon became clear, however, that admirable though this policy was in the abstract, it was not practicable. This was due not so much to the reluctance of the religious to give up the parishes they had built up—understandable in the circumstances, but which could have been overcome—but to a much more fundamental difficulty: the lack of secular priests. Two years later Philip II had to suspend the decree and look for some other solution to the problem of episcopal jurisdiction.[16] The ideal solution never did become practicable, especially in such remote parts of the Spanish empire as the Philippines. Few peninsular clergymen cared to go to such distant colonies, the Spanish population in them was too small to provide enough candidates for the priesthood, and for a number of reasons colonial policy did not encourage the formation of a native clergy.[17]

It might be asked why the regular clergy found such difficulty in renouncing their privileges and submitting to the jurisdiction of the bishops. Doubtless a certain natural and human desire for independence was behind it; but the attitude of the regular clergy was in far greater measure based on the sincere conviction that their privileges were essential to their work, that to give them up would be to sacrifice not only their freedom of action but their very existence as corporate bodies, and hence that the dilemma confronting them was either to give up their privileges or their ministry—there was no third alternative.

II

The problem gave rise in the Philippines to a series of conflicts in which not only the episcopate and the religious orders were in-

---

[15] *Ibid.*, III, 682.

[16] Cedula to the Synod of Mexico, June 1, 1585, *ibid.*, III, 683.

[17] On the causes which retarded the formation of a native clergy in the Philippines, see my article, "The Development of the Native Clergy in the Philippines," which follows in this volume.

volved, but the civil government as well. The first of these conflicts occurred in 1622, during the administration of Archbishop Miguel García Serrano; but even before that date there were rumblings of the coming storm.

In the very first diocesan synod of Manila, convoked by Bishop Salazar, himself a religious, there was already sharp discussion of the *omnimoda* faculties, occasioned by misunderstandings which had arisen between the bishop and the Augustinians.[18] In 1611 Archbishop Diego Vázquez de Mercado of Manila attempted to impose episcopal visitation on the religious parish priests. Before doing so he called a meeting of the provincial superiors and explained to them what he understood the Tridentine decrees and the royal cedulas obliged and empowered him to do with regard to the regular clergy engaged in the parish ministry. It was part of his office, he said, to inspect and if necessary to correct them, not as to their personal conduct—that was the business of their religious superiors—but strictly as to their ministry, in particular, as to the manner in which the Blessed Sacrament was reserved, the baptisteries and sacristies cared for, the parish records kept, and the general religious and moral tone of the parish maintained.

The fathers provincial replied that their papal privileges exempted them from such a visitation, and since it had never been done before, they could not consent to it now. When Archbishop Vázquez appealed to the governor for support, they served notice that they would resign all their parishes and missions rather than submit to visitation. This brought home to the governor, Don Juan de Silva, the necessity for caution. He kept putting off the archbishop and finally asked him to suspend the visitation. Vázquez did so, but in 1615 he still had not given up the idea, for we find him suggesting to the king that since the Philippines already had a normal diocesan organization, there was no longer any need for the regular clergy to retain their *omnimoda* faculties.[19]

Nothing, however, was done until Fray Miguel García Serrano, an Augustinian, became archbishop of Manila. In 1621 he wrote to the king that he was resolved to enforce episcopal visitation

[18] San Agustín, *op. cit.*, pp. 396–417.
[19] Pastells, *op. cit.*, VI, ccxcii–ccxcv, ccclvii.

because the natives "have no redress for injuries received [from the religious parish priests] because they have no superior to go to who can relieve them; for the fathers provincial, at times, because of their partiality to certain of their subjects, usually give them their support—a situation which would be remedied by episcopal visitation." On April 2, and April 3, 1622, accordingly, he caused to be notified to the fathers provincial an *auto* or official declaration which because of its importance must be summarized in some detail.[20]

Archbishop García Serrano began by explaining that there were two parts to the decree of the Council of Trent defining the authority of the diocesan prelate over religious engaged in parish ministry. The first was that in all things pertaining to the administration of the sacraments they were immediately subject to his jurisdiction, visitation, and correction. The second was that no religious, even though only provisionally appointed, might engage in the said ministry without having been examined and approved by the diocesan prelate or his vicar.[21]

The first part of this ordinance was confirmed by Gregory XIV in his brief "Cum nuper accepimus" (April 18, 1591), addressed to the archbishop of Manila. The second part was apparently suspended by Pius V for the Indies in his brief "Exponi nobis" (March 23, 1567), issued at the request of the Spanish crown. However, it should be noted that whatever might have been the force of this brief, it was revoked by Gregory XIII in his *motu proprio* "In tanta rerum" (March 1, 1572), whereby all the privileges of the mendicant orders contrary to the Tridentine decrees were abrogated.[22]

The assertion made by certain apologists of the religious orders that the execution of the *motu proprio* of Gregory XIII was suspended, was based on the solitary testimony of the canonist Fray Alonso de Veracruz. But since Fray Alonso was not even in Rome but in Seville when the papal ordinance was promulgated, his testimony was, to say the least, inconclusive. And even granting that the *motu proprio* was suspended, it could not be argued that

20 Colín, *op. cit.*, III, 690–93.
21 Sess. XXV, c. 11 (see note 11 above).
22 See the texts of these documents in Hernáez, *op. cit.*

the privileges contained in the brief of Pius V still remained in force in the Spanish dominions. For these privileges, although obtained at the instance of the Spanish crown, had been shown by later experience to be incompatible with the prior privileges of the crown itself, namely, those contained in the donation of Alexander VI and the *omnimoda* of Adrian VI. Now the crown had a perfect right to forbid that its own more ancient privileges be set at naught by privileges which it had obtained for others.[23]

And as a matter of fact, the crown *had* forbidden it. Philip II in his cedula of 1585 enjoined the visitation and correction by the diocesan prelate of religious parish priests in all that pertained to their office, and Philip III in his cedula of 1603 expanded the scope of this ordinance to include the second part of the Tridentine decree, namely, the previous examination and approbation by the diocesan prelate of religious intended for the parish ministry. There was, then, no doubt whatever as to the wishes of the crown in this matter.[24]

Having stated his case in this forthright fashion, Archbishop García Serrano began his visitation of the Franciscan parish of Dilao (now Paco) with an announcement, read from the pulpit during high Mass, commanding the parishioners to communicate to him anything they had noticed in the administration of the parish priest "which cannot and ought not to be tolerated by the citizens and inhabitants of this said town of Dilao, of whatever nation or condition they may be." Certain abuses which the archbishop particularly desired to correct were specified. For instance: Did the parish priest charge more for the administration of the sacraments than was set down in the scale of stole fees approved by the archdiocese? Did he fail to punish public sins and scandals, or (what is worse) did he collect pecuniary fines under the guise of punishing them? Did his *fiscales* (sextons and provosts) vex the native parishioners by buying rice, chickens, and

[23] Archbishop García Serrano is here turning the tables on the religious canonists, one of whose main arguments was that the privileges of the religious orders had the same juridical basis in the papal grants as the royal *patronato* and therefore stood or fell with it. On the contrary, replies the archbishop: your privileges are incompatible with the *patronato;* hence, if the *patronato* is to stay (and it must), your privileges must go.

[24] See note 14.

other commodities from them at less than the market price, or by forcing them to contribute money under the guise of alms for the church? Were there any public sinners in the parish, or persons who kept in their houses slaves and other men and women of evil life? Were there any usurers who lent money on interest, or persons who sold on credit at a higher price than they would have got in cash, or bought for less than the just price because they paid cash down? Were there any persons who practiced witchcraft, worshipped the devil, cast lots, or obtained forbidden knowledge through incantations?

When the parish priest of Dilao, Fray Alonso de Valdemoros, refused on orders from his provincial superior to submit to the visitation, he was promptly excommunicated. Upon his refusal to consider the excommunication valid, he was sentenced by the archdiocesan court to a term of imprisonment, although he was graciously permitted to choose as his place of imprisonment any religious house outside those of his own order. To enforce this sentence Archbishop García Serrano invoked the *auxilio real,* that is, the aid of the civil government; but the *Audiencia* replied on July 4 that "there was no occasion for the time being to grant to the Archbishop of these Islands the royal aid requested by him." This made it sufficiently clear to the archbishop that his visitation would receive no support from the government, and without that support he could not hope to overcome the resistance of the regular clergy. He therefore gave up the attempt, explaining in his report to the king, with some bitterness, that he preferred "to be reprimanded for laxity than for letting loose the grave scandals which I have been assured will follow from engaging in litigation with these religious." [25]

III

It will not have escaped the reader that in the clashes we have so far described the colonial government consistently maintained an attitude of reserve, preferring to continue existing arrangements by denying the aid of the secular arm to the diocesan prelates. The reason for this, as has already been suggested, was that the royal officials in the Philippines realized how indispensable

[25] Colín, *op. cit.,* III, 693 ff.

the regular clergy had become not only to the religious life but even to the administration of the colony. During the decade 1624–1634, for instance, there were only sixty lay Spaniards in the islands who resided outside the cities of Manila and Cebu. In most of the provincial towns, therefore, it was the religious parish priests who alone represented the authority of the Spanish crown. If they were to make good their threat of abandoning their posts, would not complete anarchy result? [26]

But this eminently practical consideration was apparently not fully realized in Madrid. There were two main reasons for this. The first was the attitude of the Holy See, which was interested in bringing the organization of the church in the Indies into conformity with the Tridentine decrees, wherever it seemed that the pioneering phase which originally justified the privileges granted to missionary religious no longer existed. Thus, in the very year that Archbishop García Serrano made his frustrated attempt to impose episcopal visitation, Gregory XV issued a constitution declaring in the clearest terms the subjection of religious engaged in the parish ministry to the "all-embracing (*omnimoda*) jurisdiction, visitation and correction of the diocesan prelate." [27] Here was an *omnimoda* to match the *omnimoda* of Adrian VI, and it must have had some weight with the government at Madrid.

The second reason why the royal government was anxious to strengthen the hand of the colonial episcopate was that the attitude of independence assumed by the religious orders towards the diocesan prelate was bound to lead—in fact, had already led —to an attitude of independence toward the colonial government. This touched the crown more nearly. Disregard of episcopal authority might possibly be overlooked, but not disregard of the *patronato*. [28]

In Philip IV's reply to Archbishop García Serrano's report we can see how episcopal jurisdiction had now become bound up with the *patronato* in the formulation of royal policy. The reply

[26] See the unsigned memorial on episcopal visitation in *BRPI*, XXXVI, 264–65.

[27] "Inscrutabili Dei providentia" (February 5, 1622), Hernáez, *op. cit.*, I, 485.

[28] For a brief discussion of the nature of the *patronato*, see the article referred to in note 17.

was really a transcript of a general ordinance, dated June 22, 1624, regulating the relations between the diocesan prelates, the religious orders, and the vice-patrons. According to this ordinance, the diocesan prelate had the right to impose visitation on religious parish priests in everything pertaining to their office. With regard to their personal conduct, the diocesan prelate should not correct thcm himself but should advise their regular superiors. Should the superiors fail to correct their subjects, the bishop should notify the vice-patron, who would then, if the faults were sufficiently grave, remove them from their posts. It was the vice-patron's duty to do this, the ordinance stated, "in order that the said religious may not claim in the matter of jurisdiction a right in perpetuity to the said parishes," but may subordinate themselves to the ordinary jurisdiction of the diocesan prelate and the royal right of patronage.[29]

"A right in perpetuity to the said parishes"—that was what the religious orders might in time acquire by prescription, and that was what the crown wished at all costs to prevent. They must be made to understand very clearly that no matter how long they held these parishes they still held them in complete dependence on the royal patron, who reserved the full right to take them away if and when he wanted to. In order to clinch this point the king extended to the whole empire the practice followed by the viceroyalty of Peru in the matter of parish appointments.

Briefly, the procedure worked out in Peru was as follows. Whenever a parish administered by the regular clergy became vacant, the provincial superior of the order concerned presented to the viceroy as vice-patron a list (*nómina*) of three candidates for the post, at the same time indicating the reason for the vacancy. Without indication of the cause of the vacancy the *nómina* was unacceptable; in other words, if the provincial superior wished to remove or transfer a subject, he had to tell the vice-patron his reasons for doing so. The vice-patron was the sole judge of the validity of these reasons.

If the vice-patron approved of the vacancy, he chose a successor from the superior's *nómina* or list. No new parish priest received his stipend from the government unless he had been ap-

29 Colín, *op. cit.*, III, 685–86.

pointed in this fashion. The only exceptions were the emergency replacements due to the death of a previous incumbent or his promotion to the superiorship of some other house of the religious order.[30]

In all this the intention of the crown to clip the wings of the orders is unmistakable. But no less evident is a consciousness of the delicacy of the operation. Reports had doubtless come in from other parts of the empire besides the Philippines stressing the indispensability of the regular clergy to the preservation of peace and order in the rural areas. Hence, while they must be put in their place, they must not be driven from their posts. The bishops were warned, in the same cedula of 1624, that "the religious are to remain and continue [in their parishes] and no innovation whatever must be introduced in this matter." In short, the policy adopted was to make the religious feel their dependence on the crown's favor, but to conceal from them the crown's dependence on their services.

This was clearly impossible. The religious orders knew the realities of the situation, and they made it quite clear that they did. Less than a year after this cedula was promulgated, the Spanish ambassador to the Holy See was requesting that, because of certain difficulties that had arisen, the pope might be pleased to suspend the execution of Gregory XV's constitution depriving the orders of their privileges. The request was granted by Urban VIII in 1625.[31]

In 1629, however, the crown returned to the attack. In a cedula addressed to the archbishops and bishops of the Indies, Philip IV called their attention once again to the ordinance of 1624. It was being reported that for some time now provincial superiors had been contravening this ordinance by appointing and removing parish priests "by their sole authority without giving notice to the said viceroy or persons referred to [the vice-patrons]." Moreover, they were claiming that once a religious had been approved by the diocesan prelate for a particular parish, "he had no need of any further approval for any other parish to which his provincial may send him." Worst of all, if the diocesan prelates attempted to

[30] *Ibid.*, III, 698–99.
[31] "Alias a felicis" (February 7, 1625), Hernáez, *op. cit.*, I, 488.

stop this practice, the fathers provincial haled them to the civil courts, "from which much harm and inconvenience result."

It was therefore ordered, in confirmation and extension of the ordinance of 1624, first, that whenever a parish administered by a religious became vacant, the provincial superior was to submit a list of three names from among the subjects he had available for the position to the supreme civil authority of the colony, who would select one from the list and present him to the diocesan prelate for canonical collation; second, that a religious examined and approved by the diocesan prelate for a specific parish was to be considered approved for all parishes in which the same language or dialect was spoken, but if nominated for a parish speaking a different language, he was to be examined and approved anew by the diocesan prelate.[32]

When this important cedula was received in Manila and was notified to the religious superiors for their compliance, their replies were either hostile or ambiguous. The Dominican provincial bluntly stated that "what is here ordered is contrary to the orders of his General and the constitutions of his Order"; while the Jesuit provincial tried to convey the same idea more diplomatically by saying that "the Society of Jesus wishes to serve His Majesty in whatever he may ordain, as long as the ordinance does not run counter to its constitutions and the decrees of the General." In 1638, the *autos* of the lieutenant governor demanding that the fathers provincial submit their *nóminas* for vacant parishes were politely ignored, and by 1654 the only evidence in the government archives in Manila of anything having been done to comply with the cedulas of 1624 and 1629 was one solitary *nómina* presented by the Augustinians and confirmed by Governor Corcuera in 1644.[33]

The apparent remissness of the vice-patrons in enforcing these decrees becomes perfectly understandable once it is noted that the central government at Madrid had again entered on a period of doubt and vacillation. When Governor Diego Fajardo asked for instructions as to what should be done about the bishop of

[32] Philip IV to the Hierarchy of the Indies, Madrid, April 6, 1629, in Colín, *op. cit.*, III, 686.

[33] *Ibid.*, III, 700–701.

Cáceres trying to take away the parishes of the Franciscans in his diocese, the king replied that with regard to giving aid to the bishop, "you should see what you ought to do in accordance with justice," and with regard to protecting the Franciscans, "you should conform to what is decreed by the cedulas and ordinances already issued on the matter"—not a particularly helpful reply.[34]

There came a time, however, when the *Audiencia* of Manila felt that it could not tolerate this state of affairs any longer. In August 1654, at the instance of the fiscal, Don Juan de Bolívar, notice was served on the fathers provincial that henceforth the cedulas of 1624 and 1629 would be enforced. They were to bear in mind that the authority to appoint or remove religious engaged in the parish ministry resided with the governor of the colony as vice-patron; that it was the duty of the provincial superior to nominate three religious for each vacancy that occurred in the parishes of his order; that the religious nominated must have been examined and approved by the diocesan prelate within whose jurisdiction the vacancy occurred, "in order that there may be proof that they are capable of hearing the confessions of, preaching to, and catechizing the said Indians"; that it was the part of the vice-patron to choose one among the three nominees and present him to the diocesan prelate for canonical collation; and that the diocesan prelate was empowered to make a visitation of religious parish priests "solely in what concerns their ministry as pastors and in nothing else."

The replies of the provincial superiors and procurators may be taken as a fair statement of their side of the dispute. They petitioned that the execution of the cedulas be suspended until the king could be informed of the reasons why they were willing to obey but unable to comply. These reasons may be briefly summarized here.

First of all, the rule of submitting to the vice-patron a *nómina* for every vacancy deprived religious superiors of the free disposal of their subjects and hence was contrary to their constitutions.

Secondly, it was impossible in any case to submit three names for each vacancy. Given the multiplicity of languages in the islands, they were often hard put to it to find even one priest famil-

[34] *Ibid.*, III, 687.

iar with the language of a certain parish or mission. By the same token, how did diocesan prelates intend to judge the fitness of a religious for work in the more remote districts? Who in the episcopal chanceries would be able to test the language qualifications of missionaries assigned to Calamianes, Cuyo, or Bolinao?

Thirdly, episcopal visitation would necessarily have to be conducted as a judicial process, involving the interrogation of lay witnesses, the filing of charges, the imposition of censures, and so on. Aside from the scandal this would cause, the religious parish priest would not be able to defend himself against a possible miscarriage of justice, since religious are forbidden to appeal from an ecclesiastical to a civil court.

Fourthly, the rule obliging a religious superior to manifest to the vice-patron his reasons for removing a subject from his post was not only an undue limitation on the superior's freedom of action, but a violation of the subject's right to his reputation.

Finally, the inevitable result of all this would be hopeless confusion, for instead of the religious having only one superior, they would have several, all perfectly coordinate, and extremely likely to issue contradictory orders.[35]

In spite of these representations the *Audiencia* decreed the following year that the cedulas would have to be observed; and in order to ensure fulfilment, the royal treasury officials were ordered not to release the usual stipends to the religious who could not show that their appointments had been submitted and confirmed in the manner prescribed. Meanwhile, the archbishop of Manila, Don Miguel Millán de Poblete, proceeded to make a visitation of the parishes around Manila. Wherever he met with resistance, he took the parish away from the religious and gave it to secular priests. Since these parishes were the most lucrative and convenient livings in the possession of the orders, their loss was deeply felt, and in order to persuade the vice-patron to restore them the provincial superiors had recourse once more to their old threat: renunciation of all their parishes and missions.

The religious orders had a very definite advantage in the fact that they had 254 men actually engaged in the parish ministry throughout the islands, whereas there were only fifty-nine secular priests altogether who could take their places. On the other hand,

[35] *Ibid.*, III, 700–14.

the books of the royal treasury officials revealed that there were 141 religious who received stipends from the king. These stipends had been suspended, and the suspension was beginning to be felt. The superior of the Franciscans, for instance, had been obliged to beg the governor to send his men "some rice at least, so that they will have something to eat." It was therefore a question of waiting to see which side would yield first. It was the *Audiencia* that finally did so. In September 1655 the members of that tribunal declared themselves in deadlock over the question of releasing the stipends. They co-opted a *juez acompañado* to break the tie, and he decided in favor of resuming the payments to those religious who had remained in their parishes. The full restoration of the *status quo* followed quietly soon afterwards.

However, the government appealed the case to the Council of the Indies. In his covering letter transmitting the documents Fiscal Bolívar said that, although the religious orders were clearly contravening the ordinances of the royal patron, conditions in the islands were such that it was impossible to compel them to obey. The lack of secular priests and the great number of natives still to be converted made it necessary to retain the religious in the parishes and missions on their own terms. The Council of the Indies apparently saw the point, for although it insisted—on paper —that the religious in the Philippines had to obey, that no exceptions whatever could be made in their case, and so on, nothing was done. Finally, on October 23, 1666, the whole *expediente* or file was rubricated with a laconic *"Visto"* (*"Seen"*) and sent to the archives.[36]

One more major attempt to enforce episcopal visitation was made by an archbishop of Manila before the close of the seventeenth century. But Archbishop Camacho was no more successful in 1697–1698 than his predecessors, Archbishop Serrano and Archbishop Poblete.[37] There is more than a trace of irony in Charles II's reply to Archbishop Camacho's lengthy account of his proceedings.

"I am resolved to approve," said the king, "and I do approve all

---

[36] *Ibid.*, III, 716 ff.

[37] See Diego Camacho y Avila, *Manifiesta a los M.RR.PP. Provinciales* . . . (Manila, 1697), and *Defensa canónica por las sagradas religiones* (Manila, 1698).

that you have done in this controversy; especially your decision to do nothing more about it." [38]

IV

With the accession of the Bourbons to the throne of Spain (Philip of Anjou became Philip V in 1700), the royal government began to give more resolute support to the episcopacy. To these absolute monarchs and their regalist ministers the privileges of the religious orders were not only outmoded but inconsistent with the royal prerogative. Nothing could be allowed to stand in the way of the sovereign's free disposal of his subjects.

The Society of Jesus, in particular, came under suspicion as harboring less than complete loyalty to the dynasty, and in 1767 Charles III expelled it from Spain and all the Spanish dominions. That same year a court prelate, Don Basilio Sancho de Santa Justa y Rufino, was dispatched to Manila as archbishop to assist in the expulsion of the Jesuits and to see to it that the example made of them was not lost on the other religious orders.

With full backing from Governor José Raón, Archbishop Sancho summoned the religious parish priests of the archdiocese to submit to his visitation, and when they refused deprived them of office. In their place he substituted native secular priests, many of whom he had to train and ordain in a hurry. The effect of this on the development of the Filipino clergy is discussed in another contribution to this book.[39]

In 1774 the royal government went a step further and decreed that whether the religious parish priests submitted to episcopal visitation or not, they should be replaced by seculars as they vacated the parishes either by death or retirement. By this time, however, the evil effects of Archbishop Sancho's hasty ordinations had become apparent, and the incumbent governor, Simón de Anda, took it upon himself to suspend the royal decree. In 1776 the king, better informed, withdrew his earlier cedula and restored parish appointments to the *status quo ante*, disposing that

[38] Aranjuez, May 20, 1700, in Ventura del Arco, comp., *Documentos, datos y relaciones para la historia de Filipinas*, MS. (5 vols.; Madrid, 1859–1865), IV, 204.

[39] "The Development of the Native Clergy in the Philippines," *op. cit.*

for the time being the regular and the secular clergy would keep the parishes of which each had charge. He did not, however, abandon secularization as a policy objective, and ordered that the training of native secular priests be better organized with a view to its eventual accomplishment.[40]

The next few decades saw the outbreak of the French revolution, the involvement of Spain in the wars of Napoleon, and the loss of all but a fraction of her American empire. These developments inevitably brought about a change in the government's attitude toward secularization. By the early nineteenth century the official doctrine was that the presence of the religious in the parishes was a political necessity, not so much because they were religious as because they were Spaniards, and hence to be depended upon to keep the population loyal to Spain.

Beginning in 1837, the hostile attitude toward religious orders and congregations adopted by liberal governments in Spain resulted in the emigration to the Philippines of friars for whom livings had to be found, and it was decided to transfer certain parishes in the archdiocese of Manila from Filipino seculars to the newcomers. The number of such transfers increased when the Jesuits were invited back to the Philippines in 1859 and put in charge of the evangelization of Mindanao. The parishes and missions which the Augustinian Recollects had in that island were transferred to them, and an equivalent number of parishes in the provinces near Manila taken from the native secular clergy and given to the Recollects.

The result was mounting disaffection among the native priests thus deprived or threatened with deprivation, and on the occasion of a mutiny of garrison troops in the naval station of Cavite (1872), the government found it necessary to put their principal spokesmen to death for alleged complicity in the revolt. The evidence on the basis of which these priests (Gómez, Burgos, and Zamora) were found guilty by a military tribunal of the capital charge laid against them has never been made public. Even at

[40] José Montero y Vidal, *Historia general de Filipinas* (3 vols.; Madrid, 1887–1895), II, 257–58; Charles III's cedula of December 11, 1776, in Juan Ferrando, *Historia de los PP. Dominicos en las islas Filipinas* (6 vols.; Madrid, 1870–1872), V, 83–84.

the time of their execution they were widely held to be innocent; today, they are regarded by Filipinos as national heroes. Their death, in fact, contributed as much as anything else to the emergence of Filipino nationalism.

Thus what began as a canonical controversy developed into a political issue and ended up by providing the spearhead for a nationalist revolt against colonial rule. With the transfer of sovereignty from Spain to the United States (1898) the unique relationship between church and state created by the *patronato* came to an end. By this time, the visitation controversy had become largely a dead issue, and after Leo XIII's "Quae mari sinico" (1902) and the codification of canon law (1918), an academic one. However, any assessment of Philippine Catholicism, of its strengths and weaknesses, cannot afford to ignore the long shadow that the controversy casts over its formative years.

The Development of the Native
Clergy in the Philippines*

HORACIO DE LA COSTA, S.J.

It is clear both from the repeated and emphatic declarations of the Holy See and from the nature itself of missionary activity that one of the most important tasks of the missionary, if not the principal one, is the formation of a corps of native priests who can eventually receive from his hands the administration and propagation of the Catholic church in their own country.

"First of all," says Pius XI in his encyclical letter, "Rerum ecclesiae," "let Us recall to your attention how important it is that you build up a native clergy. If you do not work with all your might to accomplish this, We maintain that your apostolate will not only be crippled, but it will prove to be an obstacle and an impediment for the establishment and organization of the Church in those countries."[1] Seven years previously, Benedict XV had couched the same idea in no less vigorous terms: "The main care of those who rule the missions should be to raise and train a clergy from amidst the nations among which they dwell, for on this are founded the best hopes for the Church of the future."[2]

Benedict XV and Pius XI were not, of course, enjoining anything new; they were merely repeating what the Sacred Congregation of Propaganda had insisted on almost from the beginning

---

* This is a revised and expanded version of an article that appeared under the same title in *Theological Studies* (Baltimore), VIII, 2 (June, 1947), 219–50.

[1] *Acta Apostolicae Sedis* XVIII (1926), 73. The translation used for this and subsequent quotations from "Rerum ecclesiae" and "Maximum illud" is that of the America Press edition of these encyclicals (New York, 1944).

[2] Encyclical letter "Maximum illud," Nov. 30, 1919, AAS, XI (1919), 444–45.

of its existence,[3] and what the Code of Canon Law imposes as a grave obligation on vicars apostolic.[4]

The specific purpose of missionary activity is the permanent establishment, in its entirety, of the visible church in those lands and among those relatively isolated groups where it is not yet firmly established.[5] The Son of God became Man in order to save all men by uniting them to Himself through membership in His Church. This imposes an obligation on the church to render herself visible to all, that is, so present and accessible that men of good will everywhere may, if they wish, participate in her life by receiving her doctrine and partaking of her sacraments. And since the need that men have of the church is a permanent need, her presence in every nation and community must likewise be permanent: she must take root. Finally, men have need of all that the church can give them; hence she must be established everywhere in her entirety, endowed with all the means necessary for the carrying out of her divine mission, which is to bring about the eternal and temporal welfare of the individual and of society.

It is easy to see how essential the formation of a native clergy is to the achievement of this missionary goal; for the church can neither be rendered sufficiently accessible, nor permanently established, nor established in her entirety, in any given nation without recruiting her clergy from among the members of that nation. All other things being equal, the native priest exerts a greater influence on his countrymen and is better able to present Christ and His message in a fashion suited to their genius and character. "Linked to his compatriots as he is by the bonds of origin, character, feelings and inclinations, the indigenous priest possesses extraordinary facilities for introducing the faith to their minds, and is endowed with a power of persuasion far superior to those of any other man." [6]

[3] Cf. *Collectanea Sacrae Congregationis de Propaganda Fide* I (Rome, 1907), notes 62, 150, 1002.

[4] Can. 305.

[5] Cf. E. L. Murphy, "The Purpose of Missions," *Missionary Academia Studies* I, 2 (New York, 1943), 8; P. Charles, *Les dossiers de l'action missionnaire* (Louvain, 1938), I, 24; Tragella, "Introduction à la missionologie," *Revue de l'Union Missionaire du Clergé* (1934), supplément.

[6] "Maximum illud," *AAS*, XI, 445.

Moreover, the church is only then securely founded when she is assured of a clergy sufficiently numerous to administer and develop her various works, and she has no such assurance as long as her personnel in any given territory is dependent for its recruitment on foreign lands. Right order demands that the church in each nation attend first to her needs before providing for the needs of her missions; and political conditions, as Pius XI points out, will not always permit her free access to those missions.

Suppose that on account of a war or on account of other political events, one government supplants another in the territory of the missions, and that it demands or orders the expulsion of foreign missioners of a certain nationality; suppose likewise (although this is not likely to happen) that the inhabitants who have attained a higher degree of civilization, and as a result a correspondingly civil maturity, should wish to render themselves independent, drive from the territory both the governor and the soldiers and the missioners of a foreign nation under whose rule they are, and that they cannot do this save by recourse to violence, what great harm would accrue to the Church in those regions, We ask, unless the native clergy, which has been spread as a network throughout the territory, could provide completely for the population converted to Christ? [7]

Finally, the church in her entirety is the church completely organized. Until the full hierarchy of bishops, priests, and laity has been articulated or at least sketched out in outline, the church cannot strictly be said to have been brought into existence in any country, as Father Charles well points out:

The native clergy, therefore, is not the coping stone of the missionary edifice; it is the foundation stone. The truth is that as long as it does not yet exist, the mission itself does not exist either. To have a clergy of their own is not a reward held out to those peoples who render themselves worthy of it; it is the necessary instrument to render them worthy of God. No one dreams of giving a stonemason a trowel because he has done a good construction job, or of placing wheels on a carriage because it has successfully negotiated a journey. . . . The Church is nowhere planted, it is nowhere established in any perma-

[7] "Rerum ecclesiae," *AAS*, XVIII, 75.

nent fashion, as long as the continuance of the priestly function is not stably assured by the inhabitants themselves of the region.[8]

We may consider it as certain, then, that one of the indispensable objectives of missionary work, intrinsic to its very nature and inseparable from it, is the formation of a native clergy, and that until that formation is accomplished, a territory cannot be said to have ceased to be a mission. Only where "an indigenous clergy adequate in numbers and training and worthy of its vocation" has been brought into existence, can the missionary's work be considered brought to a happy close; only there may the church be said to be established.[9]

In the light of these considerations, it is somewhat disconcerting to observe that after more than four hundred years of missionary endeavor, this objective has not yet been fully accomplished in the Philippines. Although it has become a politically independent nation, it remains, to a large extent, mission territory.

Claimed for Spain by Magellan in 1521, the Philippine Islands began to be effectively colonized in 1565, when Miguel López de Legazpi founded the settlement of Cebu. Manila's first bishop, Fray Domingo de Salazar of the Order of Preachers, arrived in 1581; and in 1598, Manila became an archbishopric with the creation of three suffragan dioceses: Cebu, Cáceres, and Nueva Segovia.[10] By 1605, thanks to the missionary zeal of the Spanish Augustinians, Dominicans, Franciscans, and Jesuits, the majority of the population had been baptized.[11] Since that date, the Filipinos have been overwhelmingly Catholic in numbers, and they remain so today.

At the same time, there are not nearly enough priests to take care of this Catholic population. The *Catholic Directory of the Philippines* for 1965 gives a total of 4,175 priests in the country

[8] *Missiologie* (Paris, 1939), pp. 111–12.

[9] Cf. "Maximum illud," *AAS*, XI, 445.

[10] Cf. *El archipiélago filipino* (Washington, 1900), I, 376–79.

[11] Cf. E. G. Bourne's introduction to Emma Helen Blair and James Alexander Robertson, eds., *The Philippine Islands, 1493–1898* (55 vols.; Cleveland, 1903–1909), I, 33–37 (hereinafter cited as *BRPI*). Also John Leddy Phelan's essay in this volume, "Prebaptismal Instruction and the Administration of Baptism in the Philippines during the Sixteenth Century," pp. 22–43.

and estimates that there is one priest for every 5,600 Catholics. However, this average does not give a fair picture of the actual situation, for of the total number of priests only 1,935 are diocesan priests. The rest are religious, and while most of the religious orders and congregations of men in the Philippines administer parishes and missions, a fair proportion of their membership either conduct schools or teach in them. Thus it would be closer to the truth to say that there is one priest engaged in the parish ministry for every 10,000 or 15,000 Catholics. Moreover, it must at once be added that this is an *average* figure, and that there are numerous rural and even urban parishes with a population of 20,000, 30,000, and even 40,000 Catholics.

Finally, it should be pointed out that while the diocesan clergy is composed almost entirely of native Filipinos, only 350 or so religious priests are native Filipinos. Thus, of the 4,175 priests in active service in the Philippines today, fully 1,890 are foreigners —and this four hundred years after the introduction of Christianity to the islands. It would appear then that the development of the native clergy in the Philippines has been abnormally slow. This calls for an explanation, and the purpose of this paper is to suggest by means of a brief historical survey some of the causes that have contributed to retard the formation of a Filipino clergy.

I

The Philippine Islands were evangelized within the framework of a characteristic institution of the Spanish colonial empire, the *patronato real*. This was an arrangement based on the bull "Universalis ecclesiae" of Julius II, by which the Roman pontiff granted to Ferdinand and his successors on the throne of Spain the exclusive right: (1) to erect or to permit the erection of all churches in the Spanish colonies; and (2) to present suitable candidates for colonial bishoprics, abbacies, canonries, and other ecclesiastical benefices. This concession was made in consideration of the Spanish sovereign having undertaken to promote the evangelization of his pagan subjects, and to provide for the material needs of the church in his dominions.[12]

[12] For the text of "Universalis ecclesiae" see F. J. Hernáez, ed., *Colección de bulas, breves y otros documentos relativos a la iglesia de América y Filipinas* (2 vols.; Brussels, 1879), I, 25 ff.

The Spanish kings took their patronage of the church in the Indies very seriously. In 1594, for instance, we find Philip II writing to his governor in the Philippines:

> Because I have learned that better results will be obtained by assigning each [religious] order a district by itself, I command you, together with the Bishop, to divide the provinces among the religious in such manner that where Augustinians go there shall be no Franciscans, nor religious of the Society [of Jesus] where there are Dominicans. Thus you will proceed, taking note that the province allotted to the Society must have the same manner of instruction as the others; for this same obligation rests upon them as upon the others, and it does not at all differ from them.[13]

The colonial administrators, in their turn, looked upon the authority of the Spanish crown as competent to dispose of ecclesiastical personnel. Governor Luís Pérez Dasmariñas, writing to the king, seems to consider this a perfectly natural assumption.

> For many years this colony has desired and hoped for the coming of priests of the Society of Jesus, for the benefits of their presence and for the good of souls in these Islands, in whose conversion and advancement the Society has the dexterity known to Your Majesty. . . . I request that it may please Your Majesty to command Father General [of the Society] to order the provinces of Europe to gather perhaps forty priests whom Your Majesty may send to the help of these Islands.[14]

Thus, in virtue of the *patronato*, the Spanish king wielded a preponderant and decisive influence on the administration of the church in his dominions. His right of presentation, in practice, meant that every missionary bishop and priest was appointed or approved by the crown and depended on the crown for his support; the priest was, in other words, a salaried government official. As such, the crown assigned to him the sphere of his activities, and decided any conflicts that arose between him and the

---

[13] Philip II to Dasmariñas, Aranjuez, Apr. 27, 1594, *BRPI*, IX, 120.
[14] Dasmariñas to Philip II, Manila, June 20, 1595, in Francisco Colín, S.J., *Labor evangélica*, Pablo Pastells, ed. (3 vols.; Barcelona, 1900–1902), II, 9.

civil government of the colony, or between him and other ecclesiastical officials.

This arrangement resulted in many obvious advantages. It relieved the missionaries of all financial anxiety by placing the material resources of the government at their disposal. It distributed and coordinated their activity, thus avoiding in many cases duplication of effort and conflicts of jurisdiction. It gave stability to their work, whose continuity and ordered development was assured by an imperial power at least equally as zealous for the spread of the Catholic faith as it was for the extension of its sovereignty. The comment of the sixteenth-century colonial historian Herrera has, therefore, a broad basis in fact:

> The concession which the Holy and Apostolic See of Rome made to the Crown of Castile and Leon of the ecclesiastical patronage of that New World was a measure greatly beneficial, whereby God Our Lord, who alone sees and makes provision for what the future has in store, brought about a work worthy of His great goodness; for experience has shown that if this [New World] had been governed in any other fashion, it would never have been administered with that balanced harmony and consonance which now exists between religion, justice and good government, and the [resulting] obedience and tranquillity [of the subject peoples].[15]

On the other hand, the actual working out of this close cooperation between the church and the Spanish crown circumscribed and retarded the normal development of a native secular clergy in a way that could scarcely have been foreseen. We saw above how Philip II, with a view to the equitable distribution of labor, partitioned the mission field in the Philippines among the various religious orders. He had previously decreed, by royal cedulas of 1557 and 1561, that the *doctrinas* or mission parishes which were assigned to the regular clergy could not be transferred by the bishops to the secular clergy. Secular priests were to be given parishes in territory which had not previously been assigned to any religious order. This was all very well in theory, but since, as far as the Philippines was concerned, the entire mission had already

[15] *Descripción de las Indias occidentales* (Madrid, 1601–1615), déc. 1, cap. 28.

been divided among the religious orders, what territory was left for the secular clergy? The secular priest in effect was reduced by royal legislation to being an assistant of the religious parish priest.[16]

Everyone knew, of course, that parish work was the proper sphere of the secular clergy; that the religious missionaries had charge of the *doctrinas* which they had founded only for the purpose of building them up into regular parishes; and that when this had been accomplished, these pioneers were to give way to the secular clergy and push on to the frontier. Such had always been the policy of the church, but the regime of the *patronato* placed great difficulties in the way of carrying it out.

Any transfer of parishes, as has been pointed out, required the consent of the crown, and the crown, or at least the crown administrators, were extremely reluctant to permit such a transfer. Since the Spanish religious were, in the great majority of *doctrinas,* the only colonial officials who were willing to take up permanent residence with the natives, it was thought necessary for the good government of the colony to keep them there. And as a matter of fact, the mere presence of these zealous missionaries and thoroughly loyal subjects in regions far from the capital dispensed with the expense and effort, which might otherwise have been necessary, of maintaining large armed forces for the purpose of policing the colony. Hence Governor Sarrió was merely giving expression to a long-standing policy when he wrote to the king in 1787 that

a second consideration which has decided me not to remove the religious from the *doctrinas* is that, even if the *indios* and Chinese *mestizos* [17] possessed all the necessary qualifications [for administering them], it would never conduce to the advantage of the State and the royal service of Your Majesty to hand over to them all the parishes. The experience of more than two centuries has shown that in all the wars, rebellions, and uprisings that have broken out, the religious par-

---

[16] Cf. A. Brou, "Notes sur les origines du clergé philippin," *Revue d'histoire missionnaire,* IV (1927), 541–42.

[17] Native Filipinos were referred to as *indios.* Chinese *mestizos* were persons of mixed Chinese and Filipino blood.

ish priests were the ones who contributed most to the pacification of
the malcontents.[18]

The actual functioning of the *patronato*, then, led to royal legislation and to a colonial policy which left little scope for the secular clergy, and gave no encouragement either to native candidates
to aspire for the priesthood, or to the missionaries to train them.
Nor was ecclesiastical legislation and policy in the Spanish colonies of the sixteenth and early seventeenth centuries any more
favorable. The first missionaries to the New World, it is true, and
even some of the first civil officials, were thoroughly in favor of
the immediate formation of a native clergy. Thus Father Constantino Bayle, S.J., is able to cite a certain Rodrigo de Albornoz
as writing to the king from Mexico in 1525:

> In order that the sons of the *caciques* [19] and lords be instructed in
> the Faith, Your Majesty must needs command that a college be
> founded wherein they may be taught reading and grammar and phi-
> losophy and other arts, to the end that they may be ordained priests;
> for he who shall become such among them will be of greater profit in
> attracting others to the Faith than fifty Christians [i.e., Europeans].[20]

This and similar petitions induced the king to found the famous
college of Santiago Tlatelolco, which was entrusted to the Franciscans and solemnly inaugurated in 1536. It was limited to the
sons of the native aristocracy, and was expected to serve the double purpose of forming a cultured elite among the laity and of
providing a certain number of native priests.[21]

However, the high hopes conceived in the beginning with regard to the enterprise do not seem to have been realized, for we
find the Dominican provincial of Mexico vigorously representing
in 1544 that

[18] Pedro Sarrió to the King, Manila, Dec. 22, 1787, in Sinibaldo de Mas,
Informe sobre el estado de las islas Filipinas en 1842 (Madrid, 1843), III,
33.

[19] The *caciques* constituted the native nobility.

[20] Constantino Bayle, S. J., "España y el clero indígena de América," *Razón y Fe*, XCIV (1931), 216.

[21] Cf. R. Ricard, *Etudes et documents pour l'histoire missionnaire de
l'Espagne et de Portugal* (Louvain, 1931), pp. 155–57.

the Indians ought not to be permitted to study [arts and theology], because no good will come of it; in the first place, because they will never turn out to be regular preachers, since to preach effectively it is necessary that the preacher have some ascendancy over the people, and these natives have no ascendancy whatever over their own. Secondly, because one cannot be sure of them, and the preaching of the Gospel cannot be entrusted to them, for they are but new in the Faith and it has not yet taken firm root in them. Thus they are liable to give expression to erroneous doctrines, as we know from experience some have actually done. Thirdly, because they have not the capacity to understand firmly and aright what pertains to the Faith, and the reasons thereof, nor is this language such as to be able to express them with propriety. . . . And from this it follows that they ought not to be ordained to the priesthood, for their being priests will give them no better standing than they have now.[22]

Not many years later, Bishop Zumárraga was writing to the king that "it seemed to the religious themselves that the revenues would be better employed in the hospital than in the College of Santiago, which we know not whether it will continue in existence much longer, as the best grammarians among the native students *tendunt ad nuptias potius quam ad continentiam.*" [23]

The failure of this first experiment and of others like it seems to have led to a very strong reaction against the native clergy, and under the influence of this reaction the councils and synods of the New World in the latter half of the sixteenth century passed rather drastic measures forbidding or severely limiting the ordination of natives and even their religious profession. The first Council of Mexico (1555) declared that sacred orders were not to be conferred on Indians, *mestizos,* and mulattoes, who were classed with the descendants of Moors and persons who had been sentenced by the Inquisition as lacking the good repute which befitted the sacerdotal character.[24] The third Council of Mexico (1585) repeated the prohibition, while softening it somewhat:

That respect and reverence may be shown to the order of clerics, the sacred canons decree that those who suffer from natural or other defects which, though not culpable, detract from the dignity of the

22 Letter to the Visitor of New Spain; cf. Bayle, *op. cit.,* pp. 221–22.
23 *Ibid.,* p. 223.   24 *Ibid.,* p. 225.

clerical state, should not be ordained, lest the recipients of holy orders suffer contempt and their ministry be held in derision. Wherefore this Synod forbids . . . that Mexicans who are descended in the first degree from Indians, or from Moors, or from parents of whom one is a Negro, be admitted to holy orders without great care being exercised in their selection [*sine magno delectu*].[25]

The second Council of Lima (1591), however, decided with laconic severity that "Indians are not to receive any of the orders of the Church." [26] Thus Father Bayle concludes that "after the generous intentions of the beginning had suffered shipwreck on the reefs of experience, the ordinary legislation [of the church in New Spain] was unfavorable to the native clergy, whose ignorance and natural instability inspired no confidence, and whose mean origin obscured the dignity [of the priesthood]." [27] This ecclesiastical policy was naturally extended to the Philippine mission, which was officially attached to the church of Spanish America. An interesting indication of this may be noted in the rules and regulations drawn up by Governor Corcuera for the Seminary of San Felipe de Austria, which he founded in Manila in 1641. Rule 3 provides that "the collegiates must be of pure race and have no mixture of Moorish or Jewish blood, to the fourth degree, and shall have no Negro or Bengal blood, or that of any similar nation, in their veins, or a fourth part of Filipino blood." [28]

The wisdom of this procedure has been questioned. It certainly forms a contrast with the policy of the Holy See in the missions directly dependent on the Sacred Congregation of Propaganda, and even with the practice of missionaries within the sphere of the Portuguese *padroado,* so similar in many respects to its Spanish counterpart.

In 1518, a brief of Leo X authorized the ordination of East Indians and Negroes "considered capable of serving God in their respective countries." A year before St. Francis Xavier's arrival in Goa, a native seminary had been established, and several Malabar

[25] Council of Mexico (1585), *lib.* 1, *tit.* 4, "De vita, fama et moribus ordinandorum," note 3, in Mansi, *Conciliorum . . . amplissima collectio* XXXIV, cols, 1034–35.
[26] Cf. Brou, *op. cit.,* p. 544.   [27] Bayle, *op. cit.,* p. 225.
[28] In *BRPI,* XLV, 175.

priests had been ordained. India, in fact, had its houses of formation for the native clergy twenty years before the Council of
Trent made such establishments obligatory in every diocese of
the Catholic world.[29]

As early as 1626, Propaganda had enjoined on the bishop of
Japan "to confer holy orders, the priesthood included, on such
Japanese as he shall consider suitable and necessary." Again in
1659, Alexander VII advised Propaganda to instruct the vicars
apostolic being sent to Tonkin, China, and Cochinchina that "the
principal reason for sending bishops to those regions was that
they might employ every means in their power to train native
youths so as to fit them for the priesthood, and thus be able to
ordain them and distribute them throughout those vast countries,
where they may diligently promote the cause of Christianity under their [the bishops'] direction"; and hence they should always
have this end in view, namely, "to draw as many as possible of
the most promising native youths to the clerical state, to educate
them, and in due time to ordain them." Succeeding popes were
no less clear and emphatic in their insistence on this point.[30]

The famous visitor of the Jesuit missions in Asia, Father Alexander Valignano, went even further, and in a celebrated *con-
sultum* caused the following resolution to be adopted:

It is necessary that there should be a bishop in Japan. But let him
not be sent from Europe, a stranger both to the language and the customs. It is abnormal for a Church to be without a bishop; and yet here
a foreign bishop will not do. Consequently natives must be ordained
either in Macao or in India. Let them be put to the test: we shall see
whether one of them will be worthy of the episcopate. As far as the
Japanese are concerned, there are grounds for hoping that if they are
well trained in learning and piety in the seminaries, they can become
as capable as Europeans of becoming religious, priests, and bishops.[31]

Thus the persecuted Japanese church could boast of several
martyr priests and religious at a time when there was probably
not yet a single native priest in the Philippines.

[29] Brou, "L'encyclique sur les missions," *Etudes,* CLXII (1920), 593.
[30] See the *instructio* of the Sacred Congregation of Propaganda of Nov.
23, 1849 in *Collectanea, op. cit.,* note 1002.
[31] Brou, "L'encyclique sur les missions," pp. 593–94.

We must not, however, ascribe this deficiency in the Philippine mission entirely to the royal cedulas of Philip II or to the decrees of the Spanish-American councils. A third contributing cause must be taken into account, namely, the difference in the cultural level of the two mission territories. As Father Charles points out, the establishment of the visible church which is the specific aim of missionary activity demands a certain level of civilization below which it is impossible.[32] It would be difficult, for instance, to encounter suitable material for the priesthood among a people just beginning to organize into stable political communities. Now the Filipinos during the early years of Spanish colonization were just such a people, whereas India, China, and Japan already had very high and ancient cultures of their own. Thus the failure of the Tlatelolco experiment was probably due, at least in part, to the fact that it was a little too premature; and the prohibitions of the Councils of Mexico and Lima, though perhaps too sweeping, were very fundamentally a sound precaution.

To sum up, three main causes combined to retard the formation of a native clergy in the Philippines. The first was the primitive condition of society, which had first to be raised to that level of cultural maturity required before it could provide suitable aspirants to the Catholic priesthood. This preliminary work of civilization was mainly if not solely the achievement of the first Spanish missionaries, and we need neither add nor detract from an American historian's assessment of it:

In the light . . . of impartial history raised above race prejudice and religious prepossessions, after a comparison with the early years of the Spanish conquest of America or with the first generation or two of the English settlements, the conversion and civilization of the Philippines in the forty years following Legazpi's arrival must be pronounced an achievement without parallel in history.[33]

The second cause was the framework of the ecclesiastical establishment constructed by the *patronato* in the colony, a framework which provided no suitable room for a native clergy even when the mission was ready for it. And the third was the conciliar and

[32] Charles, *op. cit.*, I, 31.   [33] Bourne in *BRPI*, I, 37.

synodal legislation of Spanish America, extended without modification to the Philippines, legislation which, while it effectively prevented the ordination of unworthy candidates, did so by excluding even the worthy from the priesthood.

The first of these causes was by nature transitory. There came a time when, thanks to the creative energy of the church even on the natural and temporal level, there was no longer any valid objection to admitting native Filipinos to holy orders. The other two causes, however, had that inelastic tenacity with which human institutions cling to existence long after they have outlived their usefulness, and so we must not be surprised to find the idea of a native clergy opposed even by those who should have been most zealous in promoting it.

II

In a report submitted to Innocent XI around 1680, the Secretary of Propaganda, Monsignor Urbano Cerri, remarked about conditions in the Philippine mission that

notwithstanding the great number of Monks in these Islands, and the progress of the Catholic faith, there are some faults; particularly the neglect of many conversions, which might be attempted without great Labour; and want of Charity towards the Sick, who are obliged to get themselves carried to Church, to receive the Viaticum, and the Extreme Unction. Besides, no Care is taken to make the Natives study; and Holy Orders are never conferred on them, though they have the necessary qualifications to be ordained.[34]

It should be noted that this disbarment of native Filipinos from holy orders was no longer based on official policy. By the second half of the seventeenth century it was generally recognized in the Spanish colonies—or at any rate in Spanish America—that there were *indios* capable of assuming the responsibilities of the Catholic priesthood, and hence that holy orders could not justifiably be refused to *indios* as a class. This more favorable attitude is clearly expressed in a guidebook for administrators of Indian parishes

[34] The quotation is from an English translation (London, 1715) entitled *An Account of the State of the Roman Catholic Religion throughout the World*, pp. 113–14.

published in 1668. To the question "May Indians receive orders without special dispensation?" the author, a bishop of Quito, replies as follows:

The Indians are not deprived by birth or blood of the right to receive holy orders. The reason is because the Church of God normally admits into her service and sacred ministry all who have the aptitude, ability and inclination for them, without respect of persons. . . .

[Hence] no special dispensation is required for Indians to receive holy orders, any more than it is required for Spaniards born in lawful wedlock, since no impediment exists in the former any more than in the latter. True, the Second Council of Lima (Part II, n. 74) forbade the ordination of Indians; but that was . . . when they were still beginners engaged in learning the rudiments of our holy religion. Later, when they had acquired a sufficient grasp of it, not only were they not excluded from holy orders, but the Third Council (*Actio* II, *cap.* 31) enjoins that those who are as familiar with the native languages as the Indians are, as well as others who possess the same facility, ought not to be prevented from taking holy orders; on the contrary, they should be encouraged and invited to do so, provided they are endowed with the aptitude and qualities necessary for an office so sublime and of such importance in the service of our Lord.[35]

However, such advanced ideas had not yet gained acceptance among the ecclesiastical authorities of the Philippines. What pre-

---

[35] Alonso de la Peña Montenegro, *Itinerario para parochos de indios* (Madrid, 1668), pp. 368–69. He goes on to say that *mestizos* may also be ordained without a dispensation being required provided they are of legitimate birth. As for negroes, they obviously could not receive holy orders if they were slaves. There was a dispute regarding free negroes. Certain canonists claimed that the color of their skin was an impediment to ordination, "because for a negro to go up to the altar to celebrate Mass would cause considerable consternation among white people whose contact with negroes is limited to those who perform the meanest offices and who are for the most part slaves. . . . But many other authorities, and weighty ones, are of the opinion that this does not in any way constitute an impediment to their being ordained; for in this part of the world where they are so numerous, and where some of them command troops and hold other military commissions, their becoming priests will be in no wise disturbing; on the contrary, it has been our experience with the few who have actually received orders that the people have been much edified by them" (*ibid*, pp. 370–71).

cipitated the decision to open the ranks of the priesthood to native Filipinos was, in fact, a rather curious accident.[36]

In 1672 Msgr. François Pallu, who had been sent by the Sacred Congregation of Propaganda to the East as vicar apostolic of Siam, Cochinchina, and Tonkin, met with stormy weather on a voyage from Siam to China and was forced to put into Manila harbor. The governor of the Philippines at the time, Don Manuel de León, decided upon the advice of his council to restrain Pallu from proceeding to his destination. His reason was that the eastern provinces of China came under the *patronato* of the Spanish crown, and hence that a Propaganda bishop had no business going there without the Spanish government's knowledge and consent.

Pallu was politely but firmly lodged in the Jesuit college in Manila, and a few months later put on board the Acapulco galleon with instructions that upon arrival in Mexico he should be sent on to Madrid. It must have been with considerable embarrassment that the Count of Medellín, president of the Council of the Indies, welcomed the indignant prelate to the court of Charles II. He tried to make up for the Philippine governor's excess of zeal by treating Pallu with the utmost consideration. Pallu, for his part, decided to bear no grudge, and the upshot was that the count and the bishop became fast friends.

Although Pallu had been under house arrest in Manila, he seems to have formed quite definite ideas about the state of the colony and the colonial church, ideas which he discussed with Medellín and which that gentleman took up with enthusiasm. Prominent among them was the need to form a native clergy, a need not only religious but political. The first was obvious; the Philippine clergy was undermanned and there was no possible way of increasing its numbers except by local recruitment. But the second was no less real. For fully a century the royal government had been trying to get the religious orders in the Philippines to accept its patronal privileges—in particular, the right to approve parish appointments. The religious superiors repelled all

---

[36] The present account is based on Casimiro Díaz, *Conquistas de las islas Filipinas* (Valladolid, 1890), pp. 701–704. This is the printed edition of a manuscript completed ca. 1718, the work of an Augustinian friar of long residence in the Philippines.

such efforts with a simple but effective formula: either the government left them alone, or they abandoned all their parishes and missions. To such an ultimatum the government had no reply, for there was no one to take over the parishes and missions from the regular clergy.

But if there were? If a native secular clergy could be formed in sufficient numbers to enable the royal patron to relieve the religious at least of the more settled parishes? The prospect could not fail to be attractive to the Council of the Indies. In 1677 a decree of the king in council went forth to the ecclesiastical authorities in the Philippines, couched in the following terms:

A certain person moved by zeal for God's service and mine has represented to me, among other matters pertaining to the spiritual and temporal welfare of the natives of those islands, the convenience and manifold advantages which would redound to the common good if the opportunity to study [for the sacred ministry] were given to Indians capable of undertaking them, in order that by this means there might be a sufficient number of ministers engaged in the conversion and instruction of those who have no knowledge of the faith; and since [Indian priests] being familiar with their language and belonging to the same race would do this more easily and with entire devotedness, this person proposes that seminaries be established and that in the meantime the colleges of your Order provide the said facilities for study.

The matter having been examined in my royal council of the Indies . . . I have seen fit to enjoin by letters of even date on the archbishop of Manila and bishops of those islands to endeavor by every possible means to provide the Indians with the opportunity of studying for the sacred ministry, admitting boys (even though they be few in number) to such studies in the existing seminaries; and, if such seminaries do not as yet exist, to put forth every effort to establish them in accordance with the provisions of the sacred Council of Trent . . . in the meantime making arrangements for such boys to be enrolled in the colleges of your Order and in due course ordaining them to the priesthood provided that they have been Christians from infancy, the sons of Christian parents, well instructed in our holy Catholic faith, and endowed with the ability, intelligence and learning required for the reception of holy orders.[37]

[37] In *Colección Pastells de Madrid*, Philippine section (hereafter *CPM Fil.*), XIV, 103v. This is a collection of transcripts of documents pertaining to the history of the Spanish empire compiled by Pablo Pastells and kept in the library of the Jesuit journal, *Razón y Fe*, in Madrid.

The reaction of the ecclesiastical establishment to this move was instantaneous, unanimous, and negative. The tenor of it may be gathered from the minute of the reply returned by Archbishop Felipe Pardo of Manila in 1680:

The archbishop stated the little inclination that the Indians have for theological and moral studies, and that there was the additional difficulty of their evil customs, their vices, and their preconceived ideas—which made it necessary to treat them as children, even when they were fifty or sixty years old. He considered even the sons of Spaniards, born in the Islands, unsuitable for priests, since they were reared by Indian or slave women, because of their defective training and education in youth. Finally, on account of the sloth produced by the climate, and of effeminacy and levity of disposition, it was evident that if they were ordained priests and made ministers to the Indians when they were not sufficiently qualified therefor, through the necessity there was for them, they did not again open a book, and with their vicious habits set a very bad example to their parishioners. That which should be done was to send from España those religious who were most zealous for the conversion of souls.[38]

Fortunately, the attorney-general of the colony, Diego Antonio de Viga, got wind of what the bishops and religious superiors were writing back to Madrid. He decided to write, too, to ensure that their arguments did not go unanswered, and Madrid did not abandon the project of training native Filipino priests for lack of local support. It is a remarkable letter. It anticipates much of what Benedict XV and Pius XI would say in favor of the idea of a native clergy two and a half centuries later. It deserves to be quoted at length.

I am reliably informed that the religious orders (to whom [Your Majesty's cedula] was duly communicated) are most unwilling to comply with it and are sending many representations against it to Your Majesty, and that the archbishop-elect of this city intends to submit a memorial to the same effect, all of them alleging that the incapacity and vices of the natives disbar them from the exercise of the sacred ministry.

[38] In *BRPI*, XLV, 182–83. Cf. James S. Cummins' chapter in this volume, "Archbishop Felipe Pardo's 'Last Will.'"

Since this is among the most important questions that can arise with respect to these islands, and since the said representations may result in irreparable harm to the well being of these natives, the adequate supply of sacred ministers and the proper administration of the royal finances, I consider it my duty as Your Majesty's servant and as advocate-general of the natives of these islands to express my opinion on the subject.

I shall mention only a few of the many reasons tending to show that natives who show themselves apt and who have made the necessary studies ought to be ordained to the priesthood. One is that such natives will thereby gain honor, esteem and good repute among their own people; on the other hand, their not being able to go the whole way in this line of endeavor may cause them to become disaffected.

Secondly, a native of standing in his community who speaks the language as his mother tongue and who has received a solid grounding in religion and civility is more likely to get results of a permanent nature in the conversion of infidels than someone to whom the language and the community are foreign, even if he shows the most ardent zeal in the performance of his duties.

Thirdly, if the number of priests is deficient relative to the size of the population, many parishes will either be badly administered or not administered at all, as is the case at present, in spite of the large number of religious of almost every religious order which Your Majesty was pleased to send and which arrived this year.

Fourthly, since these islands do not have the complement of ecclesiastics necessary to staff their parishes, we are forced to be very sparing in granting permission to said ecclesiastics to proceed to other Asian countries and do mission work there. This is a sore point with them; but we must first attend to our obligations in justice with respect to Your Majesty's subjects before undertaking works of piety and charity among foreigners.

Fifthly, this archipelago consists of many well-populated regions. The religious orders stationed here undergo great labors and perils in their conversion, and sow far and wide the seeds of the true faith. But owing to the shortage of Spanish religious the size of the harvest is smaller than may be expected from the extent of the planting. We must also consider in this connection how much it costs Your Majesty to maintain a religious here, for they all come at Your Majesty's expense. This policy cannot be discontinued, but if natives are ordained we shall have more ministers available for the parochial administration of these islands as well as for the preaching and extension of the holy gospel in this and other countries, a work which the Catholic zeal of Your Majesty and your glorious predecessors has ever striven to promote from the time these lands were discovered to the present, at the cost of so much treasure and the lives of your subjects.

As for the defects or vices which these natives generally possess, surely if they are taken in hand from an early age and trained as they ought to be trained it is possible to rectify the habits of their natural condition and render them quite capable of performing the duties of churchmen, seeing that even among their fathers there are to be found men of honor and good Christians. The financial outlay which this new enterprise may require of Your Majesty does not seem to me to be much when compared to the great fruit which may be expected from it. Given the low cost of living in this country, three thousand pesos [a year], carefully administered, can feed and clothe as many as fifty boys, or somewhat less, provided that this fund can always be drawn upon whenever necessary. [I mention this because] this treasury is at present much in arrears in its payments.

In view of the above, permit me to recommend to Your Majesty the establishment of a seminary under the immediate supervision of this audiencia in which natives with the necessary qualifications may study for the ministry.[39]

An admirable brief, but quite fruitless. No one undertook to establish the diocesan seminaries enjoined by the cedula of 1677, or even the single interdiocesan seminary proposed by Viga. When, in 1697, after a lapse of twenty years, the Madrid government inquired whether there existed in the Philippines any seminary for the native clergy, Governor Cruzat y Góngora replied (June 13, 1700) that there was not, that there never had been, and that he saw no reason why there should be.[40]

By this time there was a new king—and a new dynasty—on the throne of Spain. Charles II, the last of the Hapsburg line, was succeeded in 1700 by the Bourbon Philip V. Philip V clearly did not see eye to eye with his governor in the Philippines, for on April 1, 1702, he wrote that "since it has been ordained by the sacred canons and by pontifical bulls that there should be a seminary for young men attached to all cathedral churches, that they

[39] Manila, June 26, 1680, *CPM Fil.*, XIX, 138–41.
[40] Cf. T. H. Pardo de Tavera, *Una memoria de Anda y Salazar* (Manila, 1899), pp. 48–49.

may assist at the divine service and at the same time be trained in the sciences," there should be founded in the city of Manila a seminary for eight seminarians.[41]

A modest beginning, to be sure, but a beginning. What possible objection could the authorities in the Philippines have to a seminary for *eight* seminarians? As it turned out, none whatever. For it is one of the ironies of this phase of our narrative that the very year this cedula was dispatched from Madrid, a vastly more ambitious project was taking shape in Manila.

In 1702, that capital was honored by a visit from Archbishop Charles-Thomas Maillard de Tournon, the legate accredited by the Holy See to the court of Peking for the purpose of settling the controversy over the Chinese rites. In the legate's entourage was a certain Abbé Sidotti, an Italian secular priest who would later make a fantastically heroic attempt to reintroduce Christianity to Japan. Soon after his arrival in Manila Sidotti conceived the idea of making it the seat of a seminary which would train Asian candidates for the priesthood, candidates recruited not only from the Philippines but from all the neighboring nations in which Catholic missions had been established, in effect, a regional seminary for East and Southeast Asia.[42]

With the blessing, apparently, not only of Archbishop de Tournon but also of Archbishop Camacho of Manila, he began to collect contributions from the city residents toward the construction of a seminary building, with such success that the building was almost if not actually completed before the departure of the embassy for Peking. It stood on a favored site between the residence of the governor and the city wall, to one side of the postern gate, was large enough to house 72 seminarians, and was named the College of San Clemente in honor of the reigning pope.

Unfortunately Sidotti, or rather Archbishop de Tournon, while taking care to inform Pope Clement XI of the project, failed to inform King Philip V. Philip therefore learned about it only from the apostolic nuncio at Madrid, and as a *fait accompli.* This was a

41 *Ibid.*

42 On this whole episode see, besides Pardo de Tavera, Juan Francisco de San Antonio in *BRPI,* XXVIII, 117 ff., and Joaquín Martínez de Zúñiga, *Historia de las islas Philipinas* (Sampaloc, 1803), pp. 415 ff.

disaster. Philip, it must not be forgotten, was a Bourbon; to the extreme touchiness regarding patronal rights which he inherited from his Hapsburg predecessors he added pretty strong views on the royal prerogative. Since nobody had bothered to ask his permission to erect this seminary within his dominions, it clearly did not exist; or if it did, it ought to cease to exist forthwith.

The way in which the affair had been conducted caused such indignation at the royal court that Archbishop Camacho was sharply reprimanded and transferred to the See of Guadalajara. His Majesty ordered that all the foreign seminarians be sent away at once, and that of the rest only eight be retained, all of whom had to have the approval of the governor as vice-patron in order to enter the seminary. . . . The seminary building . . . was not to be sold or put to any other use, but demolished and razed to the ground.[43]

The College of San Clemente was duly torn down and the construction of a completely new seminary was begun on another site, a seminary which would be of the right size, for eight and only eight seminarians, and which would bear when finished the more appropriate name of San Felipe. Was it ever finished? Apparently not, for a royal letter of 1720 inquires of the governor whether it would not be a good idea if the site and foundations of the proposed seminary were to be used instead for "the erection of a building for the Royal Exchequer, the Royal Treasury, and an armory with lodgings for the infantry." [44] Thus the seminary for native priests did not advance beyond the paper stage until 1772, when Archbishop Sancho de Santa Justa y Rufina transformed the University of San Ignacio, after the expulsion of the Jesuits, into the diocesan seminary of San Carlos.

III

Earlier in the eighteenth century, however, various educational institutions which had originally been founded exclusively for Spaniards began to educate native Filipinos for the priesthood. The Jesuit historian Murillo Velarde, writing in 1752, remarks drily that "there are in the Philippines, as in other parts of the

43 Martínez de Zúñiga, *op. cit.*, pp. 415–17.
44 In Pardo de Tavera, *op. cit.*, p. 49.

world, many who are stupid and ignorant; but there are not wanting some who have wit and ability, sufficient for the study of Grammar, Philosophy and Theology, in which they have made some progress, though not much." [45]

If "some progress" had already been made in 1752, the first step must have been taken some years earlier, and this is doubtless what the Augustinian, Fray Gaspar de San Agustín, tried to prevent when he wrote in 1725:

It does not seem good that I should refrain from touching on a matter which is most worthy of consideration, and that is, that if God because of our sins and theirs should desire to chastise the flourishing Christian communities of these Islands by placing them in the hands of natives ordained to the priesthood (*which seems likely to happen very soon*), if, I say, God does not provide a remedy for this, what abominations will result from it! [46]

San Agustín's warning seems to have had little effect, for in 1750 native priests had charge of 142 parishes and missions out of a total of 569.[47] These first fruits of the Filipino clergy seem to have been equal to the demands of their vocation. The Spanish Jesuit Delgado could even say of some of them that "although they are *indios,* they can serve as an example to shame Europeans." [48] He cites two instances: Eugenio de Santa Cruz, a native of Pampanga, who became a chancery official of the diocese of Cebu and an assessor of the Holy Office, and Bartolome Saguinsin, a native of Antipolo, one of the parish priests of the suburban district of Quiapo, "omitting mention, only because brevity compels me to do so, of many others, living and dead, who are worthy of having their names mentioned in this history." [49]

The passage occurs in that part of his history where Delgado undertakes to refute the animadversions made by Fray Gaspar de

---

[45] *Geographia historica,* VIII (Madrid, 1752), 37.

[46] In Mas, *op. cit.,* III, 33; italics supplied.

[47] Cf. Brou, "Notes," pp. 546–47.

[48] Delgado, *Historia general* (Manila, 1892), p. 293. The date is that of the printed edition; the manuscript was completed in 1754.

[49] *Ibid.*

San Agustín a quarter of a century earlier regarding the Filipino character in general, and in particular its unfitness for the clerical state. Since San Agustín's letter became a kind of *locus communis* from which later controversialists quarried their arguments, and since Delgado's reply, being that of one who was himself a Spaniard, may be expected to be free from racial bias, it will not be amiss to give the substance of both.

San Agustín argued that the ordination of Filipinos to the priesthood would in no way change their character, to the detailed description of whose numerous and grave defects he devoted the major portion of his letter.

Rather, their pride will be aggravated with their elevation to so sublime a state; their avarice with the increased opportunity of preying on others; their sloth with their no longer having to work for a living; and their vanity with the adulation that they must needs seek, desiring to be served by those whom in another state of life they would have had to respect and obey; in such wise, that the malediction of *Isaias*, 24, shall overtake this nation: "It shall be as with the people, so with the priest." For the *indio* who seeks holy orders does so not because he has a call to a more perfect state of life, but because of the great and almost infinite advantages which accrue to him along with the new state of life which he chooses. How much better it is to be a Reverend Father than to be a yeoman or a sexton! What a difference between paying tribute and being paid a stipend! Between being drafted to cut timber [50] and being waited on hand and foot! Between rowing a galley and being conveyed in one! All of which does not apply to the Spaniard, who by becoming a cleric deprives himself of the opportunity of becoming a mayor, a captain or a general, together with many other comforts of his native land, where his estate has more to offer than the whole nation of *indios*. Imagine the airs with which such a one will extend his hand to be kissed! What an incubus upon the people shall his father be, and his mother, his sisters, and his female cousins, when they shall have become great ladies overnight, while their betters are still pounding rice for their supper! For if the *indio* is insolent and insufferable with little or no excuse, what will he be when elevated to so high a station? . . . What reverence will the *indios* themselves have for such a priest, when they see that he is of their color and race? Especially when they realize that they are the equals

[50] Forced labor supplied timber for the shipyards.

or betters, perhaps, of one who managed to get himself ordained, when his proper station in life should have been that of a convict or a slave? [51]

Delgado's refutation of these strictures is as devastating as it is urbane. To the charge that the native candidates for the priesthood will have no standing in the community, being congenital slaves or potential jailbirds, he replies:

Those [natives] who are being educated in any of the four colleges in Manila which are devoted to the formation of the clergy are all sons of the better class, looked up to by the *indios* themselves, and are not *timaua* or of the *olipon* class, as the Visayas—or *maharlica* or *alipin,* as the Tagalogs—call slaves and freedmen. These boys are being educated by the Reverend Fathers of Saint Dominic or of the Society [of Jesus]; they instruct them in virtue and letters, and if any of the bad habits of the *indio* cling to them, these are corrected and removed by the teaching and conversation of the Fathers. Moreover, their Lordships the Bishops, when they promote any of them to holy orders, do not go about the matter blindfolded, ordaining any one who is set before them, but with great care and prudence gather information regarding their purity of blood and *de moribus et vita,* examining them and putting them to the test before they are made pastors of souls; and to say otherwise is injurious to these illustrious prelates, to whom we owe so much respect and reverence. [52]

This is not to say, of course, that native priests have without exception lived up to expectations. To demand as much from the priesthood of any nation is to show complete ignorance of human nature.

It is possible, no doubt, that some have not justified the high regard which has been shown them in entrusting to them the dispensation of the divine mysteries; but it is bad logic to argue that because one or many are bad, therefore all are likewise bad. And it is to be noted that if any cleric or parish priest among them is bad or gives scandal, their prelates, who are holy and zealous, correct and chastise them and even remove them from their posts and deprive them of their ministry; and often, as I myself have seen, they summon them and cause them to say

[51] In Mas, *op. cit.,* III, 33–34.   [52] Delgado, *op. cit.,* pp. 293–94.

Mass and perform their spiritual duties under their eye, until they are certain of their reformation and amendment. Thus they do not permit that "it shall be, as with the people, so with the priest." Moreover, it is a gratuitous assertion to say that the *indio* seeks holy orders, not because he has a vocation to a more perfect state of life, but because of the great and almost infinite advantages which accrue to him along with the priesthood—the advantages, that is, of being a parish priest over being a yeoman, or a sexton, or a galley slave, or a jailbird. For it is common knowledge that there are also many in Spain who seek the ecclesiastical state for the sake of a livelihood; and others enter religion for the same reason. Nor may we conclude that therefore such persons did not have a true vocation; for if the Church *non judicat de occultis,* such judgment being reserved to God who *scrutat renes et corda,* much less is it permitted to any private person to pass judgment on this matter.[53]

Delgado clinches his argument by examining the supposition on which San Agustín's whole thesis is based, namely, that there are certain sections of the human race—among which the Filipinos are to be counted—which are by nature unfit for the priestly state.

Finally, I shall answer the example brought forward by the reverend author of this hyperbolical letter to prove that it is impossible for the *indios* to divest themselves of their racial traits, even though they be consecrated bishops, etc. I say, then, that this was precisely the practice of the holy apostles, namely, to ordain priests and bishops from among the natives of those regions where they preached, whether they be Indians or Negroes. And it is a historical fact that when Saint Francis Xavier arrived in India, he found many Comorin clerics, who are Negroes, already preaching the Gospel in those newly founded Christian communities. And so likewise there were in Japan many Japanese priests belonging to religious orders, and in China there are today, as we read in the printed accounts of the venerable martyrs of Saint Dominic and the Society of Jesus.[54]

We thus have sufficient warrant for saying that in spite of the official attitude unfavorable to the formation of a native clergy, in spite of the obstacles placed in its way by the clumsy machinery

[53] *Ibid.*, pp. 294–95.   [54] *Ibid.*, p. 295.

of the *patronato*, in spite of the often bitter prejudice against the *indio*—which, though perhaps unjustifiable, was in many cases quite understandable—there were not lacking, in the first half of the eighteenth century, writers to champion what the church has always held regarding the necessity of a native priesthood, and educators to carry it into effect. Delgado's reply to San Agustín reveals that by 1750 at least four educational establishments in Manila were training native candidates for the priesthood; that some of these natives had already been ordained and put in charge of parishes; that a few had even distinguished themselves and been appointed to positions of trust; in a word, that man-made barriers, and even the conscious opposition of the church's own instruments, were powerless to withstand, in this as in so many other cases, the secret springs of the church's vitality.

IV

We have seen how the regime of the *patronato* tended to keep the parishes in the hands of the regular clergy.[55] This meant, of course, that the bishop could exercise only a limited jurisdiction over the majority of his parish priests, since they were religious and hence subject to their religious superiors.

This overlapping of authority occasioned numerous clashes between the bishops and the religious orders, and it is easy to see how the secular clergy would be drawn, willy-nilly, into the quarrel. An obvious solution to every conflict was for the bishops to take away their parishes from the recalcitrant religious and hand them over to secular priests who would be completely under their authority; and the temptation was to do this even if the secular priest had no other qualification for the post save that of being amenable.

An incompetent parish priest was scarcely an improvement over a rebellious one; but incompetent or not, such tactics on the part of the bishop obviously did not make for harmonious relations between the regular and the secular clergy. Rather, the reli-

[55] The regular clergy had 427 of the 569 parishes in 1750, distributed as follows: Augustinians, 115; Augustinian Recollects, 105; Jesuits, 93; Franciscans, 63; Dominicans, 51. Cf. C. B. Elliott, *The Phillippines to the End of the Military Regime* (Indianapolis, 1917), p. 219, note.

gious in charge of parishes came to look upon the secular clergy as a standing threat to their security, the more so since within the peculiar framework maintained by the *patronato* the only way in which the secular clergy could obtain any parishes at all was at the expense of the regular clergy. This antagonism was underscored by the fact that while the religious orders admitted practically no natives into their ranks, the secular clergy in the Philippines was composed almost entirely of them. Thus, racial prejudice confused and embittered the rivalry between seculars and regulars from the very beginning, and served to account for such startling outbursts as the memorial of Fray Gaspar de San Agustín.

Another factor must be taken into consideration, and this is that until the founding of the first diocesan seminary in the latter part of the eighteenth century, the training of native priests was exclusively in the hands of religious. It is to their credit, as we pointed out, that the religious undertook this task at all, in spite of the prevailing attitude against it, although, of course, it was to their advantage to have native assistants in their parishes. And the temptation was precisely to give these seminarians just enough education to enable them to be assistants to parish priests, and no more, and to water down that "intensive, severe and solid training" [56] which is demanded by the church for all her priests, which alone could have fitted them for positions of responsibility.

The recurrent charges made by the religious of the time against the Filipino secular clergy—that it was composed of men who were ignorant, incompetent, unstable, unworthy of the high dignity of the priesthood—may have been to some extent merited, but if they were merited, could not a large part of the blame for it be justly laid at the door of the religious themselves, who failed to give them the formation necessary to render them worthy? Thus there seems to be a kernel of truth in Governor Simón de Anda's somewhat exaggerated statement that

[56] The phrase is that of a general of the Society of Jesus, Wlodimir Ledóchowski. It occurs in his letter to the superior of the mission of Kiangnan in China, Aug. 15, 1919 (*Acta Romana Societatis Iesu*, III, 122–44), which may be taken as a classic statement of the standards set by the church for the training of a native clergy.

it is to the interest of the religious orders that there should not be formed and should never be any secular clergy, for so, there being no one to take their places, they may continue in their possession of the curacies, and the King in his long-standing and thoroughly troublesome burden of sending out missionaries at his own expense, who when they arrive here are so many more enemies to his interests. In accordance with this policy and with remarkable harmony the two universities [Santo Tomás and San Ignacio] have made it an invariable rule to impart a merely cursory training, in order to spoil in this way even the small number of assistant priests.[57]

There was at least a very strong temptation, as we have said, to take this course of action, and human nature being what it is, it is very likely that the temptation was not always successfully resisted. For there can be no doubt that many Filipino priests of this period, unlike those of a generation earlier, were as a matter of fact not up to standard. The reason most commonly given for this was the innate incapacity of the national character, but aside from the fact that this had been disproved time and again by such examples as those adduced by Delgado, such an argument cannot be valid unless a fair trial is made of that character's capabilities, which certainly was not the case if a stunted education did not give it a chance for full development.

Moreover, the charge of incompetence came with very bad grace from those who were willing enough to make extensive use of these incompetents, as Archbishop Sancho pointed out:

Is it not common knowledge to all of us here [in the Philippines] that the actual spiritual ministry falls entirely on the shoulders of the secular coadjutor, the Father Minister [i.e., the religious parish priest] reserving to himself merely the task of collecting, at ease in his rectory, the parish stipends? How can they deny this, when it is so well known? If the secular priests are so incompetent, how can they [the religious] permit and entrust to them the spiritual administration of their parishes? If they are not incompetent, how dare they cast discredit on the secular clergy with the strange, not to say unjust accusation of being inept and incapable? . . . To such excesses are the religious led by the black jealousy with which they look upon the secular

[57] In Pardo de Tavera, op. cit., p. 10.

clergy; for they are afraid that by its ability and upright conduct it is bound to prove, and indeed has already begun to prove, that although the religious render good service, service of a very high order, they are nevertheless not as necessary as they assume.[58]

The argument has point; but of course, as with all the controversial writings of this troubled period, we must always make allowances for heated exaggeration in the writings of the pugnacious Archbishop Sancho. The cold residue of fact seems to be this: that the system of the *patronato* had so muddled ecclesiastical affairs in the Philippines as to create an endemic conflict between the religious in charge of parishes and their bishops, a conflict which made very difficult the normal development of the native clergy.

Moreover, not content with having thus created the elements of this conflict, the royal patron and his colonial officials were forever exerting direct pressure on one or the other side of the quarrel, thus adding a tangle of political intrigue to an ecclesiastical problem already confused by every shade of professional and racial bias.

Archbishop Sancho's administration is a case in point. We have already seen how the Spanish government was as a general rule against the religious parish priests being replaced by native clergy. Exceptions to this general rule were Charles III and his ministers, who found the most determined opponents of their policies among the religious orders. They succeeded in suppressing the Society of Jesus in all the Spanish dominions, and as a part of a plan to cripple the others, a court prelate, Basilio Sancho de Santa Justa y Rufina, was sent as archbishop to Manila in 1767.

No sooner had Archbishop Sancho reached Manila than he proceeded at once to enforce episcopal visitation on the religious parish priests. We need not delay on this vexed question of episcopal visitation, beyond noting that the religious orders looked upon the way Archbishop Sancho proposed to conduct it as an attack upon their respective institutes to which they could not in conscience yield. This was precisely the excuse the archbishop

[58] Sancho to Charles III, Manila, Oct. 1, 1768, *ibid.*, pp. 52–53.

was looking for to warrant his transferring as many parishes as he could from the regular to the secular clergy.

To the scandal and sincere regret of all good and loyal Spaniards, the Archbishop of Manila now began to hand over to the native clergy almost all the missions and parishes, wresting them under various pretexts and on different occasions from the religious who had conquered and organized them at the price of their blood and sweat.[59]

Thus in 1773 the Augustinians were expelled from their parishes in the province of Pampanga and native priests installed in their places. In addition to the vacancies thus created, the archbishop also had to provide for the parishes abandoned by the suppressed Society of Jesus. He was therefore compelled to ordain priests hurriedly, in quantity, and with little regard for the thoroughness of their training. However, this did not seem to have given him any scruples, for we find him writing complacently to the king:

At the cost of intensive labor I have succeeded in the space of a year in setting up this seminary,[60] which has supplied a sufficient number of suitable ministers for the towns which had been administered by the Jesuit Fathers; and to put it in a nutshell, I have removed its reproach from the insignificant clergy that has existed hitherto, which was a national disgrace.[61]

There were others who did not see eye to eye with the archbishop as to the merits of his achievement. The quip became current in Manila that "there were no oarsmen to be found for the coasting vessels, because the archbishop had ordained them all."[62]

[59] J. Ferrando, *Historia de los PP. Dominicos en las islas Filipinas* (Madrid, 1870), V, 35–36.

[60] What he actually did was to transform the College of San José into a diocesan seminary contrary to the terms of the endowment. Upon being taken to task by the king for doing this, he surrendered San José to the government and took over instead the physical plant of the former Jesuit University of San Ignacio. Cf. Martínez de Zúñiga, *Estadismo de las islas Filipinas*, W. E. Retana, ed. (Madrid, 1893), I, 232–35; BRPI, XLV, 123–24, 128–30.

[61] Ferrando, *op. cit.*, V, 36.

[62] M. Buzeta and F. Bravo, *Diccionario geográfico, estadístico, histórico de las islas Filipinas* (Madrid, 1851), II, 279.

And sure enough, it was not long before his hasty ordinations began to bear bitter fruit for Archbishop Sancho. In a pastoral letter dated October 25, 1771, he gives violent expression to his disappointment, and a lurid summary of the shocking reports that had caused it.

How can We refrain from weeping and lamenting, when the news comes to Us that the parish priest of such and such a town is not a father of souls, but a galley boatswain who punishes with the lash—O accursed and most execrable crime!—even the very maidens! The example of a good life, the exact fulfilment of one's duties, serious and repeated admonitions, prayer and preaching: these are the arms of our profession. Neither Jesus Christ nor our patron, Saint Peter, bequeathed to us the scourge or the whip.[63]

Then in a dramatic passage the heartbroken archbishop pictures couriers arriving at his palace from every part of his diocese, bringing sombre news of the misdemeanors of his clergy.

Here comes a messenger with another letter which pierces Our heart with the certain information that in such and such a town Father So-and-so multiplies visits to suspicious houses at suspicious hours; that the town and its parishioners are greatly shocked; that on the night of such and such a day certain persons followed said Father and stoned him. Good God! Is this a father of souls, or a ravening wolf who spills their life-blood and devours them? . . . Other messengers and letters come pouring in.

"My Lord: Father So-and-so of such and such a town is a wine-bibber, and on such a day rendered himself incapable of administering the sacraments. He has become a byword, an object of derision and contempt for old and young alike."

"This other parish priest does not observe the established scale of stole fees; he is a tyrant, a robber; he does not practice the works of mercy, nor give Christian burial to the dead of those who are unable to offer a stipend."

"And that one does not teach the catechism in the Spanish language."

"My Lord: such and such a town is in a state of revolt, disturbance and confusion, because the parish priest or vicar who was assigned to

[63] Full text in Ferrando, *op. cit.*, V, 36 ff.

it has brought with him all his relatives: aunts, male cousins, female cousins, who, puffed up with the high station of their kinsman, wish to order everything according to their fancy, and treat all the parishioners with high-handed contempt."

"My Lord: the rectory of such and such a town is wide open to all sorts of people at all sorts of hours, and on such and such a day, to the scandal of the God-fearing and discreet, it was the scene of a *fandango,* and other provocative dances in which both sexes took part."

"My Lord: this priest temporarily in charge of a parish has eaten up the fees and what silver plate the church contained, and has paid no attention to the eighths and other ecclesiastical taxes. . . ."

"My Lord: the majority of the parish priests and coadjutors look with horror and distaste at attendance at the moral conferences, and very few open a book or bother to buy one."

"My Lord: in this town and that other, the parish priests do not practice or care about almsgiving; they are very strict in exacting stipends and fees, but they want all the money for themselves, or distribute it among their relatives; the churches are bare, and they turn a deaf ear when they are asked for an alms." [64]

Allowing for the good archbishop's habitual vigor of speech, more noted for its vividness than for its exactitude, the picture of the native clergy that emerges from his pastoral is still not a very edifying one. We can easily understand the bitterness with which religious observers of the time saw the prosperous parishes which their predecessors had built up "at the price of their blood and sweat" run to seed under the mismanagement of this hastily created clergy.

It was painful to see brought to ruin [one of them wrote] all the labors of our ancient Fathers; and what was for me especially mortifying was to find that the libraries which they had left behind in some of the rectories had been entirely destroyed, having been exposed to leaks in the roof or eaten by moths through their new owners never handling or reading them.[65]

Now, indeed, Fray Gaspar de San Agustín's dire prophecy is fulfilled, and with a vengeance. Had he not—and so many others before and after him—foretold that nothing but evil would come

[64] *Ibid.,* V, 57–58.   [65] Martínez de Zúñiga, *Estadismo,* I, 479.

of trying to make priests out of this hopelessly ignorant, indolent, unreliable race? Surely the event has given proof positive of their thesis that the *indio* is congenitally incapable of the clerical state.

It may be permitted to conjecture, however, that if these essentially just and prudent men were given to stand where we stand now, outside the orbit of factional strife and with their perspective corrected by time and subsequent experience, they would admit that such a thesis is an oversimplification of what was really a more complicated reality. Enough of the evidence has been presented to suggest that the native clergy were as much victims as the religious were of a particular form of union between the ecclesiastical and the civil order which injured rather than helped the work of the church. They were, in fact, the ones more heavily victimized. For the religious orders suffered little beyond the loss of a few parishes, whereas the native clergy as a whole sustained an injury to its reputation which has crippled its growth until very recent times.

Be that as it may, Archbishop Sancho's disastrous experiment historically resulted in the general acceptance, on the part of both civil and ecclesiastical officials, of San Agustín's thesis. Filipinos, being by nature incapable of the full responsibilities of the priesthood, were to be employed only in strictly subordinate positions in the church, and were to be trained as such. This was the prevailing attitude toward them until almost the last years of the nineteenth century—an attitude, at best, of pitying tolerance, at worst, of unconcealed contempt. It recurs regularly in the writings of the period.

Tomás de Comyn, writing in 1810, reports that by that time the number of native priests and seminarians exceeded that of the regular clergy. In spite of this, he suggests that natives should be prevented from becoming parish priests.

At present there are no more than three hundred [religious], including old men, jubilarians and lay brothers; whereas the number of *indio* clerics in effective possession of curacies, temporary parish priests, assistant parish priests and seminarians exceed a thousand. And since the latter, unworthy as a general rule of the priesthood, are prejudicial rather than of real usefulness to the State, it would not be an injustice to deprive them, as a general policy, of the dignity of parish priests, enabling them merely to be substitutes in necessary cases, and aggregating them to the curacies in the role of coadjutors. In this way, in the measure that the towns are provided with suitable ministers, the said clerics will be given their respective places, and will acquire knowledge and decorum at the side of the religious, and with time may come to earn a certain amount of standing and good repute among their countrymen.[66]

Seventy years later, the publicist Francisco Cañamaque comes up with the suggestion that the limited talents of Filipinos could be more usefully employed in the development of industry and commerce than in the study of theology and Latin:

Seven hundred and forty-eight *indio* priests . . . not only indicate a deviation in the choice of a profession as mistaken as it is censurable, but to my way of thinking, given the religious fanaticism of the Filipino people, constitute political dynamite which is bound sooner or later to explode. No one gains by this policy of ordaining Filipino priests; neither themselves, because in exchange for the habit they relinquish to foreigners the practice of the national crafts, industries and commerce; nor the friars, because they find in every secular priest a jealous rival; nor the Philippines, because it is not gifted with talents in such abundance as to be able with impunity to exercise them in theology and Latin; nor the mother country which has suffered enough since the beginning of the century from the thanks that it ordinarily receives from the native clergy of the colonies. The Governors and Bishops ought to give weighty consideration to this matter, and direct the inclinations of the natives along more useful lines, until conditions in the Islands shall permit the employment along other lines of a part of its resources without fatal injury to the general interests of the country.[67]

The same author elsewhere makes clear why he considers Filipino priests such a waste of time and energy:

The *indio* priest is a real caricature. . . . He is a caricature of the Spaniard, a caricature of the *mestizo*, a caricature of everybody. He is

[66] *Estudo de las islas Filipinas en 1810*, F. del Pan, ed. (Manila, 1878), pp. 159–60.

[67] *Las islas Filipinas* (Madrid, 1880), pp. 63–65.

a patchwork of many things, and is nothing. I put it badly; he is something, after all; more than something . . . he is an enemy of Spain.[68]

And in that last phrase, the rather haphazard scalpel of Cañamaque's wit blunders upon the true political reason for discourag-
ing a native clergy in the Philippines—fear. Behind the repeated
assertion that the Filipino was incapable of assimilating any but
the most rudimentary education lurked the fear that if he should
be given more than that, he might conceivably use it to conduct
his own affairs, and eventually discover that he no longer stood in
need of a mother country. There are indications of this in the way
the few Filipino priests who managed to rise by sheer talent or
strength of will above the mediocrity to which they were condemned were immediately surrounded by large numbers of their
admiring countrymen, ready to follow their lead with a disconcerting devotion. Patricio de la Escosura, another Spanish observer, notes the symptom:

Here [in the Philippines] every time that a native priest distin-
guishes himself by his learning or his activity, every time that he is
seen to be successful in his profession, every time that he shines in one
way or another, the same moral phenomenon is infallibly produced;
public opinion marks him out as a rebel, and the malcontents seek him
out and surround him, while those who are loyal [to Spain] withdraw
more or less openly from his company. . . . It seems to me indisput-
able that as long as there are native lawyers and priests of some standing in any town or province of the archipelago, there shall rebellion
and other troubles break out.[69]

In other words, the "public opinion" to which Escosura refers
had the Filipino priest neatly pinned between the horns of a dilemma. If he was incompetent, his incompetence proved that he
could not be anything else; if he was competent, his competence
proved that he was a rebel. In either case, the practical conclusion was the same, that is, that little effort need be expended on
his formation, any zeal in this regard being either useless or dangerous. And how inadequate, as a matter of fact, this formation

[68] In W. E. Retana, *Frailes y clérigos* (Madrid, 1890), p. 100.
[69] *Ibid.*, p. 102.

5 2 5 3 3

was, may be gathered from a memorial of the *ayuntamiento,* or city council, of Manila to the king in 1804:

In the three provincial capitals which are adorned with episcopal sees, there are no seminaries in which a young man can be trained with firmness and prudence, since what are called seminaries consist practically of the mere material edifice. There are barely taught in them, by one or two *indio* clerics who speak Spanish only with difficulty, a very bad Latin and a little of Lárraga.[70]

A very bad Latin and a little of Lárraga—perhaps this is the answer to the question posed by one of the regular clergy's most enthusiastic apologists:

How many Indian theologians, canonists, philosophers, moralists [have graduated from] the conciliar seminaries? Not even one by exception, which usually is found in any general rule. . . . This lack is not due to the professors, for they were always picked men. . . . What does this signify, if not that the deficiency is in the race, and not in the professors or the books?[71]

We are inclined to think that what it really signified was "a very bad Latin and a little of Lárraga."

As was to be expected, the result of this short-sighted policy was the exact opposite of what it aimed at. The average Filipino priest received just enough education to resent the suspicion and contempt with which he was treated, but not enough to perceive the real causes for such treatment, or how to rise above it. Consequently either he relapsed into apathy, and became in fact what he was told he could not help being, or he sought to escape the vicious circle in which he was caught by political agitation and intrigue alien to his profession. In either case, the work of the church in the Philippines suffered well-nigh irreparable damage; but so did the stability of the Spanish regime. For it is always bad statesmanship, in the long run, to put political expediency before

[70] In Retana, *Archivo del bibliófilo filipino* (Madrid, 1895), I, fasc. 8, pp. 24–25. Francisco Lárraga was the author of a *Promptuarium theologiae moralis,* written in dialogue form, the first edition of which was published at Pamplona in 1710.

[71] E. Zamora, *Las corporaciones religiosas,* in *BRPI,* XLVI, 348–49.

the demands of the spiritual order, and that is exactly the measure of the failure of the *patronato* in its declining years.

The education of the native clergy improved appreciably with the arrival of the Vincentians in 1862 and their taking charge of the diocesan seminaries, but not to an extent sufficient to cope with the emergency resulting from the revolution of 1896 and the transfer of sovereignty from Spain to the United States. The nature and gravity of that emergency was well described by Archbishop Michael J. O'Doherty of Manila:

A careful analysis of after events will lead one to the conclusion that if the Spanish friars made a mistake in their policy of governing the Filipinos, it was solely in this that they failed to realize that the day might come when Spanish sovereignty in the Islands would cease. Hence they made no plans for an emergency such as happened in 1898. They neglected the Catholic principle that no church can rest upon a substantial basis unless it is manned by a native clergy. True, native priests had been ordained in the Philippines, but they were seldom, if ever, allowed to become pastors. To illustrate, the status of affairs in the Archdiocese of Manila may be cited. Of the 350 parishes under the jurisdiction of the Archbishop, only twelve were actually in his control, so far as appointment of pastors was concerned. Other pastors, although nominally appointed by the Archbishop, were really the choice of the Spanish friars.

Such being the case, it is by no means strange that the Filipino priests were wholly unprepared to cope with the situation when full responsibility for the government of parishes fell unexpectedly upon their shoulders. Perpetual curates they had intended to be and nothing more. A certain native priest of Bulacan voiced his sentiments to the bishop some years after the new regime had gone into effect exclaiming: "Your Lordship, we were never trained for this!" And his words were but too true.[72]

Along with the tremendous responsibility, however, there came at last to the Filipino clergy the freedom to develop normally along the lines marked out by the church. This is not the place to make any comparisons between the Spanish and the American regimes. Like all human institutions, both had their merits and

[72] "The Religious Situation in the Philippines," *American Ecclesiastical Review*, LXXIV (1926), 131–32.

defects, and the Filipino people would be obtuse indeed if they ever ceased to be grateful to both countries, to the one for her gift of the faith, to the other for her gift of freedom.

There is this to be said, however, for the American period, that while the separation between church and state which it introduced was sometimes taken to mean the estrangement of the state from the church, it did remove from the church the political trammels of the *patronato,* and enabled her to form a Filipino clergy in conformity with her divine constitution.

V

It is a bit premature to estimate the results of seven decades of this freedom, nor is it necessary, since the scope of this paper has been merely to suggest a historical solution to the problem of the slow emergence of a native priesthood in the Philippines. Nothing remains, therefore, but to summarize the conclusions of our study.

Even after the Filipino people had reached that level of cultural maturity required for the formation of a native clergy, two main causes retarded its beginnings and interfered with its development.

The first was the ecclesiastical legislation of New Spain, where the failure of a premature attempt to develop a native clergy resulted in a reaction unfavorable to the very idea of a native clergy. The letter of this legislation was, indeed, subsequently interpreted in a very lenient sense by canonists, and thus rendered to a great extent inoperative. But its spirit endured in a widespread if largely subconscious prejudice against a native clergy, which came to be looked upon not as a necessary means to the accomplishment of the missionary objective, but as a rare privilege to be conceded to native peoples only if they proved themselves worthy, according to more or less arbitrary standards of worth.

The second was the system called the *patronato,* whereby the Spanish sovereign, in his capacity as royal patron of the church in the Indies, defrayed the expenses of the colonial churches, and in exchange acquired the exclusive right of presentation to all important ecclesiastical posts in the colonies, together with very wide powers regarding the disposition of personnel and the division of ecclesiastical territory.

In such an arrangement, it was almost inevitable that considerations of political expediency should stir up controversies and influence decisions injurious to the church's work, and in particular to the normal development of the native clergy. To summarize only the instances given in the body of the article:

(1) The division of ecclesiastical territory in the Philippines among the missionary religious orders decreed by Philip II left no scope for a secular clergy, and antecedently condemned it to the essentially false position of a subordinate instrument.

(2) This arbitrary limitation of its scope necessarily lowered the standards of its formation. For, on the one hand, the native priest with such a future before him had no incentive to prepare himself for the full responsibilities of the priesthood, while on the other hand the advantage to his religious teachers of training him merely for a subordinate position was a strong and ever-present temptation.

(3) The attempt of Charles III and his ministers to cripple the religious orders resulted in the sudden imposition of full responsibility on a poorly trained, half-educated native clergy, with the disastrous results that were to be expected.

(4) This political maneuver also resulted in creating, or at least deepening, an antagonism between the Spanish regular clergy and the native secular clergy which rapidly degenerated into a national and racial enmity.

(5) Half-hearted attempts on the part of the home government to secularize parishes in the Philippines were stubbornly and successfully opposed by colonial officials, who suspected the native clergy of cherishing little love for the mother country, and in view of the treatment which they received, the suspicion was very often well founded.

Briefly, then, the system of the *patronato* asked for a second-rate native clergy, and got it; but it did not thereby accomplish the political objective which it had in mind—rather, it injured by such short-sighted statesmanship precisely those two great institutions which it aimed to serve and which in other ways it served so magnificently: the Catholic church and the Spanish crown.

Archbishop Felipe Pardo's "Last Will"

JAMES S. CUMMINS

The question of the sacerdotal ordination of Filipinos during the Spanish regime is still of interest, and in this connection the attitude of Fray Felipe Pardo, O.P., archbishop of Manila from 1677 to 1689, is sometimes referred to. Thus Blair and Robertson quote a letter of his written in 1680 indicating that he believed the Filipinos were not at that time ready for ordination.[1] He also thought it doubtful if youths born in the Philippines of Spanish parents would make suitable priests because of their upbringing and schooling; moreover, he believed that the climate of the Philippines had an adverse effect on character, so that any such persons, ordained out of mere necessity, would inevitably give a bad example to their native parishioners.

This short-sighted policy can only be condemned; it is a defect of judgment for which a price is being paid today and often by those not themselves guilty of such beliefs. But it should be remembered that the attitude was not peculiarly Spanish; the Portuguese abroad shared it fully in their colonies,[2] and indeed it was common among Europeans at the time.

The French members of the Paris Foreign Mission Society and the Italian administrators of Propaganda Fide were among the first to see the injustice of such theories, and it was doubtless Pardo's contemporary, Bishop François Pallu, M.E.P., who

---

[1] Emma Helen Blair and James Alexander Robertson, eds., *The Philippine Islands, 1493–1898* (55 vols.; Cleveland, 1903–1909), XLV, 182–83 (hereinafter cited as *BRPI*).

[2] C. R. Boxer, *Race Relations in the Portuguese Colonial Empire, 1415–1825* (Oxford, 1963), pp. 33–35, 56–57, 65–66, 117–19.

showed Propaganda Fide that the Philippine Islands could, indeed, become a "spiritual arsenal" in Asia.[3]

Pardo's restrictive policy was not due to any nationalistic animus, as he gave proof in his seventy-ninth year when, within a few months of his death, he wrote what may be regarded as his "last will" in this matter.[4] In this, *inter alia*, he urged the education of native and *mestizo* boys. Essentially a practical man, he had already sought to establish canon law studies with a view to settling the ecclesiastical disputes of which he had ample experience, for the archbishop had lived through "what may certainly be regarded as one of the most eventful decades in the history of the Philippines." [5] So now, in his last months of life, he sought, for an equally practical purpose, to make humanistic studies available to selected native boys. He realized that something had to be done to raise standards generally, and he saw the creation of a small but influential elite as the partial answer. Pardo's new scheme was a multipurpose one for it was intended to plant a proper ambition in the native youth ("*levanten el corazon, al servicio de Dios y de la Repca*"); to help create a more self-sufficient community; and to help spread the faith rapidly. Conceivably, such a program might later lead to the ordination of natives. Himself a Dominican, Pardo first submitted his scheme to the order's provincial chapter for consideration, comment, and approval.

He attempted to forestall criticisms that the spread of learning and the encouragement of ambition must result in unrest and rebellion, but there were other practical obstacles which he had not foreseen.[6] The chapter objected that the scheme, as proposed, would violate the foundation statutes of St. John Letran College; nor did the members feel that the financial arrangements in-

[3] U. Cerri, *An Account of the Roman Catholick Religion* (London, 1715), p. 114.

[4] Pardo's ecclesiastical household and train was composed very largely of *mestizos;* his secretary Domingo Díaz was one; cf. A. Xaramillo, S.J., *Memorial* (Madrid, 1691), pp. 14–15.

[5] H. de la Costa, S.J., *The Jesuits in the Philippines, 1581–1768* (Cambridge, Mass., 1961), p. 502.

[6] Some outsiders, moreover, saw in the attempt to found new chairs merely a shrewd move in the old interuniversity rivalry (Xaramillo, *op. cit.*, p. 87). See also *BRPI*, XXXVI, 74–88.

volved were sufficiently sound, since, to quote their example, the "Monetary Fund of the Board of Guardians" (i.e., *Mesa de Misericordia*) had paid out but two or three times in eleven years on an earlier endowment.[7] The chapter also feared that acceptance of the endowment would involve the community in tiresome lawsuits and in accusations that the Dominican friars were engaging in trading activities.

They made a counterproposal that another college for native boys (*"para niños indios"*) be founded in the grounds of Letran College which would be in conformity with royal orders (*"porq. es conforme a lo que su Magd. tiene encargado en sus zedulas"*). One hopes that this last was a reference to the royal order of twelve years earlier (1677), enjoining the education of native youths and the ultimate ordination of suitable candidates for the priesthood. This must remain a supposition, but it is worth noting that amongst the Dominicans who signed the reply to Pardo was the prior provincial, Fray Bartolomé Marrón, a man of vision and one acutely aware of the needs both of the Dominican province and of the islands themselves.

Unfortunately, however, before he could answer the chapter's reply the aged archbishop died. Nevertheless, if eight years earlier he had expressed a belief that the natives would show little inclination for theological studies, he now seemed in no doubt that they could overcome any environmental obstacles and would at any rate profit by a humanistic education. Thus the document, printed below, in translation, serves to show him as a man alerted to and anxious to meet the educational, cultural, and spiritual wants of the Philippines of his day, and it thereby throws a sympathetic light upon him. It is a matter for regret that time and fate prevented him from having his way in the end.

The text of the document,[8] dated March 12, 1689, runs as follows:

[7] For this, see *BRPI*, XLII, 160.

[8] This transcript is taken from the copy written into the minutes of the MS "Libro de consejos de provincia . . . 1621 . . . " (fols. 18v–19r) in the Archive of Santo Domingo Priory, Quezon City; there is a second copy *ibid*. at Vol. 571, fols. 109–118. The chapter's reply is quoted in part above.

To the Very Reverend Father Provincial and other Reverend Fathers of the Province of the Most Holy Rosary, of the Order of Friars Preacher in the Philippine Islands:

[The following I do] Impelled by my gratitude towards our holy Province [of the Dominican Order in the Philippines] not only as pertaining thereto, but because, while living in it, I have received more honors than my merits and efforts deserved; but also—and most especially—because the Province was my only refuge and the defense of my [episcopal] office and jurisdiction during the disputes and persecutions that this, my embattled Diocese, has suffered.[9] I wish to show my gratitude by some worthy alms from my income, and, incidentally, to make up for the heavy damage and expense which the Province suffered on the occasion referred to.

Moreover, I was urged to this also by the obligation to free this Commonwealth, and the rest of these islands, from the spiritual and temporal woes which beset them in the political and material spheres on account of the lack of studies of the humanities and secular sciences, and because of the slight knowledge of the Mysteries of our holy Faith, and of the Commandments of God and of the Church; for though countless priests have labored to teach these things they have done so with little success, as is revealed by the reports which I ordered should be gathered concerning idolatrous practices in various towns and provinces. And this state of affairs will continue in the future due to the repugnance and hatred which the natives in general feel towards every Spaniard, even though he be a Priest.

Impelled, then, by these obligations and by my own desire, I am minded to place thirteen thousand *pesos* with the Monetary Fund of the Board of Guardians so that from the interest (which will be three thousand, five hundred) five hundred shall be paid to those holding the Chairs of Law and Medicine that I wish to establish in the University of Saint Thomas. [Two hundred and fifty *pesos* are to be given, during his lifetime, to Bachiller don Francisco Espinosa de Monteros.] The remaining two thousand five hundred are to be used for the upkeep of as many Spaniards as possible in the aforesaid College, so that the College of St. John Letran may be left free to maintain as many

---

[9] The controversy to which Pardo here refers is discussed in P. Fernández, O.P., *Dominicos donde nace el sol* (Barcelona, 1958), pp. 189–93; De la Costa, *op. cit.*, pp. 489–502; *BRPI*, XXXIX, 149–275; and also by H. Ocio y Viana, O.P., *Reseña biográfica de . . . la Provincia del Smo. Rosario . . . de Filipinas* (Manila, 1891), I (1587–1650), pp. 473–526. This latter is a valuable work, based on first-hand sources.

natives [*indios*] as possible who may from their tenderest years be brought up in virtue and learning.[10] To this end they are to be given a Master, books for their lessons, and time for meditation; nor is the recitation of the Rosary of the Blessed Virgin to be omitted, for by such means they draw close to our Order and obtain every blessing from God our Lord. But after the death of the aforesaid Bachiller don Francisco Espinosa it is my wish that the said two hundred and fifty *pesos* be applied to clothing and maintaining the above mentioned Collegians of St. Thomas university.

I recognize clearly that the most fitting course of action in this matter will always be that chosen by your Reverences, but, in order to contribute to the best of my ability, it seems right to put before your Reverences the ways and means which appear to me to be most proper. That is to say: that all the scholarships in the College of our holy Father Saint Thomas shall continue to be of the standard demanded by the Statutes; that six Collegians shall be chosen who meet those requirements fully, without applying the dispensation of the eighth permitted by the Statutes; and these Collegians are to be given an emblem, a sun made of gold or silver gilt, to be worn on the breast of their academic tippets; [11] moreover none shall enter this group except there be a vacancy: and then only those students who have already spent three years as ordinary scholarship holders shall be eligible. Let there also be admitted, with academic gown, but without the tippet, all the remaining Spaniards who can be maintained, provided that they be at least *mestizos* on the father's side, excluding all the *Manteistas*.[12]

In the College of St. John Letran let there be admitted such natives [*indios*] and Sangley, Chinese and Japanese *mestizos* as may appear most capable of studies in the humanities and sciences. Thus this Commonwealth may begin to have men of status the lack of whom keeps the temporal state in confusion and disorder. Thus also there may be produced, not only from among the Spaniards, but also from the other races here, good apothecaries, surgeons, trained doctors who shall cure with some degree of accuracy and skill, thus preventing the tragedies that follow when ignorant men without even the rudiments

[10] For the history of San Juan Letrán College, see E. Bazaco, O.P., *Historia documentada del real Colegio de S. Juan de Letrán* (Manila, 1933).

[11] This emblem is associated with St. Thomas Aquinas, patron of the university.

[12] *Manteistas* were day-students, or students who, not having any scholarships, had to work their way through college. These latter were also called *capistas* or *agraciados*.

of technical knowledge set themselves up to cure. There may also be remedied the lack of attorneys, notaries, and lawyers; and many acts of injustice may be avoided by the removal of those who, though themselves never pupils, yet play the Domine. The door will thus be opened and the way made straight so that many other natives may leave off their pusillanimity and may raise their hearts to the service of God and the Commonwealth, serving it in many other employments. Then the community will be provided for and will be ennobled by a variety of professional and skilled men and thus free from its present dependence upon the Chinese colony on whom it currently depends for its upkeep. For in their hands lies the maintenance and commerce of the community even now, after the repeated alarms caused by their revolts and insurrections. Above all, the knowledge of God will spread through those thus brought up in virtue and learning, and through the children brought up by them in their turn as well as through their relatives, friends, familiars and other persons who may be moved by the good example of, and this contact with, people of their own race and of good standing (especially if the persons chosen for these studies are from the upper class). And this harvest will be gathered with incomparably greater fruit than is achieved by all the efforts of missionaries, past, present and to come, whose preaching, when backed by these means and measures will doubtless be most profitable. Over and above the wider spread of knowledge, the people will lose that horror which they have for all Europeans and they will recognize the good that has come to them through the Ministers of the Gospel. And this consequence will soon spread to all the provinces without there being any risk of a loss of faith in, or regard for, the Gospel among the natives themselves, as might happen if natives were forthwith put to study sacred theology with a view to ordination to the priesthood. For since the priests are Europeans they will always preserve that dignity which is due to their state. Nor is there any risk that the natives, due to their wider knowledge, may rebel against the Europeans, because learning does not endow men with new courage or strength; and although it serves the inclination yet it also serves to show the risks that would be run and penalties that must come upon the heels of any rising. Hence it follows that because of their knowledge of this, and their awareness of these mortal dangers we find that in all parts men of greater learning are less fitted for wars and military undertakings.

And finally, it has never been the intention of his majesty to keep the natives in slavery and ignorance, nor to rest his kingdom and empire heavily upon their backs; rather he has always sought for them liberty and the greatest degree of knowledge possible in order to set them upon the road to the kingdom of eternal happiness. These pious desires have been rewarded by the Lord Who has preserved this vast monarchy in America and these parts without any rising by the natives such as has befallen the other Europeans who have subjected other territories in the East Indies.[13] And this, without doubt, is a special act of providence by God our Lord from Whose divine goodness we may expect the continuation of this, and greater, favors, in proportion as the diligence and anxiety of his majesty is shown in his Royal Warrants which repeatedly order, command and charge that educational facilities be provided for the natives of these islands; and similarly other Royal Orders command that means be found to establish Chairs of Jurisprudence and Medicine in the University of our holy Father St. Thomas.

This Dominican Province alone is able to undertake a task of such magnitude for it is the principal bastion of the Faith in these Islands, and with its holiness, learning and good example, not only spreads the holy Gospel in the six missions on which it is at present working,[14] but also it puts a curb on evildoing through the medium of the pulpit and confessional; even more, its high standards are a continual reproach to the perversity and looseness of wrongdoers;[15] similarly the work of our Order encourages virtue in the strong and also offers a refuge and protection to the frail and afflicted (of this I have sure and wide experience);[16] and for other reasons which touch upon our Order in general, and this Province in particular, I judge that it alone has the strength to undertake such weighty tasks and to resist the power of the common enemy who, doubtless, will strive to disturb by different means so glorious an undertaking; it is this Province alone, also, that can direct affairs so that the natives may acquire civic character, and the spiritual state be extended, which is now very limited due to the serious impediments in the way of the preaching of the Gospel. These latter will be removed by the means I refer to.

Finally, in this holy Province alone will my care find rest, by its

[13] A reference to the Portuguese and Dutch. Some Portuguese seem to have shared the belief that their losses in India were God's punishment for their cruelty to the natives.

[14] These were in Bataan, Pangasinan, Cagayan, Zambales, and the islands of Babuyanes and Batanes.

[15] The Dominicans' Philippine province was celebrated throughout the order for its high standards of austerity and piety: it was called the "Pearl of the Order."

[16] A reference to his own recent sufferings; see note 9 above.

undertaking the education of these Spanish and native children in both the colleges. And so, for the sake of God our Lord and holy Mother Church, and for my own part also, I charge and exhort you, Very Reverend Fathers, and I beseech you through the merits and blood of Christ, our God, (for Whose sake you all came here from such distant parts in order to spread the holy Gospel and make these peoples worthy of such precious gifts) to receive my love for you without refusing the charges with which it is accompanied. For it is not lack of love or affection, but the force of the confidence that I have in this holy Province, and the urgent need of the State, which oblige me thus to divide my burdens and share them with those who have greater and more appropriate strength.

And since my aim is to assure this pious work, without prejudice to the good of the Province, I now make known to your Reverences that in order to remove from the malicious any opportunity of staining our holy Province's unsullied reputation for poverty, and for indifference to commerce and temporal gains, it is now my wish to place the sum referred to with the Board of Guardians until such time as his Holiness shall approve and decide that in the College of our holy Father St. Thomas a safe-deposit with three keys be made, into which the said sum be placed to be administered by two completely trustworthy laymen who are to send the capital to be invested in two parts when the galleon goes, so that the whole amount shall not go in one and the same year, even though two or more ships go in the same year, and let them inform themselves each year of the coming of the galleon and any monies brought shall be handed over to the Father Rector of the College for the purposes stated, and the Father Rector shall have one of the keys and the other two shall be held by the two laymen mentioned above. These latter are to be chosen every two years on the day after the feast of the martyr St. Catherine; they shall be chosen by the Reverend Father Rector, the Reverend Father Regent and the lecturers who shall be resident in the College, without any limitation whatsoever on their choice of candidates, so that one or both of these two lay administrators may be elected for many years consecutively.

I look to the zeal of Your Reverences to hear my supplications for the greater glory of the Faith and of God our Lord; may He keep your Reverences in much grace and happiness, as I beg of Him.
San Gabriel: 12 March 1689

FR PHELIPPE
Archbishop of Manila

Some Aspects of the British Occupation of Manila

CONRAD MYRICK

The British occupied Manila on October 6, 1762, and withdrew on June 10 and 11, 1764.[1] During this period a unique chapter in Philippine church history occurred. The efforts of a growing extern Spanish force and the help of the Spanish religious orders stymied the military and commercial conquest undertaken by the East India Company and the British crown until in accordance with the Treaty of Paris of February 10, 1763, the British had to withdraw. The Treaty of Paris did not become effective in Manila until May 31, 1764, at which time Spain's sovereignty was fully restored.[2]

This occupation was the only serious imposition of a foreign power on Spanish rule and the only outside threat to the Spanish Catholic church in the Philippines from 1565 until 1898, when that rule ceased and the islands were ceded to the United States. Only the Manila area was occupied by the British. In the rest of the colony, Spanish civil authority continued to function locally. Spanish religious authority functioned overall without British hindrance, but many in the religious orders took an active part in opposing the British occupation. This was in keeping with the Spanish concept of the unity of church and state that was carried over into the Philippines, wherein when one was touched each answered to the defense of the other.

---

[1] Great Britain, Records of Fort Saint George, *Manila Consultations, 1762* (Madras, 1940), I, 1 (hereinafter *BMC*); Marques de Ayerte, *Sitio y Conquista* (Zaragoza, 1897), p. 131, quoted in Emma Helen Blair and James Alexander Robertson, eds., *The Philippine Islands, 1493–1898* (55 vols.; Cleveland, 1903–1909), XLIX, 175 (hereinafter cited as *BRPI*).

[2] William L. Langer, *An Encyclopedia of World History* (Boston, 1963), p. 452; *BMC*, X, 9; *BRPI*, XLI, 175.

Geography and Climate

The walled city of Manila is on the west side of the northern and largest island, Luzon, and on the east side of Manila Bay. This large bay is 120 miles in circumference, 28 miles across east and west, 32 miles from north to south, and has a narrow opening into the South China Sea between Bataan and Batangas with the famous island of Corregidor in between.[3] The bay area was never completely occupied by the British, although their forces dominated its waters. The triangle of occupation was from Manila on the north to the port of Cavite some nine miles south by water, to the river town of Pasig, about nine miles east of Manila, with arcs of influence extending at each angle. All else remained as it was before the invasion.

However, since Spanish colonial policy made the capital of each colony the only great city in it, whatever power held that city imposed severe restrictions on the whole colony in all phases of its life, including religion. But in this episode there was a checkmate to this fact. Don Simón Anda y Salazar, as visitor-general of the provinces, formed a court and went to Bulacan on October 4, 1762, in apparent anticipation of a possible capitulation of the capital. When Manila was taken by storm the next day he declared himself, according to the Laws of the Indies, the royal *Audiencia sole,* since the governor-general archbishop and *Audiencia* in Manila became prisoners of the occupation.[4] Anda's opposing force in the three provinces of Pampanga, Bulacan, and Morong, north and east of Manila, was able to hem in the British and cut off their supplies.[5] Although the British had ingress and egress to Manila Bay, their base of operations was Madras in India, some 3,403 statute miles away, and communications were slow.[6]

[3] For period descriptions, Fr. Manuel Buzeta y Fr. Felipe Bravo, *Diccionario Geográfico, Estadístico, Histórico de las Islas Filipinas* (Madrid, 1850), II, 212–13.

[4] "Anda and the English Invasion, 1762–1764," in *BRPI,* XLIX, 132–37. Note that British dates are one day ahead of Spanish dates, since the British came to Manila by the Eastern route.

[5] *Ibid.,* p. 142.

[6] Rand McNally-Cosmopolitan *World Atlas* (Chicago, 1951), p. 164.

The occupation began at the close of the southwest monsoon and ended two years later at the outset of the same monsoon. In the Philippines two winds govern the islands and, in sailing days, governed its ships. The *vendavales* from the southwest blow strongly and intermittently from June to October, bringing the rainy season and typhoons which provide some relief from the tropical heat for a short period. The *brisas* from the northwest begin to blow in October and increase in steadiness and without rain until June, thus creating the dry season with its heat.[7] In the dry season the Spaniards and natives could more easily move around the rim of British control and keep the occupation force ill at ease and uncertain about their resistance movements. The freedom of religious assembly granted by the British fortuitously provided undisturbed meeting places for resistance movements within the perimeter of occupation.

The Scope

The British occupation of Manila was a small, local action, but it was enveloped in a much larger framework of international affairs known as the Seven Years' War. England, at war with France over boundary disputes in North America, also declared war on Spain in January of 1762, partly because of the Bourbon family compact between France and Spain.[8] English supremacy in India had been assured by their defeat of the Dutch in 1759. So the British East India Company and the British crown, in privileged relationship, were freer to move on the dual pursuit of commerce and colonization.[9] The English and Spanish declaration of war coincided with an expedition to the Philippines whose chief purpose was not related to the main object of the war.[10] How much of all these affairs was known to Manila is an open question, since the Philippine ports were officially closed to Europeans, and, being further from Spain than any of the other colonies, it received all news later and last.

---

[7] Fr. Joaquin Martinez de Zuñiga, *Estadismo de las Islas Filipinas* (Madrid, 1893), I, 218–19.

[8] Langer, *op. cit.*, pp. 435, 453.   [9] *Ibid.*, p. 535.

[10] *BRPI*, XLIX, 11.

The British Plan

As early as 1760, General William Draper, an employee of the
East India Company, when in Canton suggested a conquest of
the Philippines. An anonymous document, which is thought to be
the general's detailed report, set forth a plan for conquest which
in polity was later followed in 1762.[11] The plan stated that the
chief motive of the Spaniards in maintaining the Philippines was
their religious zeal and missionary interest, and that if the southern islands were subdued by the British, the Spaniards might be
compelled for the sake of their missions to concede Manila itself
to them with possible valuable grants of commercial privileges.
Also, the cost of the expedition could be retrieved from Philippine
resources. Then the plan named the islands and listed their produce of value, such as rice, hogs, poultry, wax, timber, cattle,
abaca, deer, cloth, coconuts, fruits, sulphur and gold, tobacco and
cotton, cocoa, wheat, buri, cowries, cinnamon, pepper, and salt-
peter.[12] The sources of this knowledge were not given in the
plan. The information concerning the natural resources of the islands was correct, but the assumption that the Spanish zeal for
religion did not include loyalty for its realm was not correct.

Opinions differ as to whether or not the Spaniards in Madrid
and Manila were ignorant of the plan, or simply lethargic concerning it, and as to whether or not Manila listened to rumors
from unofficial sources concerning the preparation of an expedition from Madras for the purpose of taking the Philippines in
September of 1762.[13]

The author of the British plan, however, seemed quite unaware
that he had oversimplified Spanish character and had discounted
a national loyalty not second to British loyalty. He also seemed
unaware of the fact that the majority of the Spanish friars not

[11] "Plan of an Expedition for the Conquest of the Southern Philippines,"
in *BRPI*, XLIX, 28–43.

[12] *Ibid.*, pp. 31–39. Wheat must have been a misnomer. It did not grow
in the islands and was imported. Both the wheat and altar wine for mass
have been imported by the church throughout its history here.

[13] Colonel Frank Hodsoll, *Britain in the Philippines* (Manila, 1954), pp.
6–7.

only were dedicated to their missionary work, but also were devoted to Spain.

Religion in the Period

In the middle of the eighteenth century the religious situation in England and Spain had some outward similarities as well as many differences. In both nations the church was established; each church was protected by the crown, supported by law, and granted special privileges.

By the middle of the century the Church of England was developing with serious purpose a ministry for its colonies through such societies as the Society for Promoting Christian Knowledge, founded in 1698, and the Society for the Propagation of the Gospel, in 1701.[14]

The East India Company in general was hostile toward missionary work on the basis that religious propaganda might cause native resentment and harm the growth of commerce. But in the south of India it employed German missionaries, sent by the king of Denmark for work among non-Christians, as chaplains to British troops and British subjects. These missionaries, as chaplains, used the services and rites of the *Book of Common Prayer*. All were without any episcopal assistance until 1814, when the first Anglican bishop took up residence in India.[15]

When Señor Anda justified his defense of the Philippines, in that otherwise they would have been taken over by "Calvinism and Lutheranism," he was correct at least as to the tenets of the chaplains ministering to British subjects, of whom the majority were Anglicans.[16] He was incorrect, however, in assuming that the East India Company sustained any missionary motive in the occupation of the islands.

On the other hand, Spain, for over two hundred and fifty years, had been using its mobile religious orders as overseas mission-

[14] John R. H. Moorman, *A History of the Church of England* (New York, 1954), p. 267.

[15] Stephen Neill, *A History of Christian Missions* (Harmondsworth, 1964), pp. 232–33.

[16] "Anda and the English Invasion," *op. cit.*, p. 158.

aries, spreading the Roman Catholic faith and the Spanish way of life. They held their commissions from both their king, as royal patron since 1493, and the pope.[17] Together with a conforming and often times zealous laity holding the sword and the law in ready assistance to missions, the Spanish religious spread their faith and way of life over more of the earth than the world had ever seen under one crown.

The religious orders had unity of purpose, but not always complete harmony; nor did all religious authorities and royal officials have unbroken unity, peace, and concord among themselves. For example, in the Philippines as far back as 1582, the bishop and governor disagreed over the treatment of natives and areas of authority.[18] Likewise, in the period of British occupation, there were variances of opinions among the orders as to what their relation should be with the enemy. While the Jesuits appeared more bending in their attitude toward the British, the other orders were hostile.[19] Nevertheless, there was a missionary zeal among the Spaniards which excelled that of the British at this time, and there was a commercial genius among the British which the Spaniards did not have.

In eighteenth-century England some religious toleration was being manifested between the established church and nonconformists through the Act of Toleration of 1689.[20] But the Whigs and Tories in Parliament passed an Act of 1700 for preventing the "growth of popery," which remained in force until 1778.[21] Yet, when George III ascended the throne in 1760, two years before the Philippine venture, the established Church of England had not been permitted by law to deliberate in convocation for forty-three years.[22] The unity of Britain at this time was not religious, nor was it centered in the Church of England. There was a national and insular unity and loyalty to things English, English

[17] "Inter caetera," in *BRPI*, I, 97.
[18] Ronquillo de Peñalosa to Felipe II, June 15, 1582, and Salazar to Felipe II, June 20, 1582 (MMS. in *Archivo*, Seville) in *BRPI*, IV, 316, and V, 188–92.
[19] *BRPI*, XLIX, 134.
[20] Henry Offley Wakeman, *An Introduction to the History of the Church of England* (London, 1947), p. 392.
[21] *Ibid.*, p. 405.   [22] *Ibid.*, p. 413.

ways, and English might. There was both an independence of
and unity in the British crown. The great motivation seemed to
have been trade and settlement of new lands by individuals and
groups.[23] And as for the East India Company, religion carried little weight beyond its respectability in the lives of the officials. At
this time, it happened that the king's name was George, and
militant Saint George was patron of England, and the base of operations against the Philippines was Fort Saint George in Madras.

Spain in the eighteenth century was united in religion, and its
king bore the title of "Catholic Majesty." The holy, Catholic,
apostolic and Roman faith alone was permitted in Spain and its
dominions. Spain felt a suspicion for all things foreign.[24] The in-
grained triangular tension between Catholic, Moor, and Jew left
Catholic Spain abhorrent of any form of heresy or teaching
against its profession of faith. And the Holy Office, though weak
at this time, showed no more tolerance toward British Christendom than the British Act of 1700 showed to "popery." [25]

The Occupation

On September 23, 1762, the Spaniards in Manila saw thirteen
ships sail into the bay, and the authorities thought that they were
a Chinese trading fleet.[26] When its true identity was discovered,
a Spanish officer went aboard and learned that a state of war existed between England and Spain. The officer declared that he
would defend the honor of the Catholic crown to the last extrem-
ity, but he was sent back to Manila with a message to surrender.
Meanwhile, the fleet proceeded to land a short distance below the
walled city at Malate.[27] Although the British had had an agreeable passage, their landing was made difficult due to high waves
and heavy winds which caused some loss in material. The troops
were able to establish a secure beachhead without opposition, but
their advance was slowed by weather conditions.[28] On October

[23] William Bridgewater and Elizabeth J. Sherwood, eds., *The Columbia Encyclopedia* (2nd ed.; New York, 1950), p. 255.
[24] A. S. Turberville, *The Spanish Inquisition* (London, 1932), p. 151.
[25] *Ibid.*, p. 186.
[26] Malo de Luque, *Establecimiento Ultramarinos* (Madrid, 1790), V, 238, in *BRPI*, XLIX, 82.
[27] *BMC*, I, 27.   [28] *BRPI*, XLIX, 48.

1, a typhoon struck, and heavy rains continued for several days. A siege was set, and on October 6 the British took Manila with little opposition. Immediately after the surrender, a British consultation was set up, and it ordered that the "Madeira wine and other stores" be landed "with all possible haste." [29]

Admiral Samuel Cornish and General William Draper required four conditions to be met if the city was to be preserved from plunder and the inhabitants preserved in their religion, goods, liberties, and properties. These demands were conditioned on the prompt payment of $2,000,000, with hostages and security to be given for the future payment of $2,000,000 more.[30]

The Spaniards were obviously not prepared to withstand an invasion. Archbishop Manuel Antonio de Rojo y Vieyra, the Spanish governor-general, for all his good qualities as bishop, was not a military man. Being harassed by opposing factions he put up a feeble defense, and delayed negotiations of surrender too long to save Manila from being taken.[31] However, when the British landed and took over the Augustinian convent in Malate, the archbishop promptly called on the religious orders to leave their cloisters and help defend the city. The religious as a whole gladly responded, and many friars entered the ranks.[32]

After the city was taken, the archbishop, taking the initiative, sent to the British on October 7 twelve articles which he asked the victors to accept and permit in the occupation. These were agreeable, and the British admiral and general made only four alterations. First, as to the request for freedom of the ecclesiastical government of the Spanish Catholic church to instruct the faithful, the phrase was inserted that "they must not attempt to convert any of our Protestant Subjects to the Popish faith." Second, in civil authority, self-government was subject to British superior orders. Third, the maintenance of Spanish ministers and royal officials must be supported by His Catholic Majesty; and

[29] *BMC,* I, 2, 29–30.

[30] *Ibid.,* pp. 15–16. At this time many English documents used the word "dollar" or "pillar dollar" (from the impression on the reverse side of the coin) to describe the Spanish silver coin, the *peso duro* of eight *reales,* which was about the size of a U.S. silver dollar. Its coinage ceased in 1822.

[31] Le Gentil, *Voyage* (Paris, 1781), II, 252–55, in *BRPI,* XLIX, 129.

[32] Marques de Ayerte, *op. cit.,* 30, 50, in *BRPI,* XLIX, 112.

finally, all articles were subject to British revocation if thought
necessary.[33] No objection at all was raised concerning the article
which "granted that the Catholic, Apostolic and Roman Religion
be preserved and maintained in its exercise and functions by its
Pastors and faithful Ministers." [34]

Most of the documents which recorded the negotiations on
both sides are fairly reconcilable in their differences. But this is not
so concerning the accounts of the numbers of troops, ships, and
casualties, or the account of the plunder of Manila by the British.
These were the sensitive issues for both sides. They had to do
with results, justifications, and honor.

Spanish accounts stated that the invasion force consisted of
thirteen ships and 6,830 men. British accounts said that the whole
squadron arrived except two store ships, but they gave no other
total, and in all there were 2,300 men.[35] The number of British
killed and wounded varied from Draper's account of 147 to Rojo's
account of more than 1,000. Spanish casualties were listed as 386
killed and some 300 wounded.[36]

Concerning the plunder of the city, Archbishop Rojo stated
that after the surrender of Manila, it was given over to pillage.
Although after twenty-four hours the British general ordered it to
cease, the archbishop claimed that the pillage continued for sixteen hours more, and he noted that no church was exempted.
Others also held that the general permitted the pillage with all its
atrocities against persons and property.[37] General Draper denied
these charges, stating that after the storming of the city and before the capitulation could be signed, there was pillage of abandoned houses for several hours, and that there were some robber-
ies after the signing. The general maintained, however, that
extracts from the orders of the day would show that protection
was granted to the inhabitants, and that an order had been issued
to hang any robber or plunderer.[38]

After the general's vindication of himself, he attacked the court

---

[33] BMC, I, 16–17.   [34] Ibid.
[35] D. José Montero y Vidal, Historia General de Filipinas desde el descubrimiento de Dichas Islas hasta Nuestos Dias (Madrid, 1887–95), II,
13; "Draper's Journal," in BRPI, XLIX, 81.
[36] BRPI, XLIX, 101, 128.   [37] Ibid., pp. 127, 322–23 with note 197.
[38] "Draper's Defense," in BRPI, XLIX, 327–28.

of Spain for its refusal, because of the alleged plundering, to pay the $2,000,000 honorably agreed to by the archbishop. He also charged that Spain had no case for secretly stripping the galleon *Philippina* of its treasure when it had been included as part of the capitulation.[39]

On November 2, the British military phase was considered accomplished, and Manila was turned over to the officials of the East India Company "until His Majesty's further pleasure." Mr. Dawsonne Drake, Esquire, was made governor and president of the consultation. In turn, all troops except the marines, were to remain and serve under the governor and council, while the port of Cavite was placed under the command of the navy.[40] Thence forward the archbishop became liaison between the Spaniards and the company.

Affairs were different in the provinces. The British were not prepared for Señor Anda's declaration of being governor, captain general, and the Royal *Audiencia*. In the name of Don Carlos III, Anda called for opposition against the enemy. He informed the archbishop that because of the respect and love which the natives had for their parish priests and missionaries, who understood better than any others the natives' nature and customs, the clergy could hold and incite the natives for resistance and defense against the "English enemy." He held that in spite of the fall of Manila, the islands could be preserved for their king, and he urged the archbishop to summon the clergy to action.[41]

So well did the clergy respond to Anda's call for resistance that the British a month later, on November 3 sent a notice to the inhabitants of the provinces of Bulacan and Pampanga which assured them of religious liberty, exemption from all tributes and services exacted by Spain, and the privileges of English subjects, if they would throw off all subjection to Anda y Salazar.[42] But this did little good. In less than a week the council complained of frequent murders of British people and signs of new trouble, and concluded that their "tenderness and humanity" had done nothing to reconcile the affections "of a people bigotted to Popish

[39] *Ibid.*, pp. 322–23, 329–30.   [40] *BMC*, I, 6–7.
[41] "Anda and the English Invasion," *op. cit.*, pp. 133–34.
[42] *BMC*, I, 19.

principles and of course prejudiced against us." [42] The council was constantly aware that the undercurrent of religion not only moved the people toward Spanish resistance, but also that it was moving the company out of reach of the people.

The Augustinian friars appeared more active and effective than the others. One friar preached to the natives that the English were Jews, heretics, and barbarous, and that as long as they stayed, there would be no peace.[44] At the end of November, the British considered that six Augustinians were militantly involved to the extent of being dangerous to the occupation, so they were taken from their Manila convent and put on board the *Weymouth* for exile to Bombay.[45] At the same time, when the council began to press for the ransom due, the religious orders began to stall one by one. The Franciscans, who lived by charity, declared that they had nothing. The Recollects claimed that they had suffered a loss of $70,000 in damage to their churches during the occupation, so they had nothing to give. The Jesuits answered that they had tried to keep their parishioners in peace, and that they had already given $50,000.[46] This call to pay came to naught.

But the commercially minded company did not let the matter rest, and in January of 1763, the archbishop, standing between the British demand to pay and the failure of the religious orders to meet payments, stated that the superiors of all the orders had declared in his presence that they could not pay more on the ransom. He gave their excuses one by one, mentioning poverty, plunder, robbery, and the forfeit of their church plate. He said that San Juan de Dios had to maintain its hospitals, and the Dominicans had to maintain their college and Beateria. He mentioned that the Jesuits also had obligations to their missions and schools, and that they had already paid a large sum.[47]

Captain Thomas Backhouse, commander of the troops in the field, looked on the religious situation with cold military eyes. To him it represented the enemy and must be handled accordingly. His thin line of troops stretched from Manila through San Juan, Mandaluyong, Guadalupe to Pasig, and was constantly exposed

[43] *Ibid.*, III, 4.   [44] *Ibid.*, I, 46.   [45] *Ibid.*, pp. 47–48.
[46] *Ibid.*, pp. 49–50.   [47] *Ibid.*, VI, 11, 22.

to Anda's growing force, to religious opposition, and to Spanish complaints. When they accused Backhouse of despoiling churches —and the council was sensitive to this charge—he denied it, but stated his determination to use the church building in Pasig for a defense post. Throughout this incident and during the next six months, the captain clearly stated his views about the enemy, and especially the Spanish clergy.[48]

Captain Backhouse wrote the governor and council saying that the whole country could be quickly subdued if all the clergy of "any order whatsoever" were prohibited from living outside the walls of Manila—implying that the religious were the real power against the occupation. Backhouse believed that, if the council adopted such a plan, Luzon would soon become "beneficial" to the "Honorable Company." [49] But the council determined to continue its policy of religious freedom, and notified the captain, through the archbishop, that the Augustinian friars in his area would be relieved, and seculars would take their places. As to the future, should the captain find friars in arms and acting beyond their duties, he should act as he thought proper.[50] Again, when the captain asked if he could send certain troublemakers from Guadalupe to Manila, he added that if the council approved this request it should be kept in "profound secret" because "intelligence flies amongst those Padrys [sic] like wildfire." [51] A little later he warned the council that all clergy "of what orders soever" were involved in a scheme to starve out the military garrison of Manila, while the clergy planned to supply "their brothers in the Garrison" with salt beef. This was to be sent in small quantities, and the captain claimed that he had seen a number of these parcels in the convent of Marikina.[52]

When the commander of the troops penetrated Laguna in the first part of December 1762, he again reported to the council on the religious situation. This time he said that he could assure them that these natives were far from having the attachment to the "Padrys" and the Roman Catholic religion that had been claimed. The people complained vigorously about the friars and said that their religion was troublesome. Then he counseled that if they

[48] *Ibid.*, II, 11.   [49] *Ibid.*   [50] *Ibid.*, p. 12.   [51] *Ibid.*, p. 16.
[52] *Ibid.*

took away all priests and cut the taxes in half and converted the natives to no religion at all, he would venture to bet "the first dividend of prize money" that without force he could lead the inhabitants where he pleased.[53]

Despite the continued vexations of having to deal with the inhabitants in a military way and to allow the free exercise of "the Popish faith," the governor and council did not forget that their primary purpose was commerce. William Stevenson, the company engineer, sent to the court of directors of the United Company of Merchants of England in London, who were trading in the East Indies, one of the most complete descriptions of Manila ever written, which included suggestions for mending the walls and bastions so that the city could repel any European force which might be sent to this part of the world, and also be secure from any native uprising.[54] Manila could be made a secure port for British trade. A list was made of the commodities and the quantity of them which the company could obtain in the island of Luzon. They included cocoa, wheat, cotton, sapanwood and other woods, tobacco, rice, pepper, coconuts, abaca, brimstone, indigo, sugar, cattle and gold dust.[55] Nothing was mentioned about the possibility of propagating the established church.

As to normal church life in the occupied area, no account showed thus far any interruptions caused by the British. Dealing with friars exceeding their ecclesiastical duties was one thing, but within the limits of spirituality and services the churches functioned as usual, or at least without any direct interference by the company. In Pampanga, however, Anda discovered a few days before Christmas that the Chinese had planned on Christmas Eve to kill "right and left" and "prepare the way for the entrance of the English." [56] The Chinese fled, but those who were captured were killed. The sale of wine was prohibited, and the ecclesiastics were warned to keep strict watch on all, and not to open their churches on Christmas Eve without placing guards.[57]

On February 10, 1763, the Treaty of Paris was signed between Great Britain, France, and Spain. Spain was to recover Cuba and

---

[53] *Ibid.,* pp. 17–18.   [54] *Ibid.,* I, 25, 26.   [55] *Ibid.,* III, Item 11.
[56] "Anda and the English Invasion," *op. cit.,* pp. 148–49.
[57] *Ibid.*

the Philippines.[58] This news was officially dispatched to the company in Manila through a letter from Fort Saint George dated May 23, 1763.[59] Meanwhile, in this month Captain Backhouse discovered in the floor of a church a cache filled with powder and shell which was thought to have been sent from the coast of Coromandel. The captain was convinced that Señor Anda now had a source of military supplies for continued resistance.[60]

Señor Anda's power increased until he became a threat to the British. The council warned Admiral Cornish that they were being surrounded by enemies, that it was now a risk to go beyond the walls, and that the only escape from the Spanish friar-inspired plan to starve the British out was to use naval force. Cornish responded by asking why Drake had taken over the government before Draper had brought about a complete pacification.[61] Two weeks later the council reported to London that Anda now had a force of 7,000 natives, Mexicans, and Spaniards, including a number of friars bearing arms in the ranks and several friars as commanders. It had been necessary to attack a Bulacan church which was an Anda stronghold. So determined and obstinate were those in the resistance force that it was necessary for the British to put every man of the 400 to the sword. Among these, three friars were found in arms. The council now offered a $5,000 reward for the safe delivery of Anda as a prisoner.[62]

From March of 1763 through mid-June, the council sat uneasily on Manila affairs. The archbishop complained about three Franciscans and an Augustinian being brought as prisoners from Polo to Manila, and about the wounding of a Franciscan in Dilao by a Sepoy. The council made it clear that when ecclesiastics, contrary to their profession, took up arms and excited the natives to join the resistance, they forfeited all indulgences allowed in war and could only be treated as public disturbers.[63] The council also informed the Dominican superior that since Friar Joseph Villar had been caught in arms and without his religious habit, he could expect no other treatment than as a prisoner of war.[64] Later, this

---

[58] Langer, *op. cit.*, p. 452.   [59] *BMC*, IV, 1.   [60] *Ibid.*, V, 106.
[61] *Ibid.*, p. 53.   [62] *Ibid.*, III, 34–35.   [63] *Ibid.*, pp. 42, 46, 47.
[64] *Ibid.*, p. 62.

same superior, Father Pedro Luis de Sierra, asked permission to go with two other friars to Pangasinan for the quadrennial election of a superior, but since Anda was in that territory, and the position of the province was uncertain, permission was denied.[65] This was the closest that the company came to interfering in any religious matters that were not connected with military affairs.

The British were now concerned about the defense of their position. Nonetheless, in May the council vetoed Major Fell's request to destroy Santa Cruz, Binondo, and other suburbs as a necessity to defense, despite the fact that the threat of attack from Anda's forces was great. The council did agree to the demolition of the Ermita and Malate churches, which buildings afforded a military advantage to any attacking force, but this project was not carried out.[66] When it was learned that Anda's forces were casting guns from church bells, and that bells had been taken from the Manila suburb of Tondo, the British ordered all bells in the surrounding villages to be brought to Manila. This action was explained to the inhabitants by saying that it had nothing to do with religion, but that it was a measure against trouble, and that the bells would be deposited in the city and would be returned when the existing troubles had ended.[67]

On May 26, the archbishop complained to the British that in the Quiapo church, across the river from Manila, eleven native men and one woman had been killed, the curate wounded, the church despoiled, and several homes plundered by the Chinese, who were abetted by English troops. The council investigated the matter, and on June 17 wrote its sharpest note to the archbishop, saying that contrary to the charges, the British troops had actually tried to stop the affair. The council further commented on the archbishop's readiness to complain on every occasion, when he knew full well that accidents in time of war could not be avoided. The council advised that, if a proper regard had been paid to the terms of the capitulation already agreed to, and if Señor Anda and his followers had observed the customs of war among civi-

---

[65] Ibid., V, 123.   [66] Ibid.   [67] Ibid., p. 128.

lized nations, no one would have suffered the calamities claimed.[68] Again, on the part of the company religion was not of direct interest, except in so far as it was a cause of complaint.

A letter from Fort Saint George, dated June 24, 1763, advised the council in Manila that the cessation of arms between England, France, and Spain was confirmed, and enclosed the preliminary articles of peace. Since it was thought that Manila would be restored to Spain, they were to be ready for the transfer when ordered; meanwhile, the council was advised to "take every possible method of retrenching your expenses" since those of the expedition had been "very heavy." [69] Meanwhile, extra outposts were set up around Manila to guard against malcontents.[70]

As soon as the packet from Fort Saint George arrived on July 24, 1763, the governor and council made public, through the archbishop, His British Majesty's proclamation of a suspension of arms.[71] The archbishop replied immediately, expressing his hope that a durable peace would soon prevail, and saying that he would send the message to Anda in an effort to achieve the desired effect. But Anda refused to comply because the British had not sent a dispatch to him personally. The matter seesawed on the fulcrum of proper titles for Anda until January 23, 1764, when he declared that he would be willing to conform to the preliminary articles of peace if the British would evacuate Manila before the end of February.[72]

Archbishop Rojo died on January 30, 1764, and the British gave him a solemn funeral with military honors.[73] Still Anda held out against the British, who would not leave Manila without receiving the definitive Treaty of Peace, which did not arrive until March 8. Anda waited. Meanwhile, the British could not evacuate due to the lack of ships. Then also among the British, the military and company officials began to quarrel over responsibility.[74] In all of this the matter of religion was by-passed on both sides.

Finally, it was agreed to give up the city on May 31, 1764. The new Spanish governor *ad interim*, Don Francisco de la Torre,

---

[68] *Ibid.*, IV, 121.   [69] *Ibid.*, IV, 1–6.   [70] *Ibid.*, V, 156.
[71] *Ibid.*, V, 167.   [72] *Ibid.*, IX, 12.
[73] Montero y Vidal, *op. cit.*, pp. 66–67.
[74] *BMC*, IX, 49, 54, 55, 58; and X, 1, 5, 10.

feigned illness, so that Don Simón Anda y Salazar, defender of the islands, could be the one to take possession of the city. On June 4, Anda was given a banquet with due recognition on board Captain Brereton's ship, the *Revenge*. The British vessels sailed from Manila Bay for India on June 10 and 11, 1764, one year, eight and a half months after they arrived.

The brief, turbulent, and isolated British occupation of Manila is hardly worthy of remembrance from a military standpoint.[75] The civilians and the religious remembered it for generations as simply "the war." Historically, it has been looked upon as the end of a period, and as a crisis which left the Spaniards in the Philippines with less of a sense of security than before.[76] Nonetheless, the Spanish church and state were to continue their unitive relation in the Philippines for one hundred thirty-four years more.

From the commercial standpoint, which was the primary purpose of the British occupation, there was the least to show. The English were thereafter denied trade in the Philippines, although they came anyway, often using a Moro subterfuge—having a Moro pose as captain and the English captain pose as an interpreter.[77] It was not until 1809 that Englishmen were permitted to reside in Manila, and, although some came, they did not feel secure in their residence until after 1835, when Manila became an open port.[78] Socially, the records show that no relationship of significance developed during the occupation between these two proud peoples of different language, custom, and religion, different too, as General Draper described it, in sentiment, dress, and complexion.[79] One account records that 400 abandoned prostitutes fled Manila when the British occupation troops left.[80] Natives outside the immediate area of occupation and the fringe areas of pacification experienced little of the occupation apart from the general inconvenience caused by the conflict. Their religious life was in no way purposefully hampered. The Chinese

[75] Le Gentil, *op. cit.*, ii, 264, 265, in *BRPI*, XLIX, 65.

[76] Zuñiga, *op. cit.*, pp. 219, 225.   [77] *Ibid.*, pp. 264–65.

[78] Antonio M. Regidor and J. W. T. Mason, "Commercial Progress in the Philippines," in Nicolas Zafra, *Readings in Philippine History* (Manila, 1949), pp. 382–84.

[79] "Draper's Defense," in *BRPI*, XLIX, 327.

[80] Marquis de Ayerbe, *op. cit.*, in *BRPI*, XLIX, 175.

were later expelled from the islands on the basis of not being necessary for the good of the country, according to Señor Anda, who served as governor and captain general of the islands from 1770 to 1776. In 1778 the Chinese were allowed to return.[81]

Finally, in the sphere of the religious orders, three years after the British left Manila, Don Carlos III suddenly expelled the Jesuits from his realms, without warning or trial, because of an accumulation of implications, one of which concerned their behavior with the British during the occupation.[82] Apart from the damage to their facilities in and around Manila, the other religious orders were not greatly disturbed as a result of the occupation. The Roman Catholic Church was irritated by the occupation, more by the presence of the British than by any British restrictions, but it was never seriously interrupted in its pastoral functions. The fear among Roman Catholics of Protestant intervention and domination was groundless, though logical. It was not until 1898 that the first public Anglican service was held in the Philippines, by an Episcopal chaplain with the United States Army.[83]

The Spanish clergy who gave support to Señor Anda by reporting on the enemy, exciting the natives, and in some cases by bearing arms, facilitated to a great extent the task of keeping the British within a very limited area. This containment continued until the Treaty of Paris in 1763 permitted the Spaniards to regain Manila, and enabled the British to leave without too much loss of face in the Orient.

[81] William Lytle Schurz, *The Manila Galleon* (New York, 1959), p. 98. Zuñiga, *op. cit.*, p. 261.

[82] *BRPI*, XLIX, 134, note 76.

[83] Conrad Myrick, "The Philippine Episcopal Church" (mimeographed; Manila, 1962), p. 1.

PART II

NATIONALISM, DISSENT
AND DISESTABLISHMENT

Rizal's Retraction:
A Note on the Debate[*]

EUGENE A. HESSEL

There are aspects of the life of Dr. José Rizal, the martyred Filipino national hero, which are of far greater significance than whether or not during his last twenty-four hours he retracted some of his religious views and repudiated Masonry. It is important, to be sure, to establish all the facts of Rizal's life. Nonetheless, it is unfortunate that some have not taken with sufficient seriousness what were his mature religious convictions. For some people to retract would mean little, for they have so little to retract. This was not so of Rizal. Though he did not write much in the way of formal treatments of religion, Christianity in particular, his writings as an adult contain many references to religious practices and beliefs, and his thoughts are quite uniform and systematic.[1]

To appreciate the question of the "Retraction" a knowledge of the facts of Rizal's life and thought as a whole is essential. A summary only is given here. These facts must be filled in and mastered before one is really equipped to evaluate fully what happened at the end of his life. Rizal was born some fifty-four kilometers (34 miles) south of Manila on June 19, 1861, while the Philippines was still suffering the abuses of colonial rule and knew only a more or less conservative and fanatical form of Spanish Catholicism maintained by a hierarchy which worked hand in hand with the political authorities. At the age of eleven he was already studying under the Jesuits in Manila, and at this time he was a faithful Roman Catholic. From 1878 to 1881 he

* This is a revised version of an article which appeared originally in *Silliman Journal* (Dumaguete City), XII, 2 (Apr.–June, 1965), 168–83.
[1] See the author's *The Religious Thought of José Rizal* (Manila, 1961).

studied surveying and medicine at the University of Sto. Tomás (Dominican). Very little writing from this period is preserved but enough to hint strongly at growing patriotic convictions together with some slight intimation of questions being raised with regard to his hitherto accepted traditional religious convictions. On May 3, 1882, Rizal sailed for Europe, completing three years later his medical education in Madrid. An unpublished manuscript and several articles indicate Rizal's growing confidence in reason as man's surest guide. During the following two years amid European travels and study Rizal managed to write and publish his first propaganda novel against the abuses of the Spanish regime, *Noli Me Tangere*. In the matter of religion, Rizal chiefly attacks clerical abuses, but he also expresses religious thoughts which are unorthodox. When he returned to his homeland in 1887 he was already a marked man in the eyes of the authorities, a situation worsened by a strongly worded report which he made with regard to the Dominican hacienda where his parents lived. During his second period in Europe he wrote vigorous patriotic articles and also published his even more frank and radical second novel, *El Filibusterismo*. A few days after his second return to Manila in 1892 he was arrested on charges of fomenting revolution and was exiled to the isolated town of Dapitan. Extremely valuable for an understanding of Rizal's non-Roman Catholic views during this time is his lengthy correspondence with his former professor at the Ateneo de Manila, Father Pablo Pastells, S.J. An attempt was also made to get him to repudiate his current religious views in order that he might marry in the church. When in 1896 he volunteered for medical service in Cuba he was placed on a ship bound for Spain. About this time, a revolutionary outbreak occurred. This resulted, perhaps on a pretext, in Rizal's being returned and imprisoned as an accomplice. During the last twenty-four hours before his execution (December 30, 1896), he is said to have retracted the "heretical" religious views of his mature years and his affiliation with Masonry.

There are four common attitudes toward the retraction and its bearing on the life and character of Dr. Rizal:

(1) There are those who insist that the Rizal to be remembered and honored is the "converted" Rizal. This is the official

Roman Catholic position. In the only "official" book dealing with all aspects of the retraction ("official" in the sense that it bears the imprimatur of Archbishop Santos), *Rizal's Unfading Glory*, Father Cavanna says in the preface:

Rizal's glory as a scholar, as a poet, as a scientist, as a patriot, as a hero, may some day fade away, as all worldly glories, earlier or later do. But his glory of having found at the hour of his death what unfortunately he lost for a time, the Truth, the Way, and the Life, that will ever be his UNFADING GLORY.[2]

This same sentiment is echoed in the statement issued by the Catholic Welfare Organization in 1956 and signed by the archbishop with regard to the *Noli* and *Fili*:

We have to imitate him [Rizal] precisely in what he did when he was about to crown the whole work of his life by sealing it with his blood; we ought to withdraw, as he courageously did in the hour of his supreme sacrifice, "whatever in his works, writings, publications and conduct had been contrary to his status as a son of the Catholic Church."

(2) There are those who have argued that Rizal throughout his mature life was a "free thinker and unbeliever"; thus the retraction is of necessity a lie. This is the extreme opposite of the Roman Catholic position. The major premise on which this thesis is based is questionable.

(3) A third implied view may be summarized as follows: the Rizal that matters is the preretraction Rizal; therefore one can ignore the retraction. The fundamental assumption here is held by many students and admirers of Rizal, including the writer, but the conclusion does not necessarily follow. This brings us to the fourth possible attitude toward the retraction.

(4) Scholarly investigation of all facets of Rizal's life and thought is desirable. In the interest of truth, the truth to which Rizal gave such passionate devotion, we have every right, and

---

[2] Jesus Ma. Cavanna y Manso, C.M., *Rizal's Unfading Glory*, A Documentary History of the Conversion of Dr. José Rizal. (2nd ed. rev. and improved; Manila, 1956), p. vi.

also an obligation, to seek to know the facts regarding the retraction. If scholarly research continues, fancy may yet become acknowledged fact.

Before we proceed further it would be well to say something about bibliography and method. A number of writings on the retraction merely repeat the arguments of earlier ones and add nothing new. Others are more sarcastic and sentimental than enlightening. But something of value can be gained from almost all of them. The literature belongs to two general categories, biography, and works dealing specifically with the retraction. Among the biographers Guerrero,[3] Laubach,[4] Palma,[5] and Coates [6] have given the most adequate treatment of the retraction, the first accepting it and the other three rejecting it. Of works dealing specifically with the retraction, the most objective, scholarly, and complete are those by Pascual arguing against the retraction,[7] and Father Cavanna in its favor.[8] As an almost complete compendium of information and arguments pro and con there is no book to date which is the equal of that of Father Cavanna. The second edition has 353 pages of text, appendices, and bibliographical entries totaling some 123 items. (Incidentally, Father Cavanna draws heavily upon the documents and information supplied by Father Manuel A. Gracia, the discoverer of the so-called "retraction document.")

Amongst other writers consulted, special indebtedness to

[3] León Ma. Guerrero, *The First Filipino* (Manila, 1963).

[4] Frank C. Laubach, *Rizal: Man and Martyr* (Manila, 1936).

[5] Rafael Palma, *The Pride of the Malay Race,* trans. by Roman Ozaeta (New York, 1949).

[6] Austin Coates, *Rizal: Philippine Nationalist and Martyr* (London and Hong Kong, 1968). This, the first European biography of Rizal since Retana's in 1907, is scholarly and preceptive throughout. Coates' study was published after this essay was prepared, but a comment on its contribution to the debate appears in footnote 24.

[7] Ricardo R. Pascual, *Dr. José Rizal Beyond the Grave* (Manila, 1935). A slightly revised edition was published in 1950, *Rizal Beyond the Grave.* The earlier edition, though rare, is in one respect preferable: the cuts of the retraction document and other specimens of Rizal's handwriting are much clearer. The revised edition had to depend upon reproducing the prints of the first edition.

[8] Jesus Ma. Cavanna y Manso, *op. cit.*

Collas,[9] Ricardo Garcia,[10] and Runes and Buenafe [11] should be mentioned. Garcia is a prolific popular writer in defense of the retraction; the other two oppose it. All tend chiefly to summarize what has been previously argued, although Runes introduces several new arguments which will be examined in due course. Much research time has been spent in running down various versions of the retraction document appearing in books, articles, newspapers, and so forth, in writing letters to clarify or verify certain points, and in conferring with individuals. Unfortunately, many documents were destroyed during the war. Special thanks is due to Father Manuel A. Gracia, C.M., who was most gracious in personally helping with the research, allowing examination of his own valuable documents including a splendid reproduction of the retraction document. His Eminence Cardinal Santos gave the writer a photostat copy in view of the fact that "an objective study on the matter" was being conducted. Later the hierarchy permitted the writer to study the "original" document for about forty-five minutes and to see related original documents.

The story of the retraction has been told and retold. Various newspaper reports of the last hours of Rizal were published on December 30, 1896, and the days shortly thereafter. However, the first detailed account came out in a series of anonymous articles in the Barcelona magazine, *La Juventud* (issues of January 15 and 31 and Feb. 14, 1897), and was republished some months later in a booklet entitled *La Masonización de Filipinas—Rizal y su Obra*. Some thirteen years later, Father Vicente Balaguer, S.J.,

[9] Juan Collas, *Rizal's "Retractions"* (Manila, 1960) and *Rizal at the Crossroads* (Quezon City, 1965). Mr. Collas was of great help in the preparation of the author's book on Rizal's religious thought. He handles both Spanish and English with consummate skill and has opened up to many English readers much of Rizal's thought by translating Rizal's most important minor writings.

[10] Ricardo Garcia, *The Great Debate, The Rizal Retraction* (Quezon City, 1964). Starting with a little booklet in 1960, this school-principal-turned-publisher has since published several enlargements of his original attempt to answer a number of works written against the retraction, including those by Palma, Collas, Juan Nabong, Judge Garduño, and Runes, using as his defense chiefly Cavanna.

[11] Ildefonso T. Runes and Mamerto M. Buenafe, *The Forgery of the Rizal "Retraction" and Josephine's "Autobiography"* (Manila, 1962).

the Jesuit priest who claimed to have secured Rizal's retraction, asserted that this account was his work which he originally wrote "that very same night of December 29, 1896." [12] Subsequently, on August 8, 1917, Father Balaguer repeated his story in a notarial act sworn to by him in Murcia, Spain. The only detailed account is that by Father Pío Pi y Vidal, S.J., superior of the Jesuits in the Philippines in 1896, who published in Manila in 1909 *La Muerte Cristiana del Doctor Rizal* and confirmed his account in a notarial act signed in Barcelona, April 7, 1917. In brief, the Jesuit account is this. On December 28 (the very day Governor General Polavieja ordered the death sentence) Archbishop Nozaleda commissioned the Jesuits to the spiritual care of Rizal, indicating that it would probably be necessary to demand a retraction and suggesting that both he and Father Pi would prepare "formulas." Thus, about 7:00 A.M., December 29 , two of the Jesuits arrived at the temporary chapel where Rizal was to spend his last twenty-four hours. During this day various Jesuits came in and out, together with other visitors, including members of his own family. Rizal also took time to write letters. Arguments with Rizal, with Father Balaguer taking the leading part, continued until dusk, by which time, according to the father's account,[13] Rizal was already asking for the formula of retraction. That night Rizal wrote out a retraction based on the formula of Father Pi and signed it about 11:30 P.M. The retraction contains two significant points: (1) the rejection of Masonry ("I abominate Masonry") and (2) a repudiation of "anything in my words, writings, publications, and conduct that has been contrary to my character as a son of the Catholic Church," together with the statement "I believe and profess what it teaches and I submit to what it demands." During the night there followed, according to the Jesuit accounts, several confessions (some say five), several hearings of Mass, a number of devotional acts, the asking for and signing of devotional booklets intended for various members of his family, and finally at 6:00 A.M. or thereabouts, some fifteen minutes be-

[12] Cavanna, *op. cit.*, p. 24.
[13] *Ibid.*, p. 8. Cavanna has conveniently included in his book most of the pertinent Jesuit accounts.

fore he was marched out of Fort Santiago to his execution, a marriage ceremony performed by Father Balaguer for Rizal and Josephine Bracken. So much for the story in outline. Details, including the text of the retraction, will be presented and discussed subsequently.

Before assessing the validity of the account a brief word should be said about the history of the controversy concerning the retraction. One way to arrive quickly at an overall view of the course of the debate is to read the titles and dates of pamphlets and books dealing with the subject such as are contained in any good bibliography of Rizal. A seemingly accurate description of the history of the struggle in convenient form is found in Part II of Cavanna's book which reports the various attacks down to the publication in 1949 of Ozaeta's translation of Palma's biography of Rizal. Cavanna seeks to answer the various arguments against the retraction, and in doing so makes reference to the chief works defending it. The first stage of the debate lasted for some twelve years after Rizal's death, and at least overtly was wholly one-sided. Cavanna aptly calls this period one of "Concealed Attacks." The newspapers published the reports given to them, presumably by the Jesuits. Within the first year the Jesuits published a quite complete story, for the time being anonymous in authorship. In successive years other books and booklets were devoted in whole or in part to repeating the same story, culminating in the famous full length biography in Spanish by Wenceslao Retana who incorporates the Jesuit account. Yet even in the early years of this period there were a few small voices raised in objection, quite surprisingly and probably significantly, since a totalitarian regime combining church and state was in control. Cavanna himself lists a leaflet, dated Manila, December 31, 1896, and several letters questioning the retraction.[14] Their main point, stated or implied, is that the retraction is not in keeping with the character of Rizal. It is of interest that at the end of the period, just a year after the publication of his biography of Rizal, Retana has something similar to say in an article dated December 29, 1908. Although still not denying the retraction, he adds:

[14] Cavanna, *op. cit.*, pp. 144 ff.

The fact is that influenced by a series of phenomena, or what is the same, of abnormal circumstances, Rizal subscribed that document, which has been so much talked about, and which no one has seen. . . . The conversion of Rizal . . . was a romantic concession of the poet, it was not a meditated concession of the philosopher.[15]

We may accept Cavanna's dating of the second period as covering the years from 1908 to 1935. This is the time of vigorous open attacks, many of them by Masons. Ever since, somewhat unfortunately, an active battle has been waged between Roman Catholic and Masonic protagonists. Early in the period, in 1909 to be exact, Father Pi published his booklet *La Muerte Cristiana del Doctor Rizal*. This was answered three years later in a long article by Hermenegildo Cruz in which several arguments often repeated subsequently were presented, chief of them being, Where is the retraction document? The debate drew forth in 1920 the most serious Roman Catholic answer until recent times, namely Father Gonzalo Ma. Piñana's *¿Murio el Doctor Rizal Cristianamente?* which is chiefly significant because it reports a series of notarized accounts made in the years 1917 to 1918 by the chief "witnesses." The period seemingly closes with victory for the defenders of the retraction, for after many challenges to show the actual document of retraction it was "discovered" on May 18, 1935, by Father Manuel A. Gracia, C.M., while he as archdiocesan archivist was busily sorting through a pile of documents that they might be arranged in orderly fashion in their new fireproof vault. On June 16 the news was released by *The Philippines Herald*.

One may date the last period of the debate from 1935 until the present. This is the time when, in the light of the retraction document discovery, major and minor works have been written on the subject of Rizal's life and thought as a whole and on the retraction in particular. This leads us naturally to an assessment of the chief arguments *pro* and *con* which have been raised over the years and systematically dealt with in the last thirty years.

As one examines the issues brought forth in the debate, a tabulation of the chief ones raised since 1935 (the year of the discov-

[15] *Ibid.*, p. 153.

ery of the alleged retraction document) indicates that a sort of impasse has been reached. Similar points are now made over and over again. In what follows, detailed answers to detailed arguments need not be presented. This has been done in book after book. Furthermore, as any college debater or trial lawyer knows, it is possible to present an objection to almost any statement, and the effect so far as the audience is concerned is often the result of a subtle turn of phrase or an appeal to a bit of loyalty or sentiment. Rather, we shall be concerned with the thrust of certain main positions which, taken individually and in their accumulative significance, serve to swing the weight of unbiased conviction from one side to the other. Finally, some suggestions will be offered for escaping from the present stalemated debate.

What, then, are the major arguments *for* the retraction? Although the arguments had been presented by others before him, Father Cavanna [16] gives a well-organized summary which is adopted by most subsequent defenders. The points which follow are based on Cavanna with some minor modifications:

(1) Since its discovery in 1935, the retraction "document" is considered the chief witness to the reality of the retraction itself. In fact, since then, by word or implication, the defenders have said, "The burden of proof now rests with those who question the retraction."

(2) The testimony of the press at the time of the event, of "eyewitnesses," and other "qualified witnesses," i.e., those closely associated with the events such as the head of the Jesuit order, the archbishop, and so on.

(3) "Acts of Faith, Hope, and Charity" reportedly recited and signed by Dr. Rizal as attested by "witnesses" and a signed prayer book. This is very strong testimony *if true*, for Rizal was giving assent to Roman Catholic teaching not in a general way as in the case of the retraction statement but specifically to a number of beliefs which he had previously repudiated. According to the testimony of Father Balaguer, following the signing of the retraction a prayer book was offered to Rizal. "He took the prayer book, read slowly those acts, accepted them, took the pen and saying

---

[16] Cavanna, *op. cit.*, pp. 1–108.

'Credo' ('I believe') he signed the acts with his name in the book itself." [17] What was it Rizal signed? It is worth quoting in detail the "Act of Faith."

I believe in God the Father, I believe in God the Son, I believe in God the Holy Ghost, Three distinct Persons, and only One True God. I believe that the Second Person of the Most Holy Trinity became Man, taking flesh in the most pure womb of the Virgin Mary. I believe that this Divine Lord was born of the Blessed Virgin Mary, suffered, died, arose again, ascended into Heaven, and that He will come to judge the living and the dead, to give glory to the just because they have kept his holy commandments, and eternal punishment to the wicked because they have not kept them. I believe that the true Body and Blood of our Lord Jesus Christ are really present in the Most Holy Sacrament of the Altar. I believe that the Blessed and ever Virgin Mary, Mother of God, was in the first moment of her natural life conceived without the stain of original sin. I believe that the Roman Pontiff, Vicar of Jesus Christ, visible Head of the Church, is the Pastor and Teacher of all Christians; that he holds supreme authority over the whole Catholic Church; that he is infallible when he teaches doctrines of faith and morals to be observed by the universal Church, and that his definitions are in themselves binding and immutable; and I believe all that the Holy, Roman Catholic, and Apostolic Church believes and teaches, since God who can neither deceive nor be deceived, has so revealed it; and in this faith I wish to live and die.

[17] *Ibid.*, p. 54. (A photostat of the Acts is found facing p. 57 and the translated text on pp. 57 f.) What a radical change would be involved in the signing of this creed may be noted by comparing its substance with the following statements chosen from some of Rizal's well-known writings: "I neither believe nor disbelieve the qualities that many people ascribe to [God]. I smile at the definitions and lucubrations of theologians and philosophers about that ineffable and inscrutable Being."—"Who dies on the Cross? Was it the God or the man? . . . To me, Christ the man is greater than Christ the God" (miscellaneous letters to Father Pastells).—"To mitigate somehow their terrible conception of God, they have their poetic and tender idea of the Virgin" (*State of Religiosity in the Philippines*).—The times were primitive when certain men claimed they "could make God descend to earth by merely saying a few words, . . . they ate His flesh and drank His blood and even at times allowed the common folk to do the same" (*Noli Me Tangere*).—"All your Reverence's brilliant and subtle arguments . . . cannot convince me that the Catholic Church is endowed with infallibility" (letter to Father Pastells).

The signed prayer book was among the documents discovered by Father Gracia along with the retraction.

(4) Acts of piety performed by Rizal during his last hours as testified to by "witnesses."

(5) His Roman Catholic marriage to Josephine Bracken as attested to by "witnesses." There could be no marriage without a retraction.

These arguments are impressive. Many think of them, as Cavanna does, as "irrefutable facts." But to call them "facts" is to prejudge the case or to misuse the word. That a retraction document was discovered in 1935 is a fact, but that it is a document actually prepared and signed by Rizal is the question at issue. Many opponents of the retraction use the document as *their* chief argument. So also, there *is* a signed prayer book. But a number have asked, is this really Rizal's signature? Granted, for sake of argument, that it is, what is the significance of a mere signature apart from the testimony of Father Balaguer as to *why* Rizal signed?

What about the testimony of the "witnesses"? One may dismiss the newspaper reports as being less significant though of corroborative value. Their news was secured from others. One reporter got into the chapel during part of the twenty-four hours. He states that "studies, frolics of infancy, and boys' stories, were the subject of our chat." [18] As for the actual eyewitnesses, some eight testified to having seen one or more of the acts mentioned above. Only three testify to having seen the signing of the retraction. The major witnesses are priests or government officials at a time when church and state worked hand in hand. The bulk of the testimony comes from notarized statements in 1917 or later. Having made these comments it is none the less true that the testimony is impressive. It cannot be dismissed with a few sarcastic comments. The arguments from testimony as well as the arguments as a whole can be better judged only after weighing this evidence over against the arguments rejecting the retraction.

What is the case *against* the retraction?

[18] Don Santiago Mataix, correspondent of the *Heraldo de Madrid*, quoted by Palma, *op. cit.*, p. 325.

(1) The retraction document is said to be a forgery. As has been noted, the document plays a significant part on both sides of the debate. There are four prongs to the case against the document itself.

(a) First, there is the matter of the handwriting. To date the only detailed, scientific study leading to an attack upon the genuineness of the document is that made by Dr. Ricardo R. Pascual of the University of the Philippines shortly after the document was found, a study incorporated in his book *Rizal Beyond the Grave*. Taking as his "standard" some half dozen unquestioned writings of Rizal dating from the last half of December 1896, he notes a number of variations with the handwriting of the retraction document, the following being the most significant ones according to the present writer: (i) the slant of the letters in the standard writings gives averages several points higher than the average yielded by the retraction document, and perhaps more significantly, the most slanted letters are to be found in the document; (ii) there are significant variations in the way individual letters are formed; (iii) with reference to the signature, Pascual notes no less than seven differences, one of the most significant being indications of "stops," which, says the critic, are most naturally explained by the fact that a forger might stop at certain points to determine what form to make next; (iv) there are marked similarities in several respects between the body of the retraction and the writing of all three signers, i.e., Rizal and the two witnesses, thus serving to point to Pascual's conclusion that this is a "one-man document." [19] The only scholarly answer to Pascual is that

[19] One curious fact about the document is only briefly noted by Dr. Pascual, namely, that at the upper left-hand corner of the document someone, presumably a filing clerk, has written the date of the retraction which may be read as either "29 Dbre 96" or "29 Dbre 97." When Pascual saw the document the "6" appeared a little heavier than the "7" (cf. Pascual, *op. cit.*, p. 7). This fact can be noted clearly in the reproduction of the photograph incorporated in Pascual's book. Why did someone write "97" and then change it to "96"? Could it have been that the document was actually produced at the time the filing was done, and some clerk inadvertently wrote the wrong date which had to be revised later? Another curious fact is that when the writer saw the "original" document on Oct. 26, 1965, the "7" appeared to be heavier than the "6," a fact also plain in the photostat in his possession. Has, then, some further "doctoring" been done since the "discovery" in 1935 or was Pascual's reporting inaccurate in this respect?

given by Dr. José I. del Rosario as part of the thesis which he prepared for his doctorate in chemistry at the University of Sto. Tomás (1937), although most of the details are the result of a later study which Father Cavanna *asked* him specifically to prepare.[20] Dr. del Rosario's main criticism may be said to be that Pascual does not include enough of Rizal's writings by way of comparison. On the basis of a larger selection of standards he is able to challenge a number of Pascual's statements, although the writer has noted mistakes in del Rosario's own data. Dr. del Rosario's conclusion is that the handwriting is genuine.

(b) A second prong directed against the authenticity of the document itself is based on the principles of textual criticism. Several critics, beginning with Pascual, have noted differences between the text of the document found in 1935 and other versions of the retraction including the one issued by Father Balaguer.[21] Since this kind of criticism is related to the writer's work in Biblical studies, he is now engaged in a major textual study which consists first of all in gathering together all available forms of the text. To date, it is clear that at least from the morning of December 30, 1896, there have been, discounting numerous minor variations, two distinct forms of the text with significant differences. The one form is represented by the document discovered in 1935 and certain other early records of the retraction. The other form of the text is much more common, beginning with the text of Balaguer published in 1897. Two phrases in particular are to be noted in the following comparison of the text discovered by Gracia (in italics) with that of Balaguer (in brackets): in line 6, "*Iglesia Católica*" [Iglesia], and in line 10, "*la Iglesia*" [la misma Iglesia]. There also tend to be consistent differences between the two texts in the use of capital letters. Both forms claim to be a true representation of the original.

The usual explanation of these differences is that either Father Balaguer or Father Pi made errors in preparing a copy of the original and that these have been transmitted from this earliest copy to others. Father Cavanna makes the ingenious suggestion

[20] Cavanna, *op. cit.*, pp. 176 ff. It has been stated to the writer that Dr. del Rosario is the relative of a high church official.

[21] See accompanying page for the two "texts."

TEXT OF THE RETRACTION DOCUMENT DISCOVERED BY FATHER GRACIA IN 1935 IN THE ARCHIVES OF THE MANILA ARCHDIOCESE *

Me declaro católico y en esta Religion en que nací y me eduqué quiero vivir y morir. Me retracto de todo corazon de cuanto en mis palabras, escritos, impresos y conducta ha habido contrario á mi cualidad de hijo de la Iglesia Católica. Creo y profeso cuanto ella enseña y me someto á cuanto ella manda. Abomino de la Masoneria, como enemiga que es de la Iglesia, y como sociedad prohibida por la Iglesia. Puede el Prelado Diocesano, como Autoridad Superior Eclesiástica hacer pública esta manifestación espontánea mia para reparar el escándalo que mis actos hayan podido causar y para que Dios y los hombres me perdonen.

Manila, 29 de Diciembre de 1896

José Rizal

El Jefe del Piquete   El ayudante deplaza
Juan del Fresno   Eloy Moure

* Based on a photostat of the Retraction in the files of the Rev. Manuel A. Gracia, C.M., seen by this writer.

TEXT OF THE RETRACTION AS REPORTED BY FATHER BALAGUER IN HIS NOTARIAL ACT OF AUGUST 8, 1917.*

Me declaro católico, y en esta religión en que nací y me eduqué quiero vivir y morir. Me retracto de todo corazón de cuanto en mis palabras, escritos, impresos y conducta ha habido contrario a mi calidad de hijo de la Iglesia. Creo y profeso cuanto ella enseña; y me someto a cuanto ella manda. Abomino de la Masonería, como enemiga que es de la Iglesia, y como Sociedad prohibida por la misma Iglesia. Puede el Prelado diocesano, como Autoridad superior eclesiástica, hacer pública esta manifestación, espontánea mía, para reparar el escándalo que mis actos hayan podido causar, y para que Dios y los hombres me perdonen.

Manila, 29 de Diciembre de 1896.

Esta . . . retractación la firmaron con el Dr. Rizal, el Sr. Fresno, Jefe del Piquete y el señor Moure, Ayudante de la Plaza.

* Cf. Gonzalo Ma. Piñana, ¿Murió el Doctor Rizal Cristianamente? (Barcelona: Editorial Barcelonesa, S.A., 1920), p. 155.

that Father Balaguer made corrections in the "formula" which he supplied to Rizal according to the changes which Rizal was said to have made while writing out his own, but that he didn't accurately note them all. On the other hand, one would think that the copy would have been carefully compared at the very moment or at some other early date before the "original" disappeared. It is not surprising that some have wondered if the retraction document was fabricated from the "wrong" version of a retraction statement issued by the religious authorities.

(c) A third argument against the genuineness of the retraction document which also applies to the retraction itself is that its content is in part strangely worded, e.g., in the Catholic religion "I wish *to live* and die," yet there was little time to live. Rizal's claim that his retraction was "spontaneous," is also strange.

(d) Finally, there is the "confession" of "the forger." Only Runes has this story. He and his coauthor report an interview with a certain Antonio K. Abad who tells how on August 13, 1901, at a party at his ancestral home in San Isidro, Nueva Ecija (when Abad was fifteen), a Mr. Roman Roque told how he was employed by the friars earlier that same year to make several copies of a retraction document. This same Roque had been employed previously by Colonel Funston to forge the signature of the revolutionary General Lacuna on the document which led to the capture of Aguinaldo. Runes also includes a letter dated November 10, 1936, from Lorenzo Ador Dionisio, former provincial secretary of Nueva Ecija, who was also present when Roque told his story and confirms it.[22]

On the basis of the above arguments taken as a whole it would seem that there is reasonable ground at least to *question* the retraction document.

[22] Runes, *op. cit.*, pp. 107 ff. As a first check of my own on his evidence I wrote to a professor friend of mine whom I have known intimately for eighteen years. Since he comes from the North I thought he might be able to make some comments on the persons involved. To my surprise I found that my friend is himself a native of San Isidro, knew personally all three men mentioned above, and vouched strongly for their respectability and truthfulness. All had been civic officials. My informant had not heard the above story nor read the book by Runes, but he knows the author personally and vouches for his "reliability and honesty."

(2) The second main line of argument against the retraction is the claim that other acts and facts do not fit well with the story of the retraction. Those most often referred to by writers beginning with Hermenegildo Cruz in 1912 are as follows.

(a) The document of retraction was not made public until 1935; even members of the family did not see it. It was said to be "lost."

(b) No effort was made to save Rizal from the death penalty after his signing of the retraction.

The usual rebuttal is that Rizal's death was due to political factors and that with these the religious authorities could not interfere.

(c) Rizal's burial was kept secret; he was buried outside the inside wall of the Paco cemetery; and the record of his burial was not placed on the page for entries of December 30 but on a special page where at least one other admitted nonpenitent is recorded (perhaps others, the evidence is conflicting).

It is asked by the defenders of the retraction, how else could an executed felon be treated? Perhaps the ground outside the wall was sacred also or could have been specially consecrated. To top the rebuttal, Rizal's "Christian Burial Certificate" was discovered on May 18, 1935, in the very same file with the retraction document. The penmanship is admitted by all to be by an emanuensis. Whether the signature is genuine is open to question.

(d) There is no marriage certificate or public record of the marriage of Rizal with Josephine Bracken. To say that these were not needed is not very convincing.

(e) Finally, Rizal's behavior as a whole during his last days at Fort Santiago and during his last hours in particular does not point to a conversion. Whether written during the last twenty-four hours or somewhat earlier, Rizal's *Ultimo Adios* does not suggest any change in Rizal's thought. The letters which Rizal wrote then do not indicate conversion nor even religious turmoil. In the evening Rizal's mother and sister Trinidad arrived, and nothing was said to them about the retraction, although Father Balaguer claimed that even in the afternoon Rizal's attitude was beginning to change and that he was asking for the formula of retraction. It is all well and good to point out that all of the above happened prior to the *actual* retraction. A question is still present in the minds of many.

(3) The third chief line of argument against the retraction is that it is out of character. This argument has been more persistently and consistently presented than any other. Beginning with the anonymous leaflet of December 31, 1896, it has been asserted or implied in every significant statement against the retraction since that time. It has seemed to many, including the present writer, that the retraction is not in keeping with the character and *faith* of Rizal and is, as well, inconsistent with his previous declarations of religious *thought*.

First let us look at the character of the man. Rizal was mature. Anyone acquainted with the facts of his life knows this is so. Thirty-five is not exactly young, and Rizal was far more mature than the average at this age. It is not likely, then, that he would have been shocked into abnormal behavior by the threat of death. He had anticipated for some time that the authorities would destroy him, and even the priests admit that during his last hours Rizal manifested a type of behavior consistent with all that was previously exhibited during his mature years. The present writer worked closely with prisoners for some ten years and accompanied two of them to the scaffold. Their behavior was restrained and consistent. One would have expected Rizal's to be the same. Furthermore, in the deepest sense of the word Rizal was already a "believer." The writer has argued in his book on Rizal's religious thought that Rizal was not a "free-thinker" in the usual sense of the word. He was a Christian in the best sense of the word. History is full of the unchallenged reports of real conversions, but the most significant meaning of true conversion is the change from unbelief to belief, not mere change of ideas.

Rizal's conversion is also out of keeping with his mature religious thought. It is not as though Rizal had been bowled over by confrontation with the new thought of Europe (and by antagonism toward religious authorities who had injured his family and who worked hand in hand with a restrictive colonial regime) and had never fully thought through his religious convictions. "The fact that similar views are found from writing to writing of his mature years and that they make a quite consistent whole suggest that such theology as he had was fully his own. . . ."[23] Rizal had a consistent and meaningful system of Christian thought, and it is therefore harder to think of his suddenly exchanging it for another.

So much for the debate up to the present.[24] An endeavor has been made to state fairly the arguments, and it is evident on which side the writer stands. Nonetheless, the question is not settled. What, then, remains to be done? Is there a way out of the impasse? Are there areas for further investigation?

First, let a new effort be made to keep personalities and institutional loyalties out of future discussions. It is time for honest investigators to stop speaking of the "Protestant," the "Masonic," or the "Roman Catholic" view toward the retraction. Let the facts speak for themselves.

Second, let the retraction document be subject to neutral, scientific analysis. This suggestion is not new, but in view of the present state of the debate and the prevailing ecumenical spirit it

---

[23] Hessel, *op. cit.*, p. 255. A convenient reference to the key passages in Rizal's writings which indicates views quite contrary to orthodox Roman Catholicism is the 1965 book by Juan Collas referred to in note 9. No wonder, as Mr. Collas points out (*op. cit.*, pp. 163 ff.), the authorities were eager to secure a retraction by hook or by crook.

[24] A note must be added concerning the contribution of Austin Coates's new biography to the debate (*cf.* reference in note 6). Coates deals extensively with the question of the retraction and rejects it outright as a "fraud" perpetrated by Father Balaguer personally out of desire to win the applause of the church and out of envy of Rizal himself (pp. 342 ff.). Coates reiterates most of the objections to the retraction summarized by the present writer, supporting several of them with the fruit of his own special research. Thus, with regard to the marriage of Rizal to Josephine Bracken, he indicates in a lengthy footnote based on his research in Hong Kong, that when she married there two years after Rizal's death her name is listed in the church register of marriages at the Roman Catholic cathedral not as Josephine Rizal but as "Josephine Brackin" [*sic*] (pp. 342 f.). Again, Coates's extensive analysis of Rizal's *Ultimo Adios* and the circumstances of its writing strongly suggests that Rizal in part wrote this masterpiece specifically to refute in advance "any attempt at fraud" (p. 317). Perhaps Coates's most distinctive contribution to the debate is the fact that his biography as a whole makes the retraction seem utterly inconsistent with Rizal's ultimate obedience to God. Further, his reconstruction of the events of the last twenty-four hours establishes, on the one hand, a strong circumstantial case against the genuineness of the retraction and, on the other hand, offers a reasonable view of what really happened.

would be fitting at last to carry this out. Furthermore, it would be an act of good faith on the part of the Roman Catholic hierarchy. If the document is genuine, those who favor the retraction have nothing to lose; in *either* case the cause of truth will gain. For this analysis a government bureau of investigation in some neutral country such as Switzerland or Sweden would be preferable.[25]

Should neutral experts claim that the document discovered in 1935 is a forgery, this of itself would not prove that Rizal did not retract. But it would prompt further study.

As a third step, then, to be undertaken *only* after a new evaluation of the retraction document, the Roman Catholic hierarchy should feel bound to allow its other "documents" pertaining to Rizal's case to be investigated, i.e., "the burial certificate," the signature of the prayer book, and perhaps also certain other retraction documents found in the same bundle with that of Dr. Rizal's.

In the fourth place, the story concerning the "forger" should be investigated further.

And, finally, if assurance can be given that the above steps are being undertaken then let there be a moratorium on further debate and greater attention given to the rest of Rizal's life and thought, in particular to his mature religious faith and thought. Senator José Diokno has well said:

It is because of what he did and what he was that we revere Rizal. . . . Catholic or Mason, Rizal is still Rizal: the hero who courted death "to prove to those who deny our patriotism that we know how to die for our duty and our beliefs. . . ." [26]

[25] In lieu of using a handwriting bureau abroad, could not the document at least be submitted to the Philippine National Bureau of Investigation? In conversations with officials of the bureau the writer learned that the original has never been presented to them; however, the bureau has not answered a formal inquiry from the writer concerning this and other matters pertaining to the analysis of the document. If the bureau were permitted to undertake this analysis they might assemble a board representing the two sides of the question as well as neutral experts on their staff.

[26] From the preface to Garcia's *The Great Debate*. It is surprising and heartening that the senator would write this in a book defending the retraction.

Anticlericalism during the Reform Movement and the Philippine Revolution

CESAR ADIB MAJUL

Anticlericalism during the Philippine revolution and legislative attempts to neutralize or minimize the traditional power of the church represent the last phases of a process that began in the 1870's. The various marked stages and shifts in anticlericalism represent a cumulative process. What began simply as a movement to reduce the political and social power of Spanish friars became in time an actual threat to their lives and properties. The sympathy for Filipino secular priests—a corollary to antipathy for Spanish friars—aroused attempts to use the secular priests for revolutionary aims. Initial antagonism to the Spanish nationality of friars was eventually transferred to the Spanish character and administration of the Catholic church in the Philippines. What ensued from this was encouragement for the establishment of a national church by some revolutionary leaders in spite of their commitment to the liberal idea of the separation of church and state. Earlier widespread protestations of loyalty to the church changed during the revolution to a basic questioning of the church's role and function in Filipino society.

From an historical point of view, the development of anticlericalism in the Philippines can be conveniently grouped into three stages: events in the country from about 1870 to the eve of the reform movement, the reform movement from the 1880's to the revolution in 1896, and from the revolution to the end of 1899.

Historical Background

Father H. de la Costa, S.J., in his essays in this volume, has already discussed the events which led to the visitation controversy

and the secularization controversy, together with the development of a native clergy, all of which are exceedingly important
for an understanding of the background of anticlericalism in the
Philippines.

In 1870, Archbishop Gregorio Melitón Martínez, the secular
and sympathetic superior of the Filipino clergy, sent a letter to
the Spanish regent in which he enumerated the injustices committed against Filipino seculars, explained their mounting resentment against the friars, and the serious consequences for the
colony should the government appear to side with the friars:

Now that, in the face of clear evidences, they realize that the authorities are trying to support the unreasonable claims of the regulars, and
that, in the opinion of the native priests themselves, the policy has
been adopted of reducing them into nullity, they are going over ancient barriers, are turning their eyes to a higher aim, and, what was
before but a mere resentment against the regulars, now assumes the
character of an anti-Spanish sentiment.[1]

The archbishop then warned the Spanish government that
should the bitterness and resentment of the Filipino priests not be
remedied, such feeling eventually would be extended to their
parents and relatives, and finally to the "whole Filipino people,
with whom they are in closer contact than are the regulars, with
the result that the danger would assume a grave character." As
succeeding events were to demonstrate, never were the words of
a Spanish prelate in the Philippines more correct.

At bottom, the conflict between the two clerical groups—the
Spanish friars and the Filipino seculars—was for the control of
the parishes of the country and their corollary social and economic benefits. For the Filipino priests, the step from control of
the parishes to occupying high ecclesiastical offices and enjoying
the concomitant political power would not be a difficult one—and
it was one they were ready to take.

The Rise of the *Ilustrados*

For nearly three hundred years, the majority of the Filipinos
lived in parishes under the watchful and benevolent eyes of friar

[1] The complete text is found in Nicolas Zafra, *Readings in Philippine History* (rev. ed.; Quezon City, 1956), pp. 485–98.

curates in an atmosphere characterized by some observers as "Arcadian." This innocent and generally peaceful slumber was soon to vanish. The reasons for the slow but sure awakening are numerous. The improvement of agriculture, the opening of Manila and other ports to foreign commerce, the development of Manila as a commercial center, easier and faster communication with Spain, increased educational opportunities and the offering of professional courses, and so forth, led, in the penultimate quarter of the nineteenth century, to the emergence of another elite among the native population—the *ilustrados*. By virtue of their educational attainments and adoption of Spanish cultural traits made possible by their economic base, generally classifiable as "middle-class," as well as by their ability to mix socially with Spaniards, the *ilustrados* enjoyed great prestige among the native population. Whereas up to the middle of the nineteenth century the only career that enabled a Filipino to achieve some parity with the conquerors was to be a priest, the increase in educational opportunities and professional courses opened new vistas for the ambitious scions of a rising class of well-to-do families. Meanwhile, however, because of the religious values of the people and the needs of a growing population, the priesthood still remained an attractive and relatively fruitful career.

The rise of the *ilustrados* would not have radically disturbed the Arcadian character of the colony or caused inquietude among the friars were it not for the fact that many of them were being influenced by liberal ideas emanating from the mother country. The infiltration of revolutionary ideas from France, agitation for the re-establishment of the Cortes and its essentially democratic base, and the September revolution of 1868, created expectations for the implementation of liberal reforms if not republican institutions in Spain. The political atmosphere in Spain was such that it became possible to send to the Philippines as governor-general the fiercely liberal Carlos María de la Torre (1869–1871). By encouraging the discussion of political and social questions, abolishing censorship of the press, and trying to increase government supervision of education, he alienated the friars. Contrariwise, the *ilustrados* and Filipino priests welcomed him. Organizing themselves into groups, and joined by young students from leading

educational institutions, the *ilustrados* and secular priests started
to agitate peacefully for civil rights, action unheard of before in
the colony; and naturally, too, they worked for the secularization of
the parishes. Indeed, if granted, the political rights they asked for
would enable them to be heard more effectively in Spain. Ultimately, the granting of more reforms and political rights would
increase the opportunities of the *ilustrados* to occupy more positions in the civil and military administration and even on the
municipal level. The *ilustrados* were, in effect, making a bid for
an increased share in the political destiny of the colony. The
Spanish monarchists and friars in the colony formed an alliance
against both *ilustrados* and Filipino priests. In the face of a common enemy, and on account of racial affinity as well as parallel
power aims, the *ilustrados* and the Filipino priests closed ranks.

The Cavite Mutiny of 1872 and the
Execution of Three Filipino Priests

The restoration of the monarchy in Spain under Amadeo de
Savoy brought in 1871 a new governor to the Philippines, Rafael
de Izquierdo. Completely opposed to the liberal policies of his
predecessor, and with the help of monarchists and friars, he revived press censorship, curtailed political discussions, and declared himself completely unsympathetic to secularization. Although the spirit of some of those interested in immediate
reforms was dampened, the hands of the clock could not be
turned back. Liberalism in Spain was not at all dead; neither
were the expectations which this ideology inspired in the Philippines.

On January 20, 1872, on account of oppression by their Spanish
officers, about two hundred Filipino soldiers and arsenal workers
in Cavite mutinied. In two days, the mutiny was smashed by
loyal troops. Since there was evidence that the mutineers were in
collusion with soldiers in Manila, the whole matter was judged
not merely a local revolt but one aimed at the separation of the
colony from Spain. The suspected leaders were those believed to
have been harboring liberal ideas. Consequently, three Filipino
priests—Burgos, Gómez, and Zamora—were publicly garroted on

February 17. Several dozen Filipino priests and *ilustrados* were also imprisoned or exiled to the Marianas.[2]

Priests, in general, had always enjoyed some charisma in Filipino society, and the above public execution created consternation, shock, and scandal among the people. The refusal of the Manila archbishop to defrock them, the mournful tolling of the cathedral bells during the day of execution, the secrecy of the trial, the protestations of innocence by the accused up to the very last moment, and the general knowledge that they had antagonized the friars on the issue of secularization, all these combined to produce the belief among the people that the priests were innocent and were the victims of friar intrigue. Regardless of the validity of this belief, the fact was that it became widely held. In time the *ilustrados* began to spread the explanation that the three priests were executed because they were natives who dared to challenge the established powers, and that the authorities wanted to intimidate future agitators for political rights and the secularization of the parishes. In any case, many timid souls became frightened because the demand for reforms and secularization of the parishes had now become synonymous with "filibusterism," that is, the agitation for political separation from Spain. The Spanish friars emerged as defenders of Spanish sovereignty in the colony.

It was difficult to ignore the racial implications of the execution. The executed priests were called martyrs by the *ilustrados* and other sympathizers. As perceptively anticipated in the letter of archbishop Martínez, the line between anti-Spanish friar and anti-Spaniard became thinner with dire results for Spanish sovereignty.

The above events represent a recognizable stage in anticlericalism in the Philippines, a stage equated with antifriary. However, it was an attitude initially directed to four regular orders only: the Recollects, the Augustinians, the Dominicans, and the Fran-

---

[2] For details of the Cavite Mutiny and the trial of the three priests cf. *El infame proceso incoado contra los presbiteros Filipinos, padres Dr. José Apolonio Burgos, Mariano Gómez y Jacinto Zamora con prólogo por Luciano de la Rosa* (Manila, 1963); and Nicolas Zafra, *op. cit.,* pp. 499–510.

ciscans. Not included were the Jesuits, who had returned in 1859
and were few in number, and a few Spanish secular priests.

The Reform Movement

After 1872, the reactionary policy of the government continued
unabated. To avoid persecution, a few *ilustrados* left for Europe
and nearby Asian cities. Spain proved a haven, in spite of the
Bourbon restoration, since her people were enjoying certain political rights agitated for by liberals and republicans. It is enough to
recall that the Constitution of 1876 had accommodated a few of
the principles of the short-lived Spanish republic of 1873–1874.
Eventually, in spite of educational and professional opportunities
in Manila, many young Filipino students went to Spain to study.
These *ilustrados,* brought together by a common purpose, began
to write articles, books, and pamphlets, and formed associations
to serve as pressure groups, to reveal to the Spanish government
and public the sad state of the colony. A movement, called by
historians the "propaganda movement," was thus generated.
What these reformists desired was equality of both Spaniards and
Filipinos in the colony before the law and the same political
rights then operative in Spain. To secure these demands, it had
become imperative to ask that the Philippines be represented in
the Cortes and be considered a province of Spain. To this was
added the demand for the secularization of the parishes.

The reform movement produced *La Solidaridad,* a fortnightly
newspaper that first appeared in 1889; its last issue came out in
1895, a few months before the revolution when most of its supporters had despaired of peaceful methods to secure social and
political amelioration. Among the contributors were José Rizal,
M. H. del Pilar, Graciano López Jaena, Antonio Luna, Mariano
Ponce, Pedro Paterno, and others, persons intimately connected
later on with the revolution. The *Noli Me Tangere* and *El Filibusterismo,* by Rizal, were the two most notable novels produced
by the movement.

The friars and their sympathizers tried to counteract the reformists by articles in the Manila newspapers, which they controlled, and by numerous pamphlets and booklets. Initially they

tried to dismiss the works of the reformists by belittling them as spoiled children. But when they realized that the reformists were gaining sympathy not only among their compatriots but also among Spaniards and other Europeans, the friars postulated that the introduction of liberal ideas to the colony was dangerous and might result in the loss of the colony. The stand of the friars was expected and understandable since many of the ideas of the reformists had been in 1864 already condemned in the Syllabus of Errors of Pius IX. Although such a stand was correct from the point of view of the church, within the context of the European liberal and republican movements then sweeping Europe and influencing the reformists, it was judged as utterly unrealistic. A view of some friars, considered by some reformists as imprudent, was that the rights in Spain were earned by blood and not by ink, thereby implying that Filipinos did not deserve to enjoy those rights for which they had not shed any blood.

The conflict between the reformists and the friars was inexorable. There was practically no demand made by the former that would not in some manner reduce the power of the latter as well as the traditional privileges of the church. The demand for freedom of speech, press, and association was interpreted by the friars as opening the doors to heretical ideas and secret societies like Masonry, thus endangering the faith which the king was pledged to protect and uphold. Greater civil control of education posed a challenge to what the church had always considered her cherished right in a predominantly Catholic country. More significantly, the secularization of the parishes meant that the friars would eventually have to give up nearly 700 parishes.

To the insinuations by the friars that agitation for reform was simply a disguise for separation from Spain and that they were therefore disloyal and anti-Spanish, the reformists countered that the friars in protecting their corporate interests were disregarding the more general interests of the mother country and were therefore themselves the really anti-Spanish institution. To this the friars asserted that they were the surest guardians and upholders of Spanish sovereignty in the colony. The answer of the reformists was that the friars were not necessarily an essential fix-

ture in the colonial parlor: their parishes could be efficiently handled by Filipino priests, and with more municipal autonomy and
increase of opportunities, their other functions could be taken
over by Filipino civil officials.

The controversy became more serious, and mutual accusations
more acrimonious. The reformists tried to demonstrate that the
friars, on account of their outmoded educational system, were
hindering the scientific and cultural progress of the country, forgetting all the while that they themselves were the products of
friar tutelage. The friars, not forgetting this detail, called them an
ungrateful and discontented lot. Ignoring episcopal vigilance and
disciplinary actions on lapses in the morality of curates, the reformists made it a point to expose cases of concubinage among
friars in a somewhat colored manner. Friar properties became a
special target. Agrarian troubles were blamed on them. The friars
were accused of having no titles to their lands, charging excessive
rental rates, and being ruthless in ejecting their tenants. Indeed,
the friars were the single largest and wealthiest landlord group in
the Philippines. In some agrarian troubles, some *ilustrados* were
involved. In the infamous Calamba case, the family of Rizal was
ejected from land which they had cultivated for years. *La Solidaridad* did not miss making an issue of this against the Dominicans and the government that appeared to have taken their side.

The complexity of the conflict appeared the moment the friars
claimed that to fight them was, in effect, to weaken the position
of the church, thus constituting an attack on religion. Some reformists were then constrained to attack the church as well. As
Rizal wrote to Ferdinand Blumentritt on January 20, 1890:

I wanted to hit the friars, but since they used religion not only as a
shield but as a weapon, protection, castle, fort, and armor, etc., I was
forced to attack their false and superstitious religion to fight the enemy
who hid behind it. . . . God should not be utilized as a shield and
protector of abuses, and there is less reason for religion to be used for
this purpose. If the friars really had more respect for their religion they
would not often use its sacred name or expose it to the most dangerous
situations. What is happening in the Philippines is terrible: they abuse
the name of religion for a few pesos, preach it to enrich their proper-

ties, to seduce an innocent maid, to destroy an enemy and to disturb the peace of a marriage or family, if not the honor of the wife.[3]

Of the 160 issues of *La Solidaridad*, there was practically no issue that did not criticize or make fun of friars either in lengthy articles or short news items. Some of the latter made it a point to reveal gossipy stories of priests and nuns not only in the Philippines but in Spain and Europe as well. The anticlericalism of *La Solidaridad* was not confined to friars. This, compounded by a general antichurch feeling among some *ilustrados*, signified a shift in anticlericalism among Filipinos.

To explain this shift, it is sufficient to know that many of the reformists had joined Masonry, which at that time was anathema to the church. In Europe some of the most passionate liberals and Masons were not only anticlerical but antichurch as well. The reformists could not help but breathe deeply of the environment they lived in. Moreover, some well-known scientists who sympathized with the reform movement, giving it some prestige and respectability, were themselves antifriar and devoid of traditional piety. Among these was Dr. Blumentritt, who was to a great extent one of the mentors to the relatively younger reformists in Spain, and one whose learned and antifriar articles filled the pages of *La Solidaridad*. It was this respected scientist who wrote that, should the Spanish government identify the interests of the friar with its own, a revolution against it would follow.[4] Soon the reformists would repeat him almost verbatim.

What was the position of the Filipino priests during all this? First of all, the reformists did not cast aspersions on them. Rizal even dedicated one of his novels to what he called the sacred memory of the three martyred priests. Moreover, a constant demand of the reformists was the secularization of the Philippine parishes. Not only were some Filipino priests in amiable correspondence with the reformists, but also there is evidence that some of them contributed to the funds of the reform movement. However, the alliance between both groups appears to have been

[3] *Epistolario Rizalino* (Manila, 1938), V (2nd part 1888–1896), p. 528 (author's translation).

[4] For example, see "Filibusterism," *La Solidaridad*, I, no. 8, May 31, 1889; and "Friars and Seculars," *ibid.*, II, no. 44, Nov. 30, 1890.

one of expediency. The plight of the Filipino priests was presented in Spain by the reformists, because the Filipino clergy was the answer of the reformists to the substitution of the disliked friars. The irony of it all was that some of the reformists agitating for the Filipinization of the parishes had themselves, in practice, ceased hearing Mass in parishes. Essentially, the conflict between the friars and the reformists represents a struggle between *ilustrados* desiring to have a greater role in determining the political destiny of the Philippines and an increased share in its social and economic benefits, and friars struggling to keep the *status quo* from which they derived political and social power coupled with relative economic comfort in the colony.

The Revolution in 1896

Slowly but surely the ideas of the reformists seeped to the humbler stratum of the native population. Things taken for granted or as belonging to the natural course of events began to be questioned. Lapses in morality, which did not create a fuss before, were now held against friars. Once considered as benevolent landlords, they were now pointed to as exploiters. The failure of the *ilustrados* to secure political and social reforms only brought revolutionary leadership among the masses to the fore. An atmosphere of distrust if not actual disobedience to government became manifest. The revolutionists, following the teachings of the *ilustrados,* singled out the friars as the source of most if not all the evils they were fighting against. Understandably, the friars fought the revolution as a threat to themselves and to Spanish sovereignty. They felt vindicated about their anticipations and warnings. Blaming the reformists, Masons, and Filipino priests for the armed uprising, the friars were instrumental in the arrests of many *ilustrados,* many of whom, ironically, helped unleash a violent movement they dimly anticipated but did not fully approve of.

In 1897 the fight between Spanish troops and revolutionists was temporarily halted by the Pact of Biaknabato, arranged by Pedro Paterno, an *ilustrado* connected with the movement for reforms. Emilio Aguinaldo, the leader of the revolutionists, claimed later on that during the peace negotiations the problem of reforms was discussed. Among these was the demand of the revolutionists that all the friar orders in the country be suppressed. The favorable verbal promise of the Spanish government in this regard, Aguinaldo claimed, was not put in writing so as to minimize its loss of face.[5] After the truce, however, the Spanish governor-general denied that such a promise had ever been made and insisted that the negotiations were confined to the granting of money to the revolutionary leaders.

The Friar Memorial of 1898

The uprising against Spanish rule in 1896 was, to most *ilustrados,* ultimately the fault of the friars. This view was held even by some *ilustrados* who loved the faith. For example, Felipe Calderón, who strongly propounded the unity of church and state in the Revolutionary Congress in 1898, had the following to say to the Schurman Commission on June 5, 1899:

The friar is the principal question here, and I say to you, Mr. Schurman, that I am a Catholic and have defended the Catholic faith in the Congress of Malolos, and I am certain that the friars must be expelled if we are to have peace in the country.[6]

The charge that the friars were responsible for the events in 1896 was also aired in Spain by Spaniards who had no love for the friars. Fernando Primo de Rivera, governor-general in the Philippines from 1897 to 1898, strengthened such a belief when in his memorial to the Spanish Senate he categorically stated that "upon the question of the friar depends the preservation or loss" of the colony. It was this official who also observed that the desire for social emancipation in the colony had to originate from the Filipino priests who by virtue of their relatively superior education would eventually find themselves in conflict with the friars who would like to keep the best parishes while allowing only the poorer ones for the native priests.[7]

[5] Emilio Aguinaldo y Famy, "Reseña verídica de la revolución filipina," *The Philippine Social Sciences Review,* XIII, no. 2, 185.

[6] *Report of the Philippine Commission to the President, 1900* (Washington, 1900), II, 146.

[7] Cf. Cesar Adib Majul, *The Political and Constitutional Ideas of the Philippine Revolution* (Quezon City, 1957), p. 115.

Rightly or wrongly, the friars were blamed for the events of 1896. This belief was widespread among the Filipino population. According to the Taft Commission, ". . . every abuse of the many which finally led to the two revolutions of 1898 was charged by the people to the friars. . . . The revolutions against Spain's sovereignty began as movements against the friars." [8]

The above belief and charge explain why, on April 21, 1898, the representatives of the four friar orders, including the Jesuits, signed a lengthy memorial to be presented to the Minister of Colonies in Spain.[9] Tersely denying the charges made through the press by "Masons" and "filibusters," that they, the friars, were responsible for the uprising in 1896, the memorial asserted that they constituted "the only force which has been until now the great bond of union between these beautiful lands and their dear mother, the mother country." Moreover, the interests of the church and that of the friars were not at variance but "perfectly amalgamated with religious interests." The memorial then suggested that the revolutionists adopted an antifriar attitude simply as a bait to gain the sympathy of certain quarters in Spain, for in doing away with the friars, separation from Spain would then follow easily. Furthermore, the failure of the revolutionists to blame the uprising on the excesses of Spanish colonial officials, fiscal and military abuses, and so on, was a technique to prevent them from being branded as anti-Spanish. However, unlike other institutions in the colony, they, the friars, constituted "the only permanent and deeply rooted Spanish institution. . . ."

The memorial then claimed that the blame for the uprising should be laid on the introduction of those modern and revolutionary ideas, many of which had been condemned in the Syllabus of Errors of Pius IX. These ideas, it was asserted, were the veritable germs of political and social disturbances and, before their introduction about thirty years ago, social order and religiosity reigned in the country. The lack of religiosity among some Spanish residents as well as irregularities committed by

[8] *Ibid.*, pp. 119–20.
[9] For the complete text of the "Friar Memorial of 1898," see Emma Helen Blair and James Alexander Robertson, eds., *The Philippine Islands, 1493–1898* (55 vols.; Cleveland, 1903–1909), LIII, 227–86.

colonial officials were then decried as contributing to the lessening of the prestige of the Spaniard before the eyes of the natives.

After enumerating their accomplishments in Christianizing the natives, pointing out their beneficial role in the spheres of education and morals, the friars denied that their educational system was unprogressive. The usual charges against friar immoralities were denied, and although it was admitted that there were isolated cases of lapses in moral conduct, such cases, it was claimed, were severely punished. Friar enemies were then challenged to present a known case of friar immorality that was tolerated and allowed with impunity. Also denied was the claim that friars charged excessive parochial fees.

The memorial reminded the Spanish government that, in accordance with royal prescriptions and the Laws of the Indies, Spain was obligated to send Catholic ministers to the Philippines and to guarantee the preservation of the faith in it. If the friars were to continue their sacred mission, the government had to proscribe Masonry and other secret societies in the colony, punish insults on the friars, and encourage the traditional respect for them. Furthermore, friar internal discipline, their rights to their properties, and their hold on the parishes were not to be disturbed by the government. The memorial then asked that all outrages against the clergy were to be considered as civil offenses and as a sacrilege. All government officials, from the governor-general to the lowest civil servant, were to exert effort, in public and in private, to demonstrate that they esteemed their duties to God and the church and that such duties were greater than any other kind. All these, if made to prevail, would signify the preservation of the colony for Spain.

The converse conditions which would spell the loss of the colony were then enumerated as follows: secularization of the parishes, the disamortization of friar lands, tolerance of all kinds of religious worship, and the freedom of the press and association. In passing, the friars also registered their objection to the institution of civil marriage and increased civil control of education. Finally, the memorial contended that should the Spanish government follow these recommendations, the friars would be able to "resist the enemies of the fatherland with greater force."

In brief, the friars were against practically everything demanded by the revolutionists, and their predecessors, the reformists. Opposed to many of the fundamental principles of nineteenth-century European liberalism, the friars could not have a ground of common agreement with those *ilustrados* already affected by liberal ideas.

An analysis of the friar memorial reveals that it was not merely an apology as it initially purported to be. It was, in effect, a frank and naked bid for the re-establishment of friar supremacy in the country as well as the establishment of a theocracy under their supervision or control. Yet the fact that it had become imperative for them to present a lengthy, well-thought-out, defensive document, suggests the degree to which a critical attitude toward them had developed, and that their presence and function in Filipino society had now become seriously questioned for the first time in nearly three hundred years. The claim of the friars in the memorial that the majority of the Filipinos still loved and respected them and that only a few disgruntled, half-baked educated men resented them must be judged alongside the conclusion of the Taft Commission, that

the statement of the bishops and the friars that the mass of the people in the islands, except only a few of the leading men of each town and the native clergy, are friendly to them, cannot be accepted as accurate. All the evidence derived from every source, but the friars themselves, shows clearly that the feeling of hatred for the friars is well-nigh universal and permeates all classes.[10]

Legislation against the Friars during the Revolution in 1898–1899

In 1898 when the revolutionary government was able to exercise its coercive powers over part of the Philippines, its general anticlerical orientation became clear in some of its laws and executive decrees. Some of the closest advisers of Aguinaldo, the president of the revolutionary government, were Masons who were not only antifriar but *ilustrados* interested in reducing the traditional power of the church in society. Foremost among these

[10] Senate Document No. 112, 56th Congress, 2nd session, p. 30.

was Apolinario Mabini, known as the brains of the Philippine revolution.[11]

A law passed on June 20, 1898, provided for the institution of civil marriages and the prohibition of canonical marriages without a previous civil one. There appeared, however, some objections to this law on the part of other advisers who, although antifriar, wanted to keep unreduced the prerogatives of the church. On August 22, the Secretary of the Interior reminded the municipalities about the compulsory character of civil marriages, and in June 1899, after the revolutionary government had been transformed into a republic, a reminder on the same point was made again. Since in revolutionary territory the friars had lost their power, it was now left to the Filipino priests to oppose this law. But there is no evidence of any effective opposition to it by them. The fact was that the Filipino priests were not in a strong position to do so.

Aguinaldo's message to Congress on January 1, 1899, proclaimed that all Spanish friars, whether they held high ecclesiastical positions or not, were to be expelled from revolutionary territory. To be expelled, too, were all persons leading a monastic life even if not ordained.[12] Earlier, Aguinaldo expressed the desire to have all Spanish priests, including the Jesuits, leave the country.[13] Following the message to Congress, on January 23, just after the proclamation of the republic, the president decreed that:

All regular Spanish clergy, even those who are ecclesiastical dignitaries, and also the persons who, although they are not in holy orders, are yet connected permanently with said clergy, will be expelled from the Philippine Territory.[14]

Actually about 400 friars in 1898–1899 were held prisoners by the revolutionists. Although there were a few cases of violence against them and many of them suffered humiliations and endured some privations, the evidence is that they were relatively

[11] For Mabini's attitudes towards the friars and church, see the author's *Mabini and the Philippine Revolution* (Quezon City, 1960), pp. 349–435; and *Apolinario Mabini: Revolutionary* (Manila, 1964), pp. 154–76.
[12] *The Political and Constitutional Ideas of the Philippine Revolution*, p. 122.
[13] *Ibid.*, pp. 93–94.   [14] *Ibid.*, p. 122.

well treated. Some were assigned to serve as servants to revolutionary officials, a deliberate effort to demonstrate to the inhabitants who the new masters were. American military authorities as
well as Vatican officials exerted pressure on the revolutionists for
the safety, good treatment, and possible liberty of the friars.
What is not well known is that the revolutionary government, on
the advice of Mabini, planned to keep the friars prisoner, to increase its bargaining power for having its independence recognized by both the United States and the Vatican. A letter prepared by Mabini to Nozaleda, the Manila archbishop, intended to
be signed by Aguinaldo, denied that the prisoners were held for
ransom, adding sarcastically, however, that the friars would indeed prefer to live among Filipino Catholics even as prisoners
than to be delivered to a free-thinking and infidel people such as
the Americans.[15]

The eventual defeat of the revolutionary forces by the Americans prevented the expulsion of the friars. As the revolutionists
progressively lost territory, more friars were able to flee to
Manila. Although at the beginning of the American regime a few
hundred of them left for Spain and other parts of the world, since
then their number in the Philippines has increased.

Corollary to the expulsion orders for the friars and of great significance in understanding the economic aspect of the revolution
were the laws pertaining to the final disposition of friar properties. On the eve of the revolution, the friars owned about 403,713
acres of land, mostly agricultural. Some of these represented the
best and most productive land. In the province of Cavite the
friars owned 121,747 acres of land, leading many *ilustrados* as
well as a governor-general to believe that many insurrections
originated in Cavite precisely on account of this situation. The
Malolos Constitution which went into effect in January 1899 declared in one of its additional articles the following:

From the 24th of May last, on which date the dictatorial government
was organized in Cavite, all the buildings, properties, and other be-
longings possessed by the religious corporations in these islands will be
understood as restored to the Filipino government.

[15] *Mabini and the Philippine Revolution*, p. 198.

It must be noted that the confiscated friar properties were meant initially to serve as a source of income for the government. It was not parceled among its tillers but handed to the administration of "men of means" able to furnish security in cash or in bond. A law to this effect even expressed preference for municipal officials to administer them.[16] There is evidence that against revolutionary policy, some revolutionary generals tried to appropriate some of the land for themselves. According to John Taylor, "when Aguinaldo promised to give estates in the densely populated Cagayan valley to his followers, he showed at least one motive for the insurrection of 1896." [17] At this time friar lands in Cagayan amounted to 16,413 acres. In any case, the confiscation of friar lands brought in some money to a financially hard-pressed revolutionary government as well as the hope for some people eventually to own some land.

Attitudes toward the Filipino Clergy and Church

In accordance with the plan to transform the revolutionary government into a republic, the Congress from October 25 to November 29, 1898, discussed a republican constitutional draft presented by Felipe Calderón. Although he was a passionate anti-friar, Calderón wanted to keep the Catholic religion as that of the state, providing also, however, for the tolerance of other sects. Title III, Articles 5–7, of this constitution embodied these ideas. These articles elicited the lengthiest and most controversial discussions in Congress, and many delegates normally absent made it a point to attend. It was Tomás del Rosario who proposed an amendment to Title III as follows: "The State recognizes the liberty and equality of all religious worship, and the separation of Church and State." The proponents of the amendment dwelt lengthily on historical examples regarding conflicts between church and state, papal abuses, the fact that not all Filipinos were Catholics, and even on the argument that the Catholic religion in the country, having degenerated into a "feudal theocracy," had ceased to constitute the real Christianity. Another argument proffered that the Filipinos were united in the revolution by ties other than that of religion.

16 *Ibid.*, pp. 47–48.   17 *Ibid.*, p. 48.

The argument of the Filipino clergy, who had representatives in Congress, and their sympathizers, was that to allow any other religion except Catholicism was to allow error and impiety; that a civil society constituted a moral entity and therefore needed a determinate religion. Furthermore, the Catholic religion had given the Filipinos a sense of common identity.

What resulted was that the first vote taken on the proposed amendment ended in a tie. However, on the second vote taken on November 29, 1898, the tie was broken by the chairman in favor of the amendment. This brought some disappointment to the Filipino clergy and their sympathizers to the extent that some of them began to withdraw slowly from public affairs.[18]

Discussions in Congress revealed that although most of the delegates, as well as top civil and military officials, were antifriar, not all were anti-Catholic. Indeed, many who were antifriar were also pro-Filipino clergy. What clearly emanated was that the Filipino clergy themselves were not willing to give up the traditional position and power of the church in their society. The Filipino priests supported the revolutionists to do away with their common enemy, the friars; but they had no intention of serving as agents for the dissolution of the established power of the church. Not really interested in a radically new social and intellectual order, they were mostly interested in stepping into the sandals of the Spanish friars. Sameness of race with the revolutionists and past humiliations suffered under the friars, however, enabled the Filipino priests to keep their sympathizers. More important, it was recognized that they were the first to have presented an organized stand against friar supremacy in Philippine life.

This last detail could not be neglected. What eventually took place was a compromise solution. The amended Title III was suspended and a "temporary article" was inserted into the approved republican constitution. Temporary Article 100 provided that the problem of church and state was to be discussed in a future assembly; meanwhile, municipalities needing the services of a Filipino priest had to provide for his support.

[18] Cf. *The Political and Constitutional Ideas of the Philippine Revolution*, pp. 142–43.

In revolutionary territory, it appeared that the friar problem was nearly solved. But judging from the nature of various laws, the revolutionaries were not only watchful of Filipino priests lest they perpetuate abuses associated with the friars but also attempted to utilize the Filipino clergy as tools to strengthen the revolution. There was an order for Filipino priests by means of "the pulpit and the confessional" to urge the faithful to adhere strongly to the aims of the revolution and support General Aguinaldo. Parish priests were warned to follow a schedule of parochial fees, and a government decree even went so far as to prohibit them from selling wax candles.

After the outbreak of hostilities against Americans in February 1899, the government ordered that all "parish funds and cash belonging to churches" be invested in the national loan to avoid "loss by the hazards of war." Another order declared that recognizing the Manila archbishop as an ecclesiastical superior and sending him part of parish funds was a highly unpatriotic act.[19] Although some of the measures were normally enough to tax the patience of Filipino priests, there is no evidence of any concerted effort at disobedience. On the contrary, many accompanied the revolutionists in the field to give them solace and to minister to their spiritual needs.

But the revolution never deviated from one of its aims: the secularization of the parishes. The Filipino clergy had to be rewarded for the use of its prestige to back the revolution. More important, friars were Spaniards; on both counts, they were unwanted. Since it was necessary to have Filipino bishops to ordain priests as the need arose, government officials encouraged the formal organization of the Filipino clergy to enable it to present a strong petition to the pope. High government officials had already chosen Gregorio Aglipay, a Filipino priest, to lead the clergy. In brief, the lay hand was revealed in the formation of a national church, which although still loyal to the Vatican was to be controlled by Filipino priests, from the highest ecclesiastical official to the humblest acolyte.

Filipino priests met at Panique, Tarlac, in October 1899, for-

---

[19] A number of these laws are enumerated in *Mabini and the Philippine Revolution*, pp. 427–28.

mally organized themselves, and planned a petition to the pope for a Filipino bishop, but nothing immediate came out of it. In a few weeks, the revolutionary army was disbanded into guerrilla units, and revolutionary territory began to shrink with the American advance. However, the expectations and implications raised by the prospect of a national church lay in the not too distant future, when, under the principle of freedom of worship and of religious affiliation during the American regime, the Philippine Independent Church was established under Bishop Gregorio Aglipay.

The formation of a national church can be viewed as a compromise solution to some divisive elements in the relations between the Filipino priests and the *ilustrados* closely associated with the revolution. A national church while implying the disappearance of foreign control of church activities in the country would also signify that the revolution was not against the Catholic church and religion as such. A church under the control of patriotic Filipino priests was expected to support the revolution while also satisfying their ambitions for secularization. From the point of view of the revolution, it might be easier to prevent the clerics of a national church from perpetrating those abuses that marked the pages of Philippine history. On these points, the opinion of Mabini, who was a Mason and liberal, antifriar and sympathizer of Filipino priests, a believer in God but who had lost his religiosity, and who helped inspire the formation of the national church but strongly feared church power, is relevant:

If all Filipinos advocate the cause of their countrymen-priests, it is out of love for justice which has been denied to them rather than personal love for them. These same Filipinos know that if the government that is to be definitely established in the Philippines will continue to view the Catholic parishes as public offices, the very Filipino priests, who ever they may be, once sustained by government force, would before long begin to commit abuses just like their friar predecessors.[20]

[20] "Cuestiones en relación sobre las corporaciones religiosas," *La Revolución Filipina* (Manila, 1931), II, 144 (author's translation).

Nozaleda and Pons: Two
Spanish Friars in Exodus

LEÓN MA. GUERRERO

The disaster which overtook the Spanish friars [1] in the Philippines upon the renewal of the revolution and the Spanish capitulation to the United States was not a unique experience for them. They had suffered a worse fate at the hands of their own countrymen in the riots of 1834 and would suffer even worse in the Civil War of 1936.

Indeed the liberal Cortes of 1820 had dissolved the Spanish religious orders and authorized the sale of their estates and other properties on the open market, and, when the Carlist wars broke out, the reformer Juan Alvarez Mendizábal brought back into effect in 1836 the original decrees of dissolution and *desamortización* in order to finance the war for Isabel II and, in the style of Henry VIII and the Cecils, to create a new middleclass of property owners committed by private interest to the liberal regime.

In this first ruin and diaspora of the Spanish friars, which profoundly influenced their attitudes and policies in the Philippines, the only ones to be spared in Spain were those religious houses, like the Augustinian in Valladolid and the Dominican in Ocaña, where missionaries to the Philippines were trained, since the continued presence of the Spanish friars in the colony was deemed, rightly or wrongly, to be a political imperative.

In contrast with their losses in lives and property in their own country under Mendizábal, those which the Spanish friars under-

[1] By friar is usually meant a member of the "four mendicant orders of the common law," namely, the Dominicans, Augustinians, Franciscans, and Carmelites. In the Philippines only the first three were represented, the Recollects being an independent branch of the Augustinians. The Jesuits are not friars. See *Catholic Dictionary* (New York, 1952).

went in the Philippines were comparatively light. Fair compensation was negotiated and paid by the new regime for the so-called
"friar lands," [2] whose outright confiscation had been decreed by
the republic; the religious and nonpublic character of their charitable foundations and their estates was sustained; their great
mother-houses, churches, hospitals, colleges, and universities in
the capital remained in their hands; their stocks, bonds, cash, and
other personal properties, such as escaped the Filipino revolutionary forces, enjoyed the constitutional and legal protection of
the insular government; and the town churches and rectories
(misnamed *conventos*), many of them impressive architectural
works built by the Filipino faithful under the direction of the
Spanish friars, were adjudged the property of the Roman Catholic Church and its ordinaries.[3]

Nor, it appears, were the Filipinos ever as cruel to the Spanish
friars as past and future mobs in Spain. A number of friars, who
had earned the hatred of their parishioners for one reason or another, were killed and sometimes tortured, but by and large there
was no popular "friar-hunt." For ideological and political reasons,
and also for purposes of future diplomatic bargaining, the revolutionary chieftains and later the government of the republic

[2] Governor Wm. H. Taft went to Rome in 1902 to negotiate the expulsion of the friars and the purchase of the friar lands under the erroneous
impression that the friars were under the direct command of, and their
lands owned by, the Holy See. Eventually the purchase was made in
Manila, in December 1903, more than $7,000,000 being paid for about
425,000 acres, upon authority of the Act of July 1, 1902, of the U.S.
Congress. See Pedro S. de Achútegui and Miguel A. Bernad, *Religious
Revolution in the Philippines* (Manila, 1960), I, 45–46, 146–53; Gregorio
F. Zaide, *Philippine Political and Cultural History* (rev. ed.; Manila, 1957),
II, 237; and Dean C. Worcester, *The Philippines Past and Present* (New
York, 1914), II, 836.

[3] In Barlín v. Ramírez, 7 Phil. 41, the Supreme Court of the Philippines
(then composed of four Americans and three Filipinos) held, in a decision
promulgated Nov. 24, 1906, that during the Spanish regime and at the time
of the Treaty of Paris the Roman Catholic Church, a juridical entity, had
lawful possession of church buildings in the Philippines and the exclusive
right to them for the purposes for which they were built, and as such was
entitled to the protection of the Treaty's provision that the cession of Spanish public properties "cannot in any respect impair the property or rights
which by law belong to the peaceful possession of property of all kinds of
. . . ecclesiastical or civic bodies. . . ."

rounded up about 300 friars and herded them into harsh and humiliating captivity in the northern mountains, but many friars themselves would later testify to the help openly or secretly given to them by their Filipino friends and sympathizers.

The experience of the Dominicans, perhaps the wealthiest and most powerful religious order then in the Philippines, may be taken as typical. Of the 115 taken and held prisoner during 18 months (1898–1901), nine died in captivity, six shortly after being freed and presumably as a result of their sufferings, 21 stayed in the Philippines, 12 went back to Spain but subsequently returned to the Philippines, 57 definitely remained in Spain, nine went to other countries, and the whereabouts of one is said to be still unknown. In comparison 150 Dominicans—or more than 10 times as many as in the Philippines—were killed during the Civil War in Spain (1936–1939).[4]

At this distance from such controversial happenings it is difficult to arrive at an accurate assessment of the popular feeling among the Filipinos toward the Spanish friars during and shortly after the revolution. Certainly the propaganda movement of the intellectuals was essentially antifriar, and its heirs, the revolution and the first republic, were equally antifriar in ideology, policy, and action. How much of this feeling, little short of hatred, was shared by the mass of Filipino Catholics? And how much remained after the Spanish friar had been stripped of the quasi-political authority and power which made him for centuries the symbol and the instrument of alien domination?

There is an interesting although naturally partisan study of the question by the learned Augustinian chronicler of the Philippine Independent Church, which is controverted by its equally authoritative Jesuit historians.[5]

It is alleged that Governor Taft, apparently under pressure of

[4] The Philippine statistics were furnished to the author from the Dominican archives in Madrid by Father Villacorta, 1965. The Spanish statistics are from the *Enciclopedia de la Cultura Española* (Madrid, 1965), II.

[5] Isacio R. Rodríguez, *Gregorio Aglipay y los Orígenes de la Iglesia Filipina Independiente* (Madrid, 1960), I, 80 ff., largely quoting from Salvador Pons, *Defensa Imparcial y Sincera de las Corporaciones Religiosas Españolas en las Islas Filipinas,* MS. no. 27300, Biblioteca, Colegio de Filipinos, Valladolid. For the opposite view, see Achútegui and Bernad, *op. cit.,* I, 156 ff.

the surviving idealogues of the revolution, issued a questionnairo designed to explore Filipino public opinion on the desirability of expelling the Spanish friars from the Philippines; that about 300,000 printed forms were distributed all over the country; that even in Manila only about 300 bothered to reply in spite of a campaign by the "anticlerical" or "nationalist" press, especially *El Renacimiento;* and that only about 3,000 in the whole country, constituting a majority in only 50 to 60 municipalities out of 2,000, expressed an opinion in favor of the expulsion of the friars.

On the other hand it is alleged that Governor Taft was so convinced the Filipinos did not want the friars that he went to Rome to negotiate their "withdrawal"; that President Theodore Roosevelt, presumably on the basis of official reports from the American authorities in the Philippines, explained to a friend that "so embittered are the Filipinos against the friars that we thought it best to try whether the Holy See would not take them away if we pay for their lands"; that Placide Louis Chapelle, archbishop of New Orleans, named apostolic delegate to the Philippines, had seen a "storm of indignation" breaking over his head when it became known that he favored the restoration of their parishes to the Spanish friars; and that the Filipino clergy had sent a commission of two priests to Rome in 1901 to protest against such a move, possibly because, out of 825 Filipino seculars, only 157 had parishes, the remainder being held by Spanish friars.

It is much too late in the day to take a "scientific opinion poll" in the matter, and in any case such a poll would not take into account the fundamental fact that in any democracy, and even more in a rudimentary democracy where the people, as in the Philippines at the turn of the century, are largely uninformed and even illiterate, it is an intellectual elite—"the vast minority," in a classic Spanish phrase—that makes public opinion, and renders mere numbers meaningless.

Indeed, on a strictly statistical basis the revolution and the republic should not have happened. But it is not without significance that of approximately 1,000 Spanish priests in the Philippines in 1898, only about 250 remained in 1904.[6] Thus fully three-

[6] Isidoro Alonso, *La Iglesia en Filipinas* (Madrid, 1965).

fourths, most of them friars, "voted with their feet" on the state of Filipino public opinion, and quit the country, some in anger and in bitterness; others, in fear and anguish; still others, surely, heartbroken at leaving behind their lifework and homes.

Those familiar with the history of the revolution will savour two or three names. The Augustinian Mariano Gil [7] who, as parish priest of Tondo, uncovered the daggers and oaths of the *Katipunan* in a printing press and precipitated Bonifacio's call to arms, returned to Spain in 1898 and died in the episcopal palace of Pamplona on December 11, 1903. Another Augustinian, Salvador Font,[8] who wrote the judgment condemning Rizal's *Noli Me Tangere*, also returned to Spain and died in Madrid shortly after an operation for cancer of the tongue on December 9, 1908. José Hevía Campomanes, Dominican bishop of Nueva Segovia (Vigan), who was wheedled and bullied into naming Gregorio Aglipay ecclesiastical governor of his diocese, and thus unwittingly opened the doors to the nationalist schism,[9] returned to Spain after his release from captivity, was named bishop of Badajoz, and died in the course of a pastoral visit on May 2, 1902.

The Recollect Francisco Ayarra [10] typifies another direction taken by the friars in their diaspora. As provincial in the Philippines he initiated and organized the redeployment of the Philippine Recollects to new missions in Panama, Venezuela, and Brazil. Elected superior of his order, he left Manila for Spain on

[7] See Gregorio de Santiago Vela, *Ensayo de una Biblioteca Ibero-Americana de la Orden de San Agustín* (7 vols.; Madrid, 1913–1931) for a biographical note on Gil.

[8] See *España y America*, XX, 525 ff., for a biographical note on Font.

[9] See Achútegui and Bernad, *op. cit.*, and Rodríguez, *op. cit.*, for a complete treatment of the Philippine Independent Church from two divergent but equally Roman Catholic viewpoints. Bernad is a Filipino; Achútegui and Rodríguez, Spaniards.

[10] Francisco Ayarra (Jaurrieta, Navarra, 1834—Monteagudo, 1913), Augustinian Recollect; entered his order, 1857; ordained priest the following year; arrived in Manila, 1860; served as parish priest in Hinigaran, Negros Occidental, for 34 years with slight interruptions; elected provincial of his order in the Philippines, 1897; named *definidor general* (superior) of his order and served as such, 1901–1908 (*Catálogo General de los Religiosos Agustinos Recoletos de la Provincia de San Nicolás de Tolentino de Filipinas* [Madrid, 1906]; *Boletín de la Provincia,* 1913; letter to the author from Fr. Manuel Carceller, 1965).

November 30, 1901, serving as such until 1908 when he retired to the convent at Monteagudo where he had taken his first vows. Even at the age of 89, he is said by his official biographer to have been assiduous in the observance of fasts and abstinences, and, even with his past dignities, obedient to his superiors "like a well-brought-up child," dying so poor that he still had the same suitcase he had used in his earliest days as a parish priest.

However, it is manifestly impossible within the scope of this brief study to follow the footsteps of even the more distinguished Spanish friars in their exodus; and it may be more useful to concentrate our attention on two of them, the first the Dominican Bernardino Nozaleda,[11] archbishop of Manila during the revolution.

"Father Nozaleda is the synthesis of all the friars," cried the Count of Romanones in launching the parliamentary attack against him in the Spanish Cortes of 1904, "he is not one friar, he is all of them." Indeed the charges against Nozaleda were the same charges that liberals, anticlericals, and republicans, both Filipinos and Spaniards, had been making against the Spanish friars throughout the close of the colonial regime.

Fray Bernardino, as he signed himself in office, had been named archbishop of Manila in circumstances that throw a certain light on his second nomination to an archdiocese upon his return to Spain. His original designation to the highest post in the Philippine hierarchy and to the richest see in the gift of the Spanish crown, made by Pope Leo XIII upon nomination of the Spanish government, had apparently come as a surprise not only to his flock but to himself.

There is a handwritten letter in the private and confidential

[11] Bernardino Nozaleda y Villa (San Andrés de Cuenya, Oviedo, 1844—Madrid, 1927); entered the Order of Preachers in Ocaña, 1860; went to the Philippines, 1873, where he was named professor in the University of Santo Tomás, and, 1876, prior of the Convent of Santo Domingo in Manila; elected vice-rector of the University, 1881, and rector of the Dominican College of San Juán de Letrán, 1886; named archbishop of Manila, 1889; consecrated in Oviedo, 1890, taking possession of his see the following year; resigned, 1902; nominated archbishop of Valencia by the Maura government, 1903; renounced Valencia see and retired to teach theology at the Dominican convent of Sto. Tomás in Avila (Enciclopedia Espasa; letter to the author of Fr. Villacorta, 1965).

archives of the then Queen Regent María Cristina [12] which suggests that the nomination of a Spanish friar as archbishop of Manila was unusual and unexpected in the prevailing situation, contrary to what is commonly believed. "In any circumstances," wrote Nozaleda to his sovereign under date of June 3, 1889, "so high an honor accorded by a Queen of Spain to an humble religious, an honor beyond his dreams because of his social obscurity and shortness of personal qualifications, would have given cause for extraordinary appreciation and gratitude to Your Majesty, but, in the present circumstances, when everything seemed to indicate that, not only a person as unworthy as myself, but any individual religious,[13] would not be taken into consideration in nominating an archbishop for Manila, and when it was *upon the sole personal initiative of Your Majesty, maintained against all opposition,* that such a high honor should have befallen me, . . ." And Nozaleda went on to refer to "an affectionate friend, obfuscated by an excessive attachment" who had pleaded Fray Bernardino's cause with the queen regent.[14]

It was this same "affectionate friend" who was now, upon Nozaleda's return to Spain, blamed for the Dominican's nomination to the archdiocese of Valencia left vacant by the death of Sebastián Cardinal Herrera. He can be almost certainly identified as Alejandro Pidal,[15] the *cacique* or political boss of Asturias in northern Spain and one-time *Presidente del Congreso* (Speaker of the House). Pidal and Nozaleda came from the same region, had studied together under the Dominican Ceferino (later Cardinal) González, and had become such fast friends that in later days Nozaleda would spend long seasons in his friend the mar-

[12] María Cristina of Hapsburg-Lorraine (Gross Seelowitz, 1858—Madrid, 1929), Archduchess of Austria, Queen and Queen Regent of Spain, second wife of Alfonso XII and mother of Alfonso XIII; she had just turned over the monarchy to her son at the time of the Nozaleda affair (*Diccionario de Historia de España*).

[13] That is to say, a priest belonging to a religious order rather than a secular priest.

[14] Secretaría Particular de Da. Cristina, Cajón no. 6 (Palacio de Oriente, Madrid; translation and emphasis by the author).

[15] Alejandro Pidal (Madrid, 1846—Madrid, 1913), Carlist and ultra-Catholic politican; deputy for Villaviciosa, Asturias, from 1872; yielded leadership of Conservatives to Silvela upon death of Cánovas, and to Maura upon death of Silvela (*Dicc. Hist. Esp.*).

quis's Madrid town house and there would close his eyes in death.

It was charged in the Madrid press [16] that Pidal, his huge white beard discreetly cloaked, had been seen in the palace shortly before Nozaleda's nomination was signed by the boy king on the last day of 1903. Indeed it was pointed out that the decree had been submitted to Alfonso XIII [17] by the minister in charge of those matters (*Gracia y Justicia,* that is to say, Justice, Grace, and Favor), Joaquín Sánchez de Toca, who, as it happened, was another classmate of Nozaleda and Pidal. Prime Minister Antonio Maura [18] and the Minister of *Gobernación* (Interior or Home Office) José Sánchez Guerra, were compelled to deny publicly that the queen regent had had anything to do with Nozaleda's appointment, but it was generally known that, at any rate, the matter had not been taken up in full cabinet and had been arranged privately between Maura and Sánchez de Toca.[19]

[16] Among the principal Madrid dailies of the time were *El Imparcial* (liberal-monarchist), *La Epoca* (monarchist-conservative), *El Liberal* and *El Heraldo de Madrid* (leftist), *El Globo* (liberal-republican), *El País* (republican), *El Siglo Futuro* (Catholic-Carlist) and *La Correspondencia Militar* (army). The author has chosen to rely on the press rather than on the journal (*Diario de Sesiones*) of the Cortes because the former gives more of the contemporary flavor of the controversy; and *El Imparcial* has been chosen as most representative of the Madrid press because of its high reputation as an impartial liberal newspaper and its circulation, then the largest (about 140,000 daily), in Spain. In the course of the parliamentary debate, the editor of *El Imparcial,* Ortega Munilla, also a member of the House, defended his paper from Maura's criticisms and said that it had merely examined the nomination of Nozaleda "in its political aspects" and the record of the archbishop as "a political official." See *El Imparcial,* Year XXXVIII, no. 13, 227 (Jan. 26, 1904), et. seq., Hemeroteca Municipal de Madrid; Manuel Ortega y Gasset, *El Imparcial, Biografía de un gran periódico español* (Zaragoza, 1956); and Antonio Espina, *El Cuarto Poder* (Madrid, 1960).

[17] Alfonso XIII (Madrid, 1866—Rome, 1941), posthumous son of Alfonso XII and María Cristina; born King of Spain, he assumed full powers in 1902, and reigned until the proclamation of the second Spanish republic in 1931 (*Enc. Hist. Esp.*).

[18] Antonio Maura (Palma de Mallorca, 1853—Madrid, 1925); Conservative prime minister at the time of the Nozaleda affair; originally a Liberal, he became minister of the colonies in 1892 and resigned on the issue of colonial (local autonomy) reforms, for which he is best known and remembered in the Philippines; turned Conservative under Silvela in 1902 (*Dicc. Hist. Esp.*).

[19] It should be explained briefly that, then as now, under the terms of a concordat between Spain and the Holy See, the Spanish crown and gov-

Still, the unanimity and vehemence with which the Madrid progressive press assailed the Nozaleda nomination, the embarrassed silence of the Catholic press, the feebleness of the defense in the relatively small conservative press, were totally unprecedented and immediately made what—inevitably—became known as *l'affaire Nozaleda* a serious political crisis.

The republican *El País* had led the attack as early as Christmas 1903 when the government's intentions first leaked out; by New Year's day 1904 *El País* was carrying banner headlines, then unusual in the Spanish press, such as "The Traitor Nozaleda" one day, and, the next, "Death to Nozaleda." Practically all the other Madrid dailies led off, week after week, with front-page editorials on the outrage of the Nozaleda nomination, and filled their political columns with all manner of stories on the archbishop's conduct before and during the revolution, before and after the fall of Manila, and during the first years of the American regime.

Nozaleda and the friars in general were blamed for the Philippine revolution, a theme familiar enough to its historians. Fray Bernardino personally was accused of "inspiring the murder of Rizal" and maneuvering the recall of the kindly Blanco and the appointment of the ruthless Polavieja as governor-general. It was said that the archbishop had had secret dealings with the United States forces besieging Manila, cravenly insisted on its bloodless capitulation, that he had fled from the capital on a German ship, tried to expel the wounded among the Spanish garrison from the city's churches and convents, and even called on Dewey at Cavite to congratulate him on his naval victory and to bless his arms, flags, and ships. Nozaleda, it was added, had forfeited his Spanish citizenship,[20] remained in his palace in Manila only to protect

---

ernment had the right to nominate archbishops and bishops in Spain and Spanish possessions for designation by the pope. In Nozaleda's time the pope had no choice but to approve or disapprove; at present the Spanish government proposes six names, from among whom the Holy See selects three, and the Spanish government has the final choice of one.

[20] This curious charge had two foundations. First, it was said that Nozaleda, as a nominee and paid official of the Spanish crown, should not have remained in office as archbishop (by way of contrast it was pointed out that the Spanish bishop of Puerto Rico had left the island rather than serve under the Americans, and was now bishop of Jaén). By choosing to remain he had served, not perhaps the U.S. government which maintained

the property interests of his fellow friars, and visited the pope in
Rome, without passing by Madrid, only to intervene in the negotiations for the purchase of the friar lands.

Fray Bernardino felt compelled to write a reply to these
charges.[21] His pamphlet, published too late to affect the parliamentary debate, was as ponderous and naive as his Manila pas-
torals during the revolution and the Spanish-American War, but
it made its points on the basis of solid documentary evidence.

Far from losing the Philippines for Spain, the friars had enabled the regime to survive with an incredibly small garrison for
close to three and a half centuries, and, if their warnings of a
"Masonic conspiracy" had been heeded, the revolution might
have been forestalled. Once it had broken out, Nozaleda had in
fact tried to avert the anger of loyal Spaniards against the ineffec-
tual Blanco and to rally them around the governor-general.

Rizal and others had been found guilty by military courts on
the strength of the testimony of their fellow-conspirators, and not
at all on the say-so of Spanish friars. Indeed the efforts of the
"ecclesiastical element" had saved not a few from the firing
squad; Nozaleda himself had interceded successfully for the Luna
brothers [22] and unsuccessfully for three Filipino secular priests
executed in Camarines.

He had not sneaked out of besieged Manila on a German ship;
he was being confused with Fray Arsenio del Campo, bishop of

---

the separation of church and state, but certainly the Vatican, which was
considered a foreign power under international law; and by thus serving a
foreign power, without the king's permission, Nozaleda had forfeited his
citizenship under the Spanish constitution. Secondly, it was said that Nozaleda had failed to register at the Spanish consulate in Manila as required in
the Treaty of Paris of those Spaniards in the Philippines who wished to
retain their citizenship. In reply, Nozaleda said he had been among the first
to register at the consulate, and that a Catholic bishop did not lose his citizenship merely by exercising his functions in foreign lands like the French
bishops in Alsace and Lorraine after the Franco-German war of 1870 or
missionary bishops in China and Japan.

[21] P. Nozaleda, *Defensa Obligada contra Acusaciones Gratuitas* (Madrid,
1904), 93 pp.

[22] Juan Luna and Antonio Luna were prominent members of the propaganda movement, and were imprisoned upon the outbreak of the revolution.
Antonio Luna later became commander-in-chief of the armies of the republic in the war against the Americans, and was assassinated.

Nueva Cáceres, who had left upon medical advice and with the express leave of then Governor-General Augustín. Nor had he dealt secretly with the United States forces or clamored for the surrender of Manila to save church properties from destruction.

His only contact with the enemy during the siege had taken place one day in August 1898 (perhaps August 7), quite unexpectedly, when an American Catholic priest, one "Mac-Keenon," who could hardly express himself in a barbarous "American" Latin and finally managed to make himself understood only through the aid of an English-speaking Jesuit, sought from the Manila ordinary delegated jurisdiction to minister to the Catholic United States troops that had been landed around Manila. The records of the official military investigation into the subsequent surrender would bear this out.

The minutes of a consultative meeting of military and civil authorities called on his own initiative by General Jáudenes on August 8 would likewise show that its purpose was merely to evaluate public opinion on the situation of the beleaguered city and the limits to which its defense should be carried in the face of a 48-hour ultimatum threatening a United States naval bombardment. The military commanders were under orders to "fight to the last" and had reserved their judgment, but all the civil authorities had advocated capitulation after a token resistance that would save "military honor," considering that more than 30,000 wounded and sick soldiers, and women and children in the city could not be evacuated because the Filipino revolutionary forces surrounded it by land. In these cruel circumstances the archbishop had thought it his Christian duty to express the view, in accordance with the doctrines of mother church, that a hopeless and pointless resistance, sacrificing thousands of noncombatants, was unjustifiable, as indeed it was.

Nozaleda then indignantly rejected as pure fiction the charges as to his conduct after the fall of Manila. The Americans had quartered the surrendered Spanish garrison in the city's churches in plain violation of the articles of capitulation, yet the archbishop not only had accepted this illegal and sacrilegious situation, but also had turned all the city's convents, seminaries, and religious houses into hospitals for the sick and wounded.

Of course he had had dealings with the Americans. How could this be helped when the enemy was now in sole authority by right of conquest? He had persuaded Dewey to send the *Yorktown* to rescue the Spanish garrison at Baler, and when this sortie failed, with more American casualties than were taken in the battle of Manila Bay, he had called on the American admiral to thank him for the effort and express his sympathy for the casualties suffered. This was the only time he had gone to Cavite.

In the absence of legitimate Spanish government authorities, it had also fallen on the archbishop to direct the work of finding, feeding, clothing, and protecting the Spanish prisoners-of-war held by the republic, and negotiating their liberation and repatriation.

Finally, as head of the church in the Philippines and its only remaining bishop on Luzon, with his brother of Nueva Cáceres away and his brother of Nueva Segovia a prisoner, Nozaleda could not abandon his flock, threatened as it was by an ominous schism. The records would bear him out that the pope had refused to accept his resignation of the Manila archdiocese until 1902. In all fairness it cannot be denied that Nozaleda had a strong case.

But in the field of domestic politics other questions were being asked. What folly had led the Maura government to nominate a man of Nozaleda's equivocal record to the archiepiscopal throne of Valencia, one of the most liberal, anticlerical, republican, and revolutionary cities and provinces of Spain? Had not that "old fox" Silvela, Maura's predecessor, refused to nominate Nozaleda to the vacant see of Zaragoza for fear of popular rejection? It was true there was a *Ley de excedentes de Ultramar,* providing for the "re-employment" of Spanish archbishops, bishops, and priests who had lost their livings in the "colonial disaster," but there were other colonial bishops available such as Manuel Santander, the former archbishop of Santiago de Cuba, four other former friar-bishops from the Philippines, and the former bishop of La Habana who, as the Count of Romanones pointed out sarcastically in the parliamentary debate, "still lives in retirement in his convent, where all friars ought to be." Were there no secular priests in the whole of Spain worthy of the throne of Valencia with its livings of 25,000 *duros* a year? What indeed would Spain do with the horde of "four to six thousand friars" coming home to roost?

Public meetings were organized to protest the Nozaleda appointment. Indiscreet and salacious *cuplés* were improvised in the *Teatro de la Zarzuela,* none of them very amusing if one is to judge from one sample published in *El Imparcial*:

> Antes eran los obispos
> españoles, por lo menos,
> ahora se guardan las mitras
> para los filibusteros!

which may be roughly translated: "Before, bishops were Spaniards at least; now they keep the mitres for the disloyal." But the meetings were banned by a thoroughly alarmed government, the *cuplés* were censored, and enough people were arrested in the orchestra pit of the *Zarzuela* to frighten the saucy *vedette.*

Maura felt it necessary to deny that Nozaleda would be transferred to Valladolid (where a protest movement was promptly started). The archbishop went to court in a number of libel actions in which his lawyer was Silvela himself (he won most of them although he subsequently waived the awards). If only outwardly, however, Fray Bernardino, rotund and amiable, remained calm, but surely bewildered and deeply hurt, living with his friend the marquis in the elegant street of Fernando el Santo (No. 22, noted the press), and went so far as to advise a reporter of the liberal *Diario Universal* jestingly: "Now, then, don't make me out a nice fellow. The press won't like it. You must picture me as a veritable dragon."

He was not wholly isolated. The Spanish hierarchy issued a joint letter in his behalf. And Sánchez de Toca told the *Heraldo de Madrid* that for the archdiocese of Valencia "one could not appoint a friar who knew life only from his monastic cell, or a canon who had spent all his days in the cathedral choir." It was necessary to name a man of great experience because "in Valencia too there are *Tagalogs* and *King Bonifacios* and, to deal with them, there seems to be nobody better than Father Nozaleda."

What a prospect, one newspaper critic was quick to exclaim, in contrast with the saintly Cardinal Herrera, who had lived with workers, republicans, and atheists in peace and mutual respect.

It was in this atmosphere that on January 26, 1904, the Count of Romanones [23] with the Duke of Baena and five others laid down a motion in Cortes that the House state its "displeasure at the nomination made by H.M. Government of Father Nozaleda for the diocese of Valencia without taking into account those rules of prudence and timeliness which should inspire the public powers in all their acts."

The public galleries were packed when the Count of Romanones, his handlebar moustache abristle, rose to move. In addressing the House, he said, he was not moved by a "sectarian spirit." Perhaps some of the charges against Nozaleda had been "unjust." He would press only one, that Nozaleda had remained so long in Manila after its capitulation only to protect the interests of the friars. The Masons were not behind the campaign against Nozaleda; he himself was not a Mason, and yet he was fighting this nomination; he was an old politician, and he had not seen Masonry "en ninguna parte."

When Maura rose to reply, the "blue bench" of the ministers was packed, and the public galleries, gay with elegant ladies, were hushed. Arrogant as usual, with his white imperial neatly trimmed, the famous advocate, who had slowly overcome a disastrous Canarian accent to become one of Spain's greatest orators, faced his first great challenge as Conservative prime minister.

Romanones, he began, wanted him to say that he did not know whether Nozaleda had been accused justly or not, but that, having been accused, the archbishop had lost his usefulness and should be jettisoned. That would be "abominable." The government was bound to "reason and justice" even if this should cost its life. Nozaleda had been accused of staying in Manila two years after the Spanish flag had been lowered. "What would have been said if he had then, at that moment, abandoned Manila, when

<hr />

[23] Alvaro de Figueroa, first Count of Romanones (Madrid, 1863—Madrid, 1950); Liberal politician; various times prime minister and minister until the fall of the monarchy in 1931 (*Dicc. Hist. Esp.*).

there were still prisoners in the hands of the Tagalogs and when there were still moral interests to be safeguarded?" Fray Bernardino had secured the release of the Spanish prisoners, saving Spain many millions in ransom, and, despite the change in sovereignty, only the pope himself could have released him from his spiritual duties to his flock. Yet, under the protection of parliamentary privilege, Nozaleda was now being called a traitor to Spain.

"All Spain proclaims it!" cried out Rodrigo Soriano,[24] the Republican for Valencia.

No, retorted Maura, there was no proof of it. Romanones had said that Nozaleda was the synthesis of the friars (*la frailería*). He, Maura, would not now enter into the question of whether the influence of the friars in the Philippines had been for good or evil. But was Fray Bernardino now to "pay for the policy of three centuries"? Did Romanones hold himself "responsible for the errors of that policy, maintained by all the Spanish parties, including the Liberal party of which the Count of Romanones was a member? Shall we avenge on one man the errors of the parties and oligarchies of Spain?" When his own conscience was face to face with what speakers had called public opinion, he would be on the side of his conscience.

The day was Maura's. When the count's motion was put to the vote, it was defeated, 128 to 69, with the Carlists supporting the Conservative-albeit-Alphonsine government.

The debate, nevertheless, dragged on until the first week of February. Soriano accused Maura of saying that Nozaleda would enter Valencia to take possession of his see even if he had to do it "surrounded by bayonets," a phrase that is still remembered in Spain.

"Did Your Honor say it? Yes or no."

---

[24] Rodrigo Soriano (San Sebastián, 1868—Santiago de Chile, 1944); Republican representative from Valencia (1901–1909) and later Madrid; a brilliant and much feared parliamentarian and newspaperman.

Soriano and Menéndez Pallarés, both representatives from Valencia, hotly opposed the Nozaleda nomination, together with Vicente Blasco Ibáñez, the renowned novelist and newspaperman, also representing Valencia, but a personal enemy of Soriano. Blasco Ibáñez concentrated on organizing popular opposition in Valencia and did not take an active part in the parliamentary attack on Nozaleda.

"There is a publication called the *Diario de Sesiones*," replied Maura coldly, "and what I said is recorded there."

"I know that the *Diario* does not print what I heard," retorted Soriano. "The nomination of Father Nozaleda is a challenge to Valencia so that His Honor can take his hatreds there and bathe its streets in blood. If that is so, Mr. Maura should at least have the courage to accompany Father Nozaleda to Valencia."

These exchanges will perhaps give an idea of the passions aroused by Nozaleda's nomination. Soriano referred to the Minister of the Army, General Linares, who had surrendered his command to the Americans, as "the Nozaleda of Santiago de Cuba," and was promptly challenged to a duel.

"What must you think of Nozaleda," asked Soriano bitingly, "that you consider the comparison an insult?"

The affair was settled bloodlessly; but the interpellations went on day after day, driving Maura almost to the end of his tether.

"An article was published in Valencia the other day which says: 'Entry of a traitor in Valencia. Murder of Father Nozaleda.' And this article is signed by a member of the House," he complained bitterly.

"It is signed by me," admitted Soriano, explaining that the article was a warning in fantasy, in the same way that another recent article by the famed journalist Mariano de Cavía had described the destruction by fire of the Museo del Prado and had driven the curators to take adequate precautions.

Maura steadfastly maintained that none of the charges against Nozaleda had been proven. There had been much talk of public opinion. Did not the Spanish hierarchy speak for the Spanish faithful? And did not the faithful represent more votes than newspaper readers? Did the vote taken in the House itself mean nothing? How could a man be condemned on mere suspicion? Where was the vaunted "democracy" of the Republicans?

As to the record of the friars in the Philippines, he would hate to compare it with that of their colleagues in frock coats.

Fittingly enough the debate was rounded up by Ramón Nocedal,[25] the uncompromising Catholic antiliberal leader, who

---

[25] Ramón Nocedal (Madrid, 1846—Madrid, 1907), editor of *El Siglo Futuro* and founder of the political movement called *integrismo*, which, putting aside the dynastic quarrel between Carlists and Alphonsines as rela-

said that among Nozaleda's accusers were some who "would like to have a friar for breakfast." He was grateful to the Count of Romanones for admitting frankly that Nozaleda had to be attacked because he was a friar.

"Very well," said Nocedal, "you hate friars, and I love them."

He defended the Inquisition, and called to witness the Golden Age's poet of the people, Lope de Vega, beloved of the Republicans.

A voice called out: "He was afraid they would roast him!"

Nocedal went on staunchly. The glories of Spain were the work of monks and friars; they had raised Spain to the first rank among the nations of the world, and had civilized and given identity to the colored races. "There is only one colored nation in the world, the Philippines, and that is thanks to the religious orders. They have given us glories and felicities. How many have the Republicans given us?"

Nocedal's intervention also revealed the real significance of the entire affair. Reminding the House that the pope had not yet sanctioned the nomination of Fray Bernardino, he asked pointedly: "When the bull comes from Rome, will Mr. Maura still be on the blue bench? Or will the Count of Romanones sit there?"

Indeed, in an unguarded moment earlier in the debate, the Valencian Menéndez Pallarés had exclaimed: "We are not fighting Father Nozaleda, we are fighting the government!"

The nomination of Fray Bernardino had given the Spanish "Left" an occasion and an opportunity, with irresistible overtones of patriotism and undertones of liberalism, to attack not so much the Dominican refugee from Manila, as all friars; and not so much the friars, as the Conservative government.

Alfonso was not yet 18, the regency was barely ended, Maura's was almost the boy king's first government, as indeed it was the first time that the patrician advocate himself had headed one. How could the opportunity be resisted by Carlists and Republicans, and, in between, every other political opponent of a regime barely half a century in power? Toward the end of the debate even the arrogant and self-assured Maura was to admit it on the

tively unimportant, called for a united Catholic front against all liberal parties and tendencies (*Dicc. Hist. Esp.*).

floor, ruefully, even perhaps petulantly: "If I had known the effect this nomination would have, I would not have made it."

The regency had presided over the "colonial disaster," but the responsibilities had never been openly and properly adjudged. Soriano had recalled that, when France had been defeated by Germany in 1870, those responsible had suffered "just and severe" punishment, but in Spain "the general responsible for the surrender of Santiago de Cuba is given the War Ministry, the general who lost Puerto Rico is appointed Captain-General of Madrid, the man who signed the Treaty of Paris is found at the head of a political party, and now it is sought to place on the archiepiscopal throne of Valencia the prelate who was mainly responsible for the loss of Manila."

The humiliations of the Philippine and Cuban revolutions and the Spanish-American War had inflicted on the proud Spanish people a trauma from which they would not recover for decades, and which would produce a whole new "generation of '98," disillusioned, bitter, hagridden by an inferiority complex. But, as Soriano had insinuated, the military would always take care of their own, and the politicians could take care of themselves. But the friars were fair game.

As it turned out, when Leo XIII did approve the nomination of Fray Bernardino (he is said to have exclaimed that he wished he had a Nozaleda for every Spanish diocese), Maura was no longer on the ministerial "blue bench" to put the archbishop on his throne, with or without bayonets. Almost exactly a year after the controversy began, he resigned when Alfonso insisted on naming Rizal's executioner, the Marqués de Polavieja, chief of the newly constituted Army General Staff against the advice of the Minister of War, surely an ironic *denouement* for those intransigent friars who had hailed "the Christian general" as the guardian of their fortunes. Not, as it now turned out, of Fray Bernardino's.

Nozaleda, for his part, renounced the see of Valencia when it became clear that Maura's successor felt unable to maintain the nomination. It is said that the see of Toledo was offered to him in later years, and that he turned it down. If so, he could have been a cardinal twice over. Instead he retired to the Dominican convent of Santo Tomás in Avila where he taught theology.

In season he was also to be seen frequently in the Madrid town house of his crony and protector, the Marqués de Pidal, or strolling pensively, a ghost in black and white, along the more secluded walks of the capital's great royal and popular park of *El Retiro.* He died of bronchial pneumonia on October 5, 1927, at the age of 83, and was buried in the Dominican church in Ocaña, facing his old friend and teacher, Cardinal González, under an inscription which praised him as "unsparing in his charity, magnanimous in his forbearance, sublime in forgiving those who traduced his heroic patriotism during Spain's darkest days in the Far East." His grave was desecrated during the Spanish Civil War.

In sharp contrast with the first subject of this study is its second, the Augustinian Salvador Pons.[26] Where Nozaleda is the dogmatic prelate, protégé of monarchs and ministers, Pons is a turncoat friar, drifting from prodigality to indigence, dabbling in spiritism and schism. If Nozaleda's exodus was of the body, Pons's was of the spirit.

He is described by a far from sympathetic fellow Augustinian as possessing a "well-endowed" intelligence but an "uncommon excitability," "vast theological and patristic erudition" combined with a degree of "pride and indiscipline" unusual among the Spanish friars closing ranks in defeat.

He had served mostly in obscure parishes in the central islands, unworthy, he must have thought, of his many talents. His resentments, it is admitted, were in some cases justified. The outbreak of the revolution, the flight of the friars from the provinces and their reconcentration in the mother-houses in Manila, gave his restless spirit the opportunities it craved. No longer was he to be

[26] Salvador Pons y Torres (Piérola, Barcelona, 1859—Wurzburg, Germany, 1926), alias, "Hermenegildo J. Torres," the name which marks his tomb, and "Jacinto Torres"; Augustinian; entered his order, 1878; went to the Philippines, 1884; served mostly in Visayan parishes; left his order, 1899–1900; as secular priest, sympathized with Philippine Independent Church and Protestant churches, but denied having joined any of them formally; returned to his order and to the Roman Catholic Church after a formal abjuration, 1909; retired to the Augustinian convent in Wurzburg, Germany, 1910, until his death. A study of Pons's thought and activity during the period pertinent to this article is made in Rodríguez, *op. cit.,* I, chap. x, with various documents reproduced in II.

confined in some dreary rectory on the edge of nowhere. In the vast and ancient convent of his order he could mix freely with the brooding wounded of the vanquished garrison, and, in the cobbled streets and shuttered houses of the walled city, with the now jobless placemen and the triumphant Masons and reformers.

Afterward he was to write his memoirs, but these were consigned to the flames by some pious hand.[27] It is impossible, therefore, to retrace his movements with any assurance. At some point in 1899 he seems to have left his convent or been expelled from his order. There were other Spaniards at this time who went over to the Filipino side in the burgeoning conflict with the Americans, men like Felipe Calderón, who was writing the Constitution of Malolos, or the dashing Torres Bugallón, who would die beside the generalissimo of the Filipino army. They could be forgiven, and even admired, by their compatriots because politically and militarily Spain was already out of action, and there was some satisfaction to be had from adding to the discomfiture of the "Yankees." But the Roman Catholic Church and the Spanish friars still faced an undecided religious revolution, under a new laical regime whose sympathies were at least ambiguous, and when Pons forsook his convent, as he did, it seemed to be shameless desertion in the midst of battle.

He was a man with a taste for experiment and adventure, and also perhaps with a grievance against authority, which he chose to vent in a manner that his brethren could not but resent and condemn. He testified before official commissions with all the presumed authority of personal experience and privileged knowledge, "accusing the Spanish religious, and even some bishops, of sins of impurity, and of illicit relations with Filipino women, even daring to give the number of children that each one had."[28]

[27] Rodríguez, op. cit., I, 509, n. 80.

[28] Ibid., I, 510, n. 81. La Estrella de Antipolo (Manila) IV, no. 34, Aug. 23, 1902, 567, summarizes one of Pons's attacks in the following language: "Some poor devil, expelled from a religious order, has published in various local newspapers a filthy farrago against the Dominicans and the other monastic orders in the country. In that disgusting article the exfriar describes the religious as felons, vile souls, depraved slanderers, coarse, obscene libellers and lampooners, humbugs, devilish, ignoble, immoral thieves, liars, sensualists, misers, cowards and scoundrels."

Articles in the same vein poured from his fluent pen, and brought down upon his head the wit and the wrath of the Catholic organs, *Libertas* and *La Estrella de Antipolo*. Even Taft was disturbed. He appears to have summoned Victor del Pan, the editor-publisher of *El Progreso,* to which Pons was a prolific contributor, and to have admonished him for his paper's campaign to "dishonor and discredit" the Catholic religion. Del Pan felt obliged to take Pons aside and ask him to "soften" his attacks on the friars; otherwise his articles would not be published.[29] There was nothing, however, to stop Pons from enthusiastically collecting signatures to petitions for the expulsion of his former brethren.[30]

Having thus cut himself off from his old moorings, he zestfully set sail in all possible directions, carried by every passing wind and current. He was fascinated by the table rapping and trances and ectoplasmic visions of spiritism.[31] Indeed its rapid spread in the suddenly rootless Philippine society of the revolution and the republic may surprise later generations. And yet was it so very strange, in view of the Catholic doctrines on purgatory and the after-life, that a priest like Pons and many otherwise orthodox faithful should have accepted, in the "shipwreck of faith," the possibility of guidance from the dead? Or that, nurtured on stories of miraculous interventions by the souls in purgatory, simple folk should have sought counsel of the spirits of Rizal and Bonifacio?

Soon Pons was to be seen preaching and practicing his new beliefs, churning out articles, even recklessly publishing books and pamphlets in Manila and Barcelona at his own expense, attending the *seances* in the spiritist centre on San Rafael street in Manila, followed "like a prophet" as far north as San Fabián in Pan-

---

[29] *Ibid.,* II, 20, reproducing the Pons manuscript, "*La Iglesia Filipina Independiente.*" The author has relied greatly on this semiautobiographical work.

[30] *Ibid.,* II, 22, reproducing Pons.

[31] In the Roman Catholic view, spiritism (commonly called spiritualism) is "a practice whereby one endeavours to get into communication with the souls of the dead or with other spirits." It is said to "involve the sin of superstition" (*Cath. Dic.*).

gasinan by crowds anxious to peer "beyond the brink" to the "life beyond the grave." Later he was to recall rather ruefully: "It is possible that there was no one in the Philippines who worked so much for this absurd and chimerical ideal, or in propagating this French-born error." [32]

The story of his disenchantment with spiritism is simply told by himself. Perhaps he was at the time already wary of the summonses issued by the Filipino anticlerical spiritists to such an odd medley of correspondents as St. Roch and St. Raphael, Our Lady of Sorrows, St. John, and St. Vincent Ferrer—the last-named, Pons knew, a Dominican friar and an Inquisitor. In any case it was agreed by the spiritists in Vigan to put the whole thing to a test. They would write and post a registered letter to one Amalia Soler, then a spiritist author and medium of considerable repute in Barcelona, asking her to identify which one of her own poems had been declaimed by Pons at the solemn opening of classes at the "Ilocano University." In all fairness a poster bearing the poem's title was to be displayed for three months in the school's main hall for "Father John's" benefit. Alas, we are told, receipt of the letter was never acknowledged, and the poem never named.[33]

All the while Pons had also established contact, rather gingerly, with the new American Protestant missionaries. He was seen in the company of a Mr. Hernon Williams and a Methodist, the Rev. Mr. Peterson, with whom he was reported to be wrestling in theological discussion. However, it was a long way still to Vatican II and the ecumenical movement, and nothing much came of these random conversations. Pons recoiled from baptism by immersion and would not, in his own language, "take the plunge" into Mr. Williams' pool. He was also to claim later that he was aghast at the tolerance with which the Protestants looked on one another despite their doctrinal differences, blithely sharing services and partitioning parishes, and refraining from public attacks even on the Aglipayans while sniggering and snickering at their practices in private. To a Spanish mind this was all

[32] Rodríguez, op. cit., I, 477, quoting from Pons, El Espiritismo.
[33] Ibid., I, 484, n. 35, quoting Pons.

sheer hypocrisy and the barest cynicism. Which was truth and which was error? Was there no difference between them? It all looked to him like a ganging up on the Old Church.

By his own account he was further repelled by the comparatively luxurious living of the new arrivals, cozily ensconced in the "American way of life" with their "four-horse carriages," comfortably furnished houses, abundant food, and elegant clothing. He was shocked when Mr. Williams charged an American official $70 a month for board and lodging, and virtuously recalled that the Spanish friars had collected not a centavo from the stream of official and unofficial travellers to whom they had given hospitality in the old rectories. He was aggrieved that the Americans would chat with him but would not lend him any money.[34]

The bitter fact was that, having emptied his pockets on spiritist propaganda, Pons had fallen into ever worsening want. As a rebel but not a schismatic, he was a priest without a parish, a friar without a convent. "Following St. Paul," he was not charging any fees for his religious services. And when he demanded support from the Augustinians, he was coldly told that he had no right to share the table of those he was offending daily with his "exposures" of friarly excesses and oppressions under the old regime.

"My esteemed Father Pons," José Lobo, provincial of the Augustinians, wrote him under date of August 4, 1899, "with reference to what you asked for in your letter, I cannot oblige you. I repeat what I told you the other day: that I am bound to receive you if you wish to return to the convent, but that I should not furnish you any means to live outside the cloister, nor make an exception even in the case of your personal funds. You know very well that any religious who leaves the cloister, even to become a bishop, leaves all his money to the community to which he belonged." [35]

So that was that, and Pons had to make a precarious living teaching Latin and philosophy and whatever else came to hand in the lay and Aglipayan schools that were springing up to break the old educational monopoly of the religious orders. "I am of the opinion," he wrote cheerfully enough in a letter to the editor of

[34] *Ibid.*, I, 490 ff.   [35] *Ibid.*, II, 208.

La Patria, "that the education of the young is, for now, of greater importance to the people than the practice of religious rites and ceremonies; the people need the blessings of the sciences, arts, and trades, which are God's true blessings." [36] These were sentiments admirably suited to the age, but the initial patriotic enthusiasm for the "new schools" was quickly smothered by poor facilities, inadequate instruction, not to mention a touch of scandal, and the wide efficient net of English-teaching government schools; and Pons drifted from "institute" to "college" to "seminary" in one province after another until he finally took a teaching position in the "college-seminary" run by Adriano Garcés in the large town of Dagupan in Pangasinan.

Talented and scholarly, Father Garcés had taught Latin in the Augustinian seminary in Vigan. Wrongly accused and persecuted as a subversive at the outbreak of the revolution, he had turned against the friars and the church, losing the parish of Dagupan in the process. Driven by resentment and dire need, he had then set himself up as the town's Aglipayan pastor while turning down an offer to be consecrated Aglipayan bishop of the province. Pons seems to have conceived a fondness for this kindred spirit, and it was perhaps partly for this reason that he had agreed to teach in Garcés's "seminary." At the start, according to Pons, there were exactly six students enrolled in it, but thanks to Garcés's efforts this number was gradually increased to the extent that the seminarians made quite an impression when they took their daily promenade.

For all that, Pons seems to have been poorly paid, and, in search of more remunerative employment, and also, according to him, on a confidential mission entrusted to him by certain Roman Catholics, he undertook a tour of the Ilocos provinces, then as now the stronghold of the Philippine Independent Church. His account of these travels throws a certain light on the times although it is not wholly free of polemical hindsight. [37]

Heading north Pons found in the old rectory of Badoc another

---

[36] *Ibid.,* I, 520, n. 94. *La Patria* had published an item to the effect that Pons had joined the Philippine Independent Church and was acting as one of its priests in Dagupan.

[37] *Ibid.,* II, 122 ff., reproducing Pons, *"La Iglesia Filipina Independiente."*

"seminary," this time with four students, youngsters learning the rudiments of Latin and Spanish under the nationalist pastor Mariano Espíritu. In Paoay, Batac (Aglipay's hometown), and San Nicolás, the huge rectories were empty. In Laoag, eventually to become a provincial capital, a situation had arisen which was not unusual in those times. At the start of the nationalist religious movement, José Evangelista had been parish priest, with Román Ver as his coadjutor; both had forsaken the Roman allegiance, but later, while Evangelista was in Manila conferring with Aglipay, Ver had returned to the Roman church, and, after litigation, had retained possession of the parish properties. Now Evangelista, designated bishop of Cebu in the central islands, was whiling away the time in his rich family's household as rival pastor of Laoag and director of yet another "seminary." This had five Latin scholars and one other who had apparently begun his studies in the Augustinian seminary and was now learning moral theology. "Out of courtesy" and, it may be surmised, in desperation, Pons offered his services as professor of philosophy and theology; alas, he was told, the "seminary" was not in a position to engage the services of a "specialist."

Bacarra was the seat of an Aglipayan diocese. But the nationalist pastor had retained possession of the rectory, and Bishop Pedro Brillantes had perforce to live in his own small wooden house. Five or six Latin scholars were lodged in a nearby "field hut," which in fact was the "diocesan seminary." He had to contend, Brillantes complained, with a refractory clergy who contributed nothing to the support of their bishop or his seminary, and who, when assessed a modest contribution, replied they had no obligation to do so since they had received their ordination from Rome.

"Do you know what my episcopal consecration cost me out of my own pocket?" he asked Pons. "More, much more than ₱4,ooo!" Yet he seemed to be tormented by doubts as to the legitimacy of this expensive elevation despite Pons's sympathetic display of patristic erudition. When the latter sought to discharge his confidential mission, placing in the bishop's hands a sealed communication from the junta of Catholic priests in Ilocos Sur, Brillantes knew immediately what was afoot. After a rapid glance at the document he exclaimed:

"You see, Father Pons, what did I toll you? They want us to make a solemn declaration, in a notarized document, pledging to return to the Catholic union when all the bishops in the Philippines shall be of our skin and color, Filipinos in race and nationality, and that we only temporarily withhold obedience to the pope and to the foreign bishops placed by him over us until our patriotic desires are met. Item, they also ask us to swear not to alter dogma, discipline, or ritual, preserving all without the slightest change. This is what the Romanists of the south want from us, and it is too much, Father Pons, because it is quite possible that our church will, in time, go much farther than it thought of doing at the start."

Brillantes had a proposition of his own to make to the ex-Augustinian, who had already placed the Philippine Independent Church so much in his debt with his tenacious propaganda campaign. The facts had to be faced. The "old priests" would never be wholeheartedly loyal to the new nationalist church; they would always be hagridden by the charges of schism and heresy, haunted by the curse of Rome, contemptuous of the "new priests" who knew little Spanish and even less Latin, and of the "new bishops" who had been consecrated by other priests no better than themselves. Many would sooner or later make their submission to the pope; meantime they were faithful in their fashion only because they wanted to hold on to their parishes. That was why the new seminaries were so essential.

Pons, erudite, popular, an independent spirit, could play an important part. "I would give you the best parish in my diocese," offered Brillantes, "if you were only to adhere publicly and formally to our church. I beseech you to study the matter; later you can let me know your decision by mail. Should it be favorable, then there would be nothing to stop you from founding in your parish your own college-seminary, or even a university!" This was scarcely an offer likely to appeal to Pons after what he had seen in Badoc, Laoag, and Bacarra itself; nonetheless it brings us to the heart of his problem.

Pons had much more in common with Aglipay and his priests than with the American Protestant missionaries. He might suspect the latter of sneering at him behind his back as a turncoat; not so the Aglipayans who were Catholic priests like himself, in rebellion, it was true, forbidden the exercise of their sacred office, but, at least until 1902, neither schismatics nor heretics. Almost as important, from a more worldly point of view, the nationalist movement could enable him to live once more in the security and authority to which he was accustomed, and no thanks to Father Lobo, for they could give him one of the parishes seized in the wake of the revolution, a wealthy parish, if not indeed one of the best, as Brillantes had promised. Pons knew of three other Spanish friars who had accepted from Aglipay the enviable parishes of Manaoag, with its famous shrine, Dumangas, and Carles. One was to become vicar forane in Iloilo; another, bishop in Ilocos Norte.[38]

Brillantes's offer had not been the first, if we are to believe Pons. He was later to claim that not only Brillantes but, before him, Garcés, Pío Romero, and Aglipay himself, "tireless in seeking my public and official adhesion, offered me employment, offices and honors." When he first met Romero in 1902 in Garcés's house, all three then under suspension, Romero is said to have told Pons:

"Let us get together and work together, Father Pons, let us go together as far as . . . Hell, if need be."

To which Pons claims he made the pious and cautious reply:

"To get together and work together seems all right. I need you, and you need me. But to go together to . . . Hell. . . . Well, no, that doesn't seem right to me. I want your friendship but not that of Satan, who, they say, is a very tricky customer indeed." [39]

But the real difficulty lay elsewhere, and the Spaniard in Pons was acutely aware of it. The essence of the Philippine religious revolution was nationalism; it was a rejection and a repudiation of the Spanish hierarchy and the Spanish friars, in short, of the colonial religious establishment which, for more than three centuries after the conversion, had stubbornly barred the native Filipinos from the episcopacy. Aglipay and his priests, at the 1899 Assembly of Paniqui, had made a declaration of independence from the Spanish hierarchy, but not, it should be emphasized,

[38] *Ibid.*, II, 61, 99, reproducing Pons. From Rodríguez, *ibid.*, and from Achútegui and Bernad, *op. cit.*, I, 232, the three Spanish friars may be tentatively identified as Rafael Murillo, Agustín Ran, and Pons.
[39] *Ibid.*, II, 94, reproducing Pons.

from the Roman pontiff, proclaiming their *"fides in Petrum, non politicum, non diplomaticum, non despoticum."* But however understandable such a declaration might have been at the time for the native clergy, it would seem inconsistent for them to welcome a Spanish friar or exfriar to their company and give him one of the parishes from which they themselves had been for so long excluded or in which they had been compelled to accept the subordinate positions of coadjutors. And for his part, how could the Spanish friar or exfriar feel at ease and at home in such a movement?

The history of the Philippine Independent Church is dealt with elsewhere in this volume, and, for the purposes of this study, it is sufficient to note that Pons's dilemma was quickly resolved by events. On the one hand, driven by that impetuous enthusiast, Isabelo de los Reyes, "the true founder" and exuberant theologian of the Philippine Independent Church, Aglipay and his priests "went much farther," as Romero had foretold, than they had thought at first, and flung themselves headlong from rebellion to schism to heresy, from denial of the Trinity to denial of the Real Presence, from humanism to rationalism, leaving poor Pons floundering behind.[40]

On the other hand, the decision of the Supreme Court recognizing the right of the Roman Catholic Church to the possession and control of the parish churches, rectories, and other ecclesiastical properties in the Philippines ruined whatever chances the Philippine Independent Church had ever had of emulating the Church of England. There was to be no wealthy parish for Pons when even Aglipay had to inaugurate the new church in the upper story of a chemist's shop, and no visible future in any of the new "college-seminaries" when the brilliant rector of Aglipay's own "Great Central or Archdiocesan Seminary" was soon to publish his retraction.[41]

As early as April 1901 Pons had appealed indirectly for relief and rehabilitation to the Holy Office in Rome.[42] Fourteen

40 Cf. Achútegui and Bernad, *op. cit.*, I, 279 ff., on the official doctrine of the Philippine Independent Church.

41 Rodríguez, II, 139 ff., reproducing Pons. This was Félix Sevilla Macam.

42 *Ibid.*, II, 297; in I, 508 ff., it is explained that the Holy Office required Pons to submit his petition for rehabilitation personally and not through his superiors in his order. For one reason or another he did not do so.

months later, in June 1902, he was still awaiting a decision and, despairing of one, wrote to the archbishop of Manila, informing him that he had taken employment in a school in Dagupan, where he would await Rome's decision. But one Cardinal Vanutelli demanded a complete retraction, and Pons would not be ready for that until after almost seven more years of pride, perplexity, penury, and loneliness.

Nozaleda at least had his friend the marquis, and the praises of the pope, and the comfort of staunch Nocedal's devotion to the friars, but what of Pons, a Spaniard left stranded by the ebb of his country's empire in an alien archipelago beyond the reach of Maura's celebrated bayonets, a friar among schismatics who "would like to have a friar for breakfast," a wandering scholar who did not know where his next meal was coming from. What on earth was Salvador Pons to do with his "vast theological and patristic erudition" among four or five yokels parsing *amo, amas, amat?*

There were other things preying on his mind, as he wrote to a friend after his retraction: "The almost sudden death of my friend, the Methodist pastor, Mr. Buenaflor, in Bangued, September 1908; the terrible disease of another friend, the Evangelical pastor, Mr. Williams; the sad heartbreaking death of companions in rebellion, the schismatic 'bishops' Brillantes and Garcés; all of this on top of my own personal misfortunes seemed to me to be prophetic warnings from Heaven which were meant for my good. From then on I began to reflect on my own behavior, horrified by what I had once loved in disregard of my sacred duties. Nor were these the only reasons or motives which led me once again to the path of truth. . . ." These reasons, he explained, were to be found in his publications refuting his former errors.

He began receiving visits from a former student of his, Eugenio Abalos, who was now a seminarian in the Jesuit college in Vigan. And so it was that, after four months of spiritual and physical depression, a Spanish Jesuit, Miguel Saderra Mata, on March 5, 1909, in Vigan, with one Simeón Antonio and one R. Antonio as witnesses, received the sworn submission of Salvador Pons. His Augustinian biographer denies that Pons was ever an Aglipayan; the Jesuit chroniclers of the Philippine Independent Church imply that he was. The text of the retraction is reproduced in translation in the notes.[43]

[43] *Ibid.*, I, 523 ff. The author's translation of the Spanish text follows:

"I, Salvador Pons y Torres, priest, bearing in mind the Divine Majesty that will pass judgment on me, and convinced that no one can be saved outside of the faith held and taught by the Holy, Catholic and Apostolic Church of Rome, against whom I repent having grievously offended by following, teaching and practising doctrines contrary to those which she believes and teaches, (hereby) declare and profess to believe all that is proposed for my belief by the said Holy, Catholic and Apostolic Church of Rome, the one true Church, founded by Jesus Christ on earth, to which (Church) I bind myself with all my heart, rejecting and condemning whatever she condemns and rejects.

"I therefore declare that I admit and believe what is contained in the Apostolic Creed (*símbolo Apostólico*), the decrees of the Councils and the pontifical constitutions or documents (*Concilios y Constituciones o documentos pontifícios*) and reject what is to them opposed.

"I declare that I consider expunged and withdrawn, and that I repent of, all the opinions, writings, and practices with which I have defended, favored, and taught by word of mouth or in writing doctrines contrary to the doctrines and practices approved by the Catholic Apostolic Church of Rome, and specially those which refer to schism, heresy, spiritism, the sacraments of penance and matrimony, and devotion to the saints.

"I declare that I consider expunged and withdrawn from my writings every phrase, criticism or censure offensive or injurious to the prelates of the Church, especially to the Roman Pontiff, his most illustrious delegates and the venerable bishops, whom, as a good Christian, I humbly ask to pardon such offenses, and in a special manner the former venerable bishop of this diocese, Monsignor Dennis Dougherty, and the Most Illustrious Archbishop of Manila, Monsignor Harty.

"I declare that I withdraw and expunge any phrase or writing offensive, denigrating (or) injurious to the Catholic clergy, secular and regular, and especially of this diocese.

"For those of my acts and writings which may have caused scandal to Catholic people, I ask the pardon of the faithful and of the Church, promising to follow in the future conduct proper to a faithful and obedient son of the Church.

"I hope that Our Lord by His grace will help me to carry out these my resolutions, trusting in the prayers of all the faithful.

"I beg the Most Illustrious Bishop of this diocese and the Catholic press to do me the favor of giving publicity to these declarations which I have freely and spontaneously written down in order that all may know what I am and what is my faith in matters of religion."

Rodríguez comments:

"It is necessary to note that the Catholic Church, through its hierarchy, compelled Fr. Salvador Pons to retract and repent of all the opinions and practices 'with which he (had) defended, favored and taught by word of mouth or in writing . . . schism, heresy, spiritism, etc.' But although refer-

In any case the only penance imposed on him, aside, of course, from his implied intellectual humiliation, seems to have consisted of ten days of spiritual exercises.[44] He had been advised by his physicians to return to Spain (a case of asthma?) and he did so in 1910, but life among his newly recovered brethren of the cloth was very trying, as it was bound to be. They could not forget Pons's "diatribes" and "personal attacks" in the past, and one may even now without unfairness imagine the snubs and sarcasms in choir, refectory, and cell. So it was agreed to transfer him to the Augustinian convent in Wurzburg, Germany, where he spent the rest of his life—about fifteen years—refuting his former writings.[45]

His tombstone bore the name of "P. Hermenegildo J. Torres" and the simple prayer "R.I.P." Was it a last mean repudiation by his brethren? His final act of repentance? A graveside abjuration of his troubled past? No matter. Of all the Spanish friars in the exodus of the revolution, Salvador Pons was perhaps the last to go home.

---

ence is made to defense of the Aglipayan schism, nothing is said of a formal adhesion, and consequently he is not required to retract and condemn it. . . . In all the other retractions, whenever there had been a formal adhesion to the Aglipayan schism, it was so stated in the document. We conclude therefore, in view of the documents, that Fr. Salvador Pons was in sympathy with the schism of Gregorio Aglipay and Isabelo de los Reyes, but was never a true Aglipayan" (*op. cit.*, I, 524; also 514 ff.).

Achútegui and Bernad state flatly that Pons "joined the schism" (*op. cit.*, I, 232).

[44] Rodríguez, *op. cit.*, I, 509, n. 78.

[45] Among these may be mentioned the following numbered manuscripts in the Augustinian Library in Valladolid: no. 26120, "El Espiritismo en las Islas Filipinas"; no. 26324, "El Protestantismo en las Islas Filipinas"; no. 27850, "El Protestantismo ante el Tribunal de la Historia"; no. 26408, "Volvamos a la Iglesia Católica Romana"; no. 27300, "Defensa Imparcial y Sincera de las Corporaciones Religiosas Españolas en las Islas Filipinas."

The Disentanglement of Church and State Early in the American Regime in the Philippines

PETER G. GOWING

Before the Americans Came

One of the facts of Philippine life in the three-and-a-third centuries before the United States assumed rule over the archipelago was the close alliance between the Roman Catholic Church and the Spanish colonial government. It had not always been an easy alliance, for sometimes conflict of interest led to hostility and even violence between church and state. Still, the colonial government had well understood that its control of the Philippines rested heavily on the power which the loyal Spanish bishops and especially the friar-priests wielded in the lives of the Filipino people. This power was not simply spiritual, it was economic and political as well. The dynamics operative in the acquisition and maintenance of this power are well known and need not concern us here; but something of the nature and character of that power, as it had developed up to the time of the American arrival, can be seen in the following excerpt from the Schurman (First Philippine) Commission's report to President McKinley in 1900:

It will be noticed that there is scarcely any branch of the municipal government in which the reverend parochial priest does not play an important part. It is true that his powers are limited to inspection and advising, but in practice he is said to make himself a power in the pueblo by simply using these attributes effectively.

In the first place, the parochial priest is considered a member of the principalia, but a member without a vote. He merely advises the principalia in choosing the twelve delegates. In the municipal tribunal he sits with the others and advises them in regard to their deliberations. He also assists in choosing the *cabeza de barangay*, but in this

203

case, as in all others, he does not have a vote, but simply advises.

In general, it may be said that the reverend parochial priest assists in all the meetings of the municipal tribunal, whether that body meets alone or in conjunction with the twelve delegates of the principalia. He has the right to intervene in all business conducted by the tribunal, gives his opinion in regard to the approval of bills presented by the captain, and advises the town officials whenever occasion offers.[1]

In August 1896 the Philippine revolution broke out, and it was as much a rebellion against the real and imagined abuses of the Spanish friars as against the colonial government. For many Filipinos the Spanish friars had become the symbols of tyranny and oppression. Grievances centered around exorbitant fees charged for religious services, unfair and discriminatory treatment of the native clergy, the extensive landholdings of the religious orders together with their questionable business activities, and what was seen to be the opposition of the friars to progress in general.[2] The execution of Fathers Burgos, Gómez, and Zamora in 1872, the political novels of José Rizal, the propaganda movement, the clandestine activities and secret teachings of the *Katipunan,* all this articulated the widespread antifriary of the Filipino people. The fury of that sentiment was vented on the persons of those Spanish friars who fell prisoner to the Filipinos in the course of the revolution. When the revolution started in 1896, there were 1,124 friars in the islands. During the fighting the majority were able to escape to Manila, but better than 300 of their less fortunate brothers were taken prisoner, and some fifty of them were killed. At Imus, Cavite, for example, thirteen were savagely put to death, one by being burned alive, another by being hacked to pieces, and still another by being roasted on a bamboo pole. Many friars were publicly beaten and otherwise cruelly treated.[3]

It was one of the major objects of the Philippine revolution to

[1] *Report of the Philippine Commission, 1900,* I, 57.

[2] Cf. Antonio Regidor, "The Filipino Case Against the Friars," *Independent,* LIII (Feb. 7, 1900), 317–20; and James A. Le Roy, "The Friars in the Philippines," *Political Science Quarterly,* XVIII (Dec. 1903), 675–80.

[3] *Report of the Philippine Commission, 1900,* I, 130; II, 110, 396; see also Frank C. Laubach, *The People of the Philippines* (New York, 1925), pp. 113–15.

expel the Spanish friars from the islands and confiscate their huge estates for distribution to the Filipino tenants who had tilled the soil for generations. There was also concern about advancing the status of the Filipino priests, not one of whom had been raised to the episcopate in the entire period of Spanish rule and most of whom were kept in subordinate positions as parish coadjutors or assistants to the Spanish clergy. In general, however, the devoutly religious Filipino people were antifriar without being antichurch or anti-Catholic, though many of the *ilustrados* (native intelligentsia) advocated separation of church and state.

The Spanish-American War occasioned Admiral Dewey's victory over the Spanish fleet in Manila Bay on May 1, 1898. On June 12 General Emilio Aguinaldo proclaimed Philippine independence, and in September a constitutional convention was convened at Malolos, Bulacan, to draw up an instrument of government for the infant republic.

The most exciting and dramatic debate of the convention centered on Title III of the proposed constitution. Felipe G. Calderón, the chief architect of the instrument and a good Catholic, sought to make Catholicism the official religion though tolerating the existence of other faiths. Tomás G. del Rosario, a lawyer and a Mason, was the leader of the opposition which sought separation of church and state as well as religious liberty. The final vote was taken on November 29, and, of the 51 votes cast, 26 were in favor and 25 against separation of church and state. In its adopted form, as prepared by del Rosario, Title III, Article 5, of the Malolos constitution read: "The State recognizes the liberty and equality of all religious worship, as well as the separation of Church and State." [4]

It is doubtful whether this provision represented the convictions of the Filipino people, the majority of whom were not really aware of the issues involved—and certainly it did not represent

[4] For a discussion of the religious issues at Malolos, see Nicholas Zafra, "The Malolos Congress," in the booklet prepared in 1963 under the same title by the Philippine Historical Association in Manila. The pages are unnumbered, but the discussion of the religious question begins on the sixth page of the article. See also Cesar Adib Majul's essay in this volume, "Anticlericalism during the Reform Movement and the Philippine Revolution," pp. 152–71.

the views of the Filipino clergy.[5] In any case the question was made academic by the turn of events. Ignoring the Treaty of Paris which was signed on December 10, 1898 (and which itself had completely ignored Philippine independence and transferred sovereignty over the islands from Spain to the United States), President Aguinaldo declared the Malolos constitution in force, with the exception of Title III, Article 5, on January 21, 1899. Scarcely two weeks later, the Philippine-American War broke out which ended in the forcible imposition of American rule over the islands. Even so, Title III of the Malolos constitution was not without significance. Years later, a young Filipino political scientist wrote:

It is truly surprising that a Catholic country should have taken such a liberal view regarding the separation of Church and State and the freedom of worship. It can only be accounted for because of the many abuses and tyrannies that had resulted from a union of Church and State in the Islands, and from the fact that the members of the Congress were of a superior type, many of whom were well educated and had had opportunity for travel in countries in which abuses of the Church did not exist. Many, no doubt, felt that a continuation of the union of Church and State in the Philippines would involve a continuation of the friar rule and this they desired to avoid at all costs, even to the extent of permitting other religions to enter than that to which the great majority of the Filipino people belonged.[6]

Policies and Problems of the American Regime

From the moment of its arrival on Philippine soil, the United States became involved in the religious situation prevailing in the

[5] Father Gregorio Aglipay, a Filipino patriot who was later to help found the Philippine Independent Church, was the only priest to be a delegate to the Congress. He expressed the attitude of most of the Filipino clergy at the time when he wrote: "If we continue recognizing the supremacy of the Spanish prelates or even if we remain in an expectant and neutral attitude without definitely and clearly defining our position, this might lead to the separation of Church and State in our country and, consequently, other conflicts which assuredly would not fail gravely to prejudice the interests of the clergy and above all the service of religion to which we should sacrifice all our affections and even our convictions" (quoted in Leandro H. Fernandez, "The Philippine Republic," unpublished Ph.D. dissertation, Political Science Faculty, Columbia University, 1926, p. 132).

[6] *Ibid.*, pp. 124–25.

islands at the close of the Spanish regime. The involvement began as an incident of war. The sixth provision of the terms of capitulation of the city of Manila agreed to by the Spanish forces in August 1898 stated that "its churches and religious worship . . . and its private property of all descriptions" were placed "under the special safeguard of the faith and honor of the American army." [7] Considering that the surrender of Manila to the Americans took place while thousands of Filipino troops besieged the city, this provision was very important. In effect it made the United States army the protector of the Catholic church in Manila against possible attack or seizure by the Filipino revolutionaries.

The Treaty of Paris deepened and broadened American involvement in the religious situation in the Philippines. Article VI obliged the United States government to undertake "to obtain the release of all Spanish prisoners in the hands of the insurgents"— many of them being Spanish friars. Article VIII stipulated that cession of the islands to the United States "cannot in any respect impair the property or rights which by law belong to the peaceful possession of property of all kinds, of . . . ecclesiastical bodies." And Article X provided for something which Spain herself had never granted in the Philippines: "The inhabitants of the territories over which Spain relinquishes or cedes her sovereignty shall be secured in the free exercise of their religion." [8] By these provisions the United States became committed to protecting the Spanish friars and their extensive properties throughout the archipelago, a commitment which opened her to some criticism at home. Nearly four years after the treaty, *The Nation* editorialized:

[Our Commissioners at Paris] with incredible lightness of heart and lack of foresight . . . tied up our Government by a sweeping guar-

---

[7] The full text of the Terms of the Capitulation is found in Louis S. Young and Henry D. Northrop, *Life and Heroic Deeds of Admiral Dewey* (Philadelphia, 1899), pp. 175–76.

[8] *A Treaty of Peace Between the United States and Spain,* Message from the President, 55th Congress, 3rd Session, U.S. Senate Document no. 62, part 1 (Washington, 1899), pp. 6, 7, 9.

antee of the personal and property rights of the very men who had done most to drive the Filipinos to insurrection.[9]

The United States did her best to live up to the provisions of the Treaty of Paris. American army commanders, before the outbreak of the Philippine-American War, tried unsuccessfully to persuade General Aguinaldo to order the release of all Spanish prisoners held by the insurgents; and later, the United States government indemnified church authorities for the occupation and damage to ecclesiastical property which occurred during the war. These actions aroused the suspicion among some Filipinos that the United States was interested in re-establishing the power of the friars. The behavior of General Elwell S. Otis, the American military governor (and a Presbyterian) seemed to the Filipinos to confirm these suspicions. For one thing, he returned the Paco church in Manila—which had been temporarily seized by American troops in a skirmish with the insurgents—to the jurisdiction of Archbishop Nozaleda (himself a hated Spanish friar) who in turn promptly replaced the Filipino parish priest there with a friar. Then again, Otis irritated Filipinos by the manner in which he received Archbishop Placide Chapelle of New Orleans, appointed by the Vatican to be chargé d'affaires in the Philippines for the purpose of dealing with the church situation. On January 2, 1900, General Otis sent his personal launch to meet the ship on which the archbishop arrived so as to transport him ashore.

It was cried from the housetops that the new American prelate, come to reinstate the friars, was brought ashore in the government launch, given a reception in the old governor's palace with the friar archbishop and the other friars by his side, and otherwise shown official courtesies which to Americans were merely ordinary social amenities, but to Filipinos were magnified into matters of great importance.[10]

The whole affair seemed strange indeed to Filipinos in the light of what the Americans had all along been saying about the sepa-

[9] Quoted in Robert B. Silliman, "The Taft Administration in the Philippines" (unpublished M.A. thesis, Lafayette College, 1938), p. 122.

[10] James A. Le Roy, *The Americans in the Philippines* (Boston, 1914), II, 299.

ration of church and state. It came to be believed widely that Chapelle—who seemed openly to support the friars—had the backing of the United States government.

Nor was that all. Among many other loyally Catholic Filipinos there was alarm over the arrival and growth of Protestant missions from the United States which had begun their work late in 1898. Some believed that the American government was supporting Protestant missionaries in the same way that Spain had supported the friars. Obviously Filipinos were far from understanding what Americans understood by complete separation of church and state. The matter very badly needed clarification.

Early in 1900, while the Philippine-American War raged, President McKinley appointed the Second Philippine Commission to prepare the way for, and eventually to assume the legislative power over, civil government in the islands. The new commission succeeded the Schurman—or First Philippine—Commission which had been given investigatory powers only. Headed by the Hon. William H. Taft (who was to be inaugurated as first civil governor of the Philippines on July 4, 1901), the commission was instructed by the president to see to it that no laws were made in the islands which either established religion or prevented the free exercise and enjoyment of religious profession and worship. In keeping with these instructions to the Philippine commission, General Arthur MacArthur, who had succeeded General Otis as military governor, issued a pledge to the Filipino people on July 8, 1900, which was widely circulated and which set forth in the clearest and most comprehensive terms possible the basic policy of the American regime respecting religion:

As under the Constitution of the United States complete freedom is guaranteed, and no minister of religion can be interfered with or molested in following his calling in a peaceful and lawful manner, and there must be a complete separation of Church and State, so here the civil government of these Islands hereafter to be established will give the same security to the citizens thereof, and guarantee that no form of religion shall be forced by the government upon any community or upon any citizen of the Islands; that no minister of religion in following his calling in a peaceful and lawful manner shall be interfered with or molested by the government or any person; that no public funds shall be used for the support of religious organizations or any member thereof; that no official process shall be used to collect contributions from the people for the support of any church, priest or religious order; that no minister of religion, by virtue of his being a minister, shall exercise any public or governmental office or authority and that the separation of Church and State must be complete and entire.

In pursuance of the policy embodied in the foregoing paragraph, it is apparent that congregations, by independent individual action, so far as any governmental interference is concerned, may reject any clergyman who is not acceptable to the majority of the communicants of the parish, and prevent his ministrations therein by such means as are suitable to accomplish the purpose, provided that any action in the premises be not accompanied by application of violence.[11]

This policy received the endorsement of the Protestant missionaries, of course, and helped to set at ease the minds of those Filipinos most concerned to see the Roman Catholic Church, and especially the friars, disestablished permanently. Roman Catholic authorities in the Philippines were not at all enthusiastic, and in general they held to the sentiments expressed by the Jesuit fathers of Manila in the report of the Schurman Commission:

The Filipino people . . . do not ask for nor want religious liberty, nor the separation of the church and the state; [they] are content with their Catholicism, and they do not desire anything more, nor would they suffer their government to overthrow the Catholic unity. . . . Therefore it is demonstrated that religious liberty in the Philippines is not only not advisable but adverse to public peace.[12]

American Roman Catholics, however, generally favored the principles of separation of church and state and of religious liberty as applied to the archipelago—though they vigorously warned the Protestants of the futility of sending missionaries to a land as devoutly Catholic as the Philippines.

The principles of religious liberty and separation of church and state were confirmed in the Organic Act passed by the United States Congress in 1902 which virtually served as the constitution of the Philippines until its replacement by the Jones Law of 1916.

[11] Quoted in *ibid.*, pp. 300–301.
[12] *Report of the Philippine Commission, 1900*, IV, 112.

When the American civil government finally assumed control of the Philippines from the military authorities in 1900–1901, it was fully aware of the many vexing problems it had to face in the process of disentangling church and state and maintaining peace and order. The major problems were four in particular. First, there was the problem of public education. A thorough discussion of this subject is offered in another essay in this symposium, and thus we will only mention the matter here.[13] Under Spain, the schools had been almost wholly directed by the church, and, despite several attempts to put education under governmental control, it remained very largely in the hands of the friars until the end of the Spanish period. The American regime, beginning with the military governors, sought to introduce a secular public school system patterned after that in the United States. This brought the government—military and civil—into conflict with representatives of the Catholic church, some of whom feared the emergence of "godless" education and others of whom sought the privilege of teaching their religion within the new system. Second, there was the problem of antifriary. During the fighting, hundreds of Spanish friars had gathered in Manila and were waiting to return to their parishes which had been taken over by the Filipino clergy or otherwise left vacant. The people generally did not want the friars back, and peace and order were threatened by the mere suggestion of their return. Third, there was the problem of the friars' lands. Three of the orders (Augustinian, Dominican, and Augustinian Recollects) owned vast estates which the Filipino revolutionaries had seized, intending eventually to parcel them out to the tenant farmers. The Filipinos wanted that land, and there could be no hope of civil peace if the religious orders pressed their claim of ownership. Moreover, there was some difficulty in determining which lands actually were ecclesiastical and which were formerly crown lands ceded to the United States, for in Spanish times church buildings were frequently erected by the people on crown lands without proper title being transferred to the ecclesiastical authorities. And fourth, there was the problem of the so-called "Aglipayan Schism" from

[13] See the essay which follows in this volume by Sister Mary Dorita Clifford, "Religion and the Public Schools in the Philippines: 1899–1906."

the Roman Catholic Church which, though the seeds were sown earlier, occurred in 1902. Peace and order were disturbed as schismatic congregations attempted to claim church buildings and other ecclesiastical property as their own.

There were other problems as well. The amount of indemnity to which the church was entitled for the occupation and damage of its property during the Philippine-American war had to be determined. Jurisdiction over certain educational and charitable trusts—some of them civil and others religious, but all of which had been administered by the friars under the Spanish government—had to be clarified. The problem of church control of the *Banco Español Filipino* had to be resolved. Public cemeteries where anyone (especially non-Catholics) could be buried had to be provided—in Spanish times the church had nearly complete control of burial matters in the larger towns and cities. And provision had to be made for civil marriage as well—under Spain only church marriage was recognized. By legislative decree and enactment of various laws, the Philippine Commission began to deal with some of these problems. In 1901 it arranged for a survey and appraisal of ecclesiastical lands in the archipelago.

Disestablishment of Friar Control

The American regime, with respect to the religious situation in the Philippines, found itself caught between two forces: the Treaty of Paris implied that it had a duty to protect the Spanish friars if they wished to return to their parishes and regain control of their property; on the other hand, it could not afford to offend the Filipinos by forcing the hated friars on them. This was made clear from the beginning, as when Señor José Luis de Luzuriaga, a distinguished Filipino leader from Negros, testified before the Schurman Commission in 1899. Asked what the feeling of the people of Negros was toward the friars, he replied:

It is completely hostile. They are enemies of the friars. They do not wish to see a friar there. A great many people have been shot in Negros through the unjust and calumnious denunciation of the friars. . . . In the first place, they complain of the grasping spirit of the friars. The friars wished to be the civil authority, the military authority, and they were complete owners of a man's body and soul. The friar was the personification of autocracy, and had as his object the exploitation, spiritually and materially, of the native.[14]

The Schurman Commission in the end reported to President Mc-Kinley that a genuine hatred of the friars did in fact exist. Apparently believing that the antifriary was rooted largely in the economic issues arising from ownership of so much land, the commission went on to recommend that the United States purchase the friars' lands and then sell them to the Filipinos in small parcels at reasonable rates. A year later, the Second Philippine Commission came to the same conclusion. In its report to the president dated June 30, 1901, it affirmed:

The Commission should be authorized, in case its view of the matter is approved, to issue bonds in an amount sufficient to buy the lands . . . we earnestly recommend this course. The matter is a pressing one, for the action of the courts in enforcing legal decrees in favor of the real owners of the land against the tenants will be a constant source of irritation, riot and lawlessness in the provinces where the land is, and will lead to distrust and uneasyness everywhere.[15]

While the report did not specifically recommend the withdrawal of the friars from the islands, this was nevertheless the feeling of Mr. Taft personally. In an essay written in 1902 entitled "Civil Government in the Philippines," he said:

If the purchase of the lands of the friars and the adjustment of all other questions arising between the Church and the State should include a withdrawal of the friars from the Islands, it would greatly facilitate the harmony between the government and the people and between the Church and the State.[16]

As early as July of 1900, Mr. Taft had sounded out the friars on their willingness to sell their lands to the government at a fair price, the purchase being conditioned on their agreeing not to return to their former parishes. It was the rejection of this proposal

---

[14] *Report of the Philippine Commission, 1900*, II, 421.
[15] *Report of the Philippine Commission, 1901*, I, 24–25.
[16] *The Philippines* (New York, 1902), pp. 135–36.

which later made a special mission to Rome, to negotiate over the heads of the friars, seem the only hopeful alternative. Back in Washington briefly, Governor Taft testified before the House of Representatives Committee on Insular Affairs and urged the purchase of the friars' lands. The committee approved the recommendation. Accordingly, Governor Taft was instructed by Secretary of War Elihu Root to return to the Philippines by way of Rome in order to confer with the Vatican "on the subject of the friars' lands and the possible withdrawal, at the instance of the Pope, of the Spanish friars from the Philippines." The Secretary's instructions, dated May 9, 1902, went on to say:

One of the controlling principles of our Government is the complete separation of Church and State, with the future freedom of each from any control or interference by the other. This principle is imperative wherever American jurisdiction extends and no modification or shading thereof can be a subject of discussion. . . . Your errand will not be in any sense or degree diplomatic in its nature, but will be purely a business matter by you as Governor of the Philippines for the purchase of property from the owners thereof, and the settlement of land titles, in such a manner as to contribute to the best interests of the people of the Islands.[17]

Actually, the Vatican itself had been much interested in the visit of an American commission of some sort to settle church-state questions in the Philippines. In May 1901, the Vatican Secretary of State, Cardinal Rampolla, wrote Archbishop John Ireland of St. Paul, Minnesota, asking him to inquire after the possibility, and the archbishop promptly notified Governor Taft. Later in the year, President Theodore Roosevelt (who had succeeded to the presidency after McKinley's assassination) communicated with Cardinal Gibbons of Baltimore on the same subject.

Mr. Taft (whose entourage included Msgr. Thomas O'Gorman, Roman Catholic bishop of Sioux Falls, South Dakota) arrived in Rome in June 1902 and promptly submitted a letter to Pope Leo XIII stating his business:

On behalf of the Philippine government, it is proposed to buy the lands of the religious orders with the hope that the funds thus fur-

[17] *Report of the Secretary of War, 1902*, p. 59.

ɴished may lead to their withdrawal from the Islands, and, if necessary, a substitution therefor as parish priests, of other priests whose
presence would not be dangerous to public order. . . . [18]

Weeks of talks and exchanges of memoranda followed. In the
end, the Vatican replied that while it favored the sale of the
friars' lands, negotiations for the purchase would have to be handled through the apostolic delegate in Manila in consultation
with the orders concerned. The Vatican also indicated its willingness to introduce priests of other nationalities than Spanish but
would reserve the right to return Spanish friars to their parishes
where the people were disposed to receive them. It agreed to prevent the Catholic clergy in the islands from engaging in political
activity. And, finally, the Vatican refused to command the withdrawal of the friars from the Philippines: first, because it would
be contrary to rights guaranteed in the Treaty of Paris; second,
because it would bring the Holy See into conflict with Spain; and
third, because it would seem to confirm all the accusations made
against the friars, many of which were patently false. However,
the Vatican acquiesced to an informal "gentleman's agreement"
for the *voluntary* withdrawal of the friars.[19]

Though Taft was disappointed that his visit to the Vatican had
not produced all that he had hoped for, he felt that an understanding had been reached which provided sufficient basis for
solving some of the knotty church-state problems in the Philippines. Back in Manila by August 1902, he began the long series of
negotiations which led eventually to the purchase of the friars'
lands.

This proved to be no mean achievement. More than 420,000
acres of some of the finest agricultural lands in the Philippines
were involved—275,000 of them not far from the city of Manila,
125,000 in the provinces of Isabela and Mindoro, and another
25,000 in the province of Cebu. The three religious orders which
owned these lands had, during the revolution, transferred title to

[18] Quoted in Homer C. Stuntz, *The Philippines and the Far East* (Cincinati, 1904), p. 296.

[19] For a detailed account of Governor Taft's negotiations with the Vatican, see Frederick J. Zwierlein, *Theodore Roosevelt and Catholics* (St.
Louis, Mo., 1956), pp. 46–55.

secular promoting companies in which they retained a controlling interest. The Dominicans had conveyed their holdings under a promoter's contract to an Englishman living in Manila who in turn organized a company, the "Philippine Sugar Estates Developing Co. Ltd." to which he transferred nearly all the Dominican lands. The Augustinians disposed of all their agricultural holdings to a Spanish corporation, "Sociedad Agricola de Ultramar," and the Augustinian Recollects signed over their property to the "British Manila Estates Company Ltd. of Hong Kong." The American authorities were thus obliged to deal with these corporations as well as with the friars. This complicated the negotiations considerably, especially since title to some of the lands was still in doubt. The problem was further aggravated by the fact that 60,000 tenants lived on the lands, and many of them had not paid the rents due since 1896. The pressure to settle the matter once and for all was very great.[20]

All the parties concerned were brought together in a conference called by Governor Taft. It was clear that the friars and their agents were now willing to sell, but there was no agreement on the value of the lands. The agents of the friars demanded $13,000,000. The Philippine Commission was unwilling to pay more than $6,043,219.07—a figure based on estimates of value prepared by the Filipino surveyor employed by the commission in 1901 to survey the church lands. Neither side was willing to move from its proffered figure, and months of haggling back and forth followed. The new apostolic delegate, Archbishop Giovanni Baptista Guidi, was asked by Governor Taft to use his good offices to bring the agents of the friars to terms. He did so and informed the commission that he could arrange the sale for $10,500,000. The commission refused. Later the agents indicated that $8,500,000 would be acceptable. Taft turned down the offer but said that he would try to increase the government's offer by $1,500,000. Haggling resumed and in the meantime the Augustinians arranged to sell one of their estates (about 10,000 acres) privately. At last negotiations were closed for the purchase by the

<hr/>

[20] W. H. Taft in *The Philippines*, pp. 124–27; also, *Special Report of Wm. H. Taft, Secretary of War, to the President on the Philippines, January 23, 1908* (Manila: 1909), pp. 20–21.

Philippine government of 410,000 acres (167,127 hectares to be precise) of friars' lands for $7,239,784.66. The contracts were signed on December 22, 1903.[21]

Governor Taft, who had passed up an appointment to the United States Supreme Court in order to remain in the Philippines to see the negotiations through to a conclusion, was roundly criticized in some quarters for paying what was regarded as an exhorbitant price for the lands (roughly $18 an acre). He defended the purchase by an appeal to the irrefutable facts of the case:

We had to buy the friars' lands. We had to do it in order to prevent insurrection by the 60,000 tenants of the friars, which would have followed if we restored the friars to possession, as they were entitled to be restored, because they were the lawful owners of the land. We found that if the Government would buy the land, the tenants would acquiesce as tenants. The friars gave up their claim to past rents that covered a decade. We paid a large price for the lands because we were paying for a political object. We were not making a land speculation. . . . There has thus been eliminated an open sore in the social and political body of the Islands which would have involved them in constant pain and most injurious disturbances of law and order.[22]

As it turned out, the government recovered the bulk of the purchase price in the process of selling the lands to the tenants and others on long-term payments. At any rate, the economic power of the friars in the Philippines had been effectively broken.

Prevented by local conditions from returning to their parishes, the Spanish friars gradually and voluntarily withdrew from the islands. In 1896 there had been approximately 1,124 friars in the Philippines, but by December 1, 1903, the number was reduced to 246. Of these, several were too aged or infirm to do parish work; eighty-three Dominicans had renounced parish work altogether; and most of the rest were engaged in educational work in Manila, Cebu, and Vigan. Accordingly, the Philippine commission reported in 1903 that

[21] *Report of the Philippine Commission, 1903,* I, 38–44, 204–12.
[22] "Excerpts from Ex-President Taft's Address Before the Brooklyn Institute of Arts and Sciences, November 19, 1913," in W. C. Forbes, *The Philippine Islands* (Boston, 1928), II, 503.

the policy of the church . . . in not sending back to the parishes Spanish friars where it can be avoided or where they will not be well received by the people, has been sufficiently shown by the facts.[23]

By early 1904, the last Spanish bishop had left the archipelago, and four of the five episcopal sees were occupied by American bishops. Though this was resented by Filipinos, who wished to see Filipino clergy raised to the episcopate in their own country,[24] it proved to be a wise move. The American bishops were able to give leadership in a time when the Roman Catholic Church was adjusting to the new condition of separation of church and state in the islands and could no longer look to the civil authorities to support its policies, enforce its regulations, and provide all the other benefits of "patronage." Indeed, Pope Leo XIII himself recognized the dawn of the new day for the church in the Philippines when in December 1902 his apostolic constitution, *Quae Mari Sinico,* was promulgated. Among other things, the constitution acknowledged the end of both Spanish sovereignty in the islands and the *patronato* of the Spanish crown. The constitution also suppressed the ancient privileges of the friars and enjoined the clergy to cultivate religion and not engage in worldly pursuits.[25]

With the purchase and dismemberment of the friars' lands, and with the voluntary withdrawal of three-fourths of their number from the archipelago, the control which the friars had formerly exercised over the economic, social, and political life of the Philippines was disestablished. The alien clergy who moved in to fill the vacancies they left behind entered the country on entirely different terms relative to the state than those which had pertained to the friars under Spanish rule.

Ecclesiastical Peace and Order

By virtue of its policy respecting religious liberty, the American regime in the Philippines permitted the introduction of other reli-

[23] *Report of the Philippine Commission, 1903,* I, 5.

[24] In 1905, Father Jorge Barlin was made bishop of Nueva Cáceres (Naga), the first Filipino to achieve episcopal rank.

[25] An English translation of *Quae Mari Sinico* is printed in *The American Catholic Quarterly Review,* XXVIII (Jan.–Oct. 1903), 372–79.

gious bodies which began to compete with the Roman Catholic Church for adherents. The various Protestant groups not surprisingly appealed to many Filipinos who had become disaffected from the Catholic church. In some places there was open hostility to the Protestants, and a few instances of violence and even murder are recorded. There is no evidence whatever that such actions represented a policy of the Catholic authorities, and it is certainly agreed that they were isolated instances perpetrated by overzealous and misguided individuals. The insular government acted swiftly in dealing with such cases and took effective measures to prevent their general occurrence.[26]

Ecclesiastical peace and order were greatly upset, however, with the rise of the Philippine Independent Church as a schism from the Roman Catholic Church. Highly nationalistic and anti-Roman Catholic, the *Iglesia Filipina Independiente* was organized in 1902 under the leadership of Don Isabelo de los Reyes, Sr. and Father Gregorio Aglipay. The latter was consecrated *Obispo Maximo* (Supreme Bishop) of the new church which saw a quarter of the Catholic population of the islands flock to its standard in the early years of its existence. Sometimes whole Roman Catholic parishes and their priests would join the schism, and with the approval of the municipal authorities they would bring their church buildings, *coventos*, cemeteries, and other ecclesiastical property with them. Western and Northern Luzon, particularly Ilocos Norte (Aglipay's home province), were strongly affected by the religious revolt which spread rapidly throughout the islands. It was a genuine people's movement, and in effect it continued the ideological momentum of the revolution. Because of its nationalistic character and various attempts to dabble in purely political affairs, the Philippine Independent Church and its leaders were under suspicion by the American authorities, though Governor Taft maintained friendly personal relations with both De los Reyes and Aglipay.

By 1903, conflicts between the schismatic congregations and

[26] See James B. Rodgers, *Forty Years in the Philippines* (New York, 1940), pp. 18 19; and Richard L. Deats, *The Story of Methodism in the Philippines* (Manila, 1964), pp. 22–26; see also, *Report of the Philippine Commission, 1903*, 1, 46.

Roman Catholic officials approached violent proportions as they contested ownership of the parish churches which the *Independientes* had appropriated to themselves. Governor Taft was obliged to devise the principle of "peaceable possession" which he made law by executive order. The proclamation declared that whoever was in peaceful possession of a church must be considered its legitimate occupant until the courts determined otherwise. While the policy had the effect of restoring some semblance of peace and order, it did nothing to decide the basic issue about the legal ownership of the properties in question.[27]

The Philippine Independent Church argued that since the church buildings were built by the Filipino people on lands provided by the Spanish crown, both the buildings and the lands on which they stood belonged to the people who, through their municipal officials, had a right to decide whether they should be used by *Independientes* or Roman Catholics.

The Roman Catholics argued that under Spain the king was merely the patron of the church, and did not own ecclesiastical property as such. Moreover, the Treaty of Paris specifically exempted ecclesiastical properties from the lands ceded to the United States.

The American bishops in the Philippines complained to President Roosevelt over the head of Governor Taft, citing specific instances of injustice occasioned by the "peaceable possession" principle. President Roosevelt simply endorsed their complaints to Governor Taft who in turn had them investigated. In short, attempts at administrative adjudication proved unsatisfactory, and complaints piled on complaints. A number of suits were filed in the lower courts by the Roman Catholic authorities, but the process of litigation proved much too slow. Finally, the Philippine Commission on July 24, 1905, passed Act No. 1376: "An Act providing for the speedy disposition of controversies as to the right of administration or possession of churches, convents, cemeteries and other church properties and as to ownership and title thereto." The Act gave original jurisdiction to the Supreme Court in such cases and asked that they be given priority.

Thus, at last, the insular government brought an end to its di-

27 *Report of the Philippine Commission, 1903,* I, 981–82.

rect entanglement in church affairs in the Philippines by referring
the adjudication of ecclesiastical controversies requiring decisions
of law to the proper place: the courts of the land.[28]

On November 24, 1906, the Supreme Court of the Philippines
handed down a decision in favor of the Roman Catholic Church
which in effect ordered the Philippine Independent Church to return the contested properties. It was a decision based on law and
as such was a clear demonstration that the church—Roman Catholic and non-Roman Catholic—was as subject to law as any other
institution in the nation.[29]

Conclusions

The early years of the American regime in the Philippines saw
the effectual disentanglement of church and state. As soon as the
American government assumed power it could be said that the
Roman Catholic Church was no longer the official church of the
islands under the patronage of the government; clerics no longer
held positions *qua* clerics in the civil administration, nor were
they able to censor or direct national life as before; and no longer
was public education under church control. By the end of Governor Taft's administration (early 1904), the grip which the friars had
on the economic life of the country and on 60,000 of its citizens
by virtue of their vast landholdings was released, and a serious
threat to the peace of the land was eliminated.

It took time for the real meaning of religious liberty to impress
itself on the minds of the Filipino people, but as they saw Protestant missionaries freely preaching their form of the Christian
faith, as they witnessed the unencumbered rise of the Philippine
Independent Church, as they reflected on how religious bodies
are subjected to the impartial rule of law, and as they heard frequent restatements of the principle of separation of church and
state and saw that principle rigidly adhered to time after time on

[28] *Report of the Philippine Commission, 1905,* I, 67. For a full and lucid
discussion of the issues involved in the controversies over church property,
see Pedro S. de Achútegui, S.J. and Miguel A. Bernad, S.J., *Religious Revolution in the Philippines,* (Manila, 1960), I, chap. xv.

[29] Philippine Islands, Supreme Court, Barlin *v.* Ramirez in *Philippine Reports,* 7.41 (1907), no. 2832, Nov. 24, 1906.

the part of the government, they gradually came to understand and respect religious freedom.

The Roman Catholic Church, stripped of direct power in the government of the Philippines, was left free to concentrate on its religious and social ministry far more than before. The coming of American and various European Catholic missionaries helped to liberalize the general nature of Hispanic-Philippine Catholicism. New emphases emerged in church life as Roman Catholics adjusted to the climate of democracy and pluralism fostered during the American regime.[30]

[30] An excellent treatment of the legal background to the present position of the church in the Philippines is given in Jorge R. Coquia, *Legal Status of the Church in the Philippines* (Washington, 1950).

Iglesia Filipina Independiente:
The Revolutionary Church

SISTER MARY DORITA CLIFFORD, B.V.M.

When the Sixtieth General Convention of the Protestant Episcopal Church of the United States voted to accept a concordat
proposed by the Philippine Independent Church establishing full
communion between the two bodies, an important stage in
ecumenism was reached.[1] For almost sixty years events had been
moving toward this end, not by the shortest and straightest path,
but by a circuitous and at times wobbly route which raised
doubts about the journey ever getting under way. The result of
the concordat was not a merger but an agreement between equals
that they shared the essentials of Christianity: one faith, one baptism, one Eucharist, one gospel.[2] Each remained self-governing,
self-propagating, and self-supporting, although the Episcopal
church did assume part of the financial burden of the younger
church by an annual subsidy and a shared seminary program.

The real significance of this concordat was that it recognized
the restoration of wholeness of doctrine by the Philippine Independent Church, it brought into union two strongly Catholic elements within the Philippine Christian community,[3] and it marked
the coming to maturity of a group of Christians known over the
years as Aglipayans, as the *Iglesia Filipina Independiente*, and
finally as the Philippine Independent Church. But it also left behind, outside of the union, several splinter groups in schism from

[1] Meeting in Detroit, Sept. 17–29, 1961. The vote on the concordat was
taken Sept. 22, 1961.

[2] *The Christian Century*, Aug. 14, 1964, 1013, has the official statement
of the PIC reprinted for clarification; the statement of the PEC is reprinted
in Lewis Whittemore, *Struggle for Freedom* (Greenwich, Conn., 1961), 217–
18.

[3] *The Christian Century*, Sept. 23, 1964, 1186.

the independent movement, groups so radically different that they refused to unite. Taken all together these groups number more than 1,500,000 souls of whom at least 1,000,000 are PIC members.[4] The remaining 500,000 pose a serious ecumenical problem, the solving of which may well be the final step in maturation for the PIC. This solution, of necessity, demands an honest assessment of the issues which divide them. One of the first steps toward a reunion might be a thoroughly objective study of the origins of the independent church movement at the turn of the century.

Much has already been written about the early days of the PIC, but whether it can be called history is open to question. The defensive posture of the mother church, anguished over the defection of native priests and concerned for the flock unwittingly led astray, precluded much sifting of evidence or weighing of motives when an outright condemnation appeared to be the best immediate answer.[5] The sympathetic stance of the Protestant missionaries who, if we judge by their own accounts, welcomed the schism in the hope that it would break the tight control of the Roman Catholic Church and make conversions to Protestantism easier, renders their reporting questionable.[6] The belligerence of the participants in the controversy has clouded the real issues with justifications and recriminations over even the most insignificant events,[7] while the eagerness of some ecumenists in glossing

[4] Pedro S. de Achútegui, S.J. and Miguel A. Bernad, S.J., "The Aglipayan Churches and the Census of 1960," *Philippine Studies*, XII (July, 1964), 446–59.

[5] Ambrose Coleman, O.P., *The Friars in the Philippines* (Boston, 1899); "Do the Filipinos Hate the Friars?" *American Catholic Quarterly Review*, XXX (July, 1905), 449–61; "Inside the Aglipayan Church," *ibid.* (Apr., 1905), 368–81; Evergisto Bozaco, O.P., *La Iglesia en Filipinas* (Manila, 1938), might be cited as examples.

[6] Frank C. Laubach, *The People of the Philippines* (New York, 1925); Homer Stuntz, *The Philippines and the Far East* (Cincinnati, 1904); Homer Stuntz, "Filipino Independent Church," *The Converted Catholic*, XXI (July, 1904), 205–207; John Bancroft Devins, *An Observer in the Philippines* (New York, 1905); Dwight E. Stevenson, *Christianity in the Philippines* (Lexington, 1955). Most of these books have been accepted as authoritative and have been widely quoted in modern studies of the schism, whereas most of them are in error as to dates, personages, and other very important historical data.

[7] Gregorio Aglipay, "The Independent Catholic Church in the Philippines," *The Independent*, LX (1903), 2571–75; James A. Le Roy, "The

over differences and difficulties to hasten intercommunion poses
new problems for the PIC's rapprochement with her own separated brethren.[8] Unfortunately even those studies conducted
under the direction of scholars in the universities have produced
many half-truths warmed over.[9] The most reputable study, based
on meticulous documentation and admirable collections of primary sources handled with profound scholarship, is sometimes
polemical in tone if not in content.[10]

This evaluation of work already done does not imply bad faith
or mendacity on the part of the authors. It merely attempts to
indicate the very real problems facing a historian whose only objective is to discover, with as much accuracy as possible, how this
movement came to be. Discrepancies in the testimony of witnesses, data difficult to locate, and contradictory statements in
contemporary newspapers complicate the problem, but the heart
of the problem is much deeper. It is prejudice based on painful
memories of unchristian contention on both sides that stands between the historian and the truth.

The independent church movement of the Philippines in 1898
was part of the larger resistance within the remnants of the once
great Spanish empire against a home government that dared neither to recognize the nationalist aspirations of the natives nor to
suppress completely their rising expectations. Since the mother
country relied heavily on local authority and the church to main-

Aglipayan Schism in the Philippines," *The Independent*, LXI (1904), 953–
57, written at the request of and with data supplied by Aglipay. Le Roy
had been invalided home before the schism broke out.

[8] Whittemore, *op. cit.*; Isabelo de los Reyes, Jr., "Iglesia Filipina Independiente," *Historical Magazine* [of the PEC], XVIII (1948), 132–37;
"Philippine Church Reborn," *The Christian Century*, LXXXIII (Apr., 1965),
455–56; "Iglesia Filipina Independiente Today," *Pan-Anglican*, X (Fall,
1959), 71–76; Ronald E. Joseph, "The Philippine Independent Catholic
Church," *American Church News* (Jan. 1965), 7–13.

[9] Juan Rivera, "The Aglipayan Movement," *Philippine Social Sciences and
Humanities Review*, IX (1937), 301–28; X (1938), 9–34; Francis H. Wise,
"History of the Philippine Independent Church," Master's thesis, University
of the Philippines, 1954 (mimeographed; Manila, 1965); Donald Dean
Parker, "Church and State in the Philippines," unpublished doctoral dis-
sertation, University of Chicago Divinity School, 1936.

[10] Pedro S. de Achútegui, S.J. and Miguel A. Bernad, S.J., *Religious Revolution in the Philippines*, Vol. I (Manila, 1960), Vol. II (Manila, 1966),
Vol. III (Manila, 1969), and numerous articles in *Philippine Studies*, 1957–
1965.

tain her threatened control, it is not surprising that these two sources of power became primary targets of the propaganda and revolutionary movements. Distinguishing between his faith and his allegiance to the arbitrary authority of the church in purely secular affairs was not difficult for the revolutionist, but it required only the chaos of belligerency to push him into open rebellion in religious matters as well. At first there was no outright, abrupt rejection of either the authority or the doctrines of the church, but there was a gradual worsening of relations which led inevitably to usurpation of authority and the rejection of the Spanish representatives of the church in the islands.

The movement, then, was evolutionary as well as revolutionary and may be studied in three distinct phases, each characterized by a completely different attempt to establish an independent religious authority, nationalistic, autonomous, and Christian.

The first phase, 1898–1901, is the period of revolution against Spain and of insurrection against the United States. Shortly after the outbreak of war between Spain and the United States, Don Basilio Augustín, Spanish governor of the Philippines, and Archbishop Bernardino Nozaleda, archbishop of Manila, appealed to the Filipino people to support Spain against the invasion by heretics, liberals, and "heterodox people possessed of all rancors." [11] The Filipino exiles in Hong Kong countered with a manifesto calculated to inspire resistance to Spain and to encourage hope for independence and cooperation with the United States, by declaring that America was a great Christian nation with seven million Catholics, where parishes flourished under a native clergy with a citizen hierarchy and complete freedom of worship. The manifesto promised that in the government to be established the "native clergy of the country would be those to direct and teach the people from every step of the hierarchy." [12]

This announcement gave the Filipino priests an even greater stake in the revolutionary movement than their natural desire for

[11] Philippine Insurgent Records, 1125.2, War Records, National Archives, Washington, D.C. (hereafter referred to as NA).

[12] Philippine Insurgent Records, 1125.3, NA; "Las Memorias," *Philippine Review*, LV (1919), 468, gives T. M. Kalaw's quotations from Calderón's memoirs; Murat Halstead, *The Story of the Philippines* (Chicago, 1898), pp. 208–303, gives a slightly different version.

national independence, and when General Emilio Aguinaldo returned from exile on May 19, 1898, to lead the revolutionary
army, they supported him wholeheartedly. As the Spaniards, religious and lay, were driven from their posts, Aguinaldo appointed
Father Gregorio Aglipay military chaplain to coordinate the
efforts of the native clergy, to fill vacancies in the parishes, and to
separate the common people from their allegiance to Spain and
draw them to the revolution.[13]

By the time the Malolos Congress met in September 1898 to
draft a constitution for the republic, debate over separation of
church and state already loomed so large that it threatened the
unity of the revolution. The native priests desired union of church
and state as did a large group of the delegates. Apolinario Mabini, chief adviser to Aguinaldo, a staunch supporter of separation, conceived the idea of an independent national church in
union with Rome as a necessary expedient to prevent a serious
rift and to give the republic an opportunity to seek *de jure* recognition by negotiating a concordat with Rome. He managed to
nullify the harm of the separation clause by an amendment holding its implementation in abeyance until a later date, and chose
Father Aglipay as leader of the national church.[14] The revolu-

[13] Gregorio Aglipay Cruz y Labayan (1860–1940) was born in Ilocos
Norte. He was a Catholic priest of the archdiocese of Manila serving in Vic-
toria, Tarlac, when he accepted the post of military chaplain from a secular
authority and exercised ecclesiastical authority by appointing a vicar general,
accepting promotion to military vicar general, issuing pastoral letters, ordering priests to contribute church funds to the revolution. Cited three times to
appear before an ecclesiastical court to answer for his action, he refused to
comply and continued to exercise ecclesiastical authority. On April 29, 1899,
a declaratory sentence stated that he had incurred excommunication by his
actions, and public denunciation followed on May 4, 1899 (Achútegui and
Bernad, *op. cit.*, I, 78; James A. Robertson Papers, Duke University [here-
after referred to as DU]).

[14] Aglipay makes this claim in *Cátedra (Sermonario) de la Iglesia Filipina Independiente* (official edition; Manila, 1932), p. 55. James A. Robertson claims that Mabini chose Aglipay because the latter had not opposed the
regulation concerning civil marriage at Malolos. Robertson bases this on correspondence over the years with Wenceslao Retana (Robertson Papers, DU).
Captain John Roger Meigs Taylor, in *The Philippine Insurrection Against the
United States: A Compilation of Documents With Notes and Introduction*
(ready for publication in the summer of 1906, but withheld by William
Howard Taft, first as Secretary of War, and later as President, so that only

tionary government recognized his appointment as military vicar general as the highest ecclesiastical post in the Philippine church. In this new post Aglipay at once issued a pastoral letter, drafted by Mabini, which organized the revolutionary church, excluding from the ministry native priests who would not renounce allegiance to the Spanish ecclesiastics.[15] By November 1898 he had prevailed upon the old Spanish bishop, José Hevia Campomanes, a prisoner of the revolutionists, to appoint him ecclesiastical governor of the diocese of Nueva Segovia.[16]

Doubtless Aglipay realized the irregularity of his position, but the revolutionary forces held the northern provinces, and the possibility of final victory and complete independence seemed likely. After the Treaty of Paris made America's intentions clear, and the Spanish hierarchy in Manila accepted the military government of the United States, the same reasoning which prompted the insurrection against the Americans was used to justify the continuance of the national church. In October 1899 at the Paniqui Assembly representatives of the native clergy declared their independence of the Spanish hierarchy in the islands and confirmed their allegiance to the Holy See, reiterating their determination to send a delegation to Rome to regularize the procedures they had adopted to meet the emergencies created by revolution. They also confirmed their determination not to accept any foreign bishop unless a general plebiscite of native priests approved him.[17]

This was all highly irregular, but had the Philippine revolution succeeded, Rome might very well have signed a concordat with the republic to regularize the status of the church and to protect the spiritual welfare of the millions of native Catholics. The revolutionists were obviously relying on this long chance. But the

galleys can be consulted), suggests in several places that Aglipay was chosen because up to that time the revolution was a Tagalog affair, and Aguinaldo needed Ilocano help especially after the arrest of Artacho and his difficulty with the Luna brothers (this compilation hereafter referred to as Philippine Insurrection Compilation, NA).

[15] Philippine Insurrection Compilation, A–J E–L 51, Vol. II, NA.

[16] Philippine Insurrection Compilation, A–J E–L 52, Vol. II, NA.

[17] T. M. Kalaw, *Philippine Law Journal* (Dec., 1918), 209–11, quotes the long speech of Aglipay at Paniqui; The Philippine Insurrection Compilation, M–M F–M 26, Vol. II, NA, contains a report of the action taken to send a delegation to Rome.

American forces pressing the revolutionary army northward forced Aguinaldo to disband his forces and resort to guerrilla warfare. Aglipay donned the uniform of a guerrilla and went north as a guerrilla leader. The defeat of the revolutionary forces, the capture of Aguinaldo, and the subsequent surrender of Aglipay and other insurgents by May 1901 brought about the eventual pacification of the Philippines under American control and brought the independent church back under the control of the Spanish hierarchy in Manila.[18]

Had there been at the head of the church in the islands men of heroic stature, capable of seeing beyond the bitterness of all that had happened during the three years of chaos, insubordination, and revolution, or had the apostolic delegate, Placide Louis Chapelle, who arrived in the islands in January 1900 been able to view the whole problem of the church in the islands in the light of what was best for the church in the future, perhaps a religious amnesty could have achieved in the spiritual order what the political one did in the secular order. But Archbishop Chapelle had already been recalled from the islands before Aglipay surrendered, and a Spanish friar bishop held the See of Manila. The arrogance of the righteous and the intransigence of the discredited precluded any amicable settlement,[19] although the state of the church demanded reconciliation.

At most, this attempt to set up an independent church was schismatic, although the native priests may have been heretical in

---

[18] Aglipay's surrender, brought about by the Federal Party in Manila, brought peace to Ilocos Norte, and he retired to the home of a native priest where he remained for some time before going back to Manila.

[19] Several times between 1900–1905 Aglipay was on the verge of reconciliation with the church. Father McKinnon, the chaplain who accompanied Taft and Aglipay on the northern trip in 1901, reported that Aglipay had approached him several times seeking to have the censures removed. McKinnon said that "lack of real penitence and continual dickering with the Protestants, schismatics, politicians, and Catholics to see where he could get the best terms convinced him that he could really do nothing to help Aglipay" (McKinnon to Archbishop Ireland, Sept. 2, 1902, Ireland Papers, Archdiocesan Archives, St. Paul, Minnesota); the retreat with the Jesuits at Santa Ana is also a well-known attempt at reconciliation which did not come off. Robertson and Le Roy both believed that Aglipay was seriously considering a return to the church in 1905 at a time when he was disturbed about doctrine and was not feeling well physically (Robertson Papers, DU).

their attempts to rationalize their irregular position. To dismiss the whole question with the charge that the real issue was the desire of a few native priests to become bishops is crass oversimplification.[20] The whole movement was motivated by nationalism and the desire for political independence as well as recognition of the rights of the native clergy. The subsequent attempts to set up an independent church were radical departures in doctrine as well as authority and seem to have been more political in nature than they were spiritual. One such movement had already begun even before Aglipay surrendered.

In April 1900 Pedro Paterno, president of the Malolos Congress, and Felipe Buencamino, *secretario de fomento* in Aguinaldo's cabinet, returned to Manila and offered their services to William Howard Taft, the American civil governor. By July, competition between them for Taft's favor had developed into open rivalry.[21] They were both among the group of Filipinos who with Dr. Frank Bourns and Arthur Prautch, a defrocked Methodist minister, organized the Federal party to help bring an end to the insurrection and encourage acceptance of American rule. On December 24, 1900, Taft approved the constitution of the party and from that day on used its members in political positions and for special missions, in general showing them great favor.[22]

In January 1901 Buencamino and a few other leaders of the Federal party called upon Dr. James Rodgers, of the Presbyterian mission, to ask his advice about founding an Independent Filipino Evangelical Church. The result of several preliminary meetings was a great rally of the party in Rizal theatre in Tondo, on the first Sunday of February. Here Buencamino invited those

[20] If this were the only cause, we might well raise questions about Fathers McKinnon and Fitzgerald, both of whom worked to become Archbishop of Manila.

[21] Taft to Root, July 26, 1900, Taft Papers, MS. Div., Library of Congress, Washington, D.C. (hereafter referred to as LC); Bernard Moses Diary, Vol. I, June 21, 22, 28, July 18, 1900, University Archives, University of California, Berkeley (hereafter referred to as Moses Diary).

[22] Taft, "Political Parties in the Philippines," *Annals of the American Academy of Political and Social Science*, XX (Sept., 1902), 307–12; Taft to Root, Sept. 22, 1903, Taft Papers, LC.; Methodist Mission Files, New York City, report on Prautch in India dismissed under Question 20 of the Discipline.

present for a political rally to choose between the Roman Catholic Church and the friars and the new freedom and Protestantism. After whipping up considerable emotion he proposed an independent church free from all foreign control. Membership in this church was to be a necessary requirement for membership in the Federal party. Dr. Rodgers tried to explain that a change in politics did not necessarily involve a change in religion. He did not like the political aspects of this movement and tried to steer it into religious channels.[23] Nicolas Zamora and Dr. Homer Stuntz of the Methodist Church spoke in the same vein as Buencamino. On this note the meeting adjourned to meet again the following Sunday. None of the Roman Catholic members of the Federal party appeared for the second meeting, and Buencamino pointed to this as proof that Catholics were controlled by the priests and that only increased membership in both the party and the church would break this control.

By this time knowledge of the turn taken by the Federal party reached Taft, who had no intention of aiding a politically sponsored independent church movement. He sent for the board of directors of the party and required them to pass strong resolutions disavowing any connection with the church in Tondo and stating that members of the Federal party were free to belong to any church they wished. He also demanded a strong resolution on separation of church and state. Membership in the Tondo church dropped off considerably, while the Federal party continued to grow. The second attempt to establish an independent Filipino church tied to a powerful government had failed.[24]

The third attempt to establish an independent church began in much the same way, but involved many disparate elements. It was this very diversity of groups within the movement which eventually brought about its success, for at several points it seemed as if this movement too would collapse. One of the im-

[23] Dr. James Rodgers, "Religious Conditions in the Philippines," *Missionary Review of the World*, XIV (1901), 605; *Outlook*, LXVII (1901), 471–72.

[24] Taft to Mrs. Bellamy Storer, wife of the American Ambassador to Spain, Feb. 22, 1901, in which Taft gives a report of the meeting, a copy of the resolutions, and assures her the party will not be used for religious purposes (Taft Papers, LC).

portant elements was controlled by Isabelo de los Reyes y Floren-
tina, a journalist, radical, and amateur theologian.[25] His out-
spoken revolutionary writings had brought him into conflict
with the Spanish government in 1896, and he was thrown into
prison where he addressed a Memorial, violently antifriar and revolutionary, to the Spanish governor, Primo de Rivera. For this he
was transferred to Montjuich prison in Barcelona, where his ab-
ject letters to Spanish authorities denied his antifriar writings.[26]
After his release he published *Filipinas ante Europa,* an anticlerical, anti-American newspaper, advocating continued revolution.
In 1899, after the Paniqui Assembly of the Filipino priests, he was
commissioned to negotiate for the revolutionary government with
the Spanish Papal Nuncio for the release of friar prisoners in exchange for *de jure* recognition of the Malolos government and
the rights of the native clergy. Having failed to bring this off successfully, he supported a policy of complete break with Rome and
an independent church.[27] On September 21, 1901, most of the
original members of the Malolos government having surrendered
to the Americans, the revolutionary junta meeting in London
created a "government in exile" to carry on the work for independence. Isabelo de los Reyes was given the post of Secretary of the
Interior, an office which carried with it authority to approve appointments of parish priests and other church-state relations

[25] Isabelo de los Reyes (1864–1938), born in Ilocos Sur. In a letter to
James A. Robertson, May 3, 1903, he claimed to be the founder of the Independent Church. James A. Le Roy, having read this letter to Robertson
commented: "As to the founding of the schism, there is some justice to his
claim. Without his presence Aglipay would never have taken so decided
a step; and without Reyes, the movement would have died in its beginning" (both letters in the James A. Robertson Papers, MS. Div., LC);
Lewis Whittemore, *op. cit.,* p. 106, claims that Aglipay was *not* the founder,
nor was Isabelo de los Reyes (italics his) and that this was some sort of
spontaneous revolution in which they but served as catalysts. Using a meta-
phor of "smoking flax catching fire," he tries to account for the outbreak of
the schism as a sort of spontaneous combustion. The facts do not support
his contention. The term "catalyst" was first used in a different sense by
Achútegui and Bernad, *op. cit.,* I, 180.

[26] Personal File, Isabelo de los Reyes, File 1239, Bureau of Insular Affairs, NA.

[27] Philippine Insurrection Compilation, Taylor MS., A–J E–L, 51–53, Vol.
II, NA.

under the Malolos constitution.[28] On October 15, 1901, having been fully assured of amnesty by the United States and armed with the office of Secretary of the Interior, Isabelo de los Reyes returned to the islands.[29]

On October 25 Isabelo de los Reyes appeared before the Philippine Commission seeking permission to publish and send through the mails a newspaper called *El Defensor de Filipinas,* a sample of which he brought with him. Permission was refused because of the seditious nature of the writings, but he was back with another project by October 31 in company with Pedro Paterno and Pascual Poblete, radical politicians well known to the commission. The opinion recorded by Bernard Moses, former professor of political science at the University of California, who was serving on the commission, is illuminating. He wrote:

Paterno, Poblete and Reyes . . . fancy they have a large part of the population ready to follow after them in their several careers of political leadership. As thinkers on practical questions they are simply pitiable, and are significant only by the fact that in the presence of an ignorant and benighted people they are still capable of doing much harm.

They have been thrown to the surface under a system that empha-

[28] Philippine Insurrection Compilation, Exhibit 1190, C–V, F–M, 95, Vol. V, NA.

[29] Laubach, *op. cit.,* p. 138, states that he arrived in July; Juan Rivera, *op. cit.,* claims that he arrived on July 3, 1901; Whittemore, *op. cit.,* says he returned in June or July. Yet, when Taft was making his trip through the Ilocos country in August 1901 with Aglipay and others, he received the petition of Isabelo de los Reyes for the right to return with impunity if he took the oath of allegiance. His report of this petition is dated August 27, 1901 (Taft Papers, LC). This date is very important in the light of the meeting of the junta in September. Isabelo de los Reyes himself claimed on several occasions that he had been offered episcopal consecration in London if he would return to the islands and establish a Protestant church to break the monopoly of the friars. Antonio Regidor made the same claim without naming the person to whom the offer had been made (Philippine Insurrection Compilation, Exhibit 10, F–Z, H–A, 86, Vol. I, NA) and indicated that de los Reyes closed his newspaper with the announcement that the insurrection was at an end, took the oath of allegiance, and returned to the islands. The "Memorandum Regarding Isabelo de los Reyes" in Philippine Insurgent Records, File 930, Folio 33, states that he returned October 15, 1901.

sized and laid stress on shallow egotism and gave great credit for self-assertion.[30]

On November 1 Isabelo de los Reyes appeared at open hearings to oppose the Sedition Bill which was under discussion and convinced his hearers that the position he upheld was utter anarchism. On November 15 he arranged for a meeting with Protestant missionaries in the office of the American Bible Society in the walled city.[31] Present with de los Reyes were Father Aglipay, Dr. Homer Stuntz, Dr. James Rodgers, Jay C. Goodrich, and Jesse B. McLaughlin of the Bible Society and perhaps some others. This meeting, so like that held earlier by Buencamino, was aimed at setting up an independent Filipino church, and Aglipay invited the Protestant missionaries to join the native clergy in leading a schism from the Roman Catholic Church which would split it asunder. The missionaries having listened to the plan demanded more radical changes before making common cause with them, such as making the Bible sole rule of faith, ending the celibacy of the clergy, and doing away with Mariolatry.[32] If assurances could be given that these things would be carried out, then the Protestant missionaries would consider some sort of cooperation with them. The two Filipinos promised to think these things over, but no further meetings were held with the Protestant missionaries.[33]

[30] Moses Diary, Vol. VI, Oct. 16–Dec. 12, 1901, has entries concerning Isabelo de los Reyes, usually linked with Poblete and Paterno for Oct. 25, 31, and Nov. 1, 1901. Moses was, however, an imperialist.

[31] Laubach, op. cit., p. 139, says this meeting took place in August 1902 and quotes Stuntz as proof; Stuntz in The Philippines and the Far East, p. 489, says it was August 1901. Rivera, op. cit., p. 309, says the meeting took place August 1902, but he also quotes Stuntz. Isabelo de los Reyes in his letter to Robertson, loc. cit., says the meeting was held in November. Jesse McLaughlin who wrote his report on Nov. 15, 1902, says that "one year ago today" the meeting which launched the Aglipayan schism took place in his office (Roll 21, microfilm of correspondence of the Methodist Church in the Philippines, 1898–1912, Methodist Library, New York).

[32] Stuntz, The Philippines and the Far East, pp. 489–90.

[33] Whittemore, op. cit., pp. 99–100, discusses at great length the seeming hostility of Protestant missionaries to the Filipino representatives. He also quotes Dr. Donald A. McGavran, who in Encounter (Indianapolis, Summer, 1958), chided the Protestant groups for their lack of charity and foresight. But both of these men are writing in the ecumenical climate of the present,

Instead, two meetings of the native clergy of the Ilocos were held in January and May, 1902, leading toward schism. The second of these, held at Kullabeng, May 8, 1902, is of special importance, for it was at this meeting that Ilocano clergy split on doctrinal questions, one group wishing to retain the doctrine of the Trinity as taught by the Roman Catholic Church and the other, more radical group, calling for doctrinal changes leaning toward Unitarianism.[34] At this meeting Father Aglipay was able to restrain those who wished to declare an immediate schism by calling for more time to organize all the native clergy of the islands.

When Aglipay returned to Manila he found Isabelo de los Reyes deeply involved in labor organization. The first strike, launched June 3, 1902, was against E. C. McCullough Company, a printer who did much of the government's printing. Because such work came under the supervision of Secretary Moses, Aglipay took more than ordinary interest in the activities of de los Reyes, founder of *Unión Obrera Democrática,* and his labor agitation.[35] The strike reached much greater proportions than de los Reyes had anticipated, and he was glad to settle the matter by arbitration,[36] for he already had other irons in the fire.[37] More-

---

and seemingly with little understanding of the competitive type of Christianity which was regarded as orthodox by all but a few clergymen in 1901. For those missionaries who were also imperialists, any other attitude would have been out of character.

[34] See Achútegui and Bernad, *op. cit.,* I, 162–63, on the testimony of Santiago Fonacier, second *Obispo Maximo* of the *Iglesia Filipina Independiente.*

[35] On June 3, 1902, Moses records in his diary: "In the last few days Isabelo de los Reyes has again come to the surface, this time as a labor agitator and president of a union of laborers. He is not a laborer . . . and pretends to be concerning himself with the affairs of the laborers in order to further their welfare. The facts of the case seem to be that he is an incorrigible agitator and is using the poor laborer as a means of making himself conspicuous. The morning papers in considering the latest phase of the labor movement affirm that Pedro Paterno is behind Reyes and in sympathy with his projects for disturbing social affairs in Manila" (Moses Diary, Vol. VIII).

[36] *Manila American*, June 3–9, 1902.

[37] On July 4, 1902, a parade to celebrate American Independence Day was held and Moses records: "Isabelo de los Reyes, the self-styled tribune of the people, appeared followed by a small squad of persons whom he is trying to inspire with the principles of discontent. He halted before the

over, he had found another loyal co-worker in Dominador Gómez, who had returned to the islands in February.[38] Under de los Reyes' direction the UOD was really a political party, as is evident from its newspaper *Le Redencion del Obrero*.

For almost a year negotiations had been going on, initiated by the Holy See, for a meeting to discuss problems of church and state in the Philippines.[39] These negotiations had been handled by Archbishop Ireland of St. Paul directly with the Secretary of War and the President of the United States during the winter months of 1901, and William Howard Taft's arrival in Washington late in January 1902 following absence from the islands because of illness made it possible for him to accept the mission to treat with Rome.[40] Accompanied by Judge James F. Smith, district court judge in Manila, and Major John Biddle Porter, as secretary to Taft, the mission joined Bishop Thomas O'Gorman, of Sioux Falls, in Rome. Of primary concern was the problem of the friars, their extensive agricultural lands, and other problems of lesser importance.

Agitation against the friars had increased as soon as it was known that the delegation was discussing these questions in

---

stand to give three cheers for America and to make an address to the acting-governor and then passed on. His bearing and performance helped deepen the impression which he has already made that he is a demagogue, but neither brave nor skillful" (Moses Diary, Vol. VIII). Further entries of the like nature continued during a very much disturbed summer.

[38] Dominador Gómez was born in Manila in 1866 and left the islands for Europe in 1877 to complete studies in medicine. He joined the medical corps of the Spanish army in 1895 and served in Cuba throughout the Spanish-American War. When he returned to Madrid at war's end he associated himself with Isabelo de los Reyes in *Filipinas ante Europa* to which he had contributed even while in the Spanish army under the pen name Ramiro Franko. During the summer of 1902 Aglipay and Isabelo de los Reyes visited him at his home to ask him to take over the presidency of the UOD, which he did, finally, in September, 1902 (Brief for the Appellant in *The United States* vs. *Dominador Gómez* filed by Attorneys William A. Kincaid and Rafael del Pan [Manila, 1904]; see also File 11446, Bureau of Insular Affairs, NA).

[39] Cardinal Rompolla to Archbishop Ireland, May 23, 1901; Ireland to Taft, Aug. 19, 1901; Taft to Root, Sept. 26, 1901; Ireland to Root, Oct. 13, 1901; Root to Taft, Sept. 5, 1901; Archbishop Ireland to Cardinal Gibbons, Nov. 7, 1901 (Taft Papers and Root Papers, LC; Ireland Papers, St. Paul).

[40] Formal Instructions, May 9, 1902, from Root to Taft (Taft Papers, LC).

Rome, and newspapers, theatrical performances, rallies, and other propaganda weapons against them were supported in Manila by those who wished to force the withdrawal of the friars by the Holy See.

As the summer dragged by, reports of the failure of Taft's mission were carried in the daily press, and propaganda was increased. On June 29, 1902, Pascual Poblete's newspaper *El Grito del Pueblo* issued invitations to a meeting to be held July 29 in the Zorilla Theatre for the purpose of protesting the return of the friars. The meeting, however, was banned,[41] and Isabelo de los Reyes, who had expected to be one of the speakers, called a meeting of his *Unión Obrera Democrática* for August 3, 1902, in the *Centro de Bellas Artes* for the same purpose. The meeting was held, but whether or not Isabelo de los Reyes gave his now famous speech at this meeting or only published it in the reports of the meeting is still a matter of debate with historians.[42] Certain it is that the speech was published. According to the *Manila American* Isabelo de los Reyes had proposed the inauguration of a new independent church to be called *Iglesia Filipina Independiente* and proposed an entirely original organizational structure for it. The lay council was to be composed of Pascual Poblete, Dominador Gómez, Martin Ocampo, Rafael Palma, Aurelio Torentino, José Albert, Xerxes Burgos, Paulino Zamora[43] and several other less well-known nationalists. The priestly council from which new bishops for the church would be chosen was made up of sixteen native priests. Gregorio Aglipay was named to serve as *Obispo Maximo,* while the honorary presidents were:

[41] Who banned this meeting is still a question. Whittemore, *op. cit.,* p. 102, says that Taft cabled his lack of success and that authorities banned the meeting. However, the commission received the order to ban agitation against the friars on Aug. 15, 1902, according to Secretary Moses' entry in his diary for Aug. 15 (Moses Diary, Vol. IX).

[42] Achútegui and Bernad, *op. cit.,* I, 184, quotes the statement of the secretary Hermenegildo Cruz, of the UOD, that at this meeting the church question was never even raised.

[43] Paulino Zamora was the nephew of Fr. Jacinto Zamora, one of the three priests executed in 1872, and father of Nicolas Zamora, the first ordained Filipino Protestant minister. See the essay which follows in this volume, "Nicolas Zamora: Religious Nationalist" by Richard L. Deats. Buencamino was at this time in the United States and returned on August 28, after Taft's return.

William Howard Taft, Pardo de Tavera, and Emilio Aguinaldo. Most of them had never been consulted as to whether or not they wished to take part in this new church, and one after another they began to decline the nominations.

Gregorio Aglipay was not present at this meeting, and on August 20 he sent out circulars to the native clergy inviting them to a meeting to discuss their problems, assuring them that there was no schism planned.[44] "Resignations" appeared in the *Manila American* for several days afterwards. The office of civil government refused the honor for Taft, and during his lifetime the IFI never asserted this claim, although Taft was referred to as the "grandfather" and the "president" on the occasion in 1931, when Aglipay placed a wreath on Taft's grave in Arlington Cemetery.[45]

[44] *Libertas,* Aug. 11, 1902; *La Democracia,* Mar. 20, 1904.

[45] One of the characteristics of the Independent Church from the beginning has been "name dropping" to attach some sort of prestige to the movement. Aglipay frequently does it. Lewis Whittemore does also when he refers to some sort of an understanding between Aglipay and Taft, whereby Aglipay held off the schism so as not to embarrass Taft's negotiation in Rome (Whittemore, *op. cit.,* pp. 100, 101, 105 and elsewhere). See also Richard L. Deats, *Nationalism and Christianity in the Philippines* (Dallas, 1967), p. 76, who reiterates the myth that Taft introduced Aglipay to Unitarian literature. Taft's own words make this claim absurd. He wrote to Lyman Abbott, a well-known Protestant clergyman: "The respectable Filipinos generally do not separate themselves from the Church, but they are all waiting to see what will be the real attitude of the Apostolic Delegate and unless it be quite radical I fear the Church of Rome will have a long controversy and contest on its hands with the Filipino Church. . . . I do not hesitate to say that the establishment of the church under priests of the character of Aglipay and his fellow schismatics will not be to the interest of good morals and religious betterment of the Islands" (Taft to Lyman Abbott, Dec. 26, 1902, Taft Papers, LC).

At the November 1965 meeting of the Philadelphia Branch of the Catholic Clerical Union at St. Ambrose Episcopal Church, Bishop Isabelo de los Reyes, Jr., explaining his determination to seek intercommunion with the Episcopal Church, said: "During this era (World War II) we realized every day we were praying for the return of Douglas MacArthur. Yesterday we had prayed for Admiral Dewey, and the father of Douglas MacArthur, General Arthur MacArthur, who emancipated us from Spain. Now we prayed for another great Episcopalian to emancipate us, Douglas MacArthur. Why should we not give our people, we thought, the superior brand of Christianity, of Catholicism, represented by a Church that produces men like Dewey, Pershing, and Douglas MacArthur and President Roosevelt and

Isabelo de los Reyes' labor troubles occupied more of his time than the infant church which he had announced so unexpectedly on August 3, so that when striking tobacco workers at Malabon, who were willing to return to work when their strike failed, were threatened with assassination by three members of the *Unión Obrera* and force was employed to keep them from returning to work, the hue and cry went out for the president of the *Unión*, and Isabelo de los Reyes and four others were arrested on August 12.[46] On August 17 the *Manila American* announced that the *Iglesia Filipina Independiente* seemed to have died before it was born. But there was a little life still left in the movement. Two external forces had a great deal to do with saving it. One was Arthur Prautch, and the other was the return of Taft with the results of the friars' land negotiations.

The day following Aglipay's manifesto of August 20 against the

---

Bishop Brent and all those great Episcopalians who appeared in the Philippines and made history there?" quoting from the report by Rev. Ronald E. Joseph of the Protestant Episcopal Church in *American Church News* (Jan., 1965), pp. 7–13.

Or again in explaining his acceptance of episcopal consecration from the Episcopal Church he said: "I went to the great public squares of the Philippines and said: 'People would you rather have Apostolic Succession from the Church of Benito Mussolini and his relatives or from the Church of General Douglas MacArthur who brought American G.I. boys to liberate us?' And the people answered: 'A million times we will follow the Apostolic Succession from the Church of Douglas MacArthur' " (*ibid.*).

[46] *Manila American*, Aug. 15, and *Cablenews*, Aug. 15–16, 1902, stated that after the threats became known the leaders of the *Unión* went into hiding. On Aug. 21, the *Manila Times* stated: "There is much more in the case of Isabelo de los Reyes than appears on the surface and it is probable that he will be called upon to explain certain other affiliations than those of his Labor Union. . . . In the meantime the prisoner remains in jail at Malabon."

On Aug. 15, *The Christian Advocate*, whose editor was Jesse McLaughlin, stated: "This past week witnessed an incipient ecclesiastical revolution in the Islands, the formation of the Filipino Church. What this schismatic movement will amount to only time will tell, but its beginnings are not at all propitious. Señor Aglipay, its nominal head, was the chief spiritual adviser to Aguinaldo's regime. He is, to all appearances, a cool, deliberate man. We believe that he sincerely and earnestly desires the good of the Filipino people, but he is only a figurehead. The real leaders of the movement are political fanatics. In their appointment of officials, they showed no sense of discrimination, having appointed some who are diametrically opposed to their movement and others who are absolutely disinterested."

church, Arthur Prautch defended the position of the Filipino clergy in a long article in the *Manila Times*. This was the first public defense of the movement, and it was skillfully written to serve as a rallying cry. Prautch predicted that should the leaders of the Filipino clergy not raise a hand to propagate the church, nor strive to spread the idea outside the city of Manila, still by the very nature of the abuse to which the Filipino national pride had been subjected, this movement could not die. Its impetus, he said, was from within, and therefore what did it matter if the founder of the church languished in prison, the Filipino people of their own accord would carry the movement through.[47]

There may have been little more than wishful thinking in this argument, for the three men most closely associated with the movement had not come to its support. Poblete had cold feet, Aglipay had repudiated it, and de los Reyes had more important problems to solve. But Prautch took up the same argument the following day saying:

I am simply amazed at *Libertas'* attempt to show there is nothing in the matter but the silly agitation of three bad men. Those who know Archbishop Aglipay, Poblete and de los Reyes know that they have their fingers on the public pulse, and come pretty near being able to gauge public Filipino sentiment; and if the charge be true that they are in this movement for the revenue only and if there be nothing else in the movement, they are bigger fools than their enemies reckon them.[48]

And on the day this article appeared Taft returned to the islands from Rome with the report of his negotiations with the Vatican. True, report of his failure had preceded him to Manila by cable, but still there had seemed hope of pulling success out of the failure of the mission. Had Taft been able to state categorically that the government would buy the friars' land and that the friars would be withdrawn immediately, the schism might have received its quietus, as Taft claimed and as many historians have conjectured.[49] However, had the friars been withdrawn, and

[47] *Manila Times*, Aug. 21, 1902.   [48] *Manila Times*, Aug. 22, 1902.
[49] Taft to Roosevelt, Nov. 9, 1902; Taft to Archbishop Ireland, Oct. 17, 1902; to Senator Henry A. Cooper, Nov. 24, 1902; to Salvator Cortesi for

American priests taken their places, the schism would have continued unabated since the complaint was against any foreign priests or bishops. Had no foreign priests been brought in, the Filipino clergy would have found the task impossible, since there were more than seven million Catholics and about 600 native priests at most.

Here matters stood until September. Isabelo de los Reyes was still in jail, and Dominador Gómez took over the *Unión Obrero.* At some time early in September Gregorio Aglipay decided to join the movement, and on September 22 issued under his own signature as *Obispo Maximo,* and that of Isabelo de los Reyes as Executive President, and of Simeon Mandac as Executive Secretary, the first of six Epistles which gave form and organization to the *Iglesia Filipina Independiente.*[50] No public services or demonstration took place, however, until the native clergy in the Ilocos, particularly the more radical group, took action. On October 1, Pedro Brillantes took possession of St. James Church in Bacarra as his cathedral and announced himself as Bishop of Ilocos Norte, setting the date of his consecration for October 20. Whether even he believed that this action was irrevocable separation from Rome is rather difficult to ascertain, for on the eve of his "consecration" by twenty-four of his priests he wrote to a friend:

Without being dependent or independent, I am merely Filipino, Catholic, Apostolic and Divine, and for this reason I shall be conse-

---

Archbishop Satolli, Dec. 26, 1902; and others (Taft Papers, LC); James A. Le Roy, *Philippine Life in Town and Country* (New York, 1905), pp. 162–63; James A. Robertson, "Aglipayan Schism," *American Catholic Historical Review,* IV (Oct., 1918), 315–44; Laubach, *op. cit.,* pp. 140–41.

[50] The First Epistle, Sept. 22, rationalized the position of "bishops" in the IFI; the Second Epistle, Oct. 2, denied that the church was a schism and gave further instructions to bishops; the Third Epistle, Oct. 17, concerned itself with the doctrines of the church; the Fourth Epistle, Oct. 29, concerned theological training, organization of local churches, participation of women (this epistle is very important since it was signed by fifteen "bishops" who accepted their appointments); the Fifth Epistle, Dec. 8, was an answer to Leo XIII's Apostolic Constitution for the Philippines; the Sixth Epistle, Aug. 17, 1903, was aimed at the Filipino clergy who failed to join the schism, but who also refused obedience to the Holy See, which position Aglipay thought untenable. These six became the important basic doctrinal works of the IFI.

crated *ritu divino et apostolico*. I shall recognize the Pope if he recognizes me and gives up his diplomacy and his politics which are so oppressive to Filipinos. If he turns away from his errors, I shall absolve him.[51]

By this action Brillantes, of course, incurred excommunication from the Roman Catholic Church.

The formal inauguration of the Independent Church in Manila was set for October 26, when *Obispo Maximo* Aglipay, although not yet "consecrated," was to celebrate a pontifical Mass in an improvised chapel in the living quarters of a friend over the drug store in Tondo. All of the Manila newspapers carried the story. *Libertas, Noticiero,* and *El Mercantile,* three Spanish newspapers, protested against the ceremony as a sacrilegious farce in which not even the participants had a true belief.[52] One Spanish liberal paper, *El Progreso,* commented:

Against the winds and floods and notwithstanding all the prophecies of failure which were made as soon as the idea of a Filipino Church was suggested by those who were dissatisfied with the course of Catholicism in the Islands, the Filipino Church is born and will today claim its share of authority over the consciences of the people.[53]

The four Filipino newspapers approved wholeheartedly of the schism and praised all who had any part in initiating the new movement. *La Democracia,* organ of the Federal party, announced:

The die is cast! Padre Aglipay has crossed the Rubicon of intransigency and absolutism, with the decision and energy of a Roman captain. It has been a blow, a death blow to Catholic unity in the Philip-

---

[51] Achútegui and Bernad, *op. cit.,* I, 194.

[52] Taft was anxious to know precisely what was happening and ordered that copies of all newspapers carrying the story of the inauguration ceremonies should be preserved. Clippings from Spanish, Filipino, and English language papers were collected, and translations were made. The complete story of the two days of celebration is contained in these clippings. They were later sent to the Bureau of Insular Affairs, but translations and copies of the clippings were also filed in the Taft Papers where they may still be consulted (Taft Papers, LC).

[53] *El Progreso,* Oct. 26, 1902.

pines. The spark will cause a blaze. And what is the cause of this religious secession? In appearance it is the matter of hierarchy. In reality, it is the assertion of the dignity of the people, the last consequence of the revolution, which in order to be complete requires religious liberty.[54]

Thousands of people crowded the Paseo Azcarraga to attend the pontifical Mass, and so the altar was erected out of doors where all could see. Both *El Grito del Pueblo* and the *Unión Obrero* were represented. Felipe Buencamino was also present. His mother-in-law, Saturnina S. de Abreu, and his sister-in-law, Adelaide de Abreu Hollman, became officers of the women's council, which became a very strong force in drawing members to the new church. Isabelo de los Reyes, of course, was present as a major officer of the new movement. Thus most of the forces which had been at work from early days and two previous attempts to set up an independent church came together in the end.

To further cement the nationalist tie which bound the members, Aglipay announced a special memorial Mass for the heroes of the revolution, Rizal, Burgos, Gómez, Zamora, and other heroes and for all the insurgents who had died in the struggle for freedom, to be held on All Souls' Day, November 2.

On the morning of All Souls' Day, Father Gregorio Tabar, a native priest of Peñafrancia, who had not joined the schism, went to his church to say Mass as usual. He found the door locked and the keys removed from their accustomed place, while printed on the outer wall of the church were the words "Iglesia Catolica Filipina Independiente." Father Tabar crossed out the last two words, opened the door with a crow bar, and celebrated Mass with a few women for congregation. After Mass, he locked the door and started for his rectory. On the way he met Isabelo de los Reyes, who asked permission for Aglipay to use this church for the memorial Mass. Father Tabar refused, a crowd gathered, and only the timely arrival of police saved the native priest from attack. When Aglipay arrived and found the church locked, he decided to celebrate the Mass in the open air under the *ilang-ilang* trees. Father Tabar stood disconsolately on the edge of the crowd

[54] *La Democracia*, Oct. 26, 1902.

and when asked by a reporter who he thought was the real power behind the church he answered, "I am not sure whether it is Padre Aglipay or Isabelo de los Reyes."[55]

Isabelo de los Reyes, himself, has answered that question. In his own claim to be "sole" founder of the *Iglesia Filipina Independiente,* he says:

As a result I was able to bring about the schism, against wind and waves, against the rooted Catholicism of the Filipinos, against conservative Filipinos and against Americans who looked with suspicion at any reforms as possibly leading to a political insurrection (which was an error on their part); and finally against the Filipino priests themselves, including Monsignor Aglipay, who on the 20 of that same August 1902 sent around a printed circular disapproving the schism. The only true founder, then, of the Philippine Church is the undersigned.[56]

There is a certain inconsistency in the names applied to the independent church. Although the schism was initiated by Isabelo de los Reyes, and although he composed all of the doctrinal works published under Aglipay's name and gave the church its peculiar organization and structure, it was frequently called *Aglipayan,* but was never referred to as the church of de los Reyes.

Membership in the church grew by leaps and bounds, whole congregations going over to the schism when a native priest changed his allegiance. And as the membership increased church facilities were needed. Many illegal seizures of Roman Catholic churches created a state of civil disorder, which finally came to a head in Manila when the parish priest of Pandacan, a suburb of Manila, was attacked by irate women who tried to force the priest to join the schism. He was scratched and bitten, and the keys of the church were taken. The women opened the church only for Aglipay. As the priest, Father Sorrondo, tried to retrieve his keys, he was arrested for assault, and the matter came to Taft's attention. The priest was acquitted by the court of first in-

[55] *Cablenews,* Nov. 3, 1902; also, a series of undated clippings from *Manila Times* and *Manila American* (Bureau of Insular Affairs, NA).
[56] Letter to James A. Robertson, May 3, 1908 (Robertson Papers, LC).

stance, and Taft ordered the women to return the keys; however, a group of Aglipayans, headed by Felipe Buencamino, called on Taft urging that the pastor of the Pandacan church be ousted and that Aglipay be installed, since this was the will of the people. Taft ordered the keys turned over to the chief of police to be returned to the pastor and read Buencamino a lecture on his poor taste as an official in mixing with this movement.[57]

Meanwhile the apostolic delegate, Archbishop Giovanni B. Guidi, was on his way to Manila to deal with Taft on the various matters of church and state which had been discussed in Rome. He was bringing with him the new apostolic constitution for the Philippines from Leo XIII. Taft was anxious that the discussions be fruitful and, knowing that the archbishop knew nothing of the schism, nor of the state of the church in the islands, decided that he would invite him to stay at Malacañang palace, as his guest, rather than with the friar-bishop of Manila.[58] This invitation Archbishop Guidi felt required by courtesy to refuse, as he was unaware of the tremendous impact his staying with Taft would have had on the religious situation in the islands.

The papal constitution, *Quae Mari Sinico*, was the Holy See's answer to the turmoil. It acknowledged the change of sovereignty in the islands, reorganized the Philippines with new dioceses to be created, promised positions of responsibility to native clergy, warned against participation in politics, gave directions for the seminaries, exhorted the clergy to holiness, and raised the University of Santo Tomás to a pontifical institute. The question of who should serve as parish priests was left to the bishops, and all were exhorted to return to obedience.

In many ways the papal constitution was disappointing even to the Catholics who remained faithful and who had expected greater understanding from the Holy See. For the schismatics it was completely unacceptable and became a rallying cry for turn-

---

[57] Taft to Root, Nov. 11, 1902; to Roosevelt, Nov. 9; to Le Roy, Nov. 9 (Taft Papers, LC).

[58] Taft to Roosevelt, Nov. 9, 1902; cable to Archbishop Guidi, Nov. 11, 1902; and Guidi's response from the steamer *Talpoora* the same day (Taft Papers, LC).

ing whole congregations against the Holy See.[59] From this point on there was no turning back. The schism was permanent.

Several major problems faced the new church: getting sufficient clergy to serve the tremendously large number of adherents who were supporting the church, securing buildings where religious services could be held, and regularizing the consecration of bishops, which though rationalized in the First Epistle continued to trouble Aglipay, and indeed troubled Isabelo de los Reyes himself. The solutions to these problems were needed immediately, and being decided in haste, brought their own train of secondary problems.

In order to secure enough ministers for the church, men with little or no training were ordained.[60] Each bishop tried to ordain a sufficient number to cover his own territory adequately, yet no formal seminary program was set up either by any diocese or by the central authority for a long time.

The problem of securing places of worship was solved, after Taft's "Declaration of Peaceable Possession" stated that a man in possession of a church could not be dislodged except through legal action in the courts, by seizing *visitas* and churches where no resident pastor had been appointed, or by holding the church when a native priest took his whole congregation over to the Aglipayan belief. These churches were the possession of the Roman Catholic Church and, as such, their title was protected by the Treaty of Paris. Taft, however, demanded that the church institute civil action to regain this property both for the sake of public order and to set legal precedents for future litigation. Because this took a great deal of time and expense and because the Roman Catholic Church thought the burden of the proof should fall on the usurpers, few cases were brought to court during the first few years, and the Philippine Independent Church managed

[59] Epistle V, Dec. 8, 1902, was published on the same day as the proclamation of *Quae Mari Sinico*. The contents of the document were known throughout Manila before this formal proclamation of the document which makes possible the opposition on the same day as the proclamation.

[60] David Prescott Barrows, Mar. 17, 1909, recorded in his diary that, at one place he visited, the Aglipayan bishop "makes young men into priests for one hundred pesos" (Barrows Papers, University of California).

to hold them. When court decisions began to return the church property to the Roman Catholic Church, after 1906, the tremendous boom in membership began to decline.

Other factors which influenced the decline were the steadfast adherence to the Roman Catholic Church of numerous native clergy in all parts of the islands, particularly in Ilocos, where such intransigence was punished by bodily harm; the appointment of American bishops and reopening of the Roman Catholic seminaries; the discovery and exposure of a revolt in Ilocos Norte led by Simeon Mandac, executive secretary of the *Iglesia Filipina Independiente,* and his consequent conviction for murder and sedition; [61] the failure of Aglipay to secure "apostolic succession" from Bishop Brent of the Protestant Episcopal Church or Bishop Herzog of the Old Catholic Church in Switzerland, in spite of the efforts of Miguel Morayta, a Spanish Mason to bring it about.[62]

[61] File 4865, Item 53, Bureau of Insular Affairs, NA, records: "Mandac first came to notice in 1904, when he was appointed clerk in the provincial government of Ilocos Norte, but after a short time was dismissed on account of dishonesty. He was next heard of in the campaign preceding the last political election, when he was one of 16 candidates for provincial governor of Ilocos Norte, to which he was elected by a majority of five votes. He was subsequently brought to trial for murder, found guilty and sentenced to prison for fourteen years. While on bail pending an appeal he took to the woods with a small following endeavoring to create an insurrection. . . ."

William Cameron Forbes, Journals, Series One, Vol. IV, Sept. 4, 1910, LC, records that Mandac announced that Aglipay had appointed him ecclesiastical governor of the islands and that Aglipayans, priests, and people, were bound to feed and protect him at all costs.

[62] Conversations between Bishop Brent and Aglipay relative to his consecration are contained in "Private Addendum for Bishops Only" in Bishop Brent's papers in the MS. Div., LC., File 1904. In spite of his desire to aid Aglipay, Bishop Brent believed that a certain lack of candor and refusal to state the exact terms under which he would accept consecration from the Episcopal Church made him hesitate to recommend any positive action. Aglipay was at the same time negotiating for consecration with Bishop Herzog of the Old Catholic Church of Berne. Both Aglipay and Brent received invitations to attend the convention of the Swiss National Church. Brent then began a correspondence with Bishop Herzog in which Herzog revealed that he had been brought to believe by Aglipay that he was a validly consecrated bishop in schism from Rome. When Bishop Herzog laid down the terms for consecration, Aglipay abandoned the attempt (Herzog letters, July 31, 1904, Aug. 16, 1904, Brent Papers, MS. Div., LC).

Another possible reason was the elevation, in 1906, of Father Jorge Barlin, a Filipino, to the episcopacy of the Roman Catholic Church.

In spite of all these factors which became serious obstacles, the Philippine Independent Church might still have maintained its influence had it not been for internal conflict over changes in doctrine and practice. These were introduced by Aglipay at the urging of Isabelo de los Reyes, but they were largely brought about by outside influence.

Sometime in the 1920's, Frank Laubach, Congregational missionary to the Philippines, met, while on furlough to the United States, Dr. John Lathrop, a Unitarian clergyman. The two conversed at length, and Laubach told Lathrop of the schismatic church of the Philippines which had successfully challenged the power of Rome. Dr. Lathrop sent the story on to the president of the Unitarian Association, Dr. Louis C. Cornish, who was anxious to contact this "spearhead of liberal thought in the strategic outpost for freedom in the Orient represented by the Philippines." [63] Cornish contacted Aglipay and suggested that two Unitarians who were going to India as representatives for the American Unitarian Association for the centenary of the *Brahmo Samaj*, Dr. Lathrop and Dr. Reese, should stop in the Philippines also and visit the Aglipayan church. At the conference which followed, the Unitarians and the Aglipayans discovered that they had much in common.

The following year in July 1929 Gregorio Aglipay announced that he would abolish the Mass and adopt a simple ceremony of distribution of bread, following the example of Christ on the mountain. This touched off a struggle within the Philippine Independent Church between the radicals, who followed Aglipay in his Unitarian leanings and the conservatives who opposed the changes. From this point on the Aglipayan publications became more Unitarian in thought, although possibly many of the priests continued to carry on their former practices in response to the demand of their people.[64]

[63] Francis E. F. Cornish, *Louis Craig Cornish, Interpreter of Life* (Boston, 1953), pp. 74–75.
[64] *Manila Daily Bulletin,* July 18, 1929.

In 1930 Dr. Eugene Shippen and Dr. Berkeley Blake went to the Philippines as ambassadors of good will to the Aglipayan church in spite of a warning from former Governor General William Cameron Forbes, who wrote to Louis Cornish:

Unless the Philippines' Independent Church has changed very greatly in the past few years, I would go very slowly before tying up with any of the leaders.[65]

Dr. Cornish was not only a leading Unitarian, he was also an international leader in a society to protect national and religious minorities as well as president of the Anti-Imperialist League. The report of these good-will ambassadors is interesting commentary on Aglipayan religious thought:

It will be some time before they develop a positive constructive philosophy of their own. Here is where we can help them, especially in their greatest need, the education of their leaders . . . who are wisely leading the people gently step by step by methods of interpretation and substitution rather than elimination. Give them time, give them encouragement.[66]

As a result of this report Aglipay was invited to join the International Association of Religious Liberals, and the Unitarian Association of Boston extended an invitation for Aglipay and two of his bishops to visit the United States at their expense to discuss membership and to cement the bonds of friendship.

Dr. Cornish, at Aglipay's request, arranged for a meeting with President Hoover. In preparation for this meeting, the Bureau of Insular Affairs prepared a dossier on Aglipay for the President and cabled the islands for advice. The governor-general responded:

Reference to your telegrams concerning Aglipay. Interview probably desired solely for publicity purpose here. Presume it is difficult to refuse, but if necessary to receive them, suggest that President an-

[65] William Cameron Forbes, Journals, Second Series Two, Vol. IV, Feb. 21, 1930, MS. Div., LC.

[66] Cornish, *op. cit.*, p. 76; "Aglipay Gives Ideas of God," *Philippines Herald*, July 13, 1931.

nounce that appointment was at their request and be careful to say nothing which might be used by them. First named rather harmless old man with waning influence, but second [de los Reyes, Jr.?] rather radical.[67]

Aglipay left the Philippines on March 28, 1931, with Bishop Isabelo de los Reyes, Jr., and Santiago Fonacier, former senator from Ilocos. They arrived in Boston on May 16 to attend the annual convention of the Unitarian Association, after having been feted in almost every large city of America by various local groups of Unitarians.

The whole question of Philippine independence was being discussed in the American Congress, and Boston, long the home of the Anti-Imperialist League, was very aware of the fact. The Unitarian Convention passed resolutions for Philippine independence and admitted the Philippine Independent Church into the International Association of Liberal Christianity.

During June 1935 Aglipay ran for president of the Commonwealth of the Philippines against Aguinaldo and Manuel Quezon. Isabelo de los Reyes ran for a seat in the National Assembly and used Aglipay's name on his campaign literature. Aglipay resented this, and a falling out between the two old friends resulted in Aglipay's dropping of de los Reyes' name from his approved candidates. How much this had to do with the final break which came in 1936 is hard to determine, both candidates having been defeated and their friendship not having been renewed. Isabelo de los Reyes was reconciled with the Roman Catholic Church in 1936, making a retraction of all errors contained in his more than one hundred publications for the Philippine Independent Church.[68] He received papal benediction at his deathbed, October 10, 1938.

Aglipay died at the head of his church on September 1, 1940, at

[67] Bureau of Insular Affairs cable to Governor General, Apr. 30, 1931, and reply, May 1, 1931, File 7552, Bureau of Insular Affairs, NA.

[68] J. Ma. Cavanna, *Rizal's Unfading Glory* (second edition; Manila, 1956), Appendix 4, publishes a copy of retraction of Isabelo de los Reyes. Several conversations with Isabelo de los Reyes' daughter, Sister Isabelle of the Angels, Franciscan Missionary of Mary Convent, Shinju, Taiwan, in the summer of 1962 give ample evidence from those who were with him at the time that de los Reyes was a practicing Catholic for two years when he died.

the age of eighty. Membership, once estimated by him as three million, was dwindling to about half that number in a population that had nearly doubled. As an old guerrilla fighter and patriot he was given an impressive funeral, to which the president of the Commonwealth and his cabinet and most of the high state officials, came to pay their respect. Newspapers bade farewell to the "Martin Luther" of the Philippines, and the long chapter in his search for national fulfillment came to an end.[69]

With his death, however, the seeds of dissension which had been nascent since the struggle between the radicals and conservatives in the late 1920's began to sprout. The two outstanding men claiming the right to lead the church were Bishop Severando Castro, who in 1929 had tried to block the proposed tie with Unitarianism and the abolition of external forms in the church, and Santiago Fonacier, who had accompanied Aglipay on his tour of Unitarian churches in 1931 and had been consecrated bishop in 1933. The former, an old man of seventy-seven, was persuaded to withdraw in favor of the latter, a man of fifty-five, on a promise that the church would reaffirm its belief in the existence of God, the soul, the divinity of Christ, and immortality.[70] As a result of his withdrawal, Bishop Fonacier was elected *Obispo Maximo* on October 14, 1940, for a period of three years.

The outbreak of World War II in December 1941 made a wartime convocation impossible, and by common consent Fonacier was confirmed in office and given emergency powers for the duration of the war. As soon as possible after the war a Supreme Council was convoked to assess the amount of destruction suffered during the war, to elect a supreme bishop, and to determine policy. At this convocation, though Fonacier offered to retire, so few bishops had been able to attend that he was prevailed upon to retain his high office for another year. Within a few months, however, dissension over the appointment and transfer of bishops, the failure to render financial accounts for the war years, and the removal of church headquarters from Manila to Pangasinan had reached a crisis, and Bishop Manuel Aguilar, himself under expulsion by Fonacier, called a meeting of the Su-

[69] *Manila Daily Bulletin*, Sept. 16, 1940; *New York Herald*, Sept. 2, 1940.
[70] Achútegui and Bernad, *op. cit.*, II, 19.

preme Council to indict the *Obispo Maximo* on these three counts and to challenge his expulsion of several bishops from the church. On January 22, 1946, seven of the fifteen bishops of the church met and deposed Bishop Fonacier, electing in his stead Bishop Gerardo Bayaca. Fonacier and other bishops refused to accept this state of affairs, and the church was split into two strong factions. By September 1946 two Supreme Councils were in session. The Fonacier faction elected Bishop Juan Jamias as *Obispo Maximo,* while the Bayaca faction elected Bishop Isabelo de los Reyes, Jr. The contest for church property, the right to use the official church name, and the right to define doctrine for the faithful were to drag the two groups through the courts for the next ten years. In 1955 it was the Supreme Court of the Philippines, not a Supreme Council, which decided, after reversing the several decisions of lower courts, that Isabelo de los Reyes, Jr., was the legitimate Supreme Bishop of *Iglesia Filipina Independiente.*[71]

Although many charges were brought forward during the years of litigation, and although the Fonacier faction was accused of willing collaboration with the Japanese during the war and of questionable association with Communism, the real issues were doctrinal.[72] Even before the court cases were settled, Bishop de los Reyes was initiating changes and continuing negotiations begun before the war to secure apostolic succession for himself and other bishops from the Protestant Episcopal Church of America through its missionary bishop Norman Binsted.[73]

From August 4 to August 6, 1947, the Supreme Council and General Assembly of the church met with Bishop Binsted who

[71] George A. Malcolm, *An American Colonial Careerist* (Boston, 1957), p. 303.

[72] *Time,* June 25, 1950; Isabelo de los Reyes, "Philippine Church Reborn," *Christian Century,* LXXIII (Apr. 11, 1956), 455–56.

[73] Norman Binsted, a Canadian, consecrated for the missionary district of Tohoku in Japan was transferred to the Philippines in 1940 and arrived shortly before the outbreak of World War II. During the early years before he was interned, he earned a reputation for generosity and concern in securing medical supplies, food, and whatever other comforts he could for Americans imprisoned in the Philippines. In correspondence and a conference with this author he spoke at length of his concern for the drifting Aglipayan church. He remained in the islands until his retirement in 1957.

authorized Bishop de los Reyes to petition the Episcopal House of Bishops for consecration. To make this feasible, he explained, it would be necessary for *Iglesia Filipina Independiente* to adopt the Articles of Faith, the Constitution and Canons approved by the Episcopal Church, and to make a declaration of faith.[74] The Episcopal House of Bishops, convened in Winston-Salem, North Carolina, November 4 to November 7, had to be assured that the shadow of Unitarianism had been wiped out by the declaration of faith. Bishop de los Reyes' statement that, "Never at any time did more than five per cent of the Aglipayans depart from the Trinitarian faith in which they had been grounded in their youth. . . ."[75] gave added assurance. By a decisive vote of the House of Bishops, one bishop only dissenting, it was decided that the petition should be granted, and on November 6 the House authorized Presiding Bishop Henry Knox Sherrill to take necessary steps to convey valid consecration to the episcopate of *Iglesia Filipina Independiente*.[76] The following year on April 7, in the Pro-Cathedral of St. Luke, Manila, with Bishop Norman Binsted as Consecrator and Bishop Harry S. Kennedy of Honolulu and Bishop Robert F. Wilner of the Philippines as Co-consecrators, Isabelo de los Reyes, Gerardo Bayaca, and Manuel Aguilar were consecrated bishops according to the rite of the Protestant Episcopal Church of the United States.[77]

The action of Bishop de los Reyes in accepting consecration from the Protestant Episcopal Church ended any possibility of rapprochement between the two factions of Aglipayanism, but

[74] Address of Bishop Binsted to the bishops of *Iglesia Filipina Independiente*, Aug. 4, 1947; letter of Isabelo de los Reyes to Most Reverend Henry Knox Sherrill, Aug. 9, 1947; Declaration of Faith, Articles of Religion, Constitution and Canons, all made available to the author through the kindness of Bishop Norman Binsted while in retirement in Washington, D.C., during the spring of 1959.

[75] *Christian Century*, Oct. 8, 1947, quoting Bishop Isabelo de los Reyes; George Dugan, "Episcopal Heads Study Filipino Tie," *New York Times*, Nov. 14, 1961; *Christian Century*, Dec. 17, 1947.

[76] *Living Church*, Nov. 8, 1947; Henry Mattocks, "Spirit of the Missions," *Forth*, CXII (Dec., 1947), 19–20; Isabelo de los Reyes, "Iglesia Filipina Independiente," *Historical Magazine*, XVIII (June, 1948), 132–37.

[77] Norman S. Binsted, "A Statement Concerning the Iglesia Filipina Independiente," *Historical Magazine*, XVII (June, 1948), 138–39; *New York Times*, Nov. 14, 1961.

both held out in hopes of favorable results in the court cases. When the Supreme Court rendered decisions which deprived the Fonacier faction, now headed by Supreme Bishop Pedro Ramos, of both property and name, a complete reorganization of that church was necessary. Its name was changed to Independent Church of Filipino Christians, and Fonacier continued to act as chief spokesman even though Ramos was supreme bishop. Some members of the church, fearing continual litigation as parishes in various places refused to turn over their churches to the de los Reyes faction, withdrew from the church and founded the Philippine Unitarian Church under the leadership of Bishop Pedro Aglipay and sought help from the Unitarian-Universalist Church of America and the International Association for Liberal Christianity and Religious Freedom.[78] Three years later Aglipay left this church to found another and was succeeded by Bishop Angel Bitanga. During 1962 and 1963 the Unitarians in America sent several representatives to the Philippines to try to bring about an amalgamation of the various splinter Unitarian groups, but unity was hard to achieve even though all groups desired it.[79] Splinter groups from Aglipayanism, some dating back to Aglipay's lifetime, but more dating from the 1955 Supreme Court decisions, continue to claim, each in its own way, to be *the* church of Aglipay.

The Supreme Court decisions also strengthened the de los Reyes faction which sought closer ties with the Episcopal Church. In May 1960 formal request for a concordat was sent by the Philippine Independent Church to the Episcopal House of Bishops which was meeting in Dallas, Texas, in November. The Episcopal Church in the Philippines warmly recommended that the concordat be entered into and without further delay. Consequently, during the Sixtieth General Convention of the Protestant Episcopal Church in Detroit, September 17 to September 29, 1961,

[78] Correspondence between Santiago Fonacier and John Howland Lathrop, July 17, 1962; and Lathrop to Fonacier, Nov. 9, 1959 (Lathrop Files, Berkeley, Calif.).

[79] Bishop Bitanga to Lathrop, Dec. 7, 1958, and continuously until 1966; correspondence between Edward Cahill of American Unitarians and Lathrop, 1959–1965; Dana McLean Greeley to John Lathrop, 1962–1965 (Lathrop Files, Berkeley, Calif.).

the concordat establishing full communion between the two churches was formally approved by both houses of the convention. *Iglesia Filipina Independiente* was acknowledged to be a "true part of the One, Holy, Catholic, and Apostolic Church."

The Liturgy of the Philippine Independent Church[*]

H. ELLSWORTH CHANDLEE

The Independent Catholic Church of the Philippines

During the past decade the *Iglesia Filipina Independiente* has emerged from her half-century of isolation, theological uncertainty, and internal disunity into a strong and vigorous church numbering more than 1,500,000 members. Now in a relation of full communion with most of the Anglican churches,[1] the Philippine Independent Church is an active participant in ecumenical discussion and activities in the Philippines, one of the founding bodies (1963) of the National Council of Churches, and a member of the World Council of Churches and the East Asia Christian Conference. The Independent Church and the Episcopal Church are engaged in the living out of an adventure in interchurch relations which may be unique, and which may prove to be of immense significance for the church outside the Philippines as we seek the recovery of our true unity in Christ. These two churches, sharing *in sacris,* preserve their own organizations and freedom, their own customs and emphases. Both are exploring the meaning of full communion, working in joint projects, looking to a closer unity as the spirit may direct. Each church is determined not to force some scheme of merger which would be pre-

[*] This essay was originally published in *Studia Liturgica* (Rotterdam), III, 2 (Autumn, 1964), 89–106.

[1] The terms of concordat are those of the Bonn agreement of 1931 (Cf. C. B. Moss, *The Old Catholic Movement* [London, 1948], chap. xxviii). At the time of writing the Independent Church is in full communion with twelve Anglican churches, the Lusitanian Church, the Spanish Reformed Church, and has begun negotiation with the Old Catholic churches and with the Ecumenical Patriarch. The concordat with the American Episcopal Church was signed on September 22, 1961.

mature and effect no true union at all. The Episcopal Church has no desire to make the *Independientes* over into Anglicans, nor has the *Iglesia Filipina* the purpose of bringing Episcopalians into its fold. The two churches by praying, living, and working in ever closer unity and accord are learning that each has much to give and certainly much to receive from the other. Both are praying that all may grow into a more fully manifested and realized unity in the Lord.

The Philippine Independent Church is indigenous to the Philippines. It was founded by Filipinos, is Filipino in its membership and orientation. As such it is an Asian expression of the Christian church. It is a Catholic church, reverencing and seeking to maintain the characteristic doctrines, order, and forms of worship of historic catholicism. The Independent Church is also a reformed church, concerned to remove distortions in faith and worship, cherishing and emphasizing the insights and truths recovered in the reformation. The church thus preserves and bears witness to the essentials of both the Catholic and the reformed traditions—yet in so doing it is not Anglican in origin or in expression. Being a reformed catholicism with a strong national feeling and orientation, the Independent Church is an increasingly important church in the Philippine religious scene, and may prove to be also in Asian Christianity generally. In many respects the Independent Church is ideally suited for an ever greater share of the responsibility for the evangel to Asia. The *Iglesia Filipina* therefore merits the study and increasing attention of Christians everywhere. Especially worthy of attention is the revised and reformed liturgy in which the Independent Church has embodied and expressed its traditions and its ideals.

The Background of the Philippine Independent Church

Until quite recently the Independent Church has been little known outside the Philippines, and has had little contact with other churches. Some background will therefore enable others to gain insight into the life and worship of the church.[2] When the

---

[2] Many sources are either in MSS or are not easily available. Therefore documentation is held to a minimum and only generally available works are cited.

Independent Church was organized as a body separated from the Roman Catholic Church, the majority of its members desired no changes other than a necessary reform of abuses.[3] Knowledge of European or American Christianity was then very limited in the Philippines, the knowledge of the Protestant churches even more so than that of the Roman Catholic. The Filipinos had long been sequestered by the methods of the Spanish friars, then the most powerful group in the Roman Catholic Church in the Philippines. The only pattern of worship which was known was the local expression of Roman Catholic worship, and this was assumed and taught to be the only legitimate Christian worship. But the local expression of catholicism left much to be desired not only in worship, but also in matters of faith and administration. Many abuses which Rome has fully recognized and rectified were then in the Philippines not only long-standing practices, but the only ones known to the vast majority of Filipinos.[4] Thus the *Iglesia Filipina* inherited what was assumed to be Catholic worship, but was in reality a debasement and a distortion of it. The familiar patterns of liturgy and of folk devotion were continued. The Roman service books continued to be used, while efforts were made to reform the worst abuses, and to move away from the more superstitious manifestations of the folk devotions. The average Filipino had no Latin. Accordingly, various translations of the services into Spanish and into some of the Philippine vernaculars were produced and enjoyed some circulation. But in many, perhaps most, of the Independent Church parishes, the use of Latin in the services continued on after the break with Rome. No real attempt was made by the Independent Church to produce its own liturgy.

The Hispanic and intensely Catholic background and heritage is still a very powerful force in the life and worship of the Independent Church, and it is one of the most powerful forces in Phil-

[3] Lewis Bliss Whittemore, *Struggle for Freedom* (Greenwich, Conn., 1961), chaps. iv, vi.

[4] There are now a number of seminaries for the training of Filipinos which offer excellent courses; Filipinos occupy a number of church posts to which they were never admitted in Spanish times. The discrimination against the national clergy and the low caliber of the education given them was considered a major abuse.

ippino life and culture. For many years the Independent Church drew the majority of its members from the less educated and less economically privileged sections of the population. Among the common folk of the *barrios* the old ways live on, and custom changes but slowly. Many Filipinos are still suspicious of what they think to be "Protestant." The old traditions are still apparent in the arrangement and furnishings of the churches, in ceremonial customs, and in the character of much of the popular devotions— and this not only in the Independent Church. The liturgical movement has as yet gained but little ground in Filipino church life. However, there are encouraging signs of impending change.

Other dominant influences upon the nascent Independent Church were nationalism and religious liberalism. The formation of the Independent Church was in many ways the expression in religion of that striving for national self-identity which brought about the Philippine revolution.[5] The leaders of the revolution were in many cases the founders of the Independent Church. The church has not ceased claiming to be the national church of the Filipinos. It has maintained stoutly the validity of a nationally expressed and organized catholicism, and has taken pride in its freedom from any foreign rule. This heritage is of increasing significance in these days of growing self-consciousness and national spirit among Asian peoples. Philippine nationalism has had other expressions in religion. Some Filipino leaders have contended that the ancient religion of the land was a pure ethical monotheism before foreign importations corrupted it. Proponents of this view demanded the removal from religion of all they deemed foreign, and the restoration of what they were convinced was the original religion and ought to be the only true religion for Filipinos.[6] Beginning before the revolution, and more actively after the restrictions of Spanish rule had been removed, ideas such as the foregoing, and many other new ideas, liberal and rationalist, were propounded by editorial and oration. Not always was the full import of the new ideology clearly discerned, but the dis-

[5] Gregorio Zaide, *Philippine Political and Cultural History* (rev. ed.; Manila, 1957), II, 176 ff.; cf. W. C. Forbes, *The Philippine Islands* (Boston, 1928), I, 49 ff.

[6] These extremists were called *Bathalistas*, from the name of the Tagalog chief deity.

cussion was part of the exercise of the newly obtained freedom, part of the desire and need of the Filipino to cast off the shackles which had for so long bound his mind. The leaders in the Independent Church movement shared many of these views. Some were active controversialists, some preached the new concepts, some wrote of them. With her beginnings in such an environment, the *Iglesia Filipina* has always firmly insisted upon freedom of investigation and discussion, and has always been an active opponent of any sort of obscurantism or attempt to stifle the free exchange of ideas, be it upon the part of the church or of the state.

The religious liberalism which most affected the life of the Independent Church was, curiously enough, a foreign importation. The Independent Church was in the midst of many adversities during the early years of the American occupation of the Philippines, and found a welcome friend in the person of William Howard Taft, the American governor. Leaders of the *Independientes* were brought into contact with American Unitarians, and cordial relations developed between them. It was not long before unitarian teachings began to be spread, and several of the Independent Church leaders adopted a unitarian theological position.[7] But unitarianism was ill-understood by the rank and file of the clergy, who had little theological training, and hardly at all by the laity of the church, which remained staunchly Catholic in intention.[8]

The *Oficio Divino*

These influences were brought to a focus in the first attempt to produce an Independent Church liturgy, the *Oficio Divino,* published in 1906.[9] This book is largely the work of one of the most gifted and certainly most influential laymen of the church, Isa-

[7] Among them the first *Obispo Maximo* and one of the major figures in the church, Gregorio Aglipay (cf. Isacio R. Rodríguez, *Gregorio Aglipay y los Orígenes de la Iglesia Filipina Independiente* [Madrid, 1960], I, 1–42; also Achútegui and Bernad, *Religious Revolution in the Philippines* [Manila, 1960], I, passim).

[8] Norman S. Binsted, *Iglesia Filipina Independiente* (private paper, 1957), p. 21. Whittemore, *op. cit.,* chap. xii.

[9] *Oficio Divino de la Iglesia Filipina Independiente* (Barcelona, 1906). This book is now very rare indeed and copies are next to impossible to obtain.

belo de los Reyes, Sr.[10] It seems to have been compiled rather as an experimental effort than as a service book intended for practical use. It is difficult to ascertain whether its contents represent the compiler's ideas of what the liturgy of his church ought to be, or reflect the position of the hierarchy. The *Oficio Divino* is in three sections. The first contains cento of scriptural and other material organized into sets of lessons, there being three lessons assigned to each day of the month. The sets of lessons are termed *Evangelia del dia*. The rest of the book contains the forms for the various services. In almost every service, the outline of the rite closely parallels that of the corresponding rite in the Roman missal or ritual. Virtually all of the Roman ceremonies are ordered, together with some which do not appear in the Roman rubrics but were popular usages in the Philippines. But in every service almost the whole of the Roman text has been either drastically altered or altogether replaced by new compositions. The new texts appear to have been largely original work by de los Reyes.[11] It is these new texts which embody and express the liberalism and rationalism of the time. The majority of the texts are very lengthy, the language is emotional and elaborate, exhortation abounds, and the theology is confused. Some of the texts must be pronounced unsuited for liturgical use—they are essays in unitarian, liberalist, or nationalist doctrine rather than prayer. The *Oficio Divino* makes use of Scripture in a very curious manner. There are few continuous texts or direct quotations of any length, but much free paraphrase and cento made from scattered verses drawn from many places in the Scriptures and placed in sometimes disconcerting juxtaposition. With all of this, it is also to be noted that some of the new texts have a singular dignity and beauty. Some are very appealing and characteristic expressions of Filipino devotion, and a few are brilliant liturgical composition. All of the services were supplied with copious explanatory glosses, and not a few rubrics are explanations of doctrine rather

[10] Achútegui and Bernad, *op. cit.*, I, chap. ix; Rodríguez, *op. cit.*, I, chap. viii.

[11] Some attempts have been made by the writer to ascertain what sources may have been used, without much success. The book itself claims to have used "Ancient Liturgies of the Hebrews, Romans, Greeks, Mozarabs, and Anglicans."

than directions. There are whole sections of notes. The total impression given by this material is one of marked polemical intent, and of quite limited knowledge of the theological disciplines on the part of the writer. Yet it may be remarked that in some other fields de los Reyes was no mean scholar. The resources of the ecclesiastical fields were but little available to him. The notes make it clear that the rites and ceremonies are to be continued out of consideration for the common people; the elite may dispense with them as no longer needed, and, as knowledge increases, all will come to a "scientific" understanding of religion. Then the old rites will no longer be used. The comments and notes, together with some of the liturgical texts, make the *Oficio Divino,* considered as a whole, unorthodox from the point of view of any traditional theology and a marked deviation from liturgical tradition as well.

Whether *Oficio Divino* was ever ratified by authority in the Independent Church is a matter of some doubt.[12] Nevertheless it soon became the *de facto* liturgy of the church. For the book, with all of its defects, met a very real need in the church—the need for its own expression of worship. Translations of parts of the book into Philippine vernaculars were made and widely used.[13] Thus the book also met another need of the average worshipper—the liturgy in a tongue which he could understand. It would have appeared to the average worshipper that, except for minor details, the services had been changed not at all. The *Oficio Divino* rites *looked* the same as the Roman. The vast majority of Filipinos had not understood the Latin which was read or sung in the old service. Indeed, much of the service they had been unable to hear at all, since a low or inaudible voice was used in reading it. The Independent Church clergy continued the

---

[12] The title page of *Oficio Divino* claims the approval of the *Obispo Maximo* and of the Supreme Council of Bishops—the governing authorities of the church. But Achútegui and Bernad, *op. cit.,* I, 259 ff., believe that if there was assent, it was given only very reluctantly. The present *Obispo Maximo* is extremely doubtful of constitutional action.

[13] The writer has seen old copies of the *Oficio Divino* in which old typed pages have been pasted or inserted between the leaves. Some of these are translations; some are not, but are vernacular translations of Roman materials. There are still a few printed pamphlets in Ilocano, or in one of the Visayan languages, but these are very rarely seen now.

accepted manner of conducting the rites. Thus the average worshipper did not realize that what he heard in the new services
was different from what had been said—he only rejoiced that
what he now heard in church was in a tongue which he could
understand. So it continues to this day in many parts of the Independent Church. Were a chance visitor to happen into a local
barrio church for the Sunday Mass, he would probably be somewhat surprised that no Latin was being used, for otherwise he
would likely conclude that he was in a very poor and very old-
fashioned Roman Catholic Church—and all the more so if he
were familiar with Hispanic Catholicism.

It should also be pointed out that *Oficio Divino* has almost
never been used as written. Its Mass rite, for example, was far too
long and wordy. Many portions of it were simply omitted. Alterations were made, some by official command, more by common
consent. Substitutions taken from Roman sources were made for
more unwieldy *Oficio Divino* texts. Some of the more patently
heterodox sections were corrected by omission of objectionable
matter, by insertions, and sometimes by outright substitution of
orthodox material.[14] Most churchmen probably knew little of
the contents and nature of *Oficio Divino*. For the most part the
book was not available for general inspection, since there was
normally but one copy in a parish, and that the personal property
of the parish priest. The most unorthodox parts of the book are
the notes and the explanations. These were not used in public
worship. The versions most available and used were typescript or
pamphlet translations of services, and from these the notes and
explanations had been omitted.

As thus amended, the *Oficio Divino* continued to serve as the
basic liturgy of the Independent Church from soon after its publication until after World War II. No real efforts were made to
revise it, or to compile a more suitable liturgy. Apart from the
fact that the necessary scholarship was not available to the
church, few had any interest in the matter. So many grave problems faced the church that liturgical matters seemed to be of very
little import. Both in hierarchy and in laity the church lacked

14 Very widely used were altar cards, such as may be bought in most
Roman Catholic supply shops. Few altars were without them.

alert and able leadership. The clergy were ill-trained, with almost no theology and but a minimal pastoral education. They were less and less well equipped to meet the challenge presented by the rising standards of education in the country. The financial situation of the church was disheartening. Church support was largely a matter of stole fees. In a majority of the parishes, these provided but a meager living for the parish priest, and left nothing over for other purposes. As a result the churches were small, poor, and often in sad disrepair. The Independent Church was the constant target of polemic—some of it extremely virulent—from all sides. Roman Catholics and most Protestants freely engaged in proselytizing Independent Church members. The church had no educational institutions, and as a result faced the draining away of potential leadership, since the youth of necessity had to attend either sectarian or government schools. In the former schools Independent Church students were subjected to unrelenting administrative and social pressures to defect from their church. Government schools were often not available, and in them the pressures were but slightly less severe. The Independent Church thus steadily lost ground, and its end seemed to be increasingly near at hand. During these years very few indeed thought of any connection between the kind of liturgical life lived in the parishes and the problems. Almost no one had any idea that a revitalized liturgical life might point to solution of some of the problems.

Reform and Revision

The years following upon the end of World War II were a turning point in the life of the Independent Church. The country had passed through the crucible of foreign occupation and total war. The long-cherished hopes of the Filipinos had been realized in the establishment of a free and sovereign republic. New courage and new determination were evident on all sides. The record of the Independent Church during the dreadful years of occupation was one of unflinching service to the people of the country in the cause of freedom. The church had earned a new respect from Filipinos, and had gained a new self-confidence; the future presented unlimited opportunities. Soon forward-looking new leaders were given positions of authority in the church. Most notable among the new leaders was the loved and trusted bishop of Manila and Quezon City, Isabelo de los Reyes, Jr., to whom was entrusted the highest post in the church, that of *Obispo Maximo*.[15] No one has been more instrumental in the inauguration and carrying through of reforms. De los Reyes has led the renewal of his church with unceasing courage, wisdom, and patience. Negotiations were begun with the Episcopal Church that resulted in the bestowal of the historic episcopate, and the subsequent regularization of Independent Church orders.[16] By means of a confession of faith and a series of articles, the church clarified its doctrinal position, firmly asserting its adherence to orthodox Christianity and the Catholic tradition.[17] The gravest need of the *Independientes* was a well-educated ministry. St. Andrew's Theological Seminary in 1947 had been reorganized and enlarged to provide a full education of high standards for the Episcopal ministry. The seminary was opened to candidates from the Independent Church on a completely equal basis, and St. Andrew's became the official seminary of the Independent Church.

As the sense of renewed life began to spread through the church, the need for a more adequate liturgy became evident. Clergy and laity alike expressed their desire for forms of worship which the Independent Church could call its own. The Supreme Council of Bishops, realizing that the task of revision and of the compilation of a new liturgy was a most formidable one, and that the church was not ready to undertake it, moved cautiously. It

[15] The office is analogous to that of an archbishop, with rather more jurisdiction. The first to hold the office was Aglipay, who was re-elected until his death in 1940. Santiago Fonacier succeeded but was ousted in 1946. Then Gerardo Bayaca served for a very short term until the election of de los Reyes. For a biography of the latter, see Chandlee, *De los Reyes, Supreme Bishop in the Philippines* (New York, 1962).

[16] No bishops had joined the independent movement. Aglipay attempted unsuccessfully to obtain Episcopal orders from both Episcopalians and Old Catholics. He was consecrated by a group of presbyters, and succession was thus broken. The *Independientes* never lost the desire and intention for succession, and the service consecrating three bishops was held in Manila on April 7, 1948.

[17] *Constitution and Canons of the Philippine Independent Church* (revised edition; Manila, 1961).

was decided to use the *Book of Common Prayer* as an interim rite.[18] The prayer book was widely circulated and increasingly used, especially for the Eucharist and for ordinations. In a very real sense the *Independientes* soon made the prayer book their own, for it was rarely used according to Anglican precedent or custom, or even according to its own rubrics. It was freely adapted to the needs and customs of the Independent Church services—often in a manner somewhat disconcerting to Episcopalians. It became common to find a mixture of prayer book and *Oficio Divino* in use in parish churches. Many things in the prayer book were accepted, used, and became familiar and loved to Independent Church worshippers; and it became certain that the prayer book would exert a very strong influence upon the new liturgy. Despite this, it also became certain that the prayer book, without very drastic alteration, could never serve as the liturgy for the Independent Church. Its services were too austere and cold for the average *Independiente*. Much of its English was not easily understood. It had little in the way of rubrics for the customary ceremonies of the services. It made no provision at all for rites long established and loved in the Philippines—the rites of Holy Week, for one example. But most of all, the *Book of Common Prayer* is the liturgical expression of Anglicanism. It is the expression of another culture, other times, other conditions of life. It may be an excellent liturgy for use by American or English congregations. But, as it stands, that is precisely the defect of the prayer book—it is too English, too American.[19] Many things in the prayer book, it is true, are indeed universal, many things are capable of translation into any idiom, can be used at any time or place with profit and meaning, but too much of it simply does not speak to or for Filipinos. And there were many things in the *Oficio Divino* which were good, and were excellent expressions of Filipino Christianity—all wished these to be preserved and to be used. There were many things in the Roman services equally

18 This was the present *Book of Common Prayer* of the American Episcopal Church (1928).

19 No provisions are made in the prayer book for many occasions of real interest in the Philippines—the blessing of houses, planting of grain, etc., to say nothing of such occasions as *Flores de Mayo* and local saints' and patronal days. The classical English also does not set well in this land.

good and loved—indeed, the average Independent Church wor
shipper was more at home in a Roman service than in an Episcopal one which was conducted according to strict interpretation of
the rubrics and minimal ceremonial. Thus in the Independent
Church the tendency was toward a growing eclecticism. It was
hoped that the Independent Church might be able to do what
others had done: take the universal expressions, draw upon the
resources of the liturgical tradition of the church, and so order
and adapt them that they might be embodied and expressed in a
liturgy which at once expressed the needs and insights of *Independientes* and the universal tradition of the church's worship.

The task of compiling the new liturgy was begun in 1953. In
that year, the well-known American liturgical scholar, Dr. Massey
H. Shepherd, was in the Philippines for a lecture tour. It was arranged for a small committee of Independent Church members
and of interested Anglicans to confer with Dr. Shepherd in order
to obtain his advice as to the type of liturgy best suited to the
needs of the *Iglesia Filipina* and as to the practical steps to be
taken in the compilation of a revised liturgy. The results of this
conference were further discussed, and it was decided that the
work of revision should be begun, and should be guided by the
following general principles: (1) The new liturgy should be of
the Western or Roman type as best suited to the heritage of the
church. (2) In those services in which a Roman order and outline
had been followed and were familiar, the same pattern should be
followed. (3) The materials from *Oficio Divino* should be carefully examined and evaluated, and after such revision and amendment as necessary, should be preserved insofar as possible. (4)
Wide use should be made of Anglican sources, especially of the
more recent prayer book revisions, especially for Eucharist, ordinations, and divine office. (5) The liturgy should be compiled
in English as the language of widest use, looking forward to an
eventual translation into the Philippine vernaculars.[20] (6) The

[20] By this time, of course, Spanish has long ceased to be the common
tongue. The Americans introduced English, and it is the language of education and commerce, and is spoken and understood over most of the archipelago. An attempt is being made to introduce *Pilipino*, based upon Tagalog, the language of the Manila area and part of Luzon, as a national
tongue. The use of *Pilipino* is slowly increasing.

rubrics should preserve the traditional ceremonies and should be detailed enough to provide a clear guide for the clergy in conducting services. (7) Distinctively Independent or Filipino rites should be revised and preserved.

The *Obispo Maximo* then appointed a small liturgical commission of bishops and clergy, and several Anglican advisors—of which the present writer was one—and charged the commission with carrying out preliminary work. Meeting over a period of several months, the commission studied and compared various liturgies, examined and compared prayer books, sought to examine traditional liturgical patterns, examined *Oficio Divino* material, and evaluated the needs of the church. The results were taken by the *Obispo Maximo* and used as a basis for the preparation and discussion of trial forms of service. This phase of the work was carried on by the *Independientes* themselves, with but occasional reference to Anglicans for points of expert advice. Some drafts were prepared by the *Obispo Maximo*, some by various clergy whom he called to assist. A few were produced by one of the Anglican consultants. All of these were circulated, discussed, criticized, and gone over thoroughly. Many changes and amendments were, of course, made. No meetings were held, but the work was carried out by small informal groups, by the cabinet of the *Obispo Maximo*, and by correspondence. This phase of the compilation and revision took a number of years. In the course of it, it was decided that one book would not be sufficient, and that the best procedure would be to issue a large altar-size book to contain the materials for the Eucharist and for the ordinal, the other to be a smaller volume and to contain the divine office and occasional offices. The final compilation of the missal was then begun under the direction of the Right Reverend Bartolomé Remigio, then of the cabinet of the church. The present writer and the Reverend W. Roland Foster, of the seminary faculty, with the Episcopal bishop as consultant, were appointed as proofreaders, a charge which involved much more than checking typography. Typescript drafts of services and the various propers and commons were produced by the *Independientes*, and submitted to the Anglican consultants for advice as to the correctness of doctrinal and liturgical matters; suggestions for further revision were welcomed, as were suggestions for changes in language and expression. The recommendations were given to the director and then discussed by the *Independientes,* who finally decided as to their adoption. A similar process was followed in the case of the ritual, the compilation of which was directed by the Right Reverend Horacio Santamaria, with the same Anglican consultants. However, due to certain adverse circumstances, the careful editing which was done in the case of the missal was not fully carried out in the ritual.

The Filipino Liturgy

The *Filipino Missal* was published in 1961, duly ratified by the authorities of the Independent Church and declared to be the liturgy of the *Iglesia Filipina Independiente.* The "Declaration of Faith and Articles of Religion" together with the sections of the constitution and canons pertaining to the liturgy are printed as a preface. The *Filipino Missal* is really three books in one: (1) *The Missal,* containing the calendar and tables, the ordinary of the Mass, the propers of season and saints, common of saints, and the votive and requiem Masses; (2) *The Ordinal,* containing the services for admission to minor orders and the rites of ordination for the three major orders; (3) *The Pontifical,* in which are confirmation, consecration of oils, consecration of churches, and other rites and ceremonies normally performed by a bishop. The Eucharistic rite is as follows.[21]

A. The Liturgy of the Word

(*Preparation,* said either in the sacristy or before the altar after the entrance. It is in the usual Roman form, with an alternate Confession from Oficio Divino).

1. Entrance Rite
    a. *Collect for Purity,* said before the altar; translations and adaptations of *Aufer a nobis* and *Oramus te* from the Roman rite, said silently while ascending the altar.
    b. *Introit.* This is either in the usual form of Antiphon, Verse, Gloria, Antiphon, or an invariable prayer adapted from Oficio

---

[21] The titles for the most part do not appear in the original, but are added here for convenience.

Divino. At Sung Mass the Introit is sung during the entrance while the prayers are said and the altar censed. (Prayers for the blessing of incense, translated from the Roman rite are given here and below at the Offertory.)

   c. *Summary of the Law*

   d. *Kyrie eleison,* ninefold, in English

   e. *Gloria in excelsis,* in the Prayer Book version, or a hymn beginning with the opening words of the Gloria, the rest based on a cento from Malachi and adapted from Oficio Divino. (It is omitted from nonfestal services.)

2. Ministry of the Word
   a. *Salutation,* and *Collect for the Day*
   b. *Epistle*
   c. *Gradual.* This is in either the usual Western form or Psalm 23, as in Oficio Divino. (During it the preparations for the Gospel are carried out as in the Roman rite.)
   d. *The Gospel*
   e. *Sermon*
   f. *Nicene Creed,* in the Prayer Book version with the *Holy* restored in the notes of the church. (The Creed is omitted from nonfestal Masses.)

B. The Liturgy of the Eucharist

1. Offertory
   a. *Salutation* and *Offertory Sentence.* This may be the proper *Offertorium* or a sentence from Scripture. A selection from both Prayer Book and Oficio Divino is given.
   b. *Collection of the Alms* and *Preparation of the Oblations*
   c. *Offering of Alms and Oblations.* The alms are offered first with a fine prayer adapted from Oficio Divino, said aloud. There are also prayers from the same source said aloud at the offering of the Elements. The Lavabo follows, with a versicle and response, and at Sung Masses, the usual censings.
   d. *Orate Fratres and Secret,* translated from the Roman rite, and said according to Roman customs.
   e. *The Prayer for the Church,* from the Book of Common Prayer.

2. The Consecration
   a. *Verses and responses,* translated from Oficio Divino from Psalm 103.
   b. *Salutation, Sursum corda, Prefaces* as in the Prayer Book, *Sanc-*

tus and *Benedictus qui venit.* There are given the Prayer Book Proper Prefaces and a wide extra selection from Roman sources.

c. *The Prayer of Consecration,* a new composition, based upon Anglican Prayer Book revisions. *The Lord's Prayer.*

3. The Breaking of the Bread
   a. *Libera nos,* translated from the Roman rite, said silently, except for the ending. The Fraction is made during the Prayer.
   b. *The Peace of the Lord be always with you,* etc.
   c. *Commixture of Elements,* with the Roman formula.
   d. *Agnus Dei*

4. Communion
   a. *Domine Jesu Christe qui dixisti,* said silently in translation.
   b. *Prayer of Humble Access,* from the Prayer Book, said aloud.
   c. *Communion.* The celebrant receives first with the Roman words, then the people. Communion is in both kinds. The Words of Administration from the Prayer Book are used.

5. Post-Communion
   a. *Ablutions,* with silent prayers translated from Roman rite.
   b. *Communion Antiphon,* said or sung from the Proper.
   c. *Salutation* and *Thanksgiving.* The latter is either the Prayer Book thanksgiving or a proper post-Communion Collect.
   d. *Dismissal*
   e. *Benediction,* a prayer of intercession and commendation from Oficio Divino, optional, and rarely used in said services.
   f. *Blessing,* in the Prayer Book form. (The use of the Last Gospel is optional and is always the John Prologue.)

The *Temporale* provides for all of the Sundays and the festivals and fasts of the Christian year. There is a full Holy Week rite adapted and revised from the Roman restored order. A number of local observances are provided for, including the popular *Misa de Gallo,* a series of nine solemn Masses sung before dawn beginning on December 16, and with themes in preparation for Christmas. The introits and other anthems are generally those of the Roman rite, while the collects and lessons are Anglican. The Revised Standard Version of the Bible is used for all lessons, since the English of the King James Version is not well understood in the average congregation. The *Sanctorale* provides for the usual Anglican red-letter days, with some additions of local interest.

There is a full set of commons for saints' days, since the common is directed for most of the black-letter days. The customs and pastoral concerns of the Independent Church are seen in the full sets of propers for various votive Masses, and in the requiems. The use of the same sources is followed in these, but there is less Anglican material, since Anglican sources have fewer provisions for these occasions.

The ordinal is prefaced by excerpts from the canons dealing with holy orders and an explanation of the difference between the minor and the major orders. The former are declared to be after the nature of a commissioning, not sacramental, and not canonically required. The minor orders provided for are: door-keeper, reader, acolyte, subdeacon. Admission to any of these may be given at any time, not necessarily in connection with a Eucharist. The services of admission have been built from a combination of elements from *Oficio Divino* and the American *Book of Offices*.[22] In the case of each there is a presentation of the candidate, a form of admonition or questioning, delivery of the appropriate instrument, and a commissioning in the form of a prayer or blessing. The admission to minor orders has, as a matter of fact, largely fallen into desuetude in the Independent Church, and these services are but rarely used.[23] The ordination rites themselves in the case of the major orders of deacon, priest, and bishop, very closely follow Anglican models for the general outline and texts. Much of the traditional ceremonial, including the anointing of hands in the case of priest and bishop, the delivery of instruments, and the like, has been retained in the Independent Church rites.

The *Filipino Ritual* was brought to completion and authorized just a few months after the publication of the *Filipino Missal*. In the first part of the *Filipino Ritual* are the various tables, the lectionary, and similar materials, the orders for morning and evening prayer, the litany, and occasional prayers and thanksgivings. All of these are taken from the prayer book with very slight alteration. The *Oficio Divino* had made very little provision for a di-

22 *The Book of Offices* (New York, 1960).
23 But it is quite possible that with the growing emphasis on the lay ministry these orders may again become of importance.

vine office. Theoretically the recitation of the offices of the Roman breviary was binding upon the Independent Church clergy, but in practice early given up, since the clergy could for the most part neither read the Latin nor afford the necessary books. There is almost no tradition for a public performance of the divine office in the Philippines. Except in Anglican churches, the office is almost never said or sung publicly, and most worshippers both in the Roman and Independent churches have never attended an office. Various popular devotions, the rosary, novenas, and the like are substituted for the divine offices and there was virtually no customary use of the offices and no Independent material upon which to draw. The authorities of the church were anxious to provide a form of office suitable for both public use as parish service and for ordinary recitation by the clergy; for both of these purposes the prayer book offices were admirably suited. The prayer book Psalter was also adopted and printed at the end of the *Filipino Ritual*.[24] The use of the divine office, especially evensong, is growing in the Independent Church, and it will doubtless become more popular and widespread when a vernacular translation becomes available.

The *Book of Common Prayer* has had considerably less influence upon other parts of the *Filipino Ritual*. The rite of baptism, for example, follows the Roman order much more closely than it does the Anglican, and preserves a considerable amount of the *Oficio Divino* service, carefully edited and revised. Confirmation in local custom is most frequently administered in infancy, soon after baptism. The service closely follows the Roman order, with some Anglican elements. Both unction and the laying on of hands are prescribed. The service of matrimony presents the same picture of fairly close adherence to the traditional rite with some Anglican elements. The local customs of placing the humeral veil around the couple being married, and the giving of money, flowers, and the like are retained. In other parts of the *Filipino Ritual*, such as the administration of penance, and the ministries

---

24 It is perhaps unfortunate that the language of the Psalter was not simplified. An omission was the printing of the collects for the day. Recently, however, the collects were printed in a pamphlet for insertion into the *Filipino Ritual*.

to the sick, the dominant influence has been the *Manual for Priests,* published by the American Province of the Society of St. John Evangelist.[25] This book enjoyed a wide circulation immediately after the inauguration of relations with the Episcopal Church. Very soon it began to be the book most often used by the clergy in their pastoral ministrations, and accordingly large portions of it were simply incorporated in the *Filipino Ritual* as being the customary practices. The traditional Filipino pattern is retained for the burial rites, and Anglican influences are less noticeable here than anywhere else in the ritual. There is a service at the house of the deceased, a procession with stations, an abbreviated matins of the dead, the dismissal or absolution of the body, full provision for requiems, and the like—all of these being very traditional customs. The *Filipino Ritual* also reflects the common customs in the extensive provisions for various kinds of blessings. Many of these are used on occasions of social festivities, such as the blessing of a new house.

The liturgy is now in process of assimilation by the church. It is becoming more and more widely used, especially for the Mass and for ordinary ministrations. But it is still not used in many parts of the church, or used only in part. The revival of the Independent Church is still in the initial stages, and the authorities have wisely chosen to allow the acceptance and use of the revised liturgy to be gradual and the result of the wishes of the parishes, rather than to force what would, for many parts of the church, amount to a liturgical revolution. As the liturgy is more and more used, it is being found to be of signal help in fostering revival of church life. But, as pointed out earlier in this article, in many places the old ways live still, and change is apt to be resisted unless the reasons for it are clearly understood. The church faces a gigantic task of instruction of her people, after generations of very little education for the laity indeed. Part of the need is being met by a series of education conferences sponsored by the Division of Education of the Joint Council of the Independent and Episcopal churches. These conferences are being held in carefully selected centers, and draw in clergy and laity from the sur-

[25] *A Manual For Priests of the American Church* (Cambridge, Mass., 1944).

ɪ0uuding areas. The liturgy is one of the major topics of instruction and discussion, and there is always an instructed Eucharist,
while popular and common participation are stressed in numerous services during the conferences. The theological seminary is
probably the most important means of dissemination of liturgical
information and training. The seminary curriculum includes four
required courses in liturgics with two additional required courses
in the conduct of public worship. In the latter the candidates for
the ministry of both churches are trained carefully in the use of
the Independent Church service books. The seminary chapel
seeks to set an example in the use of both *Filipino Missal* and
Filipino Ritual. In the chapel services and ministrations, both
books are used on an equal basis with the *Book of Common
Prayer*.

The conservatism and lack of education are, however, not the
main reasons why the revised liturgy has not as yet come into full
use. Two factors which most militate against its general use are:
(1) the lack of vernacular translations; (2) the lack of the books
for the people. Observers have frequently asked, why, when in
the average Independent Church parish the vernacular was commonly used in liturgy, did the church publish the new liturgy in
English—why not at once in the vernacular? But in the Philippines there is no such thing as *the* vernacular. There are many
vernaculars. For the Independent Church to have produced liturgical books which could be used over the whole church, it would
have been necessary to publish the books in at least five major
languages—and there are many more less widely used tongues.
This was simply not possible with the resources at hand. The
church considered that the immediate need was a liturgy which
could be used and understood by the most members, and English
is probably the most widely understood tongue. The other need
was for a standard, a model liturgy, which could serve as the
basis for future translation. This had to be in English, for the
sources are in English, and not in the Philippine tongues. The
work of translation into four of the major Filipino languages is
now being undertaken by committees, and use is also being made
of translations of the prayer book, as these are produced. It is
hoped that the necessary resources for publication of the transla-

tions will become available. As to the second point above, it was necessary, given the customs and conditions in the Independent Church, that a complete and full altar book as well as ritual should be made available. This made anything like the prayer book format hardly feasible with the high costs of printing and binding. And for the size of edition necessary for general distribution to all the people, at a price which they could afford, the financial resources were simply not available to the church. A popular devotional manual, containing the Eucharist, has been made available by the cooperation of the American Order of the Holy Cross at a very reasonable price. In the near future it is hoped that a people's prayer book may be published, to contain Eucharist, the offices of the morning and evening prayer, the Psalter, and the more commonly used occasional offices.

It may be said in closing that there is no question but that the new liturgy represents the mind of the Independent Church, and that it will be more and more accepted and used throughout the church as soon as practical difficulties can be surmounted. The liturgical revival in the Independent Church—and in the Episcopal Church in the Philippines—has certainly begun, and everywhere there is increasing participation and understanding. And, if one may hazard a prediction as to the future, when the Philippine Episcopal Church arrives at that point in its development where it is free to produce its own liturgy, that liturgy will be considerably closer to the *Filipino Missal* and *Filipino Ritual* than to the present American *Book of Common Prayer*.

PART III

PROTESTANTISM
AND PLURALISM

Providence and Politics behind Protestant Missionary Beginnings in the Philippines

GERALD H. ANDERSON

Edward McNall Burns begins his book *The American Idea of Mission: Concepts of National Purpose and Destiny* by saying that "one of the principal clues to knowledge of America is the sense of mission which has run like a golden thread through most of her history. To a greater extent than most other peoples, Americans have conceived of their nation as ordained in some extraordinary way to accomplish great things in the world." [1] In a series of scholarly studies, John Edwin Smylie has documented this sense of American destiny among Protestant clergymen from 1865 to 1900. Dr. Smylie demonstrates that "the theological basis for this feeling of destiny was the common doctrine of providence," [2] a conviction that God works through nations to accomplish his purpose, and an assumption that the United States was to be "the primary agent of God's meaningful activity in history." [3] Smylie's

[1] New Brunswick, N.J., 1957, p. vii. Cf. Ernest Lee Tuveson, *Redeemer Nation: The Idea of America's Millenial Role* (Chicago, 1968); Gustav H. Blanke, "Die Anfänge des amerikanischen Sendungsbewusstseins: Massachusetts-Bay 1629 bis 1659," *Archiv für Reformationsgeschichte*, LVIII, 2 (1967), 171–211; K. D. Bracher, "Providentia Americana: Ursprung des demokratischen Sendungsbewusstseins in Amerika," in *Festschrift für Erich Voegelin* (München, 1962), pp. 27–48.

[2] Smylie, "Protestant Clergymen and American Destiny," *The Harvard Theological Review*, LVI, 4 (1963), 297.

[3] Smylie, "National Ethos and the Church," *Theology Today*, XX, 3 (1963), 314. Cf. Sidney E. Mead, "American Protestantism Since the Civil War—From Denominationalism to Americanism," *The Lively Experiment: The Shaping of Christianity in America* (New York, 1963), pp. 134–55. We shall see that, as Will Herberg has pointed out, in its crudest form this identification of religion with the "national purpose generates a kind

279

study shows that among the clergy in this period there was a profound and pervasive idea of mission for their country—"that America had a special work to do in history"—although there was no uniform opinion as to exactly what that work was to be.[4]

The idea of Manifest Destiny—of a national mission assigned by providence—arose in America in the mid-1840's. "It meant expansion, prearranged by Heaven, over an area not clearly defined," for extending the blessings of American freedom to neighboring peoples who wanted to achieve self-realization.[5] Herman Melville (1819–1891) expressed something of this sentiment when he wrote, "We Americans are peculiar, chosen people, the Israel of our times; we bear the ark of the liberties of the world." [6] Definitions of the scope of the doctrine were debated and enlarged as the century wore on. But the gospel of Manifest Destiny had its roots in the concepts of Anglo-Saxon racial superiority, of America as the center of civilization in the westward course of empires, the primacy of American political institutions, the purity of American Protestant Christianity, and the desirability for English to be the language of mankind.

Until the 1890's Manifest Destiny was thought of primarily in terms of continental expansion, the absorption of North America, with the consent of the people about to be absorbed and with a view toward their admission to citizenship and statehood. In the 1890's, however, when the United States had reached the limits of prospective continental expansion and as the nation's economy reached maturity, there developed considerable agitation for expansion beyond the continent of North America, to

---

of national messianism which . . . sees God as the champion of America, endorsing American purposes, and sustaining American might" (*Protestant-Catholic-Jew* [Garden City, N.Y., 1960], p. 264).

[4] Smylie, "Protestant Clergymen and America's World Role, 1865–1900: A Study of Christianity, Nationality, and International Relations" (unpublished Th.D. dissertation, Princeton Theological Seminary, Princeton, N.J., 1959), p. 560 (cited henceforth as "dissertation"). The writer is greatly indebted to Dr. Smylie for his excellent study and for permission to quote from it.

[5] Frederick Merk, *Manifest Destiny and Mission in American History: A Reinterpretation* (New York, 1966), p. 24.

[6] Quoted by Burns, *op. cit.*, p. 1, from Melville's *White-Jacket*.

permit further growth in the nation's economy, to provide out-posts of national defense, and to allow the benevolent spread of American benefits to those less fortunate.

Professor Frederick Merk maintains that the insular and imperialistic expansion of the 1890's was the antithesis of the earlier Manifest Destiny because now "it involved the reduction of distant peoples to a state of colonialism."[7] But many scholars today would agree with Walter LaFeber that "the United States did not set out on an expansionist path in the late 1890's in a sudden, spur-of-the-moment fashion. The overseas empire that Americans controlled in 1900 was not a break in their history, but a natural culmination."[8] And many Protestant clergymen, when faced with the issue and opportunity of American expansion into Asia in the 1890's, attempted to explain it and justify it "in terms of the categories of historic destiny and ethical obligation which had been forming for a generation," says Smylie.[9]

Especially important in preparing the attitude of the churches for the new phase of Manifest Destiny were the writings of the Reverend Dr. Josiah Strong (1847–1916) of the Congregational Home Missionary Society and later General Secretary of the Evangelical Alliance of the United States. His works, especially *Our Country: Its Possible Future and Its Present Crisis* (1886), and *The New Era; or, The Coming Kingdom* (1893), "did much

[7] Merk, *op. cit.*, p. 257.

[8] *The New Empire: An Interpretation of American Expansion, 1860–1898* (Ithaca, N.Y., 1963), p. vii. Robert L. Beisner agrees: "The Spanish-American War was not a sudden and totally unexpected outburst of American expansionism. An expansionist mood had been growing for years, and the war of 1898 was more a culmination of past developments than an isolated aberration," in "The Anti-Imperialist Impulse: The Mugwumps and the Republicans, 1898–1900" (unpublished Ph.D. dissertation, University of Chicago, 1965), p. 9. See also Whitney T. Perkins, *Denial of Empire, The United States and Its Dependencies* (Leyden, 1962), pp. 194 ff.; and the following unpublished doctoral dissertations: Philip Wayne Kennedy, "The Concept of Racial Superiority and United States Imperialism, 1890–1910" (St. Louis University, 1963); Edwin Berkeley Tompkins, "The Great Debate: Anti-Imperialism in the United States, 1890–1920" (University of Pennsylvania, 1963); and R. F. Weston, "The Influence of Racial Assumptions on American Imperialism, 1893–1946" (Syracuse University, 1964).

[9] Smylie, dissertation, *op. cit.*, p. 530.

to develop the idea of the part America should play in fulfilling Anglo-Saxon destiny as a civilizing and Christianizing power." [10] Anson Phelps Stokes says that "no other book in the fourth quarter of the nineteenth century did as much to get people interested in the application of religion to the problems of the nation as did" *Our Country*,[11] which sold 175,000 copies over a period of thirty years.

Austin Phelps, professor *emeritus* at Andover Seminary, wrote the Introduction to *Our Country*, in which he said that Americans should

look on these United States as first and foremost the chosen seat of enterprise for the world's conversion. Forecasting the future of Christianity, as statesmen forecast the destiny of nations, we must believe that it will be what the future of this country is to be. As goes America, so goes the world, in all that is vital to its mortal welfare.[12]

In this small volume, Strong had a chapter on the peril of "Romanism" for America, in which he argued that there was an irreconcilable difference and inherent contradiction between the fundamental principles of Romanism and "our free institutions." There was also a chapter on "The Anglo-Saxon and the World's Future" in which Strong vigorously expressed belief in the superiority of the Anglo-Saxon race as God's chosen people. The Anglo-Saxon, he asserted, as the premier representative of civil liberty and "a pure *spiritual* Christianity," was "divinely commissioned to be, in a peculiar sense, his brother's keeper." [13] Jurgen Herbst says that *Our Country* wove together a radiant faith in America's future, "a faith composed of the Protestant version of belief in the chosen people, a secular, science-supported theory of progress, and a nationalistic sense of manifest destiny." [14] And, says Herbst, when Strong wrote

[10] Anson Phelps Stokes, *Church and State in the United States* (New York, 1950), II, 311.

[11] *Ibid.*, II, 262.

[12] P. 11. All references to *Our Country* are taken from the revised edition of 1891, as reprinted and edited by Jurgen Herbst (Cambridge, Mass., 1963).

[13] *Ibid.*, pp. 200–202.   [14] "Editor's Introduction," *ibid.*, p. xxv.

of Romanism, the liquor power, and the extremes of wealth and poverty, when he related these themes to the antagonism between native Anglo-Saxons and foreign immigrants, between Protestants and Catholics, he was using the language of politics.[15]

In the closing pages of *The New Era*, Strong summarized his "enthusiasm for humanity" in these words: "Surely, to be a Christian and an Anglo-Saxon and an American in this generation is to stand on the very mountain-top of privilege." [16]

Following the outbreak of the Spanish-American War, when the Philippines fell suddenly and unexpectedly into American hands as a result of Admiral Dewey's defeat of the Spanish fleet in Manila Bay in May 1898, the issue that emerged immediately and provoked intense debate in America was whether or not the United States should keep the islands.

An eloquent and impressive minority, including former presidents Harrison and Cleveland, William Jennings Bryan, Andrew Carnegie, Mark Twain, Samuel Gompers, Jane Addams, William James, Henry James, President David Starr Jordan of Stanford University, President Henry W. Rogers of Northwestern, President Charles W. Eliot of Harvard, the Rev. Edward Everett Hale, the Rev. Henry Van Dyke, and the Rev. Charles H. Parkhurst, joined in an anti-imperialist movement to oppose the acquisition of a colonial empire.[17] But the burden of public and politi-

---

[15] *Ibid.*

[16] New York, 1893, p. 354. Senator Albert J. Beveridge expressed similar enthusiasm when defending the annexation of the Philippines he said, "And of all our race, He [God] has marked the American people as His chosen Nation to finally lead in the regeneration of the world. This is the divine mission of America, and it holds for us all the profit, all the glory, all the happiness possible to man. We are trustees of the world's progress, guardians of its righteous peace" (quoted in Sidney E. Mead, *op. cit.*, pp. 153–54). Leon Wolff says that "duty, destiny, dollars and divinity" reached a new high in the ultraimperialist addresses of Senator Beveridge on the Philippines issue (*Little Brown Brother* [Garden City, N.Y., 1961], p. 303). See also H. Richard Niebuhr, *The Kingdom of God in America* (New York, 1937), p. 179.

[17] Cf. Fred H. Harrington, "The Anti-Imperialist Movement in the United States, 1898–1900," *The Mississippi Valley Historical Review*, XXII, 2 (1935), 211–30; and Beisner, *op. cit.*, pp. 2 ff. See also Robert L. Beisner, *Twelve Against Empire: The Anti-Imperialists 1898–1900* (New York, 1968).

cal opinion swung toward "retention" of the islands for commercial, diplomatic, military, humanitarian, and religious reasons. It was felt that a new dimension of American destiny had become manifest and that to deny it would be both unfaithful and unpatriotic.

Among the "clerical expansionists," some tried to distinguish between national policy and missionary interests with respect to expansion, "between what the nation might or might not do for political, economic or military reasons, and what the Christian church was obligated to do *if* the nation should choose to retain the Philippine Islands." [18] Dr. Smylie concludes in his study that, "despite this intellectual distinction which it made, the missionary element in the country was so far-sighted about the *possibility* of new openings, and so active in preparing itself for the *contingency* of imperialism, that the cumulative effect of their words and deeds weighed heavily on the side of expansionism." [19] Kenneth M. MacKenzie, in his book *The Robe and the Sword: The Methodist Church and the Rise of American Imperialism,* comes to a similar conclusion:

While the Methodist Church did not in itself instigate American imperialism, either consciously or unconsciously, it did help to develop a *rationale* which would make this type of venture more palatable to individuals who might ordinarily have been exceedingly critical.[20]

The faith that America's course of action had the approval of divine providence seemed to be confirmed by the swift and complete triumphs of American arms.[21] Religious spokesmen saw parallels between the American victories and those of Israel in Biblical times. The editor of *Christian and Missionary Alliance*

[18] Smylie, dissertation, *op. cit.,* p. 489.   [19] *Ibid.*

[20] Washington, D.C., 1961, p. 3. As in the case of MacKenzie's study, so also in this present essay, references to the Methodist church are almost entirely concerned with the Methodist Episcopal Church. Cf. James E. Kirby, "Matthew Simpson and the Mission of America," *Church History,* XXXVI, 3 (1967), 306: "What is operative in the thought of Methodism's late nineteenth century spokesman is the identification of the message and mission of the Christian faith with the national destiny of the United States of America."

[21] Cf. Julius W. Pratt, *Expansionists of 1898: The Acquisition of Hawaii and The Spanish Islands* (Baltimore, 1936), pp. 289 ff. I am indebted to Pratt for most of the comments from the religious press in this section.

said that the story of Dewey's victory "read almost like the stories of the ancient battles of the Lord in the times of Joshua, David, and Jehoshaphat." [22] Alexander Blackburn, writing in the *Standard,* a Baptist publication, said, "The magnificent fleets of Spain have gone down as marvelously, I had almost said, as miraculously, as the walls of Jericho went down," and he maintained that the nation now had a duty "to throw its strong protecting arms around . . . the Philippine Islands" and to practice an "imperialism of righteousness." [23] President Butler of Butler College, an institution of the Disciples of Christ in Indianapolis, said that the guns of Manila were "God's own trumpet-tones summoning his people out of their isolation into the broad arena of the world's great life." [24] And within a few weeks after Dewey's victory a Presbyterian writer could say that the religious press was practically unanimous "as to the desirability of America's retaining the Philippines as a duty in the interest of human freedom and Christian progress." [25] Thus, as one scholar observes, "Missionary opportunity as a wartime interest—so conspicuously absent during the prewar period—had its inception in the Manila victory, and by midsummer became a major objective." [26]

MacKenzie, in his study, shows that "one of the strongest supporters of American acquisition of the Philippines was Bishop James M. Thoburn, who was known to advocate American possession from the very commencement of the war. . . . Praising the success of the American navy at Manila, and looking upon this as the work of God to extend his gospel to the Orient," this Methodist bishop serving in Southern Asia "expressed himself as 'delighted,' as he believed all Protestant missionaries were, to hear that public opinion in the United States was rapidly turning toward acceptance of the permanent occupation of the Philippines by the United States." [27] Methodist Bishop Hurst shared his colleague's views concerning the Philippines:

[22] XX (May 18, 1898), 468.   [23] XLV (Aug. 6, 1898), 913.

[24] *Christian-Evangelist,* XXXV (July 7, 1898), 13.

[25] *The Interior,* XXIX (Aug. 25, 1898), 1040.

[26] William Archibald Karraker, "The American Churches and the Spanish-American War" (unpublished Ph.D. dissertation, The Divinity School, University of Chicago, 1943), p. 280.

[27] MacKenzie, *op. cit.,* p. 88.

Whatever becomes of the political status of the four hundred islands [*sic*], . . . Protestantism must enter. . . . The missionary aspirations of the American Church will add this new people to its map for conquest. . . . The elimination of the evils from the present subtle compounds of idolatry and such low types of Christianity . . . will be conditions of success at even the first stages of the new evangelistic effort. . . . Never has there fallen, at one stroke of the bell of destiny, such a burden upon the American Church.[28]

The *Baptist Union* agreed that "The conquest by force of arms must be followed up by conquest for Christ." [29]

The Presbyterians were the first to take action. Three weeks after Dewey's victory the Presbyterian General Assembly, meeting at Winona, Indiana, on May 25, enthusiastically endorsed the following section in the report of its standing committee on foreign missions, the Rev. George F. Pentecost, D.D., chairman:

We cannot be deaf or blind to the startling providence of God which is just now opening up new and unexpected fields for foreign mission work. The peace-speaking guns of Admiral Dewey have opened the gates which henceforth make accessible not less than 8,000,000 of people who have for 300 years been fettered by bonds almost worse than those of heathenism, and oppressed by a tyrannical priesthood only equalled in cruelty by the nation whose government has been a blight and blistering curse upon every people over whom her flag has floated, a system of religion almost if not altogether worse than heathenism. . . . We cannot ignore the fact that God has given into our hands, that is, into the hands of American Christians, the Philippine Islands, and thus opened a wide door and effectual to their populations, and has, by the very guns of our battleships, summoned us to go up and possess the land.[30]

On June 20 the executive council of the Presbyterian board unanimously adopted a report concerning the expediency of

[28] "The Religious Significance of the Philippines," *The Christian Advocate,* LXVIII (June 30, 1898), 1049–50.

[29] VIII (Aug. 27, 1898), 631.

[30] Quoted by Arthur Judson Brown, *The New Era in the Philippines* (New York, 1903), pp. 173–74. We would raise the question here: To what extent does the "New Era" theme in Brown's work share and sympathize with the "New Era" concept put forth by Josiah Strong ten years earlier?

opening mission work in the Philippines. It said "that the Christian people of America should immediately and prayerfully consider the duty of entering the door which God in His providence is opening," and it recommended that an early conference be held with representatives of other Protestant missionary agencies to plan the new work cooperatively.[31]

The following day, June 21, the board of managers of the Missionary Society of the Methodist Episcopal Church, meeting in New York, resolved that "there are strong providential indications that, through the agency of the navy and army of the United States, the Philippine Islands . . . will be open at an early day to Protestant missionary endeavor," and that Methodist representatives should meet with those from other boards to plan the new work along the lines of Christian comity.[32]

The suggested meeting of mission board representatives took place at the invitation of the Presbyterian board in their New York offices on July 13. "The result was the unanimous adoption of resolutions declaring that the duty of Protestantism to give a purer faith to the people of our new possessions represents the deep and solemn Christian patriotism of the country, and that support will be given to the Boards for this purpose." [33]

On September 20 the board of managers of the Methodist Missionary Society met again and ordered that the following resolution be forwarded to the American members of the Peace Commission in Paris:

To the Hon. Wm. R. Day,
President of the U.S. Peace Commission
Paris, France

Dear Sir:

Disclaiming all desire to interfere with the prerogatives of the United States Government in determining the political destiny of the Philippine Islands, we nevertheless most earnestly urge that in the future there shall prevail in those islands absolute religious liberty. . . .

[31] *Ibid.*, pp. 175–77.
[32] Minutes for June 21, 1898, board of managers of the Missionary Society of the Methodist Episcopal Church, XVII, 221.
[33] Brown, *op. cit.*, p. 178.

We most earnestly desire that such guarantee of religious liberty may be secured in the peace negotiations now pending between the United States and Spain, as shall render the intolerance of the past absolutely impossible in the future.

> By order of the Board of Managers
> of the Missionary Society of the
> Methodist Episcopal Church.[34]

Three boards indicated their intention to open missionary work in the Philippines, namely, the Board of Foreign Missions of the Presbyterian Church, U.S.A., the Missionary Society of the Methodist Episcopal Church, and the American Baptist Missionary Union. Representatives of these three societies met again in New York on November 17, 1898, at which time the Baptists and Methodists reported that for financial reasons they could not enter the Philippines at present, but the Presbyterians were prepared to move ahead, and accordingly they transferred the Rev. and Mrs. James B. Rodgers from their Southern Brazil mission to Manila, where Mr. Rodgers arrived on April 21, 1899.[35]

Meanwhile, a wide range of churchmen in the United States were aroused to a sense of interest, obligation, and support for the prospects of missionary opportunities in the Philippines. In June 1898 the Methodist editors of *World-Wide Missions* were already anticipating that because of Dewey's victory

[34] Minutes for Sept. 20, 1898, board of managers of the Missionary Society of the Methodist Episcopal Church. It is an exaggeration, however, to suggest, as does Margaret Leech in her book *In the Days of McKinley*, that the General Missionary Committee of the Methodist Episcopal Church was "one of the most active of the expansionist pressure groups" (New York, 1959), p. 344.

[35] James B. Rodgers, *Forty Years in the Philippines: A History of The Philippine Mission of the Presbyterian Church in the United States of America, 1899–1939* (New York, 1940), p. 2. Dr. Rodgers also reports here that the Rev. William H. Lingle, D.D., had visited Manila in December 1898, on behalf of the Presbyterian Board to appraise the missionary possibilities of the situation, "and had recommended very strongly that no mission be established because of the evident fact that there were so many needy places in China where the Board ought to send its missionaries that he felt it would be a fatal mistake to open another mission and so divert funds from the needier work in the older missions in China. However, the Board had already taken action and we were on our way before his report reached the office."

we are no longer compelled to go to a foreign country to seek raw
heathen. When patriotism and evangelism can go hand in hand, the
one strengthens the other. If it should result that the Philippine Islands are to remain under a protectorate of this country for years to
come, it will be our immediate duty to establish a Mission there. And
how glorious it would be to think that we have one Mission in the
heathen world with the starry flag afloat above it! [36]

Later in the summer, Dr. Adna B. Leonard, one of the secretaries
of the Methodist Missionary Society affirmed that "the Christian
Church must follow the army and occupy the territory conquered
by the war power of the nation." [37] The East Ohio Conference of
the Methodist Church at its annual meeting in 1898 referred to
the "glorious consummated war with Spain," and saw in the "overthrow of Spanish rule . . . the voice of God calling the Church"
to give the freed territories "a pure Protestant Christianity." [38]

The Puget Sound Conference of the Methodist Church, meeting in Tacoma in September 1898 sent a telegram to President
McKinley congratulating him on his "statesmanlike conduct of
the war," and it further resolved that "through the short but
glorious war just closed, we are brought face to face with impera
tive duty in Cuba, Porto Rico, and the Philippines. Civil liberty is
really found only under the shadow of the evangelistic gospel,
and that the fruits of holy sacrifice and blood may be fully secured, a free gospel should be sent as this nation's best gift to
those who lately sat in chains and darkness." [39] Bishop C. C.
McCabe, who presided at the conference, was somewhat of an
episcopal maverick, and at the close of the conference—apparently carried away by the emotion of the occasion—he abruptly
appointed one of his ministers, the Rev. Charles A. Owen, to
"First Church, Manila," without any provision for his continuing

[36] X (June, 1898), 4. There was some debate and discussion, at least
among the Methodists, as to whether the Philippines should be classed as
home missions or foreign missions, if the islands came under the American
flag.

[37] *Gospel in All Lands* (Aug., 1898), p. 363.

[38] *Minutes of the East Ohio Conference of the Methodist Episcopal
Church*, Sept., 1898, pp. 16, 27.

[39] *Journal of the Puget Sound Annual Conference of the Methodist Episcopal Church*, Sept., 1898, pp. 36, 51.

support and without consultation with the Methodist Missionary Society.[40] Owen arrived in Manila in mid-November and on January 2, 1899, he wrote:

> I have preached more than forty times, held revival services eighteen nights, and eight were converted. I baptized one by sprinkling, and on December 18 I baptized four candidates by immersion in the Pasig River. . . . In looking over the field I find that we will make the most headway with this people by establishing mission schools and teaching the children, and they in turn will change the minds of their parents in regard to the pure religion of Christ.[41]

In terms of Methodist polity, the appointment of Owen was highly irregular, if not illegal, because Manila was within the jurisdiction of Bishop Thoburn's area, where McCabe had no authority, and the general missionary committee of the church had not yet officially established a mission there. Hence Owen was not recognized by the general missionary committee and received no support from it. He returned to the United States with his wife in the summer of 1899, suffering from ill-health, and from frustration over the misunderstanding concerning his appointment.[42]

Owen was not, however, the first Protestant minister to preach in the Philippines. It is claimed that Chaplain George C. Stull of the First Montana Volunteers, a Methodist minister from the Montana Conference, "held the first Protestant service on shore in the Philippines." [43] In his journal for Sunday, August 28, 1898, Chaplain Stull in Manila made the following entry:

[40] *Ibid.*, pp. 14, 23. His name is elsewhere mentioned as Owens, but here in the official record of his appointment by the bishop, he is listed as "Rev. C. A. Owen."

[41] *World-Wide Missions*, XI (Sept., 1899), 6.

[42] A report on the irregularity of Owen's appointment appeared in *The Christian Advocate*, LXXIII (Nov. 24, 1898), 1900. A brief notice that Owen had returned to the United States appeared in *The Christian Advocate*, LXXIV (Aug. 3, 1899), 1230. I am indebted to the Rev. J. Tremayne Copplestone for calling this episode concerning Owen's appointment to my attention.

[43] Homer C. Stuntz, *The Philippines and the Far East* (Cincinnati, 1904), p. 415; but Stuntz is not altogether reliable and his "facts" must be accepted with caution. An Episcopal army chaplain was also holding services in Manila in August 1898, but his name and the exact dates are not known.

What a wonderful day this has been! Arose early from my bed in the Mortuary Chapel and looked about for a place to hold services. The most acceptable place was one of the old Spanish dungeons facing the bay. Dark and gloomy. But the sun was shining, and the men came, and the natives sat about on the outside and near the door and barred windows. How we sang; how the place was transformed; how the people wondered at our service! My text was, "The power of God." How He showed Himself to us. Eight responded to the invitation at the close of the service to identify themselves with God's people; not to start a Methodist Church, but to band together to honor God. This was the first distinctive Protestant religious service, so the people tell me; for to hold any but the State service heretofore meant death. That the power of God will use this day to make a good Catholic better, any weak American stronger, any backslider ashamed, and the gloomy old dungeon the beginning of wonderful things in these Islands, is my prayer.[44]

In the United States churchmen continued to express themselves vigorously in favor of keeping open the doors for missionary work in the Philippines. A representative of the Christian and Missionary Alliance was reported in their church magazine for September 28 as

visiting Washington this week for the purpose of interviewing the President and Secretary of State . . . to impress upon the administra-

[44] *Ibid.*, pp. 415–16. Actually, the first public Protestant service in the Philippines was apparently held by two laymen, Charles A. Glunz and Frank A. Jackson, representatives of the Y.M.C.A. who entered Manila with the army of occupation on Sat., Aug. 13, 1898, and held a service the following day. See: *An Effort to Help. Report: Army and Navy Department . . . Young Men's Christian Association* (Philippines, 1901); W. Cameron Forbes, *The Philippine Islands* (Boston, 1928), II, 65; T. Valentino Sitoy, Jr., "Nineteenth Century Evangelical Beginnings in the Philippines," *South East Asia Journal of Theology*, IX, 2 (1967), 54; and Sitoy, "An Abortive Spanish Protestant Mission in the Philippines," *Silliman Journal*, XV, 2 (1968), 243–80. It would also be useful and interesting to have a study made of the contribution of Mr. and Mrs. Arthur W. Prautch, who had been Methodist missionaries in India for a time, but then came to the Philippines in the fall of 1898 and established themselves in business in Manila, where they maintained an active interest in the advancement of Protestant missionary work. Bishop Thoburn contacted them when he visited Manila early in 1899 and left Prautch in charge of the Methodist congregation started by the bishop, until regular Methodist missionaries could be appointed.

tion . . . the importance of securing an open door for missions in the Philippine Islands and holding the advantage which God has given to the American government in the interests of religious liberty and Christian evangelization in this important region.[45]

Julius W. Pratt, in his book *The Expansionists of 1898,* says, "We may conclude that the great preponderance of vocal religious sentiment, in the summer and fall of 1898, was in favor of retaining the Philippines. . . . President McKinley, with whom the decision rested, was neither unaware of this sentiment nor indifferent to it." [46] Even Mrs. McKinley talked to friends about her interest in "converting the Igorrotes [*sic.*]."

In his speeches in the mid-West during October 1898, President McKinley (who once said, "I am a Methodist and nothing but a Methodist") declared:

[At Omaha] The faith of a Christian nation recognizes the hand of Almighty God in the ordeal through which we have passed. Divine favor seemed manifest everywhere. In fighting for humanity's sake we have been signally blessed. . . . Now, as then, we will do our duty.

[At Chicago] My countrymen, the currents of destiny flow through the hearts of the people. . . . And the movements of men planned and designed by the Master of men, will never be interrupted by the American people.[47]

After noting the reception and response of the public and press to his speeches concerning the duty of assuming colonial burdens, the president returned to Washington and finally came to a decision to retain the Philippines as a sacred trust, as a mission of "benevolent assimilation." Later, when a delegation from the general missionary committee of the Methodist Church called on him in his office, he described to them how he had arrived at his decision:

The truth is I didn't want the Philippines, and when they came to us as a gift from the gods, I did not know what to do with them. . . . I sought counsel from all sides—Democrats as well as Repub-

---

[45] *Christian and Missionary Alliance,* XXI (Sept. 28, 1898), 300. Quoted by Pratt, *op. cit.,* p. 315.

[46] Pratt, *op. cit.,* p. 314.   [47] *Ibid.,* p. 338.

licans—but got little help. . . . I walked the floor of the White House night after night until midnight; and I am not ashamed to tell you, gentlemen, that I went down on my knees and prayed Almighty God for light and guidance more than one night.

The president's prayers were finally answered.

And one night late it came to me this way—I don't know how it was, but it came: (1) that we could not give them back to Spain—that would be cowardly and dishonorable; (2) that we could not turn them over to France or Germany—our commercial rivals in the Orient—that would be bad business and discreditable; (3) that we could not leave them to themselves—they were unfit for self-government—and they would soon have anarchy and misrule over there worse than Spain's was; and (4) that there was nothing left for us to do but to take them all, and to educate the Filipinos, and uplift and civilize and Christianize them, and by God's grace do the very best we could by them, as our fellow-men for whom Christ died. And then I went to bed, and went to sleep, and slept soundly, and the next morning I sent for the chief engineer of the War Department (our map-maker), and I told him to put the Philippines on the map of the United States, and there they are, and there they will stay while I am President.[10]

48 The interview took place on Tuesday, Nov. 21, 1899, but the account of it was not published until more than three years later in an article by one of the members of the Methodist delegation, General James F. Rusling, "Interview with President McKinley," *The Christian Advocate*, LXXVIII (Jan. 22, 1903), 137–38.

Commenting on McKinley's explanation of how he came to this decision by way of prayer, Pratt says, "The answer that thus seemed to McKinley to have come from above may easily have grown from seed planted in his mind by the clergy and the religious press," *op. cit.*, p. 316. Margaret Leech says, "He betrayed his intellectual limitations, not by the hard choice to which he had been reluctantly led, but by an explanation which belittled a great quandary of statesmanship to resolve a dilemma of conscience. The President's political instinct was never more sure than in adorning the territorial acquisition with the bright leaf of duty and the rose of spiritual salvation," *op. cit.*, p. 345. Thomas A. Bailey says, "It is possible that McKinley heard the voice of the people rather than the voice of God, for this statement has most of the earmarks of imperialism," in *Diplomatic History of the American People* (7th ed.; New York, 1964), p. 474. Reinhold Niebuhr has spoken of the "self-deception," "hypocrisy," "dishonesty," and "fiction" that accompanied McKinley's "heavenly vision," in *Moral Man and Immoral Society* (New York, 1932), pp. 99–103. Samuel Flagg Bemis, in his *Diplomatic History of the United States* (3rd ed.; New York, 1950), describes

In November the nation went to the polls for midterm elections and gave McKinley a working majority in both houses of Congress for the two remaining years of his term.

During the winter the treaty of peace was negotiated with Spain and signed in Paris on December 10, 1898, and then debated by the Senate until it was ratified on February 6, 1899. According to the terms of the treaty, Spain relinquished sovereignty over Cuba and ceded to the United States Puerto Rico, Guam, and the Philippines.

Encouraged by these events, American Protestant churchmen expounded further on the providential aspects of duty and destiny that were manifest, at least to some of them. The Rev. John Henry Barrows, D.D., president of Oberlin College, said that America had not only divine guidance, but "a divine mission." Referring to the events leading up to the Spanish-American War, he said, "God has been speaking of late with a voice which nothing can drown. The unexpected has happened. This means that God has intervened." The war itself, he maintained, was "righteous and necessary. . . . Providence pointed the guns of Manila Bay which destroyed the Spanish cruisers. . . . Mastered by powers mightier than ourselves, we have pondered, and now accepted our destiny. . . . God himself has brought us to the position we are now in." [49]

During the winter of 1898, Dr. Barrows delivered the Morse lectures on "The Christian Conquest of Asia" at Union Theological Seminary in New York City. In these lectures Barrows pointed out that "the United States possesses at the present hour stepping stones for its commercial and moral pathway across the Pacific." He believed that "God has placed us, like Israel of old, in the centre of the nations. . . . And wherever on pagan shores the voice of the American missionary and teacher is heard, there is fulfilled the manifest destiny of the Christian Republic." [50]

As Americans debated the expansionist dimensions of their des-

---

the whole Philippine venture following upon McKinley's decision as "the great aberration" (p. 463).

[49] "God's Hand in Recent American History," *The Interior*, XXIX (Nov. 24, 1898), 1441–42.

[50] *The Christian Conquest of Asia* (New York, 1899), pp. xi, 238, 248.

tiny, Rudyard Kipling wrote a poem urging them to "Take up the white man's burden." But Kipling, who has been described as "a minor prophet and a major poet of British imperialism," [51] also warned Americans through the defeatism and pessimism that pervaded his poem, against the perils of imperialism:

> Take up the White Man's Burden—
>   Send forth the best ye breed—
> Go bind your sons to exile
>   to serve your captives' need;
>
> And when your goal is nearest
>   The end for others sought,
> Watch Sloth and heathen Folly
>   Bring all your hope to naught.[52]

The obstacles appealed to the Protestant sense of obligation, and the opportunities attracted a benevolent paternalism—toward "our little brown brother." [53]

The largest Protestant denomination in the nation at this time, the Methodist Episcopal Church, had officially delayed beginning a mission in the Philippines due to financial difficulties. The board of managers of the Missionary Society had, however, indicated its interest for work in the Philippines as early as June 21, 1898. On July 21, Dr. Adna B. Leonard, corresponding secretary of the society, requested Bishop James M. Thoburn, who had episcopal jurisdiction for southern Asia, to prepare to visit the islands and survey the missionary opportunities. A cable of the one word "Go," sent by Secretary Leonard from New York to Bishop Thoburn in Bombay on January 22, 1899, gave the signal to proceed. It was not until February 28, however, that Thoburn arrived in Manila, coming from Penang where he had presided over the Malaysia Mission Conference. The following two Sundays, March

---

[51] Bailey, *op. cit.*, p. 476.

[52] Kipling's poem was first published in *McClure's Magazine*, XII, Feb., 1899. See Albert K. Weinberg's discussion of "The White Man's Burden" in *Manifest Destiny: A Study of Nationalist Expansionism in American History* (Baltimore, 1935), pp. 301–23.

[53] The phrase was used by William Howard Taft when he arrived in Manila in June 1899. Cf. Leon Wolff, *op. cit.*, p. 313.

5 and March 12, he held public services in a rented theater in Manila, and during the course of his two-week visit he contacted as many people as possible. In his report of the visit, which was published in *World-Wide Missions* for June 1899, Thoburn spoke of "the seeming providential tokens which indicate the missionary duty of our Church in this remote field." [54] The first point he mentioned was that all the Americans whom he met in Manila agreed that the United States could not withdraw, but rather should assume permanent responsibility for the government of the islands in order to prevent "prolonged anarchy and bloodshed throughout the Islands." As to the providential opportunities, Thoburn urged that Methodist missionary work should be started "without further delay" among the Roman Catholic Filipinos, whose religion, he said, was "to a great extent, a mere superstition." He felt that the great desire among Filipinos to learn English, the need for girl's schools, and the desire for literature, all provided openings for the most effective beginnings of missionary work. In response to Thoburn's recommendations, the first regular Methodist missionaries were sent to the Philippines early in 1900.

The report of Thoburn's visit and views aroused considerable interest in the Philippines among Methodists in the United States, and the July issue of *Methodist Review* carried an article by John P. Brushingham on "American Protestantism and Expansion" that endorsed an aggressive missionary campaign in the islands. The writer said that the first shot of the American guns at Cavite "was heard round the world and became a revelation and a prophecy." Dewey's victory, he said, placed the opportunity and responsibility upon "our American republic . . . to give the blessings of a modern form of government and Anglo-Saxon civilization. . . . The distant echo of Dewey's guns was a prophecy that under God, and baptized by the divine Spirit, we are equal to the responsibility of this great providential opening." He claimed that McKinley was the "Abraham Lincoln of the new emancipation," and that every argument being used against expansion now "had been used over and over again for the past century against foreign missions in general." He believed that, if American Protes-

[54] XI (June, 1899), 6–7.

tants would only go to the Philippines "in a Christlike spirit, the people will soon take knowledge of us and learn to love the truly Christian as thoroughly as they have learned to hate and despise those who have robbed them." The reference was to the Spanish Roman Catholic Church, for the writer felt that

the most serious problem in the future of the Philippines is to correct the abuses which natives and Spanish alike have had to suffer at the hands of those who represented the Church. It may be said that American Protestantism in these fields would goad Roman Catholicism to a higher standard.

In closing, this Methodist writer endorsed and emphasized a statement made by Senator Davis of the Peace Commission, "America *is* the evangelist of the world." [55]

When Methodists came to their annual conferences in the summer of 1899, the Eric Conference said, "Clearly God has given us the Philippines." And as one scholar has shown, "In no case was there any [Methodist] Conference which offered resolutions criticizing in any way the war or its consequences for the country and the church." [56]

Anti-Roman Catholic sentiment was a definite factor in arousing missionary concern among Protestants in the United States for work in the Philippines. There was a predominant feeling that Anglo-Saxon, Protestant, republican America was God's measure and means for the establishment of His Kingdom on earth, and Protestants then generally viewed Roman Catholicism as a sub-Christian, if not anti-Christian, force. MacKenzie, in his study, shows that this kind of sentiment was widespread by 1890. In 1889 the Northern New York Conference of the Methodist Episcopal Church "drew attention to the increasing dangers from immigrants and their un-American ideas, and especially the Catholic Church." [57] In 1891, the Maine Conference referred to the dangers of "rum and Romanism." [58] And as soon as the war broke out, even before the battle of Manila Bay, the *Christian and Missionary Alliance* editorial of April 27 displayed an interest in

[55] LXXXI (July, 1899), 585–94.   [56] MacKenzie, *op. cit.*, p. 86.
[57] *Ibid.*, p. 27.   [58] *Ibid.*, p. 28.

the Philippines along with Cuba and Puerto Rico, and said that the war was God's instrument for striking another blow "at that system of iniquity, the papacy." [59]

There is no evidence that any responsible Protestant church body or authority, except in the Protestant Episcopal Church, considered the predominant position of the Catholic church in the Philippines as a reason for *not* starting missionary work there, but, to the contrary, it was widely held that the presence and power of Roman Catholicism was evidence of the need for the "pure witness" of Protestantism. The Rev. R. G. Hobbs wrote an article on "The Philippine Islands" that was published in *The Christian Advocate* for September 1898, and was reprinted in part in *The Gospel in All Lands* for October, in which he said:

The Philippines show the legitimate fruits of Romanism. The Roman Church is supreme. She has taught the natives to tell their beads, but has taught them nothing else. . . . The priests, the black angels of the islands, are just what their predecessors were in Spain in the days of the Inquisition. They are as bigoted, cruel, and unclean as those old torturers were. . . . May it not be that Providence has something to do with the fact that this great Protestant nation is about to secure control of the splendid Philippine group? Will it not seem likely to Christian people that we have an obligation resting upon us to plant a pure form of Christianity there?

Whatever else the United States does for the Philippines she owes it to humanity to see to it that religious liberty is secured to the people. Break the clutch which Rome has put upon those people, and give them a chance for a civilization which is something more than Christianized paganism. . . . The taking of the Philippines is part of one of the holiest wars ever undertaken by men. . . . This is our opportunity to give the Gospel and liberal Western ideas and institutions to a people in the Far East.[60]

One of the strongest supporters of Protestant, Anglo-Saxon civilization in opposition to "politico-ecclesiastical Romanism," was the Rev. James M. King, a Methodist minister and general secretary of the National League for the Protection of American In-

[59] Quoted by Pratt, *op. cit.*, p. 287.
[60] *The Christian Advocate*, LXXIII (Sept. 1, 1898), 1410–11.

stitutions. In his large book *Facing the Twentieth Century: Our Country, Its Power and Peril,* which was completed in January 1899, King maintained that, properly seen,

the Spanish-American War was a war between Rome and Washington; between the papal power and republican power; between ecclesiasticism and liberty; between the bondage of superstition and the freedom of truth. It was the severest blow to the arrogant pretensions of political ecclesiasticism which has been struck in a century of time.[61]

He spoke of "that notoriously vilest type of Romanism intrenched in the Philippines," and insisted that the people of these islands "must adjust and accommodate themselves to our institutions, but we must not adjust our institutions to any features of their mediaevalism. . . . It is not our mission to travel back through the centuries and meet an inferior civilization . . . but to flood it with our better light, and when its iniquities are thus revealed, compel them to be promptly forsaken by entering upon this better way." [62] In conclusion, the author proclaimed that "manifest destiny, divinely ordered, is upon us," and the duty of America for "the greater twentieth century" is to extend "Anglo-Saxon Christian civilization in its perfect work" to the far corners of the earth.[63]

In all this there was undoubtedly a genuine concern and compassion for the spiritual condition of the Filipino people, despite an identification of Protestant missionary obligation with American patriotism and Anglo-Saxon civilization. After twenty years in the Philippines, the first regularly appointed Protestant missionary there looked back to the beginnings and explained once again, in words of personal faith, what had brought Americans to the Philippines:

In the beginning God! . . . Who else but He could have been so moved by the cries of a suffering people which went up to heaven? Who else could have taken a nation of peaceful neutrals in the world's affairs and driven them across the seas and caused them to take over

[61] New York, 1899, p. 462.   [62] *Ibid.*, pp. 473, 475.
[63] *Ibid.*, p. 593.

the mandate for these islands? Isolated America . . . Patient Philippines, and God moved.[64]

[64] James B. Rodgers, *Twenty Years of Presbyterian Work in the Philippines* (supplement to the *Philippine Presbyterian*), 1919, p. 3. Homer C. Stuntz, one of the early Methodist missionary leaders in the Philippines, summarized more specifically why American Protestant missionaries had come to the Philippines: "Protestantism is in the Philippines . . . because her testimony is needed to counteract those errors of Roman Catholic teaching which put in peril the salvation of the individual sinner, and thus jeopard the whole program of Christ for this world as well as the next" (*op. cit.*, p. 364).

Religion and the Public Schools in the Philippines: 1899-1906

SISTER MARY DORITA CLIFFORD, B.V.M.

The failure of the Catholic church in the United States to assume responsibility for the religious development of the Philippines when the sovereignty of those islands passed from Spain to the United States has never been honestly admitted by American Catholics. Until it is, there is little likelihood that questions such as proselytism in the public schools, discrimination in the hiring of teachers and the promotion of superintendents, and the introduction of biased textbooks into the schools, which were the major problems relating to education in the early days of occupation, can be discussed with any degree of candor or freedom from polemic. Such an admission is based on the records of appeals from the American hierarchy in the islands which went unheeded,[1] and from statistics in War Department records which indicate a lack of response on the part of Catholic laymen to government and church invitations to serve as teachers in the Philippines.[2]

The lack of American response was due, at least in part, to the feeling that sending missionaries to the islands might imply that American Catholics accepted as true the charges of scandal, negligence, and tyranny leveled against the friars.[3] But after Rome refused to expel the friars and sent an American archbishop and three American bishops to the archipelago, this excuse was no longer tenable, yet the response did not improve. The age was

[1] Michael J. O'Doherty, "Religious Situation in the Philippines," *American Ecclesiastical Review*, LXXIV (1926), 129–38.

[2] Bureau of Insular Affairs File 470, National Archives, Washington, D.C., (hereafter referred to as BIA File, NA).

[3] Bishop Thomas A. Hendricks to James Cardinal Gibbons, June 2, 1908, Hendricks Papers, Nazareth College, Rochester, N.Y.

one of competitive Christianity, and American Catholics seemed willing to fight Protestant efforts to proselytize, but not to assume their own burden. And when, as frequently happened, bigotry raised its ugly head, it was as likely to be a Catholic as a Protestant one.

The last two decades of the nineteenth century had not made for understanding among Christians. The American Protective Association (A.P.A.) attacks on the Catholic Indian schools in 1892,[4] and their concerted effort to rule Catholic school graduates out of teaching positions in the city-charter election of 1894 in San Francisco,[5] had developed within a part of the Catholic community an almost perpetual state of belligerency easily roused and willing to believe any charge against a Protestant without investigation. This spirit was fully reciprocated by militant Protestants. Both groups supported a species of "yellow press" which published protests "on cue" and under most Christian names. It was against this background that an inexperienced America embarked on her first colonial experiment, transporting a secular public school system to a predominantly Catholic country.

Under the Spanish government in the islands public instruction had been one of the many duties assigned to the church, and, although the salaries of teachers were paid from the royal treasury, the educational policies and practices were determined largely by ecclesiastical authorities.[6] For many reasons, involving a whole range of problems too numerous to discuss here, the primary school system had never been able to achieve the level of excellence desired by the government and the church. Certain policies and practices dictated at first by necessity had become sanctified

[4] Henry J. Sievers, "Catholic Indian School Issues and the Election of 1892," *Catholic Historical Review*, XXXVIII (1952), 129–55.

[5] Joseph S. Brusher, "Peter C. Yorke and the A.P.A. in San Francisco," *Catholic Historical Review*, XXXVII (1951), 129–50. James F. Smith was a member of the Liberal League, a nonsectarian group working against bigotry, established by Peter C. Yorke.

[6] Frederick W. Fox, "Primary Education in the Philippines, 1565–1863," *Philippine Studies*, XIII (1965), 288, quoting Feodor Jagor's report; see also Fox, "Some Notes on Public Elementary Education in Iloilo Province, 1885–1899," *ibid.*, II (1954), 5–19; and Sister Maria Carmen, "The Superior Normal School for Women Teachers in Manila, 1893–98," *ibid.*, II (1954), 217–30.

by age and custom so that any proposals for radical change were considered a form of attack. During the insurrection against the Spanish government in 1896, education had come to a standstill, and school buildings commandeered as barracks or hospitals did not reopen until about three weeks after the American army of occupation had taken Manila in 1898.[7]

The decision to reopen the schools was a military one aimed at pacification rather than an attempt to formulate an educational policy for the Philippines. Consequently, the school personnel was made up largely of officers and soldiers detailed for this work by General Elwel S. Otis, military governor of the islands.

General Otis appointed Father William D. McKinnon, chaplain of the First California Volunteers, to supervise the work of education. Under his direction seven schools opened in Manila on September 1, 1898. The success of these first American schools, primitive though they were, was due to many factors, but chief among them was the fact that the transition from Spanish to American sovereignty had left education under the supervision of the Catholic chaplain who was *en rapport* both with the Spanish ecclesiastical and American military authorities and who spoke Spanish very well.

But the change of sovereignty also brought separation of church and state. To militant Protestants this meant that the walls of opposition to missionary work in the islands had come tumbling down and that the field was wide open.[8] To Catholics, on the other hand, it meant that various Protestant churches, more or less under the protection of the American flag, could now make frontal attacks upon the faith of an already Christian people.[9] Catholics, therefore, tended to oppose the retention of the islands

[7] *Report of the Philippine Commission, 1900*, Part III, pp. 456–76, BIA Files, NA.

[8] Arthur J. Brown, *Report on a Visitation of the Philippine Mission* (New York, 1902), p. 173, reporting to the Presbyterian General Assembly at Lake Winona, Indiana, in May 1898, might be taken as indicative of the Protestant attitude. See also the essay in this volume by Gerald H. Anderson, "Providence and Politics behind Protestant Missionary Beginnings in the Philippines," p. 286.

[9] J. Church, "The Truth about the Catholic Church in the Philippines," *Catholic World*, LXVIII (1899), 289–303, is representative of the Catholic viewpoint.

while Protestants clamored for their possession. As the peace conference deliberated, both groups, armed with righteousness, watched each other warily, militantly, with little charity and no trust, while the Catholics and Protestants who realized the deeper tragedy of competitive Christianity found no avenue of communication open with each other. Government officials charged with the obligation of absolute impartiality had no easy task and no assurance that anyone would credit them with acting in good faith. The accumulation of protests and complaints against every American assigned to the post of supervisor of education in the Philippines during the first ten years of American administration of the islands by adherents of various Christian churches gives ample evidence that even men who acted honestly and impartially were subject to attack, usually most severe from their own coreligionists.

The first great wave of bigotry against the administration of the schools was set in motion by the Rev. N. H. Harriman, a Protestant chaplain from Tacoma, who had stayed on in the Philippines to work for the British and Foreign Bible Society, when he published an article intended to stimulate sleeping Protestants to accept the missionary challenge.[10] He charged that Catholics were using the United States government to obstruct the work of Protestants in the islands, that bell towers in Manila were sending out signals to aid the insurgents against the American forces, and that

---

[10] "The Catholic Church Has the Field," *The Independent*, LI (Sept., 1899), 2795–2800. This article was quoted, reviewed, and reprinted in many Protestant newspapers and periodicals throughout the country, and letters of protest about one or another of the charges began to pour into the offices of President McKinley and Secretary of War Root. BIA File 1158, NA, contains numerous letters from the *Baptist Union, Baptist Standard, National Advocate,* the American Bible and Tract Society, the Y.M.C.A., and many private persons protesting the action of General Otis in "giving Catholics a free hand" in the islands. Otis was described as an "incubus around the neck of the administration," a "man proving himself totally incapable," and an "incompetent by reason of turning the schools over to a Catholic." The Bureau of Insular Affairs cabled Otis about some of these charges on Nov. 9, 1899, and after his cable the following day answering negatively to charges of obstruction, Root sent form letters to all who had complained denying that the military commander was working against Protestant churches in the islands. The overall result was an upsurge of Protestant missionary activity.

Catholic chaplains were being supplied to the army in disproportionate numbers. He singled out Father McKinnon for special attack claiming that in his position as superintendent of schools he would see to it that only Catholic teachers were sent to the Philippines. He charged that sending parish priests into the public schools to bless the children was unconstitutional, and that Colonel Smith, a Catholic lawyer who had assisted McKinnon, had been promoted to the governorship of Negros in order to see that Protestants made no progress there.

As a matter of fact, at the time the article appeared Father McKinnon was already on his way back to the United States on leave and had been summoned to Washington to confer with President McKinley on problems of church and state.[11] Meanwhile, his successor Lieutenant George P. Anderson, a Protestant and a graduate of Yale Divinity School had assumed charge of the schools in June 1899.

Whatever other virtues Anderson may have possessed, he seems to have lacked perception and tact. When he took over the educational work of the islands, the schools were an adjunct to an army engaged in quelling the insurrection which was proving more costly and of much longer duration than had been anticipated. Consequently, as schools were set up in town after captured town, school personnel was harder to find. While some military supervisors worked to gain the good will of the people and recommended that the aid of parish priests be enlisted to allay the fears of parents about public schools,[12] Anderson pursued a policy hostile to Catholic sensibilities and lost much of the good will that Father McKinnon had built up. In March 1900 Captain Albert Todd was detailed to take over the supervision of the whole archipelago, and Anderson continued to supervise Manila

[11] On Oct. 27, 1899, McKinnon was promoted to Captain by President McKinley. At Secretary Root's recommendation he went to New York where on Oct. 29 he delivered an address, "American Policy in the Philippines," and to Boston on Oct. 30, where he lectured on "Our Flag in the Philippines." He returned to the Philippines in Dec. 1899, but not to educational work.

[12] Recommendations of Colonel W. E. Birkhimer, 28th Infantry, and Brigadier General W. A. Kobbe (Senate Document No. 129, 56th Cong., 2nd Sess., 1900).

schools until after the arrival of the second Philippine Commission under William Howard Taft in April of that same year.

On board the *Hancock*, April 21, four days out from San Francisco, the commission met to discuss the instructions Taft had received from Secretary of War Elihu Root, delegating to the commission the authority to establish civil government and to legislate for an educational system which, without removing the schools from the jurisdiction of the War Department, would place the administration in civilian hands with education rather than pacification as their goal.[13] They agreed to offer the direction of this system to Frederick W. Atkinson, a Harvard man, serving as principal of the high school in Springfield, Massachusetts, who had been proposed by Charles W. Eliot, president of Harvard.[14] The commission had been advised of the importance of establishing good relations with the church, and Taft had studied the problems and talked at length with Archbishop Ireland of St. Paul and with Maria Longworth Storer, wife of the new minister to Madrid, about the problems involved in establishing civil government in a Catholic country.[15]

Taft had hoped to avoid friction in critical areas, such as education, by making all concessions possible within the framework of the constitutional provision for separation of church and state.[16] To his consternation he discovered that a great deal of antagonism already existed over Anderson's arbitrary manner, and he decided that dismissal was called for. In explaining this action to Root he said:

[13] Memorandum for the Secretary of War prepared by Felix Frankfurter, Apr. 11, 1913, reviewing all instructions and acts relative to the government in the Philippine Islands, BIA File 141–16, NA.

[14] Taft to Root, Apr, 21, 1900, Taft Papers, MS. Div., Library of Congress, Washington, D.C. (hereafter referred to as LC). See also Edward Atkinson to Bishop Charles Brent, 1902, Brent Papers, MS. Div., LC. Atkinson's twin brother, Edward, was the pastor of the Episcopal Church of The Transfiguration in Boston, and this laid the superintendent open to the charge of being a clergyman although he was not even a member of that church.

[15] Maria Storer to Taft, May 17, 1900, and Taft to Maria Storer, July 12, 1900, Taft Papers, LC.

[16] Taft to Maria Storer, June 22, 1900, Taft Papers, LC.

The man whom General Otis selected as superintendent of schools after Father McKinnon left is a man of no discretion whatever, and has alienated Catholics by his rough method of dealing with questions certain to arise in public schools in a Catholic country. The sooner we get rid of Anderson the better. He has in his schools in Manila about 4,000 pupils whereas he ought to have 15,000 to 20,000. . . . Anderson, as I have already intimated, has made a misstep here, and I look to Atkinson to retrace it.[17]

When Atkinson arrived, Taft advised him to secure some Catholic school teachers with experience in public schools to counteract the adverse criticism of the Manila schools.[18] He also enlisted the aid of Benjamin Ide Wheeler, president of the University of California, requesting him to confer with Father Ramm of St. Mary's Cathedral, San Francisco, for the same purpose. He assured Wheeler that in dealing with a Catholic country it was essential to have as many capable Catholics in educational work as possible since they could count on the opposition of the Jesuits and others to the public school system.[19] At the same time he set one member of the commission, Bernard Moses, to the task of drafting a school bill that would provide for free, compulsory primary education without in any way interfering with private church schools and with due consideration for the religious education of children who would attend the public schools.[20] He suggested the Faribault plan introduced by Archbishop Ireland in Minnesota, which provided that schoolhouses could be used for religious instruction before and after school hours, as a feasible one.[21]

In December 1900 after many weeks of discussion, revision, and amendment, the final draft of the school bill, Act Seventy-four, was ready for public hearings and the final vote of the com-

[17] Taft to Root, July 26, 1900, Taft Papers, LC.

[18] Taft to Root, Aug. 6, 1900, Taft Papers, LC.

[19] Taft to Benjamin Ide Wheeler, Oct. 17, 1900, Taft Papers, LC, thanking him for help in getting teachers and explaining the need for Catholic teachers.

[20] Taft to Root, Dec. 14, 1900, Taft Papers, LC.

[21] Taft to Maria Storer, July 12, 1900, Taft Papers, LC. He describes the Faribault plan in detail and hopes for its success. Atkinson also favored it.

mission.[22] In executive sessions most of the disagreements had been ironed out, and passage was expected to be uneventful. However, this was not the case. Section 16, which provided for the use of school buildings after school hours for religious instruction and forbade schoolteachers to teach religion or to influence, ridicule, or criticize the religion of their pupils, drew a great deal of fire at the public hearings.[23] American teachers in Manila opposed it because they thought it compromised the independence of the public schools. Protestants opposed it as much because it forbade schoolteachers to teach religion as because it gave the church the right to use the buildings for religious instruction. The Federal party, anticlericals, based their opposition on fear that friars would return and get control of the schools. The commission supported the bill as written, and Taft spoke strongly in favor of the religious provisions, in part because he was anxious to forestall suspicion of interference in religion and because he thought the law perfectly compatible with separation of church and state.[24] He also acted from expediency ". . . giving Catholic parents a hook," on which to hang excuses for sending children to the public school if the church raised objections.[25]

There was little interest among Catholics concerning the bill until the opposition mounted,[26] then the editor of *Libertas* appeared before the board as representative of the *Centro Católico*, a club of Catholic laymen, to defend the provisions. When he de-

[22] Taft to Root, Dec. 27, 1900, Taft Papers, LC.

[23] In references to this Act, Taft refers to the section on religion as Section 15, but in the copy of the Act of 1901, which I have before me, Section 16 is the religious section, and Section 15 provides for the hiring of 1,000 teachers. It seems obvious in the letters which discuss it that when Taft refers to Section 15 he is referring to the religious question. I have used Section 16 throughout. See Taft to Root, Jan. 9, 1901, and frequently elsewhere, Taft Papers, LC.

[24] Taft to Root, Jan. 18, 1901, Taft Papers, LC.

[25] Taft to Root, Jan. 9, 1901, transmitting a copy of the bill with some comments on the hearings, and Taft to Root, Jan. 13, 1901, a complete report of the hearings, Taft Papers, LC.

[26] Father McKinnon to Archbishop Ireland, Jan. 19, 1901, Ireland Papers, Archdiocesan Archives, St. Paul, Minnesota (hereafter cited as AASP). McKinnon strongly favored the provision for religious instruction and wondered at the little interest shown in it by Catholics.

manded that Section 16 should be amended to read that only Catholic teachers could be employed in the schools and only the Catholic religion could be taught there, Judge Ide and Professor Moses withdrew their support. Ide claimed that he had doubts about the legality of Section 16, and Moses opposed it because he felt that the church would never accept the provision in the spirit in which it was proffered, so that it would be better to forbid the use of the schools for any such purposes, thereby eliminating the issue completely, than to run the risk of continual misunderstandings.[27] Taft, Worcester, and Wright continued to support the bill, and it passed by a 3 to 2 vote on January 21, 1901.[28]

The importance of the provision for the use of schoolhouses for religious instruction seems not to have been appreciated for some time, for, although Pope Leo XIII, in his Encyclical to the Philippines in 1903, counseled bishops to ". . . make every effort that the minds of the young instructed in public schools should not lack a knowledge of religion," [29] there are many indications that the time and place provided for religious instruction were not used to good effect.[30]

---

[27] Taft to Maria Storer, Jan. 18, 1901, Taft Papers, LC. Taft adds the comment, "They do not at all understand the spirit of American tolerance and they laugh at the idea of separation of church and state."

[28] Taft to Root, Jan. 21, 1901, Taft Papers, LC. Taft reports the passage of the bill and comments that he has been so attacked in the Catholic papers of the United States that he thought a complete report of the proceedings was called for.

[29] "Encyclical for the Philippines, 1903," Part VII, American Catholic Quarterly Review, XXVIII (1903), 377 (tr. into English by the editor).

[30] James P. Monaghan, S.J., "Conditions in the Philippines," Catholic Mind (Winter, 1912), 305–30. In an address to the national convention of the Knights of Columbus at Colorado Springs in August 1912, Father Monaghan told of 600,000 children in the public schools of the Philippines "studying from English textbooks and reciting their lessons in English, but that scarcely one of them has heard a word of Catholic instruction in fourteen years" (ibid., p. 310).

Just prior to the election in 1912, when Taft ran for president a Protestant politico-religious periodical, The American Citizen, made this statement: "Taft then recommended that Roman Catholic teachers be sent to teach the public schools in the Philippines, and had a law passed allowing Rome to teach her doctrines in the public schools at certain times, and had a Romanist ('Jim' Smith) put at the head of the Philippine Board of Educa-

Section 15 of the school bill providing for 1,000 American teachers of English had met no opposition in the hearings in January, but it was this provision which caused the islands' administration the most difficulty, brought forth charges of proselytism, favoritism, and discrimination, and led directly to the adoption of the civil service examination as a method of selecting teachers for the schools. The provisions of this section added enormously to the powers of the general superintendent of public instruction, and Atkinson had in his appointive power not only ten superintendencies of divisions, an almost unlimited number of principalships, but also 1,000 positions for teachers. He had the power to fix salaries for all of these positions within general limits set by the law.

The commission issued no guidelines for the selection of candidates for these positions, except Taft's advice to find some good Catholic teachers, and so Atkinson was left free to make all the top-level decisions in regard to teachers. Even the Bureau of Insular Affairs, usually so jealous of proper channels of authority, knew very little about how this great power was being exercised until inquiries, complaints, and suggestions began pouring in.[31]

tion. Today the papal catechism is taught in virtually every public school building in the Philippines" (undated clippings in BIA File 1534, NA).

This was picked up by many other Protestant papers, and Frank R. White, Director of Education, called upon Dr. James B. Rodgers, of the Presbyterian Mission to investigate the charges. Dr. Rodgers replied in the negative: "I may say I have consulted my colleagues who all agree that they know of no cases at the present time where the tenets of any Christian communions are taught, either legally or illegally, in the schools under your direction. It is a matter of surprise to us that no advantage is taken of the permission given by law for religious instruction after school hours . . . " (BIA File 1534, NA).

In 1915 Bishop Charles Brent wrote to Rev. H. Masterson saying: "Secular education is playing havoc with the traditional religious ideas of the Filipinos and unless a wise and earnest effort is made to appeal to students, the coming generation will be apathetic of all religion or worse" (Brent Papers, LC).

In 1926 Archbishop Michael O'Doherty complained: "When English became the language, native priests were looked down upon by the rising generation because they could not speak English. Because of this they were debarred from public functions and of course were not able to gain admission to the public schools" (O'Doherty, op. cit., p. 135).

[31] Clarence Edwards, Chief of the BIA, to Taft, Sept. 20, 1900, BIA File 470, NA.

By the time the bureau was aware of difficulties it was too late to direct, it could only try to correct.

Between January 21, 1901, when the school bill passed, and May 20 of that same year, Atkinson had already appointed nearly 800 of the 1,000 teachers needed for the islands.[32] To have accomplished this in so short a time and from such a distance required a great deal of assistance in the United States, but no official assistance was asked for nor given. By private arrangements with presidents or chaplains of universities, colleges, and normal schools, Protestant, Catholic, and nonsectarian, Atkinson delegated the authority to appoint a fixed number of applicants for teaching positions. He did the same with county and state superintendents of education in almost all of the states and personally chose more than 175 teachers from the 15,000 or more applications which had come to him from various sources.[33] Finally, he made arrangements with two teacher-employment agencies, Fiske in San Francisco, and Pratt in New York, to engage the remainder.[34]

Taft made a real effort to see that a fair proportion of the teachers should be Catholic. He wrote to Attorney General Henry M. Hoyt, a Catholic, suggesting that in order to avoid all charges of discrimination he thought at least 200 of the 1,000 teachers should be Catholics and intimated that he would not hesitate for a moment to give them a larger proportion if applicants could be found.[35] He contacted Father Fitzgerald, secretary to the apostolic delegate Archbishop Chapelle, in Manila and asked him to get the names of some Catholics who would make good teachers in the islands.[36] The apostolic delegate contacted pastors of

[32] Frederick Atkinson to Chaplain Charles C. Pierce, Episcopal Chaplain at Fort Meyer, Va., May 20, 1901, BIA File 470, NA.

[33] Typed copies of appointment lists in BIA File 470, NA.

[34] Senator Platt of New York to Clarence Edwards, complaining that Fiske and Pratt Teacher Employment Agencies charge applicants a fee of $3.00 for registration and 5% of salary for the first year if appointed; he also claimed that proprietors of the agencies were personal friends of Dr. Atkinson and used pressure to get appointments; and Edwards to Atkinson, July 30, 1901, saying, "Secretary of War disapproves of employment of school teachers through agencies charging commissions" (BIA File 470, NA).

[35] Henry M. Hoyt to Edwards, July 24, 1901, BIA File 3263, NA.

[36] Taft to Hoyt, May 26, 1901, BIA File 470, NA.

churches in heavily Catholic areas across the country, but not even 100 volunteers [37] were found and many of these were women. Each of the Catholic colleges, whose presidents had been invited to choose teachers, failed to fill its quota. Father John Whitney, S.J., of Georgetown, reported, "Owing to the apparent unwillingness of our graduates to accept positions which I have been authorized to tender them, I find myself unable to designate anyone for appointment." [38] Lists, kept by Dr. Atkinson, however, indicate that Georgetown did send two teachers later on. The lack of enthusiastic volunteers among Catholics to match the number of eager young Protestants weakens considerably the charges of discrimination against the Department of Public Instruction in the hiring of teachers.

Many of the teachers appointed early left for Manila from April to June, but then the Bureau of Insular Affairs took over the transportation and arranged for large groups to travel together. Most publicized of these were the 500 who sailed on the *Thomas* July 23 to arrive in Manila August 21. En route this group organized along religious lines. Forty-five Masons and Eastern Stars held lodge meetings; C. E. Steele organized the Y.M.C.A. and Y.W.C.A. with Bible study clubs, Spanish classes, and singing groups; and the Captain held Episcopal services on Sundays.[39] It is hardly to be wondered at that the ten lonely Catholic teachers, representing Catholic University, Georgetown, Holy Cross, St. Louis College, Notre Dame, and St. Mary's felt discriminated against. And they knew nothing of the lack of Catholic volunteers.

[37] Lists of Fathers Ramm, Baart, Kelly, and Flavin, BIA File 470, NA. Lists of Archbishops Ireland and Katzer, and Bishop Messmer, Root Papers, MS. Div., LC. Correspondence between Ireland and Hoyt; Atkinson and Hoyt; Hoyt and Root; Fitzgerald and Hoyt; Fitzgerald and Root; July to Oct. 1901, Root Papers, MS. Div., LC. All lists would receive careful attention. Most of the appointments were made. All men were appointed; no women would be sent unless they had relatives in the islands.

[38] Copy of a letter in BIA File 1534, NA. It was also published in the *Catholic Universe*, Aug. 15, 1902, and elsewhere.

[39] Diary of Blain Free Moore, a teacher on the *Thomas*, a Protestant whose relations with the Filipino priest in his *barrio* were warm and friendly (Moore Papers, MS. Div., LC). See also *The Log of the Thomas*, a memorial booklet published for the voyagers, and *The Briny Bucket*, published during their stay in Honolulu (Moore Papers, MS. Div., LC).

Catholic attacks on the Taft administration began in October 1901 with a series of articles in the *American Catholic Quarterly Review* and continued unabated through the spring and summer of 1902 while Taft was in Rome on the friars' land negotiations.[40] The most virulent attack was launched by a disgruntled Catholic from Catholic University, who had gone to the islands, highly recommended, to take a superintendent's post, but who was dismissed from the service because of habitual drunkenness.[41] The attack appeared in the *Catholic Citizen* of Milwaukee and was reprinted in the *Catholic Times* and *Freeman's Journal* and quoted by many others. The paper charged that Atkinson and all but one of the other division superintendents were ex-ministers, that proselytism was the rule in all of the public schools, and that Catholic teachers were shunted out to the *barrios* and barred from promotion. Catholic societies, affiliated with the Catholic Federation, sent identical memorials to the president demanding fair treatment of the church in the Philippines.[42]

President Roosevelt and Secretary Root, fearing the effect of this protest on the negotiations in Rome tried to squelch the charges promptly by published statements from Acting Governor-General Luke Wright and Father McKinnon that the charges were untrue.[43] Archbishop Ireland preached a sermon denouncing the agitation on the eve of the second national convention of the Catholic Federation in Chicago August 5 to August 7, hoping to end further protest.[44] However, Father O'Reilly, an Augustin

[40] Bryan J. Clinch, "The Work of the Philippine Commission," *Catholic World*, XXVI (1901), 625–43; and "The Language of Despotism," XXVII (1902), 369–88.

[41] Memorandum in the case of Dr. Edmund Briggs, by Henry M. Hoyt, July 28, 1902; Edwards to Major Devol, Aug. 16, 1902; Devol to Edwards, Aug. 20, 1902; Edwards to Taft, Aug. 16, 1902, Taft Papers, LC.

[42] *Memorial Bearing upon the Philippine Schools, July 12, 1902,* sent from Hartford, Columbus, New York, and many other places, BIA File 1534, NA. Ireland and Gibbons had opposed federating clubs because it appeared to be "a Catholic APA." See Bishop James A. McFaul to Ireland; Ireland to McFaul; Ireland to Gibbons, all from March 21–26, 1901, Ireland Papers, AASP.

[43] Cable, Wright to Root, July 9, 1902, which McKinnon read and approved, and Atkinson to Root, July 7, 1902, a long report by mail answering the charges in detail, BIA File 470, NA.

[44] Root to Ireland, July 19, 1902; Roosevelt to Ireland, July 23, 1902;

ian, gave an address enumerating the good effects of the agitation, charging that for certain members of the hierarchy, ". . . Party interests have prevailed and more zeal has been shown apologizing for a Republican administration than in defending the rights of our brethren." [45]

Father McKinnon defended the administration publicly, but admitted privately that he was going back on the school board in Manila to help Catholic teachers and to prevent any missionary work in the schools. He said, "I think there is an inclination in the department to favor Protestants, but I can assure you there will soon be a change in the head of the Bureau and then we can hope for some improvement." [46] Strangely enough, Taft agreed with Father McKinnon and wrote a letter to Root trying to explain why a shake-up was needed in the Department of Public Instruction:

Atkinson's selections while they might have been good in a state where there is no issue of Catholicism, I am afraid have been unfortunate in bringing to the front as educators in the Philippines some retired ministers, who feel called upon every time there is a missionary or evangelical meeting to appear and make themselves prominent by speeches and otherwise. Of course the extreme attacks by the ultra Catholics are most unjust, but it seems impossible to pump into Atkinson, although I have talked to him a good deal about it, the necessity of going out of his way to convince Catholics that there is nothing being done to discriminate against them.[47]

Taft believed that Atkinson was no longer an asset to the department and that it was expedient that a Catholic should be appointed to the commission as the Secretary of Education. He was, therefore, happy to accept the resignations of Moses and Atkinson and explained his reasons to Lyman Abbott, a liberal Protestant editor:

Roosevelt to Taft, July 29, 1902, Ireland Papers, AASP. All indicate that Roosevelt and Root considered the school protests, the friars' land protests, and Ireland's bid for a cardinalate to be part of the same problem: the contest between conservative and liberal churchmen in the Catholic church.

[45] *Proceedings of the Second National Convention of Federated Catholic Societies* (Cincinnati, 1902), p. 70.

[46] McKinnon to Ireland, June 14, 1902, Ireland Papers, AASP.

[47] Taft to Root, from Rome, July 5, 1902, Taft Papers, LC.

The controversy between Atkinson and Moses was quite unfortunate. Dr. Atkinson is a good man, but he loved exploitation in the newspapers too much and spent more time writing reports to be published than he did in thorough organization of his department. The commission at first, for more than a year gave him complete control. When the departments were reorganized in September 1901 Professor Moses was put in charge of the Department of Education. Atkinson never understood what would be palpable to a lawyer that he became subordinate to the Secretary of the Commission. Professor Moses is a fine man, but he had been a professor at UC and had acquired there a position which did not require very hard work and was loathe to undertake any work that required the tremendous energy necessary in that department. So he therefore acquiesced in Atkinson's view that he alone was responsible for the Bureau of Education and Atkinson was allowed to run it for the better part of another year with very little supervision from Dr. Moses. During my absence the Commission discovered that Moses knew very little about the department and stirred him up; he began to intervene and his intervention stirred Atkinson up.[48]

He nominated James F. Smith for the commission post. Smith had served in the islands longer, and in more different branches of service, than any other American in the Philippines. A Californian, educated at Santa Clara University and Hastings Law School, he had come to the islands in command of the California Volunteers, had served as military governor of Negros, where he inaugurated one of the best school districts in the command, and recommended, even at that early date, that competitive examinations should be held to identify the best teachers.[49] In 1900 he was appointed Collector of Customs in Manila, where he cleaned up a corrupt department and increased revenue for school expenditures. In 1901 he was appointed to the Supreme Court of the Philippines in which capacity he was serving when he accompanied Taft to Rome for the friars' land talks.[50] Taft noted that he thought Smith should ultimately become governor of the islands because he understood Filipinos better than any other man

48 Taft to Lyman Abbott, Dec. 26, 1902, Taft Papers, LC.
49 "Education in the Philippines," Senate Document No. 129, 56th Cong., 2nd Sess., 1900, pp. 52–53.
50 For succinct summary of services, see Smith Papers, State Historical Society, Tacoma.

he knew and because he was an honest man ". . . who knows men." [51]

Smith was very reluctant to accept the post. He loved the law and believed that it was his first obligation, but he finally accepted the post and the secretaryship at Taft's urging.[52] As General Superintendent of Education Taft appointed Dr. E. B. Bryan, of Indiana, a Baptist, who had a good reputation in educational circles in the islands. Bryan lodged with Dr. Homer Stuntz, one of the most militant members of the most militant Protestant group in the Philippines. He was presiding elder of the Methodist Episcopal Church. As superintendent of Manila schools, Bryan chose George P. O'Reilly, superintendent of schools in Vigan, who had made a good name for himself in a very difficult territory.

Smith took hold of the new position with characteristic firmness. He talked over with Taft the possibility of inaugurating an examination system to end all charges of discrimination in the hiring of teachers. During the last weeks of his term, Atkinson had tried to make appointments of about 250 teachers needed for the coming year, but Taft had stopped him. Taft now suggested that an effort be made to find as many Catholic teachers as possible to fill out the quota for that year and then to place the appointment of teachers under civil service examinations.

Archbishop Ireland and Bishop O'Gorman were asked to help locate Catholic teachers, but even though they contacted bishops East and West and secured the contributed services of a Catholic publisher and church goods merchant, Daniel H. McBride, to make the need for Catholic teachers known they were able to locate only 89 teachers by July 1, 1903.[53] Arrangements had gone forward with the civil service commission, and when the Catholic

[51] Taft to Root, July 5, 1902, Taft Papers, LC.

[52] Taft to Root, Oct. 14, 1902, Taft Papers, LC.

[53] Taft to O'Gorman, Oct. 17, 1902; McBride to Ireland, June 2, 4, 5, 8, 1903; Ireland to Magoon, June 28, 1902; and Magoon to Ireland, July 9, 1902, Ireland Papers, AASP. Smith to Ireland, Nov. 14, 1902, Smith Papers, State Historical Society, Tacoma. In this letter Smith begs Ireland to get good teachers saying, "With some brilliant and conspicuous exceptions, the Catholic teachers have not been up to the mark."

failure became quite apparent, on November 7, the request for examinations was sent to the civil service commission.[54]

Civil service examinations for the Philippines were announced and administered with the regular examinations held at stated times throughout the United States. The examination papers were graded, and all those who passed were requested to send health certificates, photographs, and recommendations, all of which were forwarded to the Civil Service Bureau in the Philippines which certified those eligible for service and sent their records to the Bureau of Education where the choice of teachers was made. Dr. Bryan resented the loss of the old appointive power and was never completely in favor of the system,[55] but it brought an end to discrimination charges since there was no statement of religious preference on the applications. In all probability civil service did nothing to increase or decrease the number of Catholics in the school system.

Smith had been a controversial figure from the moment he moved up to the commission. A Catholic had succeeded him on the Supreme Court and this, to the militant Protestants, made island government top-heavy with Catholics.[56] When an Ameri-

[54] Smith to the Civil Service Commission, Nov. 7, 1903; Civil Service Commission to Smith, Nov. 11, 1903 (by BIA cable) BIA Smith Personal File, NA.

[55] Series of letters from Leon C. Pepperman to L. C. Washburn, both of the Civil Service Commission, March 11, 1905, indicates the opposition within the Bureau of Education until David Barrows took over (BIA File 470, NA).

[56] Philippine Christian Advocate, June 1, Dec. 1, 1903, and Feb. 6, 1904, might be taken as samples of a kind of innuendo practiced by Protestant periodicals such as the Religious Telescope, The Independent, The Northwest Christian Advocate, and Catholic papers such as The Leader, The Freeman's Journal, and others. Dr. Stuntz published an article in the Homiletic Review charging the administration in the islands with obstructing Protestant work by "silent disapproval" even in the educational department. He charged that "all teachers were given to understand that they were to have nothing to do with missionary efforts." He also charged that not a member of the commission was to be found in the house of God on Sunday. E. F. Baldwin, editor of The Outlook refused to pick up "the cue" which most Methodist papers did, and started a private investigation of the allegations. He wrote to Taft and to Bishop Charles Brent of the Episcopal church for clarification. Brent wrote a seven-page rebuttal of the charges

can, Archbishop Harty, came to the See of Manila and three American bishops came to Jaro, Cebu, and Vigan in quick succession, a wave of anti-Catholic prejudice swept the Protestant newspapers and journals. But it was not only from militant Protestants that Smith suffered criticism. He was also attacked, and even more bitterly, by militant Catholics.

The Catholic attack came from the *Centro Católico* in Manila. A quarrel, sometimes quite petty, had begun between Smith and the leadership of the organization of which he was one of the first members. Shortly after Father McKinnon's sudden death, in 1903, the *Centro* had federated several clubs, including Father's Young Men's Institute, and refused to accept Filipinos as members. Smith fought this furiously and sometimes intemperately. He aroused the fighting instincts of two Irish-American Augustinians, Father O'Mahoney and Father McErlaine, who had come out to represent their order to the American administration. Shortly after Smith became commissioner a delegation came to him to protest that Catholic teachers were not being promoted to superintendents and named five men whom they demanded that he promote. Three of these were members of the club whom Smith knew well. In a rather heated meeting he refused categorically to make a man's religion the test for promotion, accused the club of being anti-American, because it still used Spanish colors for decorations at civic affairs and had refused to carry an American flag when it welcomed the archbishop to Manila. Many of the members were former army officers and were anticivil government. They became Smith's bitter enemies, campaigned against his appointment as governor-general a few years later, and created

___

and singled Smith out as a "devout Catholic who lives as he believes and practices his religion fearlessly." This opened even more attacks against Smith. See E. F. Baldwin to Bishop Brent, May 25, 1903; Brent to Baldwin, July 14, 1903, Brent Papers, LC. Dr. Stuntz evidently did not know that Act Seventy-four forbade teachers to take part in teaching religion, preaching, proselytizing, or other missionary works. He may have thought that Smith was merely making this decision on the basis of his own faith. Items 78 to 92 are all complaints that teachers cannot teach religion in the islands (see BIA File 1534, NA). They were all triggered by the Stuntz article. The opposition of Stuntz to Smith was personal. Both Taft and Roosevelt refer to this animosity in several letters written in defense of Smith (Taft and Roosevelt Papers, LC).

the impression in the American press that he was a Catholic who had "sold out." [57]

Smith refused to be intimidated by either side. When he received complaints that public schoolteachers were using various kinds of intimidation, pressure, or overt influence on children or parents to force attendance at public schools, he ordered investigations and punished offenders by suspension, cleared the records of those who were not guilty, and tried to walk the narrow path between Catholics and Protestants with impartiality.[58]

Two other problems held over from Atkinson's administration caused Smith considerable trouble: the use of biased textbooks in the schools and the placing of Filipino exchange students to the United States in Protestant colleges or state universities where they were lodged with Protestant families.

The first problem admitted of no easy solution since no adequate textbook in Philippine history was available, and omitting their own history from the curriculum would have been thought the crassest colonialism. Adeline Knapp, one of the *Thomas* teachers, had come to the islands to write a textbook in Philippine history for the elementary school. Her little book, *Story of the Philippines*, was most inadequate. It was written hastily, contained many inaccuracies, many misconceptions of Spanish rule in the islands, much Protestant propaganda, and was without merits of style or clarity. In April 1904, Bishop Rooker complained against the use of this book, and Smith, after reading it and the criticism submitted, concluded that the book was indeed unsuitable. He withdrew it at a loss of $10,000 to the government.[59] A text by Professor Jernigan, submitted to the secretary while still in proofs, was sent by Smith to Archbishop Harty's secretary, Monsignor Fowler, with a request that corrections, or

[57] Richard Campbell to Ireland, July 14, 1903; Roosevelt to Ireland, July 31, 1903; McDonough to Ireland, Sept. 13, 1903; Governor General Wright to Roosevelt, Sept. 15, 1903; Bishop Rooker to Ireland, Feb. 11, 1904; Rooker to Roosevelt, May 9, 1904; and many more, Ireland Papers, AASP.

[58] File of all controversies regarding proselytism in the Philippines, BIA Files 18732, 67420, 41835, NA. Copies of these files were sent to Archbishops Riordan and Ireland by Smith.

[59] Rooker to Smith, Apr., 1904, Smith Papers, State Historical Society, Tacoma. See also Exhibit "A," BIA File 1534, NA.

annotations be made, if necessary, to make the book an accept-able text for the schools. Smith waited seven months for a reply and then called it to the attention of the archbishop again. One month later it was discovered that the proofs were lost, and a new copy was furnished. Three more months passed without word and finally a page-by-page critique of the text was deliv-ered. Smith, himself made every correction in the text and incor-porated every suggestion made by the archbishop's reviewer and even modified statements which he thought might seem biased. After the book was published, with all the corrections, it came in for lashing reviews by the archbishop in letters to the United States.[60] Finally when Dr. Bryan retired because of ill health, he was succeeded by Dr. David Barrows, a former superintendent who had been working in the Bureau of Non-Christian Tribes. Barrows had been working on a small book on Philippine history and had just signed a contract with American Book Company for its publication as a text for the Philippines. He and Smith decided that it would not be proper to decide in favor of his own text, but in spite of this four papers condemning this book for use as a text in the Philippines were sent by Archbishop Harty to the Catholic papers in the United States for publication at a time when it was rather common knowledge that the book was not in use.[61]

The second problem was not any simpler, and caused an even greater clamor in the press. As early as 1900 several colleges, Yale, Harvard, Columbia, and others, had offered scholarships for good Filipino students. At first few suitable candidates were found, but gradually there were more, and the commission ap-propriated money to provide for transportation and lodging in tuition-free institutions. Many of the students were sent to small Protestant colleges or normal schools, where the dangers to their faith were many. Archbishop Riordan and Bishop Montgomery asked Smith to see if anything could be done to see that those who wanted to go to Catholic institutions were able to go. While Smith was working on the problem, a furore was created by an

[60] Exhibit "B," BIA File 1534, NA.

[61] David Barrows to James A. Le Roy, and Le Roy to Barrows, regularly from 1905–1909, James A. Robertson Papers, Duke University, discussing the problems of the Philippines schools, textbooks, personnel.

article written by Father Wynne of Fordham protesting the snubbing of Catholic colleges. The records of the Bureau of Insular Affairs indicate that this charge was, at least in part, justified. Although William Sutherland, who was in charge of students brought to the United States to study, claimed that all students were placed in institutions where they were not required to attend compulsory religious worship, no provisions were made for attendance at their own church services and gradually many gave up church attendance altogether. In other cases they resided in the homes of Protestant families and feared to offend their hosts by not attending family worship. In part, however, the charge was not justified. Some Catholic colleges which claimed to have been overlooked had never even returned the questionnaires sent out by the Bureau of Insular Affairs requesting information about requirements and fees. Others, which did reply, named requirements and costs which were prohibitive. As a result of the agitation in the press, however, Notre Dame University and University of Santa Clara waived all fees and offered scholarships to the academically able, and these were immediately snapped up for competent students. Other Catholic institutions followed suit, and another area of discrimination was ruled out.[62]

The constant bickering and contradictory directives issued by Dr. Moses and Dr. Atkinson during their last year as heads of the Department of Education had left the department in turmoil.[63] David Prescott Barrows, who had served in Manila for one year under Atkinson and then resigned to work among the Non-Christian Tribes, threw himself into the work of reorganization. Up to 1903, more than 1,074 American teachers had been brought out to the islands and distributed throughout the provinces. Once assigned to a *barrio* they were on their own and received little or

[62] Edwards to Smith, Oct. 6, 1904; Leon C. Pepperman to various Catholic periodicals, Oct. 10, 1904; Edwards to Wright, Oct. 11, 1904 (cable); Edwards to Pepperman, Oct. 11, 1904; Roosevelt to Taft, Oct. 11, 1904, BIA File 1534, NA. See also William Sutherland, *Not by Might: The Epic of the Philippines* (Las Cruces, New Mexico, 1953) which relates the story of the first students and their subsequent careers.

[63] Bernard Moses Diaries, 9 vols., University Archives, Berkeley, California. During June–August, 1902, the diaries give a caustic commentary on a running battle between the superintendent and the director which accounts for much of the disorganization which existed when Smith took over.

no direction from the Manila office, except official letters. Superintendents of school districts frequently had many islands to cover and no adequate transportation, or areas so widespread that general supervision was totally lacking. Smith insisted that supervision had to be adequate in order to support the teacher in the field, and Barrows agreed. Almost immediately the number of superintendencies was increased, and school districts were made identical with province boundaries. By 1903 hundreds of teachers had been lost to the schools by death, by sickness, by transfer to other work, both military and civil, by resignation, and by desertion. The human element which had been so lacking in supervision was partially responsible for this attrition.[64] Summer camps and institutes for teachers with the possibility of receiving credit for courses taken, lectures, and other in-service programs were initiated to keep the teacher-in-the-field in contact with the Manila office. Visits of the director to all parts of the archipelago, supplemented by suggestions and directives from the Manila office, brought the whole teaching staff into better rapport with the central administration. In later years much of the credit for this was given to Smith and rightly so.[65] It should be shared, however, by Barrows and his two assistants Gilbert Brink and Frank White and by Harry Hawley, a civil service man who transferred to the department and made the administration of selection much smoother.[66]

Smith's success in establishing civil service for the selection, promotion, and dismissal of teachers and superintendents, his courageous stand on the textbook issue, and his complete reorganization of the Department of Education made him a logical candidate for the governor-generalship when it fell empty in 1906 as

[64] Blaine Free Moore writes in his diary of his teaching years in the Philippines, of the need for supervision, contact, and concern by the Manila office for those in the *barrios* (Moore Papers, LC). Numerous letters of complaint to the BIA and stories of men who lost their minds, "went native," etc., because of isolation, make this quite clear (BIA File 1534, NA).

[65] Barrows Diaries, University Archives, Berkeley, California, 1903–1909, reiterate the friendship and confidence inspired by Smith. When Smith resigned as governor-general in 1909, Barrows resigned also rather than work under his successor, William Cameron Forbes.

[66] Paper prepared by Barrows and read at several scholarly meetings in 1946, Barrows Papers, University Archives, Berkeley, California.

a result of Luke Wright's resignation and the Vice-Governor Henry Ide's desire to leave the Philippine service. His appointment was bitterly opposed by Homer Stuntz and the Methodist Church in the Philippines and by the publications and church groups in the United States which they supplied with propaganda against him. His appointment was likewise opposed by Father O'Mahoney and the *Centro Católico* in Manila and by a disgruntled Catholic teacher whose promotion to superintendent outside the civil service structure Smith had refused to arrange.[67] In spite of this organized opposition which kept mail bags busy to the Bureau of Insular Affairs and the President, both Taft and Roosevelt supported Smith and sent his name to the Senate for confirmation. Smith accepted the post reluctantly, knowing that he would probably please no one. He offered to resign at any time if his unpopularity should compromise the administration, saying:

For more than two years now some Catholics and some Protestants, however they may have differed as to matters of doctrine, have been in complete accord in their unqualified condemnation of me as Secretary of Public Instruction, but for different reasons. . . . Protestants whose approval I fail to gain, have charged that I am a bigoted Catholic whose principal business in life is to make it unpleasant for those not of my creed, and Catholics who disapprove of me have charged that I am an enemy of Catholic interests, whatever that may mean. . . . The fact of the matter is, I have tried to the best of my ability to give Protestants just such consideration as I would expect a Protestant Secretary to give to Catholics and to Catholics just such treatment as honesty, justice, impartiality and a decent respect for their rights entitles them to receive. It goes without saying I did not please that small class of Protestants who believe that no Catholic can faithfully discharge official duties without fear or favor. Neither did it please that limited contingent of Catholics who believe that Protestants have no rights which a Catholic official is bound to respect—nor did I expect to.[68]

When Smith accepted the governorship in 1906, he was replaced in the office of Secretary of Education by W. Morgan

[67] BIA Smith Personal File, NA: Richard Campbell to Archbishop Ireland, July 9, 1905; and George Reilly to Ireland, July 12, 1905, Ireland Papers, AASP.

[68] Smith to Roosevelt, June 13, 1906, BIA File 1534, NA.

Schuster, a man whose preparation for the portfolio of education was nil and who had been intended for the portfolio of finance except for Forbes's unexpected return to the islands. It was due to Smith's continued interest in the Department of Education as governor-general that Barrows stayed on as general superintendent until 1909 and that the measures which had been adopted to eliminate discriminatory practices were continued.

Nicolas Zamora:
Religious Nationalist

RICHARD L. DEATS

Religion and nationalism are forces which have been closely linked together in the past century of Philippine history. The family background and life of Nicolas Zamora, an early Protestant convert, are an important example of this fact.

The great uncle of Nicolas Zamora, Fr. Jacinto Zamora, was one of the three priests charged with involvement in the Cavite Mutiny of 1872. Jacinto Zamora, born in Pandacan on August 14, 1835, studied theology and canon law at the University of Santo Tomás and eventually was assigned to the Manila cathedral. There he met the brilliant José Burgos, curate of the cathedral. The two priests, along with the elderly Fr. Mariano Gómez, moved into prominence among a large group of Filipino clergy and laity who were championing the cause of the native priests, especially in respect to the secularization of the parishes. The developing sense of nationalism in this group was focused on the injustice of the continued dominance by the foreign missionaries of so many of the choice parishes in the country. The great risk these nationalist-priests were taking became tragically evident at the beginning of 1872, when the Cavite Mutiny occurred when veteran soldiers decided to rebel because of the tribute they were being forced to pay. Father Zamora had attended the Sampaloc fiesta on January 20, the day the short-lived revolt began. On the flimsiest of evidence, he, along with Gómez and Burgos, was arrested and taken to Fort Santiago on charges of having instigated the revolt. Having long since aroused the ire of the friars and the governmental authorities because of their vocal nationalism, their fate was sealed. After a secret trial—the proceedings of which have yet to be published—the three priests were executed.[1]

The execution of Jacinto Zamora did not quench the independent spirit in the Zamora family; indeed, as often is the case, the martyrdom made the fires of nationalism burn all the more intensely. Fr. Zamora's nephew, Paulino Zamora, was a man of high ideals and a seeker after truth. The well-read Paulino, embittered at the friars, did not hesitate to defy their religious authority by paying a sea captain to smuggle a Spanish Bible into Manila for him. Curious to learn about this book that had launched the Protestant Reformation in Europe, Zamora moved with his family to Bulacan, where they could be away from the scrutiny of the authorities. In Bulacan he read the Bible to his family at night and then began to call in the neighbors to study the Bible with him. Word of his independent religious activities became known, however, and one evening shortly after the outbreak of the revolution, his house was surrounded, he was arrested and, without trial, Don Paulino Zamora was exiled to Chefarina Island, a Spanish penal colony in the Mediterranean Sea.[2]

His oldest son, Nicolas, born on September 10, 1875, in Binondo, had inherited the independent religious spirit of the Zamoras before him. The mother of Nicolas, Epifania Villegas, died when he was young, but his father sought to compensate for this loss by giving the boy much affection and by providing him with the best education his means would allow. The father sent Nicolas to study with the well-known tutor Don Pedro Serrano. Later Nicolas was sent to his uncle, Fr. Pablo Zamora, then curate of the cathedral. The uncle wanted the promising Nicolas to become a lawyer or a priest and helped him enter Ateneo de Manila, where in due course he obtained the Bachelor of Arts degree. During this time Nicolas was keenly interested in religion and, like his father, studied the Bible in secret. Gradually his interest turned from the priesthood to law, and, upon graduation from

[1] Sancho Inocencio, *Biography of Father Jacinto Zamora* (Manila, 1954). See also Horacio de la Costa, S.J., "Gomez, Burgos and Zamora: Priests and Citizens," *Bulletin ng Kapisanang Pangkasaysayan ng Pilipinas* (Philippine Historical Association), No. 3 (March, 1958), pp. 89–92.

[2] Frank C. Laubach, *Seven Thousand Emeralds* (New York, 1929), pp. 68 ff.

Ateneo, he enrolled at the University of Santo Tomás in order to study law. During this period he married Isabel de Guia in Bulacan. When the revolution broke out in 1896, the young nationalist left his studies in order to join the army of General Gregorio del Pilar. He took his Bible with him and read it to the soldiers, translating it from the Spanish into Tagalog. Nicolas distinguished himself in the army and rose to the rank of lieutenant colonel.[3]

When the Treaty of Paris was signed in 1898, the father, Paulino, was allowed to return to the Philippines. On his way home he visited Spain. Already a Mason, Paulino Zamora sought out Protestants in Madrid, and there attended his first public Protestant services.[4] His companion in Madrid was Moises Buzon,[5] a Filipino who had been banished with Zamora for a similar "crime" and who years later was to become a bishop in the independent *Iglesia Evangelica Unida de Cristo.*

When Paulino Zamora landed in the Philippines, his son Nicolas joyfully told him of the new atmosphere of religious liberty in the islands and of the Protestant services that the Americans were holding in Manila. The father shared with his son his deepening religious convictions and showed him Protestant literature he had obtained in Spain.

The first Protestant work of any permanent consequence in Manila began in March of 1899 when Methodist Bishop James M. Thoburn of India, assisted by a licensed local preacher by the name of Arthur Prautch, held a series of evangelistic services, attended largely by American servicemen in the city. Several Filipinos, including the Zamoras, were intensely interested in the services, and in June of that year Prautch began holding evangelistic meetings at the *Teatro Filipino* specifically for Filipinos.[6] The meetings were announced in the Spanish newspapers. Twelve

[3] Felix V. Bayot, "The Life Story of Nicolas Zamora," translated and condensed by Juan Nabong, *Philippine Christian Advance*, II, 4 (Apr., 1950), 5–7. Also, written interview with Lazaro G. Trinidad, bishop and general superintendent, IEMELIF, Oct. 23, 1965.

[4] Homer C. Stuntz, *The Philippines and the Far East* (Cincinnati, 1904), pp. 417 f.

[5] Written interview with Cipriano Navarro, general treasurer of the United Church of Christ in the Philippines, Oct. 29, 1965.

[6] Richard L. Deats, *The Story of Methodism in the Philippines* (Manila, 1964), pp. 3 ff.

came to the first meeting,[7] including the Zamoras and another outstanding father and son team, Don Luis and Teodoro Yangco. Luis Yangco had read the Bible since 1888 and thought of himself as the first Filipino Protestant.[8] His son was to become famous as a philanthropist who gave a great deal to worthy causes, especially to Protestant work and to the Y.M.C.A.

On the fourth Sunday of the services, thirty were in attendance. The Spanish interpreter did not appear, and Prautch asked Paulino Zamora to speak to the gathering about his religious convictions.[9] The noble old gentleman was not a speaker, but he indicated that his son would speak. Nicolas told the group of the execution of his great uncle in 1872 and of his father's suffering on behalf of his independent religious convictions. Then he related his own pilgrimage of religious discovery and of the power of God in speaking to men's hearts through the Bible. He was an excellent speaker and was received with a great deal of enthusiasm.[10] He was asked to speak again the next Sunday. The event was announced in the papers and a large crowd came to the service.[11]

From this point on, the Zamoras, father and son, gave themselves tirelessly to developing Protestant work in the islands. Paulino opened his home at 50 Beaterio, Intramuros, for the use of missionaries in holding religious services, and he helped find other homes where additional services could be held. On October 22, 1899, James B. Rodgers, a Presbyterian and the first regularly appointed Protestant missionary in the Philippines, received into church membership at the Beaterio home Paulino Zamora, his three sons and daughter, and four others. Nicolas Zamora preferred to be a Methodist and made it clear that his membership would be transferred to the Methodist Episcopal Church as soon as its work was established in the islands.[12]

During the rest of that year, the young Zamora was frequently

---

[7] Frank W. Warne, *A Filipino Evangelist: Nicolas Zamora* (New York, n.d.), p. 5.

[8] Laubach, *op. cit.*, p. 69.   [9] Warne, *op. cit.*, p. 6.

[10] Laubach, *op. cit.*, pp. 69 ff.   [11] Warne, *op. cit.*, p. 6.

[12] James B. Rodgers, *Forty Years in the Philippines. A History of the Philippine Mission of The Presbyterian Church in the United States of America, 1899–1939* (New York, 1940), pp. 32 f.

called upon in the evangelistic services being held throughout the city to testify of his faith. When Bishop Thoburn returned to Manila in February 1900, with Bishop Frank Warne, he was highly impressed with Nicolas Zamora, who by then was preaching in seven different places to large audiences. After Thoburn heard him speak and examined him about his beliefs, Zamora told the bishop of his fervent desire to become a minister.[13] According to the rules of the Methodist Episcopal Church, no one could be ordained before becoming a member on trial of an Annual Conference (i.e., diocese), ordination following reception into trial membership. At the time Bishop Thoburn was in the islands, no Asian annual conference was in session. Therefore he decided to take the extraordinary step of cabling, via the New York office of the Missionary Society, to the South Kansas Annual Conference, which was in session, and asking Kansas Bishop Vincent to receive Zamora into membership on trial, elect him to deacon's orders under the missionary rule, and then transfer him to the Malaysia Mission Conference (which included the Philippines) for ordination. This highly unusual request was granted by the South Kansas Conference due to the circumstances surrounding the case. As soon as Bishop Thoburn received the affirmative cable in reply, he ordained Nicolas Zamora in Manila on March 10, 1900, as a deacon in the Methodist Episcopal Church. This, said the bishop, enabled him

to place an intelligent pastor over the Filipino converts, and thereby greatly strengthen the brave company of those who had come out from the house of priestly bondage. In that hour of need I felt devoutly thankful that I serve a Church which had a flexible economy.[14]

Commenting later on the reasons for Zamora's ordination, another Methodist bishop, Frank W. Warne wrote, "He was a good man, educated, married, converted, eloquent, knew his Bible and abundantly qualified to preach." [15] The father of Nicolas was present at the ordination service, held in the Soldier's Home in "a room with a dusty floor, without pulpit or altar and with only a

[13] Warne, *op. cit.*, p. 6.   [14] Stuntz, *op. cit.*, p. 433.
[15] Warne, *op. cit.*, p. 7.

few rough chairs." Afterward, Paulino Zamora embraced Bishop Thoburn and said in Spanish, "God, now lettest Thou thy servant depart in peace, according to thy word, for mine eyes have seen thy salvation." [16]

Within the first few years of Protestant work in the islands, Nicolas Zamora thus became the first ordained Filipino Protestant minister. This appears all the more striking when one recalls the tragically long struggle for an indigenous priesthood in Philippine Catholicism.[17]

Following ordination Zamora was sent to Shanghai for a few months of seminary study.[18] The rapidly expanding Protestant work and the great need for workers precluded his being able to study for a longer period of time. Upon his return from China, Zamora was entrusted with significant evangelistic opportunities. He was appointed by the Methodist mission as an itinerant evangelist, and his fame as a preacher became well known in the Tagalog region. Many were converted in his frequent services at Plaza Goiti in Manila. By 1903 he was making regular reports that were printed in the mission journal. Thus, for example, he reported for the year 1902 as having preached 209 sermons and having baptized 70 infants and 285 adults as well as having performed 267 marriages and having officiated at four funerals. In that same year he reports having had a public debate with a priest in Caloocan where his "brother" was *presidente* of the municipality.[19] Discussing with the priest the subject of prayers

[16] *Ibid.*, p. 8.

[17] Whereas Roman Catholic missions began in the Philippines in 1565 and spread rapidly throughout the archipelago, it was not until the first decade of the eighteenth century that a Filipino was ordained to the priesthood. Even to the present day, there is a critical shortage of Filipino priests. See the essay in this volume by Horacio de la Costa, S.J., "The Development of the Native Clergy in the Philippines"; also Richard L. Deats, *Nationalism and Christianity in the Philippines* (Dallas, 1967).

[18] Gil Abesamis, "The Pastoral Ministry of the IEMELIF Church" (unpublished B.D. thesis, Dasmariñas, Cavite: Union Theological Seminary, 1965), p. 10.

[19] Zamora does not make it altogether clear in his report whether this was his blood brother, or, more probably, simply a fellow Protestant. He said, "On June 1st, 1902, I went to Caloocan to preach the Gospel there for the first time, at the request of our brother, the Municipal Presidente."

to the saints, Zamora said, "I asked him if during the 370 years in which we had been under the spiritual direction of the friars and Roman clergy he had ever heard of the canonization of one Filipino saint?" [20] This was a question that Filipino nationalists were —and still are—fond of asking Roman Catholics. The following Sunday Zamora took his Hebrew, Greek, and Latin Bibles to the *convento* to continue the discussion with the priest (the degree to which he knew these languages, especially Hebrew, is not certain). He asked the priest to bring up any questions he would like from his own Roman Catholic Bible. A large crowd had gathered, but the debate did not last long. Zamora reports that it ended when the priest, in exasperation, tried to strike him on the face and then retired to his *convento*.[21] Zamora's experience in debating while studying law served him well in his frequent debates during these years of incessant evangelistic work.

The earliest center of Zamora's work outside of Manila was at Malibay, where his preaching was highly effective. By mid-1901 in that place, Homer Stuntz reports there was "a total of members and probationers such as exceeded the total visible missionary results that were secured in China for fifteen years." [22] The services in Malibay were held in the large, old, Roman Catholic Church which had been damaged during the war with America and which was being left unattended by any priests. In addition to the preaching, Bibles and New Testament portions were sold, and house visitations were made. On Christmas day of 1901 Presiding Elder Stuntz received over three hundred probationary members into the church. He writes:

After receiving eight times over as many people as could stand in a double row in front of the altar, we had the sacrament of the Lord's Supper. It was the first time many of these poor people had ever received the cup. The wafer was all that had ever touched their tongues. There was perfect reverence, and deep spiritual interest. . . . Here were over four hundred partakers of the Holy Supper, nearly all of

---

Official Journal of the Philippine Islands District of the Malaysia Annual Conference of The Methodist Episcopal Church, 1903 (Manila, 1903), p. 42.
    [20] *Ibid.*, pp. 42–43.   [21] *Ibid.*, p. 43.   [22] Stuntz, *op. cit.*, p. 442.

whom were in the possession of as clear and definite a knowledge of the forgiveness of their sins and their acceptance in Christ as any whom I had ever ministered to in settled pastorates in the twenty years of my ministry. . . . [23]

Thus is seen the dynamic response made by the Filipinos to the evangelistic efforts of one of their own countrymen at the turn of the century.

Pastor Zamora was ordained as elder in 1902, and in 1903 he was appointed as the first pastor of the Cervantes Church (Cervantes Street being the original name of Avenida Rizal) or, as it was also called, the First Filipino Church.[24] This church became the focal point of Methodist work in downtown Manila, and it grew rapidly under the forceful leadership of the Rev. Mr. Zamora.

In addition to his pastoral responsibilities, Zamora's evangelistic work continued. One of those still living, who heard him preach, gives a colorful account of those experiences. Dr. D. D. Alejandro (retired Methodist bishop), writes:

It was my happy privilege to have listened several times to Pastor Zamora's preaching way back in 1906 and 1907 at the *Teatro Rizal* on old Ilaya Street, corner of Azcarraga. The theater, with a seating capacity of over a thousand, was always full on every Sunday I worshiped there. He was a great speaker, oratorical, somewhat bombastic in style, but mighty and sincere in expression. He had a terrible booming voice that could easily be heard all over the place and outside where a throng of late comers always could be found. He used good, very good Tagalog, embellished with Latin quotations from the Bible and interspersed with Spanish phrases.[25]

Pastor Zamora was also called upon for teaching responsibilities. As there was as yet no seminary, the earliest training of church workers was done through Bible Institutes. These courses began in 1903 and each generally lasted for about one month.

[23] *Ibid.*

[24] Today this church is known as Knox Memorial Church. Still on Avenida Rizal, it is one of the largest Protestant churches in Asia, having over 4,000 members and services in English and three Philippine languages weekly.

[25] Written interview, Oct. 27, 1965.

The courses were taught by the missionaries, but Zamora was asked to deliver lectures on such subjects as the life of Christ and on the life of John Wesley.[26] Later, when the first seminary opened, he lectured there and at the deaconess training school as well.

Because of his great ability, Zamora was frequently called upon by the missionaries to help settle difficult situations that arose from time to time. In 1906 he was sent to the Tondo area of Manila because of a great deal of unrest that had developed there. A number of Methodists wanted to start their own church under Filipino leadership. They had started a society known as *Katotohanan* in order to foster religio-patriotic sentiments, and they were advocating both political and ecclesiastical independence. Zamora was initially able to quell the unrest, and the work in Tondo began to grow once more.

However, the members of the society gradually began to win Pastor Zamora over to their side. Their slogan was, "While God has given other nations the right to serve and administer the religious life of their people, the Filipinos were also endowed by the divine Providence with the same right." [27] This independent spirit proved attractive to the grandnephew of Fr. Jacinto Zamora. Despite his outstanding accomplishments in the Methodist work, Zamora had chafed under what he felt was the small voice Filipinos were given in the actual policy-making decisions of the mission. As one who fought in the Philippine revolution, he had seen the eclipse of hopes for early independence from the Americans. Although the new colonial regime was far better than the old, it was still a bitter fact for the revolutionists to accept decades more of colonialism. By the same token, Zamora—like Aglipay before him—found himself in a church whose life was controlled by foreign funds and personnel. Strides were being made in self-leadership, but they were not fast enough for the Tondo *independistas*.

There were other factors that entered the picture as well. Tensions between Zamora and some of the missionaries had become

---

[26] *Official Journal, op. cit.,* 1904.

[27] Marcelino Gutierrez, "The IEMELIF—First Indigenous Church in the Philippines," *Philippine Christian Advance,* II, 4 (April, 1950), 3–5.

hard to contain. Not a few of the missionaries were paternalistic toward the Filipinos and expressed this paternalism in ways that could not but be offensive to a highly capable nationalist like Zamora. Once at a Bible Institute, for example, he overheard one of the missionaries say that Filipinos would never make good pastors.[28] Another wrote of Filipinos, "For all their veneer," they are still "primitive and childlike." The same writer further stated that the trouble with people like Zamora was due to visiting Americans who came around talking about independence of the islands and thus unnecessarily stirred up the nationals.[29] The missionary bishop for Methodist work in the Philippines at that time, William H. Oldham, wrote:

There is . . . amongst the Tagalog . . . a strong desire to assert themselves as not needing either tutelage or direction. This feeling in itself is praiseworthy; but there is mingled with it a certain lack of judgment, a headiness and a touch of arrogance that the present ability to manage affairs scarcely warrants.[30]

Then, as now, Western smugness was the source of no end of difficulty in relationships across national boundaries. In the missionary writings of the period, many writers revealed keen sensitivity to Filipino national hopes and aspirations; but others— riding on the crest of America's first taste of colonialism—showed little such sensitivity. This same dichotomy, of course, was seen in American attitudes of the time toward Western imperialism generally and was reflected on a national scale in the public controversy that developed as the United States went against her own heritage and became a colonial power at the close of the nineteenth century.

There was still another factor in the growing difficulties between Zamora and the mission. Its importance should be neither exaggerated nor forgotten, but seen rather as part of the total picture and remembered as a demonstration of the fact that men's motives for momentous decisions are often not as unambiguous as

[28] Bayot, *op. cit.*, p. 6.

[29] *Philippine Christian Advocate*, VIII, 10 (Sept., 1909), 6.

[30] William H. Oldham, "The Zamora Defection," *Philippine Christian Advocate*, VIII, 3 (Mar., 1909), 4.

we might wish. Some of the missionaries believed that Pastor Zamora had been charging high fees for performing weddings and that he had solemnized some marriages under questionable circumstances, as in marrying minors without parental consent. He had already been reminded by the district superintendent that such practices were against church discipline, and in early 1909, when the superintendent brought up the issue once more, Zamora rejected the counsel and announced that he was withdrawing from the Methodist Episcopal Church.[31]

On February 28, 1909, at St. Paul's Methodist Church in Tondo, Pastor Zamora announced before a congregation of several hundred persons, the formation of *La Iglesia Evangelica Metodista en las Islas Filipinas,* a church that was to be completely free of foreign control and leadership.[32] A short time later, he said in one of his sermons, "It is the will of God for the Filipino nation that the Evangelical Church in the Philippines be established which will proclaim the Holy Scriptures through the leadership of our countrymen." [33]

Evaluating the schism twenty years later, Frank C. Laubach wrote that "the demand for self-determination and proper recognition, which is like a rising tide in every country, came more rapidly than the mission could prepare themselves for it." [34] The new church continued to hold the same discipline and doctrines as the Methodist Episcopal Church, thus illustrating the non-theological nature of the split and demonstrating, as in the case of the *Iglesia Filipina Independiente,* the strong hold of nationalistic sentiments on Filipino religious leaders.

The *Iglesia Evangelica Metodista,* or the "IEMELIF" as it is called today,[35] spread mostly among the Tagalogs in the Manila area. Four of the nine Filipino conference members and one-fifth of the local preachers (25 out of 121) went with Zamora

[31] "Bishop Bashford in Manila," *World-Wide Missions,* XXI, 7 (1909), 6–7.

[32] Gutierrez, *op. cit.,* p. 3.

[33] *Aklat Pang-Alaala Sa Ika—50 Anibersario ng Iglesia Evangelica Metodista en las Islas Filipinas, 1909–1959* (Manila, 1959), p. 78.

[34] *The People of the Philippines* (New York, 1925), p. 305.

[35] The shortened name comes from combining the first letter of each word in the full Spanish title, "Iglesia Evangelica Metodista en las Islas Filipinas."

from the Methodist Episcopal Church. In the first year about 1,500 out of the total of 30,000 Methodists in the Manila district joined the schism.[36] Noteworthy is the fact that "not a Bible woman, a deaconess, or a young person trained in the public schools and able to speak English . . . [was] drawn into the new organization."[37] This then was a movement largely among the older Tagalog Filipinos who had lived through the fires of the revolutionary period. The younger generation was more moderate in its outlook and more accepting of the American colonial policies. Zamora's followers, however, thought of him as "the man God chose to preach the Gospel to us in Tagalog and [the one who] showed us that we Filipinos can take care of ourselves spiritually."[38] Today the IEMELIF leadership thinks of its divine mission as "that of bringing Christ to the nation the Filipino way."[39]

The IEMELIF established itself firmly among the Tagalogs of the Central Luzon region and is at present the largest of the completely independent and indigenous Protestant groups. It has suffered from inadequate financial resources and from a lack of well-educated leadership. In addition, the IEMELIF experienced a number of schisms from its own ranks, leaving it in 1965 with 66 churches, 106 pastors, 65 lay workers, 51 deaconesses, and approximately 15,000 members.[40]

Nicolas Zamora became the general superintendent of the IEMELIF and guided it through its early years of growth and development. His life, however, was tragically cut short during a cholera outbreak in 1914. He died on September 14 of that year when he was 39, only two years older than Fr. Jacinto Zamora was when he was executed. Despite the early death of these two members of the Zamora family, they both left an important milestone in the religious history of the Filipino people, a history in which nationalism has been a prominent factor.

---

[36] *Annual Report of the Board of Foreign Missions of The Methodist Episcopal Church, 1909* (New York, 1909), p. 349.

[37] "Bishop Bashford in Manila," *op. cit.*, p. 7.

[38] *Ang Ilaw*, Feb., 1928, p. 1.   [39] Abesamis, *op. cit.*, p. 4.

[40] *1965 Directory of Workers, IEMELIF* (mimeographed; Tondo, Manila, 1965).

"An Engineer's Dream"—
John Staunton and the Mission
of St. Mary the Virgin, Sagada

WILLIAM HENRY SCOTT

When the newly converted peoples of the Mountain Province speak of a Christian community, they mean one in which the younger generation is baptized, public education is available, and there are plenty of houses with galvanized-iron roofing. The adjective they most frequently apply to such a community is "progressive." By these standards, the Igorot municipality of Sagada in western Bontoc Sub-Province qualifies as a veritable model.

Here, more than half a population only three generations removed from raw head-taking paganism are baptized and support their own rector in their own parish church. A people who in 1900 could boast only three men able to write their names now enjoy two of the best primary schools in the province and a high school that recently ranked ninth in the whole nation, and send more than 500 of their children hundreds of miles away to college every year. Old men who as youths carried Sagada's first G.I. sheets up from the lowlands can now look out over acres of tin roofs on a hospital, church, chapels, public buildings, stores, and hundreds of private dwellings, not lacking even a scattered few with electricity, running water, and flush toilets. To visitors from the lowlands the town appears fit for a mountaintop idyll with neat, clean streets and fresh, pine-clad environs, and those with a background of Rousseau are tempted to fancies of a pure and primal Christianity superimposed on a noble and innocent savagery.

It might seem an unwarranted fondness to name any one man as the author of changes so profound, and yet in Sagada's case the pattern was set and the fabric constructed through the single-willed if not single-handed efforts of one pioneer missionary. It was in recognition of this fact that the sobriquet, "an engineer's dream," was first applied to this Episcopal church mission by the Rev. Vincent V. H. Gowen in his 1939 *Philippine Kaleidoscope,* in which he wrote of the man and the mission in the following terms:

The Rev. John Armitage Staunton, Jr., was not only a priest; he was an engineer.[1] He planned with the boldness of an engineer. . . . Without exaggeration the Mission of St. Mary the Virgin can be said to have been built to a blue-print. It was not, as is usually the case, the product of casual, even accidental, growth. Fr. Staunton was carrying it in his mind when he and Mrs. Staunton first settled in the squalor of a goat shed twelve feet square and in these cramped quarters taught school, treated the sick, offered divine worship, and baptized more than a hundred converts. Such were Sagada's simple beginnings, but the blue-print projected a great industrial mission occupying a whole countryside and beginning with the external direction of a primitive people, all that was believed possible at first, and proceeding to the internal direction of their children who, it was hoped, would be better fitted by education to receive it.[2]

That was in April 1905, and before the year was out the old goat shed was replaced by a grass-thatched house of reeds only

[1] John Armitage Staunton, Jr., was born on April 14, 1864, in Adrian, Michigan, where his father, a native New Yorker, was rector of Christ (Episcopal) Church. He graduated from the Columbia School of Mines with the B.M.E. degree in 1887, earned a B.A. degree from Harvard in 1890, and then entered the General Theological Seminary in New York. Ordained deacon and priest in the Episcopal church in 1892, he married Eliza M. Wilkie that same year. After six years' assisting at the Church of St. Mary the Virgin, New York, he became rector of St. Peter's Church in Springfield, Massachusetts, where, in 1901, he volunteered for missionary service in the Philippine Islands. There he opened the first Episcopal church in the Mountain Province (the Church of the Resurrection, Baguio), and then founded the Mission of St. Mary the Virgin in Sagada, which he served as priest-in-charge for 20 years. Leaving the Philippines in 1925, he took charge of St. Michael's Mission, Seattle, but gave up his Episcopal ministry and entered the Roman Catholic Church, in which, after his wife's death, he was ordained at the age of 70. He died in Hammond, Indiana, in 1944, leaving no children.
[2] New York, n.d. [1939?], p. 41.

slightly less humble, which the Stauntons shared for the next six years with twelve Filipino boys and girls as wards. Mrs. Staunton was a trained nurse who went around the town making house calls, and quickly set a pattern of compassion that has become legendary by venturing out at night in tropical storms on horseback. Father Staunton conducted two services daily, gave instruction in hymn singing and devotional exercises to almost 40 Christians and pagans, and made trips to neighboring villages to invite people to Christian worship in the municipal center. Having established his ministry, he then turned his attention to that engineer's dream—the vision of a progressive community growing up around the mission church like a pioneer settlement in colonial America, until it included sturdy pine buildings with limestone foundations to house shops, stores, and schools. The initial stage would be the erection of an industrial plant for the double purpose of providing steady employment and incentive for natives to learn new trades and raise their living standards, and of making the mission itself eventually self-supporting. The Christian faith would meanwhile be firmly established on Anglo-Catholic lines by surrounding the Sacraments with awe-inspiring beauty and ceremony, and by bringing their benefits as soon as possible to the people without the delay of long instruction in complex Western theology and Elizabethan English.

The local living standards which Father Staunton hoped to raise were simple in the extreme. The people of Sagada subsisted off rice from irrigated terraces carved out of precipitous slopes, or on sweet potatoes grown by a farming technique which completely denuded the mountainsides of foliage. Few vegetables were known; meat was enjoyed in the form of chickens and pigs at the time of religious sacrifices; and diet was varied seasonally by tiny fish and shellfish, snails, insects, mushrooms, berries, fruit, and birds, with hunters occasionally taking a deer or wild boar. Clothing consisted of G-strings and wraparound skirts of barkcloth or cotton, and thin blankets handloomed of thread carried up from the lowlands provided warmth in temperatures that dropped to below 50° at night. Almost all work was accomplished with a kind of large jungle knife or machete (which had only recently served also as a weapon), and some iron-shod sticks as agricultural tools. Beyond this, a few clay pots, wooden bowls and utensils, bamboo containers, and woven baskets made up a household inventory so restricted a scissors showed up as a rather sophisticated instrument. Low windowless houses with tall thatched roofs were closed up tight against the cold nights, and smoke rose up to holes under the ridgepole, providing warmth and dryness, preventing the mildew of grain stored in the attic, imparting an ebon patina to all household objects, and causing the eyes of the old folks to be rheumy and red-rimmed.

Father Staunton's attack on this primitive economy began with the importation of American, Chinese, Japanese, and Filipino workmen from Manila, and the construction of a water-powered sawmill which was in operation in 1907, selling lumber to the government in Bontoc in 1908, and self-supporting and employing 40 natives by 1912. An American physician arrived with his family in 1907, and that same year the pioneer missionary was operating a planer, a shingle mill, limekiln, and charcoal pits in addition to the sawmill itself, had opened a stone quarry, constructed a very respectable church, and was directing such diverse activities as logging, carpentering, blacksmithing, repair work, blasting, excavation, and stonecutting. In 1909 he received his first ministerial assistance, and in the same year an American schoolteacher arrived. By August the church, bell tower, office building, shop, and dispensary were shingled, and extensive sites had been leveled for a hospital and a school. When the Stauntons finally moved into a permanent American-style house in 1912, the policy of importing lowland workers to train the local people had borne fruit: 14 native stonemasons were employed under a Japanese foreman, an Igorot boy was skillfully occupied in fulltime manufacture and care of stone chisels, and a Chandler & Price job press was being operated by one of the boys the Stauntons had originally taken into their home. The next year Father Staunton's enterprises had become so vast that the annual report of the Mission of St. Mary the Virgin covered 21 printed pages in the *Convocation Journal* and was written by eight different people.

By 1915, just ten years after the Stauntons first settled in Sagada, the mission was already known as one of the outstanding achievements of the American occupation of the Philippine Islands. Visitors intrepid enough to reach the savage heights of the Cordillera Central on horseback could stand on the Stauntons' stone verandah and look down in dumbfounded amazement at 80 acres of activities connected by 20 miles of telephone wire. Four stone quarries were in operation and two limekilns; long lines of Igorots carried lumber in from the sawmill, and a planing mill reduced it to timber, boards, and shingles; electric-lighted gasoline-powered machine and carpenter shops turned out tools and furnishings. Sweet spring water was piped into the compound under sufficient pressure to make coiled fire hoses practical in many of the 20 buildings which housed the shops, stores, supplies, and considerable herd of cows, water-buffalo, and horses. Vegetables were grown by schoolboys and professional gardeners; the mission employed a shoemaker, tailor, and laundress; and schoolgirls were already producing salable lace and handwoven cloth. Photographs of the day (developed and printed locally) show American lady missionaries with pompadours pouring tea at wicker tables in rose-trellised gardens, and Father Staunton himself dictated letters to a secretary on stationary printed on his own press in an office with three telephones on his desk. Fifty apprentices were under industrial training and 150 others on the payroll; 175 school children were receiving instruction, and the beautiful frame church where daily services were conducted listed 2,000 baptisms and 600 communicants, all of whom were privileged to make purchases in the Igorot Exchange whose $10,000 worth of stock had been hauled in on bull carts over a trail surveyed by the priest-in-charge himself.

But the most thrilling aspect of the view from the Stauntons' front porch was the promise of things to come. Already discernible were the massive foundations of the great stone church which was to be the engineer-priest's crowning achievement—nine years in the building—whose altar was to become the wellspring of a new way of life, whose cross was to rise like a beacon above the heads of pagans seeking a better goal, and whose tower clock was to symbolize the changes that would accompany the process. It was this cathedral-like Christian temple towering above the grass roofs of Sagada which would refocus the attention of the younger generation from the sacred trees that were the center of their ancestors' worship, and replace the old seasonal, pig-sacrificing vengeance ceremonies in their affections with the Feast of the Conception of the Blessed Virgin Mary. This patronal fiesta on December 8 quickly became the big event of the year for the new Sagada.

In preparation for the event, a lowlander was hired a month or two in advance to make the plans, to rehearse the amateur dramatists in the *moro-moro* or *zarzuela* to be presented, and to contribute such entertaining stunts himself as sending aloft a lighted hot-air balloon at night. Sentinels were stationed down the trail to give warning of the bishop's approach, and he, vested in cope and mitre, would be met by a throng of rejoicing Christians, and escorted into the compound in procession to the sound of pealing bells and a lusty hand-cranked siren in the church tower. First Vespers on December 7 was followed by a program in the social hall in which one of the American missionaries played the reed organ or lowlanders played mandolins while the little Igorot school children joined in the Virginia Reel and other dances that went on into the middle of the night. Ilocano-style refreshments were served, and the genteel culture to which the new society aspired was indicated by programs printed in English and Spanish, and a formal *Rigodón de Honor* danced by the lowlanders present. Before the main service of the fiesta, the Virgin's statue was carried around the church in solemn procession, and after the festive Mass, visiting Christians and athletes from villages with outstations began playing softball, basketball, and volleyball, with men of the town sometimes coming up to look on and to engage in a tug-of-war. Food was served after the noon Angelus, pealing of bells and firing of *bombas y morteretes;* the Second Vespers was followed by another program, with still more games following Mass on the 9th, and, finally, a program for the distribution of such prizes as pencils, notebooks, handkerchiefs, and *camisetas.*

This annual fiesta, in its rich Catholic ceremonial and church-oriented focus, its American games, Spanish dances, and Ilocano cooking, and its attendance by Igorot children not living under their parents' custody or according to their customs, rather nicely summed up Father Staunton's program for converting and civilizing Sagada. As he himself phrased it, "There is no hope for the

Christianized savage who does not want to be cleaner in body, better clothed, better fed, better housed, better educated, more industrious, and to push his children upwards by giving them the advantages which were denied to him." [3] The Igorot Exchange, with its eyeglasses, Colgate toothpaste, and select clientele, helped "to inoculate him with the germ of discontent, to establish in his system cravings, desires, and necessities which his savage and heathen life cannot satisfy." [4] Part of this program was an educational regimen which kept children in school twelve months a year. "They must stay in our dormitories," the principal explained, "until living like an Igorot becomes for them an impossibility." [5] It was not inappropriate that the citation of the honorary doctor's degree awarded Father Staunton by St. Stephen's College in 1923 read, "For distinguished service to civilization in the Philippine Islands."

Life in Sagada, however, was not always so placid as it might have appeared before the great fireplace in Father Staunton's book-lined *sala*, and he and his colleagues had to face many discomforts and not a little danger. Seasonal storms could create lakes forty feet deep amidst craggy hills, drive through walls to destroy books and foodstuffs, and carry away roofs, bridges, communication lines and even whole sections of the sawmill. Basic necessities required by the American way of life had to be hauled in over two mountain ranges, and supplies of flour and tinned milk, salmon, and baked beans were expensive and unavailable when Sagada was cut off for weeks at a time by typhoons or landslides. With neither a resident physician nor medical laboratory available, one missionary died of intestinal parasites diagnosed too late, leaving her fellow workers to wonder uneasily about their own physical condition. New and enthusiastic appointees came out with no more training or knowledge of what to expect than reading Father Staunton's tracts and exposure to his per-

[3] "Sagada Report," *Journal of the Ninth Annual Convocation of the Missionary District of Philippine Islands* (Manila, 1912), p. 64.

[4] "An Opti-Pessimistic Outlook," *Spirit of Missions,* LXXX (November 1915), 753–54.

[5] Blanche E. Massé, "Sagada Report," *Journal of the Eighteenth Annual Convocation of the Missionary District of Philippine Islands* (Manila, 1924), p. 58.

sonal magnetism, and natives of East Coast cities sometimes arrived without even knowing how to sit a horse. Horses themselves
were not always trustworthy on those dangerous trails Mrs.
Staunton used to frequent on her errands of mercy; the school
principal once hiked in from an outstation with a broken jaw and
collarbone after her horse had carried her off the side of the
mountain. Galling frustrations in obtaining men and materials
added to the tensions of a group of dedicated, strong-willed
Americans bound together by social isolation from the community in which they lived, and some of Father Staunton's subordi-
nates departed abruptly.

If Father Staunton's ability to raise up a buzzing industrial
plant out of pristine limestone seemed magical, his ability to raise
the necessary funds was no less remarkable. On his first furlough,
his old parish gave him $1,000, another church $2,000, and a lady
in Philadelphia wrote out a check for yet another $1,000, while
alumni of his class in the Columbia School of Mines promised
$6,000 for a hospital. In addition to the gifts he received person-
ally, a speaking tour in 1916 resulted in more than $21,000 pass-
ing through the mission office as "specials" for Sagada the next
year. An old mission bookkeeper remembers regular Christmas
gifts of $1,000 and once entered a single check in the amount of
$10,000, but Father Staunton also received smaller donations such
as $10 from the United States Shoe Company in Manila and
$4.35 from the township of Sabangan toward his proposed high
school. His ingenuity left no stone unturned. When ordering a
"Gammeter Multigraph" he asked for a discount on the grounds
that it would be the first of its kind in the islands where, as Post-
master of Sagada, he would gladly demonstrate it to passersby,
and near his desk he kept a shelfful of social registers with the
names of Episcopalians underlined.

The churchmen who made these contributions felt amply rewarded by the joy of participating in the great spiritual adventure which Father Staunton's mission was. For years he answered
with long letters in his own hand, and for more years his press
turned out such a stream of postcards, pictures, prayer cards,
leaflets, and pamphlets that he and his work became the best-
known mission in the Episcopal church. A whole generation of

mission-minded Episcopalians thrilled to Father Staunton's color-ful reports written on stationary with naked spear-brandishing savages on the letter head, and which often included pictures of little boys in G-strings operating modern machinery or a self-addressed form to be filled out and returned with the names of other Americans who might be interested. Episcopalians traveling in the United States could expect to run across fellow churchmen who shared this common involvement in Father Staunton's work, and could even see the results of their efforts flashed on the silent screen of a newsreel theater above the caption, "The most won-derful missionary work done by any Christian body anywhere." [6]

Yet Father Staunton's magic as a fund-raising visionary was not matched by corresponding fiscal acumen, and the dreams from that grand blueprint often inspired him to juggle funds about as required by the existential situation in Sagada in the firm convic-tion that "there is not a shadow of a doubt that there are as many friends and funds for our work hidden away in the American church as we need." [7] In 1918 he built a building for a postoffice and when the Government refused to pay the rent he asked, moved the printing press into it and charged the cost to an ap-propriation earmark for a technical high school, and from this same source he withdrew funds to send back to the United States two laymen whom he had personally brought out but for whom no salaries could be obtained. An official visitor from mission headquarters in New York reported the following year, "I was as-tonished to find that he was completing a hospital building with funds given for the technical high school on the ground that a part of the hospital would be used, temporarily at all events, for the high school and that later he hoped to make an appeal for a hospital, reimburse the technical high school funds and then erect a separate hospital building." [8]

News of America's declaration of war on Germany in 1917 was quickly followed in Sagada by a cable from Sears, Roebuck &

[6] S. C. Brock, "Work at Sagada" (letter to the Editor), *The Living Church*, LXXIII (Sept. 5, 1925), 617.

[7] "Sagada Report," *Journal of the Third Annual Convocation of the Mis-sionary District of Philippine Islands* (Manila, 1906), p. 44.

[8] Letter from John W. Wood to the Rt. Rev. Charles Henry Brent, Jan. 2, 1919, in the Archives of the Church Historical Society, Austin, Texas.

Company that $325 worth of goods ordered would now cost $475, which was only a foretaste of the disappointments to come. The expectations of increased giving began to fade away in the intensity of America's involvement in her first European war, and no new salaries were forthcoming for faculty or industrial workers. Plans for a high school were set aside, a proposed hydroelectric plant had to be abandoned, all power equipment was stilled by the high cost of fuel oil, and Father Staunton found himself with two nurses, without a doctor or a hospital, and an engineer, an electrician, and an industrial foreman with neither power nor machinery. Ironically, Sagada's own progress made the position untenable without increased funds. That magnificent edifice whose construction had provided steady employment for a decade was consecrated on December 8, 1921, and a small army of laborers, stonemasons, carpenters, machine operators, mechanics, carters and printers could find no new employer for their skills. Projects then under development like the combined hospital and high school (which was able to function as neither) would aggravate rather than relieve the financial pressure. The decision by the government to limit its own construction in Bontoc deprived the sawmill of its last market, and negotiations to sell the equipment itself came to naught. Attempts to cut the prices of merchandise by the operation of a store and establishment of a transportation line depended on the purchases of the 15 Caucasians resident in Sagada, which Father Staunton in desperation soberly recommended as a "vital reason why our staff should not be reduced." [9] The final blow came with the adoption of a new church policy whereby all mission work would be supported directly by a central office, and no further private appeals would be permitted. The policy was designed to redress such disproportions as a domestic missionary district's being operated at six or eight times the scale of a self-supporting diocese, a condition which seemed almost to penalize progress to a diocesan status, but it was also a kind of fatal handwriting on the wall for such highly personalized enterprises as Father Staunton's.

The firm conviction that he knew what was best for Sagada

[9] Letter to Bishop Mosher, July 9, 1924, in the Archives of the Church Historical Society, Austin, Texas.

which had moved Father Staunton to keep accounts like the chancellor of exchequer of some sovereign domain also characterized his relations with his episcopal superiors. When Bishop Gouverneur Frank Mosher took oversight for the district in 1920, he was startled to find that the Sagada payroll exceeded all other diocesan expenses, while the only Anglican house of worship in the metropolitan center of Baguio, for instance, was in such a state of imminent collapse that its priest considered it too dangerous to house the Reserved Sacrament. But his attempts to redeploy the forces canonically at his disposal soon took on the aspects of a private war with Father Staunton, in which the pioneer missionary, seven years his senior, would speak of "my work" and "your work," and accuse him of snuffing out the life of one station to support the work of others that had already demonstrated their lethargy. Moreover, Father Staunton's devotion to Anglo-Catholic forms of worship were, at sixty, as rigid as ever and less likely to change, and the fact that other Philippine stations did not conform to Sagada standards made him challenge the bishop's overall leadership of the district. When it finally became obvious that he was not going to be able to carry out the grand blueprint of that engineer's dream, the great Christian civilizer decided to tender his resignation.

This was not the first time that Father Staunton had offered his resignation, but the only time it had been accepted, he promptly reconsidered. Now, in July 1924, he gave notice that he would not return for another term of duty, and requested transfer to another station where he would not have to witness the eclipse of Sagada's glory, and in September unambiguously stated, "I must ask to be relieved of all that heavy responsibility which I carry as Priest-in-Charge of this group of Missions not later than December 31st, 1924." [10] As reasons, he named lack of financial support from the church in the United States and moral support from the bishop in the field, and attempted to dramatize these accusations by a sober recommendation that the work of the Episcopal Church in Sagada be handed over to the Roman Catholics. Bishop

[10] Letter to Bishop Mosher, Sept. 24, 1924, included in "Report of the Committee on Sagada to the National Council," in Archives of the Church Historical Society, Austin, Texas.

Mosher's prompt response was equally unambiguous: he accepted the resignation and cabled the details to New York.

It is hard to believe that Father Staunton was really prepared to leave that home whose beams and stones had been hewn out of a pagan wilderness according to his own plans by workmen he himself had baptized and trained. He had always spoken of his desire to die among his beloved people, and now he began one last struggle to stay among them. Pressure was brought to bear on Bishop Mosher both in the United States and in the Philippines; telegrams of protest were originated by Igorots in Sagada, a furloughing staff missionary frankly campaigned among influential churchmen at home, and Father Staunton himself cabled New York that it was rumored that Bishop Mosher was going to resign. A special "Committee on Sagada" set up at church headquarters, however, concluded that further delay would seriously embarrass the bishop's authority and in December notified Father Staunton, "Your resignation and retirement from Sagada is regarded by the Department of Missions as an accomplished fact and final." [11]

For twenty years Father Staunton had run what in the Navy would be called "a taut ship," and although he considered himself a commander relieved of his command before making port, to the people of Sagada he will always be the Good Captain who successfully set their course out of the past and into the present. The readiness with which resistance to his will crumbled, the dignity with which he conducted his priesthood and the aura of sacred mystery which he imparted to the sanctuary of his church, his aloofness from village affairs and failure to lay hands on the Igorots' pigs, chickens, or women, all enhanced his godlike reputation in local eyes for multiplying Sagada prosperity, and he is remembered by pagan old gentlemen today as the greatest public benefactor since Biag, a deified seventeenth-century founding father with a King Midas touch. The present governor of the Mountain Province remembers having been held up as a child to see the great man, and the suffragan bishop for Northern Luzon recalls having crouched in the bushes to look out in awe at his long legs striding by as he paced up and down in the moonlight

[11] *Ibid.*

planning bigger and better things for Sagada. The good food and clothes and shelter which the people of Sagada had been praying for for generations, Father Staunton, too, wanted for them, and Christians who as children received candy from him at Christmastime or flour when the rice crops failed remember him with an admiration and affection which amounts to reverence.

There is probably not a Sagadan over fifty alive today who does not believe that Father Staunton loved them as he loved himself because he wanted them to have good things. This is no small reputation.

An Appraisal of the
Iglesia ni Cristo

ALBERT J. SANDERS

The story of the *Iglesia ni Cristo* is that of an aggressive, materially successful, indigenous movement which in a period of fifty years became a religious movement of major significance in the Philippines. In 1963, forty-nine years after its founding, it claimed a membership of 3,500,000, the possession of 1,250 local chapels, and 35 large concrete cathedrals.[1] Its distinctive temples and chapels have become familiar landmarks in many parts of the archipelago.

The success of this religious group is due primarily to its founder, Felix Manalo, who in 1914 started the *Iglesia* on its way and who for 49 years promoted its growth, controlled its ministers and finances, and served as its "Executive Minister." On April 12, 1963, Felix Manalo died, and the mantle of leadership passed to his son Eraño, who had been under the tutelage of his father since he was a small boy. In becoming heir to his father's responsibilities Eraño declared that he would change nothing in the teachings of his father or in the organization of the church.[2]

History of the Movement

This story centers in the life, the personality, and the aggressiveness of Felix Manalo, the so-called "angel" or "messenger from God referred to in Revelation 7:1,2." Manalo was born May 10, 1886, in Tipas, Taguig, in the province of Rizal. Although he was reared in a devout Roman Catholic home, in 1902, at the age of 16, he declared himself a Protestant after having listened in

[1] Felix M. Caliwag, *Sunday Time's Magazine*, Apr. 28, 1963, p. 22; and R. V. Asis, *The Manila Chronicle Magazine*, Apr. 27, 1963, p. 22.
[2] Leticia V. Jimenez, *Manila Bulletin*, Apr. 18, 1963.

Manila to an open-air debate between a Roman Catholic priest and an American Protestant missionary. Manalo was impressed with the missionary's knowledge of the Bible and the skillful manner in which he marshaled verses to establish his points. He determined that he would become an ardent student of this "book" which an uncle priest had tried to teach him to despise.[3]

He joined the Methodist Episcopal Church in 1904, later attended for a short period classes at the Ellinwood Bible School operated by the Presbyterian mission,[4] and then affiliated himself with the Disciples mission, where for one year he served as an evangelist.[5] In 1912, after undergoing a year of indoctrination, he was admitted to the Seventh Day Adventists, was ordained and became one of their most popular preachers, and a teacher in a Bible school operated by the Adventists in Malabon, Rizal. After this stint he left, or was requested to leave, the Adventist group. Directly thereafter he experienced a brief period of doubt during which he completely lost his faith in God.[6]

The period of depression prompted him to engage in an intensive study of Roman Catholic catechisms and Adventists' teachings, comparing their respective positions with the Bible—a study which opened his eyes to "discrepancies" and "inconsistencies" in both.[7] Then in November 1913 he spent three days in seclusion giving himself to fasting and meditation.[8] Immediately following this retreat he began his personal preaching mission by expounding the Scriptures to a mere handful of listeners in a small room at the worker's quarters of the Atlantic Gulf and Pacific Company of Manila, Inc.[9] Soon, however, the meetings were moved out into the open. His first converts, about 12 in number, were baptized early in 1914, in the river at Sta. Ana.[10]

The *Iglesia ni Cristo* had its formal beginning on July 27, 1914,

---

[3] Julita Reyes-Sta. Romana, "The Iglesia ni Kristo: A Study," *Journal of East Asiatic Studies* (University of Manila), IV, 3 (1955), 331, 332.

[4] *Encyclopedia of the Philippines* (Manila, 1950), IX, 393.

[5] James B. Rodgers, *Forty Years in the Philippines* (New York, 1940), p. 179.

[6] Teodoro Locsin, *Philippines Free Press*, Feb. 11, 1950.

[7] Sta. Romana, *op. cit.*, p. 333. [8] *Ibid.*, p. 334.

[9] Quijano de Manila, *Philippines Free Press*, Apr. 27, 1963, p. 46.

[10] Dolores C. Garcia, *The Sunday Times*, July 26, 1964.

when it was registered with the government. The articles of incorporation state that the head of the society is Felix Manalo, that the objective for which it was formed is "to propagate the doctrines of the Gospel of Christ in the whole Philippine Archipelago, and that its existence will depend upon Public Charity." Its rule and faith was to be the Bible.

In the first few years of the movement the preaching and teaching by Manalo and his associates was confined to the people of Manila and its environs. Then it began to spread to barrios and towns north of Manila. In the years following these early successful efforts, ministers were sent north to Central Luzon, to the Ilocos region, south to Bicol, the Visayas, and to Mindanao. By the time World War II broke out in 1941, groups were found in almost every province of Luzon and in a few of the provinces in eastern Visayas.[11] After the war, groups continued to spring into existence, and chapels were erected at a fairly steady pace.[12] In this postwar period until 1963, Felix Manalo constructed the fabulous mansion costing ₱3,000,000 in San Juan, Rizal,[13] near Manila, and more than 35 concrete church buildings of cathedral-like proportions. One writer has commented that the *Iglesia* chapel in San Juan makes the Manila cathedral of the Roman Catholic Church appear as "a cheap, ungainly house of devotion in spite of its beauty and worth in cement and marble." [14] The chapel in San Francisco del Monte, finished in 1963, one of the most beautiful church structures in the Philippines, seats 3,000 people.[15] The total worth of these structures is estimated at ₱60,-000,000.[16]

The *Iglesia* has members in Hawaii and on the western coast of the United States. The expansion of the movement outside the Philippines has come about through emigrants moving to these locations overseas.[17] Although the rank and file of its members have been drawn from the masses since World War II, it has also taken into its membership men and women from the professional

---

[11] *Ibid.*   [12] R. V. Asis, *op. cit.*
[13] Sta. Romana, *The Sunday Times*, July 31, 1955.
[14] R. V. Asis, *op. cit.*   [15] *Ibid.*   [16] *Ibid.*
[17] Quijano de Manila, *op. cit.*, p. 46.

classes.[18] There has been a steady rise in the literary rate among the members.[19]

Although Eraño Manalo declared in 1963 that the membership of the *Iglesia* was 3,500,000, many informed observers dispute this claim and regard the figure as grossly inflated. The 1960 census registered 270,104 members of the *Iglesia*. The members are concentrated in the greater Manila area, especially in Rizal province.

The political influence of Manalo was widely recognized. Candidates on both the local and national level sought to secure his backing; it is believed that Manalo decided upon a list of candidates to be supported in each election, support which in some instances constituted the margin of votes necessary for victory.[20] Eraño, it is reported, is continuing the role of his father by seeking to guide *Iglesia* members in casting their votes.

The Major Doctrines

The principal doctrine of the *Iglesia* is that Felix Manalo was called as the messenger of God according to the prophecy found in Revelation 7:1–3. The first of three trips made by the executive minister to the United States was in 1919 where it is alleged he attended classes in the study of the Bible for a year at the Pacific School of Religion in Berkeley, California.[21] Two years after his return from the United States he claimed that it was revealed to him that he was the "angel ascending from the east." [22]

The passage in Revelation 7 is designated as "heaven's ultimate epistle of salvation to mankind." [23] There is no mention of this passage in the articles of incorporation, filed in 1914, but in the 1948 amended articles, the following sentence was included: "The advent of the Church is in conformity with Biblical proph-

18 Sta. Romana, *Journal of East Asiatic Studies, op. cit.,* p. 344.

19 *Ibid.*

20 Felix M. Caliwag, *op. cit.*

21 Sta. Romana, *Journal of East Asiatic Studies, op. cit.,* p. 337. (However, the present head of this school has found no record of his enrollment or attendance there.)

22 *Ibid.,* p. 381.

23 *Pasugo* (Feb. 1954), p. 41. (*Pasugo* is the official organ of the *Iglesia.*)

ecy, Rev. 7:2–3, Isa. 46:11; 43:6–7." It is explained, quite correctly, that the word "angel" is used in the Bible in two senses, one referring to a heavenly being, the other to an earthly man who is a messenger sent by God to carry out a mission here in the world. The word "angel" does not, it is claimed, designate the nature of this being but his office. Manalo began in 1914 to preach what he felt was "the word of truth" to fulfill this prophecy: "He called with a loud voice to the four angels" (the "Big Four" of World War I: Lloyd George, Wilson, Clemenceau, and Orlando), and with his coministers continued this preaching ministry.[24] They believed that this explanation was substantiated by Isaiah 46:11 and 43:6–7, the former of which reads: "Calling a ravenous bird *from the east,* the man that executeth my counsel *from a far country. . . .*" Another passage frequently quoted is Isaiah 24:15,16, "Wherefore glorify ye the Lord in the fires, even the name of the Lord God of Israel in *the isles of the sea.*" It is maintained that the Philippines, being a far country, in the East, made up of isles of the sea, is the country alluded to in Scripture.

Another basic tenet is that Jesus Christ founded the church in Jerusalem in 33 A.D., that over the years it became apostate, as was predicted by Jesus and the Apostles, and that the appearance of an "angel" in the Far East in 1914 marked its rebirth. Accordingly, it is believed that the Church of Christ was for many centuries nonexistent, that there was a complete "blackout" of the people of God during a long stretch of history.[25] The Roman Catholic Church is charged with fostering this apostasy and as being the very embodiment of this iniquitous movement. It is concluded therefore that the Roman Catholic Church cannot be regarded as the true church, nor can any of the Protestant denominations. The true church is the *Iglesia ni Cristo.* It alone is the embodiment of truth, and outside its walls there is no salvation.[26] Various New Testament passages are employed to support this claim, notably Romans 16:16 which, it is taught, is a direct reference to the *Iglesia ni Cristo.*[27]

A third fundamental and chararacteristic tenet concerns the

[24] *Pasugo* (Mar., 1957; Dec., 1953), p. 52; (May, 1959), p. 38.
[25] *Ibid.,* Feb., 1957, p. 30.   [26] *Ibid.,* Aug. 1955, p. 35.
[27] *Ibid.,* Apr., 1956, p. 40.

person of Christ. "To the *Church of Christ*, Jesus Christ is a man." [28] It is explained that he is not a *mere man* but *the Man*.[29] He is designated as Son of Man, Son of God, as Lord, even as Lord of lords.[30] He is not God nor can divinity in any form be attributed to him. Both the Incarnation, which is branded as "an atrocious belief," [31] and the doctrine of the Trinity are flatly denied.[32] He was appointed to be a Savior and does not fill that office by virtue of what he is. His Lordship is not inherent but is an honor conferred on him by God.[33]

Factors Contributing to the Growth of the Movement

A number of factors, six of which can be discerned rather clearly, have given impetus and support to the spread of this movement in the Philippines.

First has been the dynamic leadership of Felix Manalo who dominated the movement for a period of forty-nine years. Quite early in his life he manifested eloquence in speech, skill in argument, facility in the use of the Scriptures, and mastery in organization. During the half century of his leadership he exercised sole authority in biblical interpretation, in the ordination of ministers, in the preparation of the outlines for their sermons,[34] in the payment of their salaries, in the endorsement of candidates for elective positions in the government of the nation.

When in 1922 he identified himself with the angel of Revelation 7:2, he greatly added to his stature and influence.[35] Philippine history indicates that particular honor and trust is given to one who claims to be a religious leader, especially if he shows an interest in the people and maintains that he is sent from God and claims to possess God's truth. It is ironic that although the Spanish priests taught the people to despise the Bible (the Protestant Bible which they mistakenly characterized as being quite different from the Roman Catholic Bible), Filipinos nevertheless have a high regard for one who can freely and impressively quote from it.

[28] *Ibid.*, Feb., 1958, p. 38.　　[29] *Ibid.*, Feb., 1955, p. 40.
[30] *Ibid.*, Nov., 1955, p. 37.　　[31] *Ibid.*, Oct., 1957, p. 37.
[32] *Ibid.*, Jan., 1958, p. 37.　　[33] *Ibid.*, May, 1956, p. 39.
[34] Sta. Romana, *Journal of East Asiatic Studies, op. cit.*, p. 350.
[35] *Ibid.*, p. 407.

The working class who by and large constitute the membership in the *Iglesia* congregations are thought to be readily influenced by an eloquent, knowledgeable, dynamic personality and leader such as was Manalo. It is no doubt correctly reported that from time to time members attempted to kiss his hands and shoes but that he refused this kind of obeisance. For two weeks after his death his body lay in state, first at the plush chapel in San Juan, then at Taguig, his home town, and then in the temple at San Francisco del Monte. Thousands filed past the bier to observe the remains of this great religious leader; many of them, mostly women, were seized with paroxysms of grief, collapsing in violent spasms, writhing and moaning on the floor. Of these many had to be carried away "stiff and cold and unconscious." [36] The police estimated that two million people participated in the mammoth funeral procession. Members were seen weeping, wailing, fainting outright, swooning into fits of anguish during the funeral rites which took all of five hours.[37] Such was the spell this man had exercised over his humble followers.

A second major element of strength consists in the indigenous nature of the movement. The *Iglesia* came into being through the preaching and the ingenuity of a Filipino. Filipinos have been responsible for its evangelistic activities, its program of religious education, and the administration of all of its affairs. Money for the construction of all of its large and small buildings, the support of its hundreds of ministers, the financial undergirding of its growing operations, comes from the Filipino people. Manalo made his second trip to the United States to solicit contributions for the construction of a spacious main chapel, but he became ill, and it is believed that his mission to raise a minimum of $300,000 was unsuccessful.[38]

Tagalog, or some other local language or dialect, is employed in all the preaching and teaching services, thus reaching the innermost core of the common man's heart. The songs rendered by the local choirs are in the vernacular. The official publication,

[36] Quijano de Manila, *Philippine Free Press*, Apr. 27, 1964, p. 46.
[37] Leticia V. Jimenez, *Manila Bulletin*, Apr. 25, 1963.
[38] Sta. Romana, *Journal of East Asiatic Studies*, *op. cit.*, p. 339.

the *Pasugo*, contains articles mostly written in Tagalog, and occasionally an article or two in another Filipino language or dialect. In order to reach those unfamiliar with Tagalog, an English section has been added in most editions. The writings of Dr. José Rizal, the national hero, are frequently referred to or quoted. The portions quoted, however, usually if not always are polemics against the Roman Catholic friars and the practices of the church of Rome.

The *Iglesia ni Cristo* has come to its present measure of strength riding the crest of the wave of nationalism. This is a period in history when any cause is materially enhanced and greatly buttressed if it is rooted in native soil and nourished by that soil. The *Iglesia* is the largest of the multifarious indigenous religious groups in the Philippines, where neither Protestantism nor Roman Catholicism has yet become truly indigenous in terms of structure and support.

As a third contribution to the growth of the movement, it is apparent that the *Iglesia ni Cristo* meets the need of people for human community. One of man's deepest needs is for community, to be closely associated with people, to work and to worship with others. This need is only partially satisfied by family life. It is more fully met when one becomes an integral part of a larger unit than the family. Today, urbanization and industrialization are definitely undermining the cohesiveness of the Filipino family. Individuals coming from the provinces to a big city such as Manila experience a sense of lostness and loneliness. For these people membership in a "community" meets a crying and growing need. An *Iglesia* congregation often will become the home of a "lonely soul," for here he finds congenial fellowship with people like himself, is given what he regards as a responsible God-appointed task, and enters with others in the common worship of God. These congregations are close-knit, self-contained, and separatist in nature. They are havens which separate and protect the individual from the world with all of its ungodly ways and temptations.

Iglesia members recognize that in the communities of which they are a part and in the nation as a whole, they belong to a minority group. Moreover, because of their adherence to unorthodox teachings and practices they undergo ridicule and, they claim, occasional persecution. But they do not appear to be embarrassed by their minority status, and they rejoice in ridicule and "persecution" because they believe they are fulfilling the Scripture, for Christ declared, "Blessed are those who are persecuted for righteousness sake, for theirs is the kingdom of heaven." The belief that they are members of a group that is reviled—also predicted in Scripture—tends to draw them together into a closer "community."

Another element in this experience of community is the feeling of security that comes in at least two ways: first, with respect to the salvation of their souls, since they are well indoctrinated in the belief that their membership in the *Iglesia* is a guarantee of their salvation; and second, with respect to their securing and maintaining jobs. Members, as a rule, do not belong to the ranks of the unemployed. It is said that contractors make it a practice to go to Manalo or someone else in the church in order to secure a crew of workers, since these men have the reputation of honesty and dependability. Fellow members will help an unemployed member to find a job. A member wishing to start a newspaper business, a poultry or a piggery project, or the like, will be given a small loan.

Their sense of community spirit is further enhanced by their awareness of unity. This feeling of unity undoubtedly was fostered during the years that Brother Manalo served as executive minister of the *Iglesia*. He propounded a simple, brief, understandable set of beliefs to which all subscribed. He instructed "the flock" how to cast their votes in local and national elections. There is no reason to doubt that since Felix Manalo's death this sense of unity continues to be a viable element in the life of the members.

A fourth point is that the *Iglesia* has helped to make members feel important and responsible. It is sometimes stated that the rank and file of the people who come to the *Iglesia* possess normally a feeling of inferiority because of their poverty, their lack of educational advantages, and their subjection to persons of wealth and authority. In becoming a vital part of this movement, however, persons with this mind-set are furnished with various compensations, a factor which may well attract a sizable number into the *Iglesia* fold.

For example, the high respect and recognition given to Manalo by some government officials and candidates for office would appear to make belonging to the *Iglesia* worthwhile. The late Manuel L. Quezon, president of the Philippine Commonwealth, befriended Manalo, addressing him as "bishop." [39] From that time on it became the practice of candidates for the presidency, the vice-presidency, governorships, and others seeking office to cultivate his friendship and court his influence over his people.[40] The members are proud that "Brother Felix Manalo" mingled with the high and mighty of the land. The fact that these men paid him courtesy and respect, thus acknowledging his leadership and influence over his people, raised the members' morale and helped compensate for their feeling of inferiority.

Again, the construction of expensive and beautiful chapels makes members proud to belong to the *Iglesia*. These buildings, some of which can be called "temples," costing millions of pesos to construct, serve as a compensation for the poverty of the people. They are the symbols of the "success" of the movement and the sign of God's favor. They undoubtedly bring a sense of elation to their members.

Furthermore, members are well instructed in the tenets of their faith and can defend their membership. They are carefully taught the few fundamental tenets which Manalo formulated. They memorize Scriptural verses which they believe confirm their faith. In dealing with nonmembers they can readily quote chapter and verse to "prove" their doctrines. They are, for the most part, expertly skilled in employing verses to point out how the Roman Catholic Church replaced, in the early part of the Christian era, the New Testament Church; how the Roman bishops and priests led the people astray; and how in 1914 Felix Manalo was "used" of God to fulfill Revelation 7:1–3 by reconstituting the "true church" in the Philippines. They have the satisfaction of being able to give a reason for "the faith" that is in them.

Again each member is given an assigned task in an evangelistic

[39] Quijano de Manila, *op. cit.*, Apr. 27, 1964, p. 44.
[40] Sta. Romana, *Journal of East Asiatic Studies*, *op. cit.*, p. 407.

effort which serves to develop a sense of mission that gives meaning to their lives. Both the men and the women seek with enthusiasm to convert others to the *Iglesia* doctrines and encourage
them to join their church. This evangelistic responsibility is given
expression by serving on a committee consisting of eight or ten
persons.[41] Homes of nonmembers in the community are visited by
the committee, and sometimes arrangements are made for participation in meetings held in the open air. Members of this committee share the responsibility of trying to keep other members from
becoming indifferent or faithless.

A final compensation is that members believe they are God's
elect. In sermon after sermon from their pulpits and in article
after article in the *Pasugo* the members are told that they are
God's elect because they have entered the *Iglesia ni Cristo*. Members believe that they are entrusted with the most important mission under the sun. They are taught that salvation is their portion,
while all outside of the *Iglesia* are condemned to perish in the
lake of fire which burns for ever and ever.[42] As a corollary, it is
taught that only those within the *Iglesia* "are given by God the
right to serve him. . . ."[43]

A fifth factor contributing to the growth of the *Iglesia in Cristo*
is what must be considered the religious illiteracy of Roman
Catholics [44] and Protestants who are too often poorly instructed
in their own doctrines. A considerable majority of the Philippine
Roman Catholics are woefully uninformed as to the meaning of
orthodox Roman Catholicism. This statement has particular rele-
vance to those in the rural areas, where in many places, the
people may see a priest only once in a year. Even in the urban
areas the instruction received in catechetical classes is often unsatisfactory.

A similar appraisal can be made of some Protestant churches
and groups, although in some instances, as might be said with
reference to Roman Catholics, the members have a commendable
grasp of the essentials of the Christian faith.

---

[41] *Ibid.*, p. 353.   [42] *Pasugo*, June, 1958, p. 39.
[43] *Ibid.*, June, 1958, p. 40.
[44] Rev. Manuel P. Alonzo, Jr., *A Historico-Critical Study on the Iglesia ni
Kristo* (Manila, 1959), p. 15.

In the Philippines, he who can glibly quote from the Scriptures may quickly and easily gain respect and secure a hearing. The common man is sometimes profoundly impressed when he hears an eloquent preacher, particularly one with little schooling, cite verses which are purported to be the very "words of God." The Roman Catholic will be approached by an *Iglesia* member quoting Bible verses which, it is asserted, refer to faithless and heretical priests and to the apostasy and corruption of the Roman Catholic Church. The Protestant on the other hand will be told that no Protestant church is referred to in Scripture. *Iglesia* members emphasize the weakness of the Protestant movement by ridiculing the existence of many denominations and sects, and they unfairly or mistakenly declare that the Protestant movement is on the decline in the Philippines.

The *Iglesia* then can marshall verse after verse in dealing with a Roman Catholic or Protestant, selecting verses, which it is asserted, have specific reference to Manalo, to the *Iglesia,* and to the doctrines of that movement. The proof-text method is most effectively employed against people who have only a nominal faith and are at the same time in search of spiritual help and guidance.

Finally, the use of fear to encourage conversion and to threaten expulsion has served in the Philippines as a contribution to the growth of the movement. Articles in the *Pasugo* quite frequently contain statements which seek, through the exploitation of the sense of fear, to convince and convert the reader. Preachers, in open-air meetings, declare to the nonmembers that outside the *Iglesia ni Cristo* there is no salvation. A characteristic statement is the following:

There are those who accept Christ but refuse to enter the *Church of Christ* but you cannot accept Christ and repudiate His church. Likewise you cannot accept the church and abandon Christ.[45]

This same article drives home the point that those not within the *Iglesia* "shall be spurned by the Lord, come judgment day," as is documented by Matthew 7:2–23. And again the member is

[45] *Pasugo,* Jan., 1958, p. 39.

taught that he "has to make a firm resolve to remain steadfast, for he that is separated will be cast into the lake of fire to be tormented with fire and brimstone, and the smoke of their torment ascended up forever and ever; and they shall have no rest day or night."

Moreover, the threat of expulsion from church membership is held over each member. Reference has already been made to the organization of each congregation into committees of eight or ten, one purpose of which is to keep a watchful eye on members.[46] Meetings are held weekly at which time the conduct of members is discussed, what they have done or should have done for the church and what they should do the coming week.[47] Members can be expelled from the *Iglesia* for (1) excessive drinking or gambling; (2) disagreement with the administrative policies; (3) apostasy; (4) marriage outside the church; (5) immorality.[48]

Prospects for Continued Growth

Will the *Iglesia* continue to grow in strength? The indications are that in the immediate future this movement will make gains. Some had predicted that after the death of Felix Manalo the organization would begin to crumble. It is still too early to assess how the demise of its dynamic leader will affect the life of the movement. Eraño Manalo, who succeeded his father as the executive minister, is educated and eloquent, and it is said that he moves easily among the socially elite of the country. Candidates for elective positions court his favor as they did his father's. Eraño is received with warmth and respect as he visits in different parts of the country.

Is there not the likelihood of the *Iglesia's* being splintered now that Brother Felix Manalo no longer exercises his influence? This is possible but perhaps not within the near future.[49] The *Iglesia*

[46] Sta. Romana, *Journal of East Asiatic Studies, op. cit.,* p. 353.
[47] *Ibid.*   [48] *Ibid.,* p. 379.
[49] Dr. Douglas J. Elwood of Silliman University in a research project has discovered at least 4 offshoots from the *Iglesia,* one of the first occurring in 1922, and one as late as 1957. These splinter groups are quite small except for one which claims a membership of 15,000. It would appear that the causes of schism have been both doctrinal and nondoctrinal in nature. See the essay in this volume by Elwood, "Varieties of Christianity in the Philippines," note 28.

is well organized and maintains careful discipline with respect to both its members and ministers. As the young republic continues to pass through an uncertain period of critical economic stress, the working people already attracted to its folds will continue to be attracted. The *Iglesia* provides a needed haven for them in a time of economic uncertainty and fulfills as well a measure of spiritual hunger.

But can a movement built upon indefensible Scriptural interpretations and incredible assertions grow in strength? False ideologies and unorthodox groups in the past and present have and are flourishing, such as Communism and Jehovah's Witnesses. Protestants, and Catholics too, regard Felix Manalo's claim, and the members' unquestioning acceptance of that claim, that he was the fulfillment of Revelation 7:1–3, as an extravagance and a delusion. His success in impressing this interpretation upon his members elevated his own prestige, but put his movement outside the mainstream of historic Christian faith and thereby made it suspect in the eyes of most Protestants and Roman Catholics.

The insistence that from the first century until 1914 the church was nonexistent implies that God's work of salvation suffered an eclipse for nearly twenty centuries. It is an untenable repudiation of the facts of history which regretfully are not readily accessible to the vast majority of the members of the *Iglesia*. Even though many are now literate they do not have, in their own language, ready access to literature which gives a clear account of the history of the church through the ages, during which time the Spirit of God continued the work of salvation. And if books on church history were easily obtainable their contents would undoubtedly be questioned and disputed by the *Iglesia*.

The corollary to the doctrine concerning the eclipse of the Church of Christ is that salvation can be known and experienced only within the *Iglesia*. This teaching is not peculiar to this Philippine religious group, but, like the doctrines above, it is quite untenable and understandably objectionable to the traditional Christian churches.

Nor is the *Iglesia's* Christology unique. It is a form of Arianism which has had followers since the early centuries. Attention is focused on Jesus as "the Man," who is some kind of an intermediate being, neither God nor man in the full sense, but something in between. It is this concept of Christ that is substituted for the richness and the depth of the New Testament presentation of the Incarnation of Christ, the view generally adhered to by the mainstream Christian churches, both Protestant and Catholic.

However, it must be admitted that the language found in the classical creeds in which this doctrine and the related doctrine of the Trinity have been couched is often confusing, if not meaningless, to many people. The terminology in ancient creeds and particularly when these terms undergo translation can become, and sometimes do become, a barrier to the understanding of Christ as he is seen in the New Testament writings. Manalo and the writers in the *Pasugo* freely employ the New Testament designations of Christ but fall short in putting the rich New Testament content and meaning into them. They refer to Christ as the Man, Son of God, Savior, Lord, the Lord of lords, but they refuse to recognize or accept the implications of divinity contained in those terms. We would raise the question: Can the Christian faith exist over an extended period without a strong Christology, one that is firmly rooted in the Scriptures?

The *Iglesia ni Cristo* and its members have been derided, ridiculed, and at times slandered. This has been, in part, an inevitable reaction to the *Iglesia's* vituperative attacks on the Roman Catholic Church [50] and the extravagance of certain of its doctrines. This attitude and practice, from the Christian standpoint, is indefensible and therefore should lead to repentance. Instead of ridiculing the *Iglesia* and its beliefs, efforts should be made to better understand them, by entering, when possible, into a dialogue with its leaders and members. Adherents of the *Iglesia*, it must be assumed, are earnestly seeking for the fulness of God's truth. The Bible for them is the only rule of faith and practice. God's oneness and Creatorship are recognized, and Jesus Christ is accepted and trusted as Lord and Savior, although in an attenuated sense. The members are well-disciplined churchmen, and they are exemplary citizens of the nation.

These are points of vital contact and mutual concern for discus-

[50] See Joseph J. Kavanagh, S.J., *Philippine Studies*, IX, 4 (Oct., 1961), 657.

sion with the *Iglesia*. And, obviously, out of any dialogue and discussion, Christians of other traditions may learn some valuable lessons from this body which has become the fastest growing religious movement in the Philippines.

Varieties of Christianity
in the Philippines

DOUGLAS J. ELWOOD

Religious dissent in the Philippines can be traced to the first half of the nineteenth century when, under Spanish Catholic rule, a few indigenous revolutionary movements began to emerge. Since the beginning of the American "occupation" all registered religious bodies have enjoyed the same legal status, in principle at least, and a condition of "religious pluralism" prevails.[1] An important difference, however, between the Philippines and the American scene is that in the United States "denominational pluralism" has developed out of the necessity of an actual pluralistic situation in which no single church commanded a majority of the population. In the Philippines, by contrast, the Roman Catholic Church claims 82 per cent of the population. Observing this difference, Professor Chester Hunt, in his *Sociology in the Philippine Setting*, comments that "in other countries religious divisions have made tolerance a necessity, but here it can only be based on a type of brotherhood which combines loyalty to one's own church with a tolerance of those who are outside the fold of the major religious organization."[2]

Within this climate of unrealized pluralism the Protestant Christian community in the Philippines (not including Independent Catholics) has grown from no membership at all in 1898 to approximately 4 per cent of the population in 1964. At the same time, an almost unparalleled proliferation of organized Christian

[1] A comparative study reveals that the Philippine Constitution is even more explicit on individual religious liberty than the U.S. Constitution on which it is based. See J. R. Coquia, *The Legal Status of the Church in the Philippines* (Washington, D.C., 1950), p. 40.

[2] Rev. ed., Quezon City, 1963, p. 188.

and quasi Christian movements has occurred. Within the rela tively short period of 70 years, and in a predominantly Roman Catholic society, some 300 separate groups of national or regional scope have registered with the Philippine Securities and Exchange Commission, and at least 280 of these apparently have survived to the present day. To this figure one must add at least 70 nonregistered but organized groups, bringing the total number to an estimated 350 separate organizations.[3]

The total non-Roman Christian constituency in the Philippines is believed to exceed 3,500,000, or about 12 per cent of the general population. This constituency may be divided conveniently between Protestants (*Evangélicos*) and Independent (non-Roman) Catholics (*Independientes*),[4] as well as a number of other non-Catholic Christian bodies. A further division must be made between ecumenical Protestants, affiliated with the National Council of Churches in the Philippines, and independent Protestants, outside the National Council. We have, thus, five distinct branches of Christianity in the Philippines: Roman Catholics, Independent Catholics, ecumenical Protestants, independent Protestants, and other non-Catholic Christians (those who identify with neither the "catholic" nor the "evangelical" tradition). The National Council embraces five of the largest non-Roman bodies,* in this numerical order: Philippine Independent Church

[3] Undocumented material in this chapter is drawn from questionnaires, public records, interviews, and supervised student reports—all of which are part of a comprehensive study of independent religious movements, sponsored by the Silliman University Cultural Research Center, Dumaguete City, Philippines. This essay represents only a preliminary evaluation of the data gathered, and conclusions here are but suggestive of a fuller sociological and theological analysis. Results of the first phase of this research are available in a monograph by the writer, entitled *Churches and Sects in the Philippines: A Descriptive Study of Contemporary Religious Group Movements* (Dumaguete City, 1968). The findings are also summarized in an article by the writer, "Contemporary Churches and Sects in the Philippines," *South East Asia Journal of Theology* (Singapore), IX, 2 (Oct., 1967), 56–78. The *Iglesia ni Cristo,* critically estimated to have 400,000 members, is included here under the category of Independent Protestants.

[4] The Philippine Episcopal Church is included here in the category of Independent Catholics.

* After this essay was written, the Lutheran Church in the Philippines joined the National Council of Churches in the Philippines. This national church is related to the Lutheran Church—Missouri Synod—in the U.S.A.

(Catholic), United Church of Christ in the Philippines, The United Methodist Church, Convention of Philippine Baptist Churches, and Philippine Episcopal Church. Included also are two smaller, indigenous Protestant church bodies: *Iglesia Evangelica Metodista En Las Islas Filipinas* and *Iglesia Evangelica Unida de Cristo*. The National Council's formula for membership is identical to that of the World Council of Churches to which it is officially related. Thus, alongside the proliferation of Protestant church bodies and movements there has been a parallel development toward unity which is marked by significant achievement. In addition to the National Council, a merger of denominations has taken place in the United Church of Christ in the Philippines which has not yet been possible with the parent denominational bodies in the United States. Ecumenical leaders in the Philippines also played a prominent role in developing the East Asia Christian Conference, a regional council of churches which is related to the World Council. The Concordat of Full Communion between the Protestant Episcopal Church and the Philippine Independent Church is another important achievement in the parallel movement toward Christian unity, because it draws the *Independientes* into the wider orbit of non-Roman ecumenical relationships.[5] Actually the most inclusive organization in the Philippines is the Philippine Bible Society which embraces in its member bodies as many as 33 different denominations and service organizations. Other Philippine interdenominational organizations include the Interchurch Language School, Y.M.C.A. and Y.W.C.A., the Student Christian Movement in the Philippines, Inter-Varsity Christian Fellowship, and a new national council of fundamentalist bodies to which a special section of this chapter is devoted.

The total number of Protestant communicants (including the *Iglesia ni Cristo*) may be estimated at approximately 1,000,000, or 3 per cent of the general population.[6] If we include, however,

[5] This means that the Episcopal Church is more closely associated with the Independent Catholic movement than with the Protestant community in the Philippines, whereas it is usually associated with Protestantism in the United States.

[6] *Cf.* Peter G. Gowing, "Christianity in the Philippines Yesterday and Today," *Silliman Journal*, XII, 2 (Second Quarter, 1965), 140. See also T. Valentino Sitoy, Jr., "The Search for Unity Among Non-Roman Christians in the Philippines," *Silliman Journal, ibid.*, pp. 196–210.

the many syncretistic groups of greater or lesser Christian orientation, the total figure representing non-Catholic communicants comes to 1,350,000, or roughly 4 per cent of the general population. Of this total, 274,000 full members are found within the denominations of the National Council, representing about 20 per cent of non-Catholic Christianity in the Philippines. Independent or separatist non-Catholic Christians—those outside the National Council—would then total approximately 1,076,000, or about 80 per cent of non-Catholic Christianity. This latter percentage becomes more significant when we are reminded that Protestant Christians constitute a small minority of the national population; that Southeast Asia—outside the Philippines—is only about 2 per cent Christian; and that the rate of growth among Protestants in the Philippines is lower than that of the general population.

While it is true that only a few of the independent Protestant movements are numerically significant, taken together they constitute what may be called a "third force" in non-Roman Christianity in the Philippines, representing nearly four-fifths of the Protestant population. Some of them are influential far beyond their numerical strength, others are Philippine branches of large and growing world movements, and still others are fully indigenous and bear some of the marks of permanence. It is also important to view this situation in world perspective. The independent Protestant movement on a world scale represents more than one-third of the total numerical strength of Protestant Christianity and is clearly the fastest growing branch of world Christianity.

Varieties of Christianity may express either positive or negative motifs in Christianity as professed and practiced by believing Christians. In so far as they are expressions of the inherent diversity and vitality of genuine Christian faith and experience, they are positive. In so far as they are expressions of human pride and "the cult of the individual," they are negative. To the extent that they call the established churches back from their over-accommodation to existing social customs and conditions, they are constructive. To the extent that they needlessly undermine the united witness of Christians in a non-Christian world, they are destructive. It is important to recognize, however, that ecumenical and independent forces run through denominational bodies and independent movements as well as between them, as seen, for example, in the "Evangelical Fellowship" within the Anglican Church and in the recent ecumenical currents within the Lutheran Church—Missouri Synod. In the light of the dynamics of religious group movements, one should be cautioned against prejudging any movement which claims the name of Christ, either by too broad or too narrow a definition of terms, and least of all the indigenous groups which often have much to teach others about how to make practical Christianity culturally relevant.

Factors Facilitating the Growth of Independent Protestant Movements

In addition to the factors which are universally recognized as contributing to the rise and growth of independent movements, such as the institutional insularity of the traditional churches and their failure to meet the religious needs of the whole populace, certain growth factors—political, social and cultural, and religious—have special reference to the Philippine setting.

Perhaps the most obvious is the newly found freedom of religious expression which is guaranteed by the Philippine constitution. This guarantee was written into the Bill of Rights from the early days of the revolutionary congress. It says that "the free exercise and enjoyment of religious profession and worship, without any discrimination or preference, shall forever be allowed." [7] A perusal of the incorporation records reflects, understandably, an eagerness on the part of the Filipino to exercise this newly acquired right after four centuries of religious domination.

Another obvious factor is nationalism, against which Christianity is sometimes seen to be a "Western import" superimposed on Philippine cultural patterns. Historically the Philippine Independent Church has suffered from schism because of nationalism, each schismatic group claiming to be more nationalistic than the other. Many otherwise "Catholic type" groups venerate national heroes in place of Western saints and stress literal obedience to the law of the land. Groups like *Iglesia ni Cristo* use Christianity as an instrument of continuing nationalism.

[7] Article II, pg. 7.

An important indigenous factor is regionalism and the consequent development of churches in relative isolation. Separated by geographical, linguistic, and cultural barriers, as only an archipelago can be, religious differences develop, and the group itself does not always recognize them as deviations from historic Christianity. More importantly, perhaps, the group may too easily assume that its doctrines are distinctive enough to justify separation from other Christian communions, when in fact they may not be distinctive at all. Nothing is more obvious, from a review of the data collected, than that most of the independent groups either do not know of the existence of other very similar groups or are not aware of the similarities.

Studies have shown that new religious movements often arise where people feel uncertain of their own culture, yet are unable to take over the culture with which they have contact. The Filipino's search for cultural identity is a basic factor in the development of independent movements. Liston Pope concludes his study of the relation between the economic life of a North Carolina county and its churches, with this observation: "Such groups thrive wherever a considerable portion of the population exists on the periphery of culture as organized. . . . Members of the new religions do not belong anywhere—and so they belong, and wholeheartedly, to the one type of institution that deigns to notice them." [8]

Extreme poverty is also a factor. The underprivileged and "disinherited" are attracted to some of these movements because the promise of other-worldly rewards compensates for their "fate" in this world.

There is a tendency among Filipinos to accept and adopt American patterns too readily and uncritically. The psychologist George Guthrie has observed that "imitation" is one of the traits of Philippine national character.[9] This has contributed to the reception of numerous separatist movements from abroad.

Hypersensitivity is a trait of the Filipino personality which is often a contributing cause of splinter movements, although this

[8] *Millhands and Preachers* (New Haven, 1942), p. 136.
[9] *The Filipino Child and Philippine Society* (Manila, 1961), p. 116. See also J. U. Montemayor, *Ours to Share* (Manila, 1966), pp. 258 f.

trait is by no means peculiar to the Filipinos. A noticeable number of new groups, however, have organized separately because a pastor was refused ordination or an aspiring bishop was not elected.

Many of the new organizations are clearly rooted in an anti-Catholic bias which derives from their distant memory of the oppressive rule by the Spanish friars. A widespread Catholic "nominalism" and vestigial anticlericalism contribute to the growth of "free churches." [10] The large number of "Catholic type" organizations, that is, churches with strong Catholic elements, reveals an unfulfilled yearning for a full-scale church reform in the Philippines which, unfortunately, never really flowered. The separation of religion from morality, characteristic of the traditional "folk Catholicism," has been a further stimulus to the rise of a number of "ethical culture" movements which tend to substitute morality for religion.

The spiritual vacuum that followed in the aftermath of World War II led to the birth of new and untried versions of Christianity.

The breakdown of the 1901 Protestant Comity Agreement following World War II, due partly to the population shift but also to the fact that the new mission agencies from abroad, and a few mainline denominations, felt no obligation to observe it, opened the floodgates to widespread proselytism among Protestants.

The shift, after 1938, of the major Western home base for missions from Europe to North America facilitated the postwar influence of American mission agencies in the Philippines. Whereas in 1938 only 40 per cent of all missionaries sent abroad were sent from North America, today it is 60 per cent.[11]

No less important a factor was the expansion, after 1938, of the independent or "faith mission" movement in the United States, stimulated by the Fundamentalist-Modernist controversy of the

[10] The national average of Roman Catholic churchgoers is estimated as low as 10 per cent, according to the Rev. Georges Piron, C.I.C.M., in "The Church in the Philippines Today: A Partial Analysis," in *Dialogue* (Manila), I, 2 (June, 1965), 8 ff. *Cf.* H. de la Costa, S.J., "The Catholic Church in 1955," *Sunday Times Magazine* (Manila, Feb. 15, 1955), pp. 6 f.

[11] Harold Lindsell, "Faith Missions Since 1938," *Frontiers of the Christian World Mission,* ed. by Wilber C. Harr (New York, 1962), pp. 190 f.

1920's which had reverberations as far away as the Philippines. In 1925 more than 81 per cent of all the missionaries sent abroad from North America represented ecumenical agencies, whereas today only 37 per cent represent such agencies.[12]

The theologically conservative mission agencies do not allow deference to the indigenous church principle to become a hindrance to evangelism. The older mission agencies tend to leave the responsibility for evangelism in the hands of the "younger churches." This is because the older agencies have long since outgrown the concept of "voluntary missionary societies of the church" and replaced it with the more Biblical concept of "the church as a missionary society." But many of the newer independent missionary societies still follow policies which characterized the older mission boards and agencies in the nineteenth and early twentieth centuries. "These newer bodies, conservative in theology, untrammeled by relationships, footloose to history, but profoundly moved by the constraints of the Gospel, have no inhibitions. . . . Nor are they always immune to the attraction of proselytizing other Christians whom they probably regard as indifferent, unconverted or apostate." [13]

Chinese Communism is an indirect influence in the growth of new and independent movements in the Philippines because many Protestant groups, not hitherto represented there, transferred their work from the China mainland to work among overseas Chinese in the Philippines and later expanded their work throughout the country.[14] The Southern Baptists provide a case in point. Baptist missionary refugees from China, in 1948, organized a language school in Baguio City with the help of teachers they brought with them from Peking. By 1951, more than 100 former American missionaries in China had transferred to the Philippines.

A number of American G.I.'s and chaplains, while stationed in

[12] Cf. W. R. Hogg, *One World, One Mission* (New York, 1960), pp. 75 f.
[13] Kenneth Grubb, ed., *World Christian Handbook* (London, 1962), Preface.

[14] In 1952, the Chinese residents of the Philippines numbered around 900,000 (150,000 ethnic Chinese; 750,000 mestizos), according to the *Anderson-Smith Report on Theological Education in Southeast Asia* (New York, 1952), pp. 53 f.

the Philippines during World War II, became convinced of a need for evangelizing the country, and upon returning to the United States raised funds from among interested independent mission agencies. For example, Far Eastern Bible Institute and Seminary (FEBIAS), in Manila, was started by such a group associated with the Far Eastern Gospel Crusade, a "faith mission" affiliated to both the Evangelical Foreign Missions Association and the Interdenominational Foreign Mission Association.

Newer Protestant Movements from Abroad

In this chapter attention is drawn to the organized Protestant movements of national or regional scope which presently function independently of the traditional Protestant Christian bodies in the Philippines. One may with good reason speak of them as "newer" movements in the sense that they represent a more recent and distinct line of development alongside the historic Protestant community in that country. Traditional Protestant churches in the Philippines—albeit a short tradition—are those major Protestant church bodies which either came into being or began missionary work at or near the turn of the twentieth century, including mergers and some of the offshoots of such churches. All these are affiliated to the National Council of Churches in the Philippines, with the exception of the Christian and Missionary Alliance which began work as early as 1902, and now is one of the six largest Protestant communions in the Philippines.[15]

Prior to World War II, at least twenty different independent Protestant agencies from abroad had begun missionary work in the Philippines, ranging from the Assemblies of God and the Church of the Nazarene to Jehovah's Witnesses. Immediately following the war a number of new denominations and mission agencies from the United States began work in the Philippines, so that by 1949 the number of churches and mission agencies from abroad had increased to thirty. Whereas just before the war there were only 250 American Protestant missionaries in the Philippines, and 75 per cent of them represented ecumenical bodies, to-

[15] Another early arrival from abroad, although a minor movement in the Philippine setting, is the Church of Christ, Scientist, which began work informally among military personnel in the Philippines as early as 1901.

day there are 1,413 missionaries at work in the Philippines, and only about 23 per cent of them represent churches abroad which cooperate in the wider ecumenical movement.[16] More than 150 of the estimated 350 separate organized Christian bodies in the Philippines today originated abroad or have some foreign ties in the way of financial support, personnel, or literature. These observations clearly indicate that the growth period has been postwar, and that the growth concentration has been among the independent and separatist Protestant movements from abroad.

It is an error, however, to assume that all independent mission boards and agencies are nonconciliar. The truth is that the vast majority of them are conciliar; it is only that their circle of relationships is intentionally circumscribed. It is not yet widely known that in addition to the Division of Overseas Ministries of the National Council of Churches of Christ in the U.S.A., there are in the United States three distinct associations of mission agencies through which independents enjoy wider relationships. These are the Evangelical Foreign Missions Association, the Interdenominational Foreign Mission Association, and the Associated Missions of the International Council of Christian Churches —all of which are well represented in the Philippines.

As recently as 1965, a new rival "national council" of churches was organized in the Philippines by a number of strong independent denominations and service organizations from abroad, called The Philippine Council of Fundamental Evangelical Churches. Charter-member groups include the Conservative Baptist Association of the Philippines, who provided the first president in the Rev. Fred Magbanua; Christian and Missionary Alliance; International Foursquare Gospel Church; Inter-Varsity Christian Fellowship (affiliated to the International Fellowship of Evangelical Students); New Tribes Mission; and a number of nondenominational congregations sponsored by such service organizations as Far Eastern Gospel Crusade, Far East Broadcasting Company, Overseas Missionary Fellowship, Philippine Missionary Fellowship, and Fellowship of Indigenous Fundamental Churches of the Philippines (FIFCOP). Formed after ten

[16] Cf. W. N. Roberts, *Survey Report on Theological Education in the Philippines* (Quezon City, 1962), p. 33.

months of planning and begun less than two years following the reorganization of the National Council of Churches in the Philippines, the new fundamentalist council has a present constituency of 20,000 compared to the National Council's 2,500,000. According to Eustaquio Ramientos, Jr., reporting for *Christianity Today*,[17] the Philippine Council has a potential constituency of 240,000.

The most obvious reason behind the formation of a fundamentalist equivalent of the National Council of Churches in the Philippines was "a lurking fear among independents that the National Council of Churches in the Philippines might declare itself the official voice of Protestantism before the government and become the accrediting body for foreign missionaries." [18] Other probable reasons are the suspicions among conservative evangelicals of "theological compromise" on the part of the denominations associated with the East Asia Christian Conference and their "apparent obsession for organic union" which may lead to eventual union with Roman Catholics (an understandably acute fear in the hearts of most Filipino Protestants). Fears of this kind were not in the least quelled by the reception, in 1963, of the Philippine Independent Church (Catholic) into membership in the National Council. Still another reason may be based on the social conservatism of most independent Protestants in the Philippines. They believe that the mainline denominations are guilty of "social compromise," and prefer instead to take an uncompromising stand on the principle of "spiritual separation from worldliness." It is evident that the prime movers in the formation of the new council were denominations from abroad which are affiliated to the Evangelical Foreign Missions Association. The Christian and Missionary Alliance is the largest—and the Conservative Baptists one of the four largest—missionary-sending agencies affiliated to that association. It is not yet known whether the new council will replace the former Evangelical Fellowship of the Philippines and seek a wider relationship through the World Evangelical Fellowship. Serious objections have been raised by more moderate conservative leaders regarding the negative purpose behind the formation of the council. According to a recent

[17] X, 2 (Oct. 22, 1965), 43.   [18] *Ibid.*

report of a meeting held in Manila in June 1966, consideration is being given by other conservative leaders to organizing a more inclusive national fellowship, structured along the lines of "Evangelical Fellowships" in other parts of the world which include individual members of other denominations as well as congregations, denominations, and service organizations. Indications are that the Philippine Council of Fundamental Evangelical Churches will have to yield to the desire for a larger fellowship or face the consequences of a major split within the ranks of the conservative Protestant force in the Philippines.

It is apparent that the strength of independent Protestantism in the Philippines rests with the denominations and missionary-sending agencies which are related to the Evangelical Foreign Missions Association (EFMA), the mission arm of the National Association of Evangelicals (U.S.A.). Fully 20 of their member bodies are at work in the Philippines, largest of which is the Christian and Missionary Alliance—both inside and outside the Philippines—with 328 missionaries in East Asia. In addition to five of the charter members of the new Philippine Council, which are related to EFMA,[19] other related agencies are the American Advent Mission Society, Free Methodist Church, Christian Reformed Church, and such service organizations as Overseas Crusades, World Vision, International Child Evangelism Fellowship, and Christian Literature Crusade. These 20 agencies represent a missionary force of 342 in the Philippines, 1,351 in East Asia. Usually regarded as moderately conservative in the United States, EFMA-related organizations are expected to observe comity and to subscribe to a conservative doctrinal platform. The worthy slogan of the National Association of Evangelicals, which is a member of the World Evangelical Fellowship, is "cooperation without compromise."

The Interdenominational Foreign Mission Association (IFMA) is also represented in the Philippines through such service organizations as Overseas Missionary Fellowship (China Inland Mission), International Missions, Berean Mission, and Missionary Aviation Fellowship. Far East Broadcasting Company and Far

[19] Overseas Missionary Fellowship is affiliated to the Interdenominational Foreign Mission Association.

Eastern Gospel Crusade are affiliated to both IFMA and EFMA. All these groups together represent an additional missionary force of 120 in the Philippines, 1,846 in East Asia.[20] The doctrinal platforms of the two associations—IFMA and EFMA—are basically the same, except that the IFMA Statement of Faith makes "the personality of Satan" an essential article of faith. More rigidly doctrinaire, many IFMA members consider EFMA personnel to be "neo-Evangelical," although more recently a neo-Evangelical wing has emerged in the IFMA as well. A large and growing measure of cooperation is now evident between the two associations, as seen in the jointly sponsored Congress on the Church's World-wide Mission held in 1965. The differences between them are essentially two: (1) the EFMA includes pentecostal-type societies in its membership whereas the IFMA does not; (2) IFMA includes only nondenominational mission agencies, whereas EFMA includes both denominational and nondenominational agencies.

The Associated Missions of the International Council of Christian Churches (TAM-ICCC) constitutes a third association of independent mission agencies represented in the Philippines. Related organizations include the Association of Fundamental Baptist Churches in the Philippines (Association of Baptists for World Evangelism), Baptist Bible Fellowship International, Independent Bible Baptist Missionary Board, World Baptist Fellowship Mission Council, and Bible Protestant Missions. It is known that the Association of Fundamental Baptist Churches and the Baptist Bible Fellowship together have about 90 missionaries in the Philippines. Although statistics are hard to come by, if the other agencies, taken together, have at least ten, a total missionary force of 100 would be a conservative estimate of the strength of ICCC-related mission agencies in the Philippines.

The Association of Fundamental Baptist Churches in the Philippines functions as one of the 20 "national councils" under the ICCC, and enjoys wider relations in East Asia through the

[20] These figures do not include missionary personnel of the Far East Broadcasting Company or Far Eastern Gospel Crusade, which were already included in the EFMA totals. Forty-eight of the O.M.F. missionaries in the Philippines are from British Commonwealth countries.

Far Eastern Council of Christian Churches which is one of five area councils of the ICCC. This virtually means, for fundamentalist Baptists at least, a third distinct "national council" of churches alongside the new Philippine Council and the older National Council. The foreign counterpart of the Association of Fundamental Baptist Churches in the Philippines is the Association of Baptists for World Evangelism, a mission arm of the General Association of Regular Baptist Churches which is the largest denomination affiliated to the American Council of Christian Churches. About 85 per cent of the missionary personnel connected with the ICCC are employed by two mission boards of the Regular Baptists. Furthermore, 80 per cent of all the monies collected by the ICCC for missions comes from this single denominational source.[21]

The churches related to the International Council do not associate with any churches or mission agencies in the other two associations—IFMA and EFMA, whom they regard as "ecumenical fence sitters"—and least of all with those of the World Council of Churches. Like the IFMA, the ICCC does not admit pentecostal-type groups into its membership. Like the EFMA, it was organized initially to counter the strength and influence of the National Council of Churches of Christ in the U.S.A. The method of operation of both EFMA and IFMA, however, is more positive and constructive than that of the ICCC. The distinguishing feature of the ICCC is that it represents an extreme right-wing separatism and is militantly opposed to the National Council of Churches (U.S.A.), regarding it as apostate. Their doctrinal platform is similar to that of both the IFMA and the EFMA, except that total separation from such "ecclesiastical organizations . . . as the National and World Councils of Churches"[22] is made a condition of membership.

In addition to the EFMA-, IFMA-, and ICCC-related organizations represented in the Philippines, there still remain at least 22 denominations and missionary societies from abroad which exist in "a state of splendid isolation," unrelated to any larger denomi-

[21] Lindsell, op. cit., p. 220.
[22] Doctrinal Statement of the Association of Baptists for World Evangelism.

national or nondenominational association. Prominent among them are the Southern Baptist Convention; Wycliffe Bible Translators (prior to 1960 a member of IFMA); New Tribes Mission, largest of the unaffiliated, nondenominational agencies; and Christian Missions in Many Lands (Plymouth Brethren).[23] In doctrine most of these groups correspond to the member organizations of the three associations of mission agencies discussed above. In policy regarding relations with other Christian bodies, there are varying degrees of affinity, some corresponding to the more cooperative attitude of the EFMA and IFMA (e.g., Wycliffe Bible Translators, and Southern Baptists at the local level); others resembling the more exclusively separatist attitude of the ICCC (e.g., Christian Missions in Many Lands, and Churches of Christ). These unaffiliated groups represent a missionary force in the Philippines of approximately 222.

The four categories discussed above, taken together, represent a missionary force in the Philippines of approximately 1,084, or 77 per cent of the total number of missionaries from abroad (1,413). Missionaries in the Philippines who are related to agencies affiliated to the World Council of Churches total only about 329, according to the 1962 *World Christian Handbook,* or 23 per cent of the total missionary force from abroad. While this is certainly not the only, or even the primary, basis on which to measure the comparative strength of ecumenical and independent Protestant forces in the Philippines,[24] it is an indication of a trend in the growth pattern when viewed side by side with the postwar increase of independents to more than half of Philippine Protestantism.

Independent Indigenous Movements

Churches in the Philippines, as elsewhere overseas, range from the openly "mission-directed church" with no pretense of being

[23] Missouri Synod Lutherans and Seventh Day Adventists are associate member-boards of the National Council of Churches' Division of Overseas Ministries (U.S.A.), and therefore are not included among "independent Protestants" in this paper.

[24] It is now well known that the older denominational boards and commissions increasingly subsidize national churches and support national personnel whereas independent boards rarely do so.

indigenous, to the more or less "indigenized church" with varying degrees of mission leverage, and finally to the "fully indigenous church" which is either one generation removed from missionary influence or has sprung out of the national culture independently of direct missionary influence.[25] In the first and second categories fall most of the so-called "younger churches"—which, paradoxically, are among the elder Protestant churches in the Philippines —and their offshoots and mergers. In the third category are many of those "nativistic" movements which are often admixed with pre-Christian elements, or the relatively few churches of earlier missionary influence which have since taken into themselves some currently operating processes of enculturation as a normal part of their growth.

It is difficult at this time to evaluate the numerical strength of indigenous groups due to the problem of obtaining accurate membership estimates. If it is true, as estimates indicate, that there are approximately 1,076,000 non-Catholic communicant members outside the National Council of Churches, and if approximately 240,000 of these are of fundamentalist persuasion— as the new Philippine Council estimates—this would leave another 836,000 distributed among groups which, if foreign in origin, do not always follow the orthodox Protestant tradition, or, if domestic in origin, belong often to "nativistic" movements. The largest indigenous church is the Philippine Independent Church (Catholic), and the second largest is the *Iglesia ni Cristo*, both of which merit special treatment because of their numerical strength and influence.[26] These and others admit of varying degrees of indigenousness and show a greater or lesser affinity for historic Protestant or Catholic faith and practice. The Sons of God, for instance, of Caloocan City, teach that members are to be received only when it is "proven" that they have been "chosen by the Holy Spirit" to be "Sons of God." Two tests are used to determine this: (1) The candidate is handed three lighted candles. "Should any of these candles, through their prayers, change the color of the light, then he is proven to be a member and he will be baptized

[25] *Cf.* Eugene Nida, "Indigenous Churches in Latin America," *Practical Anthropology* (Mar.–Apr., 1961).

[26] See chapters 11, 12, and 17 in this volume.

spiritually"; (2) "A cross shall be hung steadily over his head, and should the cross move distinctively, then he is considered a member and he will be baptized spiritually. . . . The Holy Spirit descends over the head of the applicant and can be seen by the audience. . . ." This is a pentecostal-type movement which today traces its origin to the time of Christ, but somehow for nineteen-and-a-half centuries the idea behind the "Sons of God" has been "forgotten."

A millennial group, the Pentecostal Assembly of Christ Elect, adds a new dimension in its interpretation of the rapture (I Thess. 4:16-17). Its members believe that "the elect" shall be chosen before the advent of the "Great Tribulation" and shall be brought to places of safety . . . in divinely provided spaceships so that they shall not suffer the terrors and horrors, the pangs and agonies, of the Great Tribulation."

By the beginning of World War II, 30 indigenous groups which still exist had registered with the government, including several offshoots of the Philippine Independent Church [27] and the *Iglesia ni Cristo*.[28] Of the more than 200 independent domestic groups of national or regional scope, which now exist, indications are that nearly half are the products of schism. Examples are the Church of Christ (Wolfe Group) which separated from the Disciples in 1926, and the Association of Fundamental Baptist Churches in the Philippines (ABWE) which split from the American Baptist Mission in 1927. Divisions also occurred among the Adventists, Jehovah's Witnesses, Pentecostals, and Churches of God.

Unique among the independent indigenous movements are the Filipino Assemblies of the First Born, the Equifrilibricum World Religion (Equality-Fraternity-Liberty), the International Christian Churches, and the World Peace Crusaders' Mission ("Lamp-

---

[27] These are carefully listed by Pedro S. de Achútegui and Miguel A. Bernad in "The Aglipayan Churches and the Census of 1960," *Philippine Studies*, XII, 3 (July, 1964), 446–59.

[28] *Iglesia ng Dios kay Kristo Hesus* ("Church of God in Christ Jesus"), *Iglesia Edificada de Jesucristo* ("The Church Built by Jesus Christ"), *Iglesia ni Kristo Itinatag sa Herusalem* ("Church of Christ Founded in Jerusalem"), and *Iglesia Itinayo ni Jesucristo sa Malayong Silangan* ("The Church Founded by Jesus Christ in the Far East") are among the *Iglesia* offshoots.

lighters"). Although very different movements, they have a common history in that all were first officially organized among Filipino emigrants in California or Hawaii, and later brought to the Philippines.

Worthy of special mention are the Christian Mission in the Far East, the Philippine Missionary Fellowship, and the Asian Evangelists Commission, which have developed under Filipino initiative as a result of the threatening conditions of the Japanese occupation and the subsequent closing of the China mainland to foreign missionaries. These are pioneer missionary-sending agencies whose purpose is to prepare and send Filipino missionaries or evangelists to other countries of East Asia as well as to other parts of the Philippines.

Probably the largest number of indigenous groups in the Philippines would fall under the heading "nativistic," by which is meant those groups that are rooted in the traditional (pre-Christian) religion and culture, but which tend to use Christian concepts and practices to revitalize that tradition. Some of these are quasi-Christian when they are too far removed from historic Christianity to be considered a viable "heresy" or when they have added some extraneous or esoteric element such as a private revelation.

Religious dissent among Filipinos—as already mentioned—can be traced to the nineteenth century when, under Spanish Catholic rule, a number of indigenous revolutionary movements emerged. Some of these were led by former Filipino members of a Catholic religious order. Apolinario de la Cruz, for example, was founder of the Confraternity of St. Joseph, in 1840, and was known among his followers as "King of the Tagalogs." [29] In 1892, a secret society came into being, called *Kataasang Kagalang-galang Katipunan ng mga Anak ng Bayan,* meaning "the highly respected Society of the Sons of the People." [30] Two years later the *Pulahan* movement (meaning "Red Turbaned") emerged, was crushed, revived at the turn of the century, suffered a second de-

[29] J. Chesneaux, "Les Heresies Coloniales," *Rech. Int. Marx,* VI (Mar.–Apr., 1958), cited in Vittorio Lanternani, *The Religions of the Oppressed: A Study of Modern Messianic Cults* (New York, 1965), p. 222.

[30] *Ibid.*

feat, then reappeared following the war. Its members fought both the Spanish and the Americans, and their battle preparations consisted of "bottles of holy oil, prayer books, consecrated *anting-anting* (amulets), and other religious paraphernalia," along with bolo knives, spears, and other deadly weapons.[31] One year before the American "occupation," 1897, the *Colorum* (outlaws) joined forces with the *Katipunan*. Its followers claimed to have received guidance from the spirit of José Rizal, their national hero, who had been shot by the Spaniards during the struggle for independence in 1896. In his name they announced the approach of the millennium and the end of the Spanish rule. Still intact today in Calamba, Laguna, which they believe to be the "promised land," they stress the worship of the Holy Family and of the eternal spirits of national heroes. Their leader, Ignacio Coronado, is believed to be 400 years old and to possess supernatural powers. Now peace loving, the group moved to the "promised land" in fulfillment of a prophecy made in 1914 by a *Colorum* leader, Felipe Salvador, that they would finally find complete happiness and lead a movement for world peace.[32]

The Rizalist Movement and a spirit of extreme nationalism have flourished in a number of active religious groups which venerate José Rizal; at least ten groups deify him. Nationalism has played an obviously important part in the development of nativistic religious movements in the Philippines. A student comment describes the mood of these groups: "The foreigners are not superior, after all, because we have our own 'God' (namely, Rizal) and our own 'angel' (namely, Manalo) who can understand us better because they are one of us." Some of the early *Colorum* and *Pulahan* movements regarded Rizal as divine. In 1903 he was canonized as a Filipino "saint" by the Philippine Independent Church, although he is no longer so regarded by that church. A still unknown number of existing religious organizations give special honor to their national hero.[33]

<hr/>

[31] Vic Hurley, *Jungle Patrol*, p. 124, cited in Richard Arens, "The Early Pulahan Movement in Samar and Leyte," *Journal of History*, VII, 4 (1959), 304.

[32] Filemon V. Tutay, "The 'Colorum' Today," *Philippines Free Press*, Dec. 8, 1956.

[33] See M. A. Foronda, Jr., *Cults Honoring Rizal* (Manila, 1961).

As recently as 1949, a new Rizalist group was organized in Manila under the name *Iglesia Sagrada ng Lahi* (Holy Church of the Race), now claiming 40 congregations. They are even more emphatic than the better known Rizalist groups in asserting that Dr. Rizal is "the God of the brown race . . . omnipotent, omniscient and omnipresent. . . ." Their doctrines, they believe, are based on the original beliefs of their Malayan forefathers prior to the colonization of the Philippines by foreign powers. A sacred book entitled *Narito Na Ako* (I Am Here) is a second Bible to the members of this group. As the Old Testament tells the story of the beginnings of the Hebrews, so this small book of 83 pages purports to tell the story of the beginnings of the Malay people from as early as 400,000 B.C. The contents of this book are believed to have been revealed by "the God of the Malays" to one Placido Bronto hundreds of thousands of years ago, but were kept secret until the appearance of "God on earth" in the person of José Rizal.

The organized *Espiritista* movement in the Philippines owes much of its apparent success to the fact that belief in good and evil spirits is "a value orientation in Filipino culture." [34] The movement was started in Manila as early as the turn of the century by a Filipino Attorney, Juan Ortega, returning from abroad as a follower of the internationally known medium Allan Kardec. The organization he started was incorporated under the name *Union Espiritista Cristiana de Filipinas,* with present headquarters in Malabon, Rizal. According to a recent article in *The Manila Times,* the organization now has about 500 chapels and estimates its membership at upwards of 500,000. [35]

There are still many apparently isolated indigenous movements that seem to defy exact classification. [36] Among these are the Uni-

[34] Mary Hollnsteiner, "Philippine Spiritism as a Social Movement" (an unpublished research paper of the Institute of Philippine Culture, Ateneo de Manila University Graduate School), p. 2.

[35] "Spirit Surgery," *The Manila Times,* Sept. 30, 1965.

[36] Many of these are listed in B. I. Guansing, ed., *Philippine Christian Yearbook* (Manila, 1962), pp. 1–12, 159–61; also in W. N. Roberts, *op. cit.,* pp. 195–98. See also the *Philippine Missionary Directory* (Manila, 1968). A complete directory (alphabetical and classified) of the 350 organized groups included in this study is available in a volume by the writer, cited earlier in this essay, under the title *Churches and Sects in the Philippines.*

versal Family of Yahweh, which accepts only the Hebrew names for God and Christ; The Church of the Living God, which claims that God is physically alive and present today in the person of a twenty-year-old boy whose name is Emmanuel Salvador del Mundo (meaning "God with us, Savior of the World"); and Catholic Apostles Initiated by the Holy Spirit, which began as an unofficial "order" in the Roman Catholic Church but became a separate organization when its members were denied the Sacrament. This latter movement is a very interesting example of an original blending of Catholic and Protestant elements of Christianity by a fully indigenous organization.

In the Philippines, in proportion to the Protestant population, there is probably a greater variety and number of separate Christian groups than in any other country in Asia, with the possible exception of Japan. The countervailing forces for unity and for division appear to be about equal at the moment. Which will prevail in the next decade is the unanswered question. As the Philippine churches break out of their isolation, through industrialization and urbanization, and see themselves increasingly in the larger context of Asia and the world scene, special religious differences will doubtless become less important, and the forces for unity will prevail. The challenge of the coming decades is the same, in principle, as other Christian nations face, that is, how to develop a style of Christian "unity with diversity" that will allow for full and varied expression of the wholeness of Christianity, so that the periodic breakup of unsatisfying unities, characteristic of the history of Christianity, will no longer be necessary. Seventy years ago in the Philippines it was important to stress division in order to break up the monolithic "unity" which characterized Hispanic Catholicism. Today, however, there is an obvious need to stress Christian unity if the small minority of Protestants, now divided into more than 350 separate entities, is to become a creative minority. In terms of both numerical strength and missionary personnel, the separatist movement clearly constitutes a major "third force" in non-Roman Christianity in the Philippines, alongside the ecumenical Protestant and the independent Catholic movements.

BIBLIOGRAPHICAL SURVEY

CONTRIBUTORS

AND INDEX

A Bibliographical Survey of
Philippine Church History

By JOHN N. SCHUMACHER, S.J.

and GERALD H. ANDERSON *

I

The Roman Catholic Church

It is ironical that the Roman Catholic Church, which provided almost all Philippine historiography for three centuries, still lacks a scholarly comprehensive history of its own work. Zaide's *Catholicism in the Philippines*,[1] the only work to attempt any overall view of the church, is rather a collection of information on various aspects of the church than a continuous history. Nonetheless, much has been written on the history of the church in four centuries, and an attempt will be made here to indicate a selection of those works most useful for obtaining a comprehensive view of Catholicism.

The most extensive and complete bibliography of the Philippine church is the well-known mission bibliography of Streit and Dindinger, which devotes five of its volumes, in whole or in part, to the Philippines.[2] Still of great value, though dealing only with the Spanish period and not exhaustive in coverage, is the *Aparato*

---

* Part I of this essay was prepared by Father Schumacher; Part II, by Dr. Anderson.

[1] Gregorio F. Zaide, *Catholicism in the Philippines* (Manila: Santo Tomás University Press, 1937), viii, 239 pp.

[2] Robert Streit, O.M.I., and Johannes Dindinger, O.M.I., *Bibliotheca Missionum* (21 vols.; Münster/Aachen: Verlag der Aschendorffschen Buchhandlung, 1916–1955). The principal volumes dealing with the Philippines are: IV (1560–1599); V (1600–1699); VI (1700–1799); IX (1800–1909); XXI (1525–1950).

bibliográfico of Retana.[3] Though not limited to church history, it contains most of the important Spanish works in this field, frequently with lengthy annotations, many of which were adopted by Streit.

An important documentary collection, not limited to church history, but largely devoted to it, is that of Blair and Robertson, covering the entire Spanish period with documents in translation.[4] BRPI is an invaluable collection, not only for its documents, but because it reproduces, either completely or in summary, many of the older chronicles no longer easily available. Its translations, unfortunately, are not always completely accurate. Many of the papal documents for the Philippines up to the nineteenth century are to be found in the collection of Hernáez.[5]

The papal and royal documents relative to the *Real Patronato de Indias,* that institution whose understanding is essential for the study of the church in the Spanish overseas empire, may be found, together with English translations and extensive commentary, in the study of W. Eugene Shiels, S.J.[6] Brief synthetic accounts are those of Antonio Ybot León and León Lopetégui, S.J., in their volumes on the history of the church in Spanish America.[7] The theological-juridical problems which were so passionately discussed at the time of the occupation of the Philippines

[3] W. E. Retana, *Aparato bibliográfico de la historia general de Filipinas* (3 vols.; Madrid: Minuesa de los Rios, 1906). Further guidance to bibliography may be found in the exhaustive *Bibliography of Philippine Bibliographies, 1593–1961,* compiled by the late Gabriel A. Bernardo, and edited by Natividad P. Verzosa, containing 1,160 entries (Manila: Ateneo de Manila University Press, 1968).

[4] Emma Helen Blair and James Alexander Robertson (editors), *The Philippine Islands, 1493–1898* (55 vols.; Cleveland: The Arthur H. Clark Co., 1903–1909). Henceforth this will be abbreviated as BRPI.

[5] Francisco Javier Hernáez, S.J., *Colección de bulas, breves y otros documentos relativos a la Iglesia de América y Filipinas* (2 vols.; Bruselas, 1879).

[6] W. Eugene Shiels, S.J., *King and Church: the Rise and Fall of the Patronato Real* (Chicago: Loyola University Press, 1961), xiii, 399 pp.

[7] Antonio Ybot León, *La Iglesia y los eclesiásticos españoles en la empresa de Indias,* in "Historia de América y de los pueblos americanos," ed. by Antonio Ballesteros y Beretta (Barcelona: Salvat, 1954), I, 293–346; León Lopetégui, S.J., Felix Zubillaga, S.J., and Antonio de Egaña, S.J., *Historia de la Iglesia en la América Española desde el Descubrimiento hasta comienzos del siglo XIX* (2 vols.; Madrid: Biblioteca de Autores Cristianos, 1964–1966), I, 123–163.

are treated in an overly apologetic but solidly based study by
Francisco Montalbán, *El Patronato español y la conquista de
Filipinas*.[8] A more extended treatment of these and other related
problems may be found in the work of J. Gayo Aragón,[9] while
some of the pertinent documentation has been reproduced in the
collection of Hanke and Millares Carlo.[10]

The story of the evangelization of the Philippines is essentially
that of the religious orders, and indeed it is in the chronicles of
these orders that we find our principal source even for the general
history of the Philippines. Since the entire country was divided
up among the orders by the king, the principal source for each
region will be the chronicles of the order under whose care that
region was, though all held parishes in the Manila area. Unfortunately the religious have done relatively little to provide modern,
scholarly accounts of their work, and we are reduced for the most
part to the use of the old chronicles, and for some periods not
even these exist.

For the Augustinians, Juan de Grijalva's chronicle of the
Augustinians in New Spain [11] provides much information on the
early mission efforts in the years before a Philippine province of
the order was constituted, though Grijalva was never himself in
the Philippines. The informative work of Gaspar de San Agustín [12] narrates the years up to 1614. Its continuation by Casimiro
Díaz, only published in the nineteenth century, is very largely
based on San Agustín's notes, and brings the story up to 1698.[13]
A useful complement to these chronicles is the recently edited

[8] Francisco Javier Montalbán, S.I., *El Patronato español y la conquista
de Filipinas,* in "Bibliotheca Hispana Missionum," vol. IV (Burgos: "El
Siglo de las Misiones," 1930), x, 140 pp.

[9] Jesús Gayo Aragón, O.P., *Ideas jurídico-teológicas de los religiosos de
Filipinas en el siglo XVI sobre la conquista de las Islas* (Manila: Imprenta
de la Universidad de Santo Tomás, 1950), 242 pp.

[10] Lewis Hanke and Agustín Millares Carlo (editors), *Cuerpo de documentos del siglo XVI sobre los derechos de España en las Indias y las Filipinas* (Mexico: Fondo de Cultura Económica, 1943).

[11] Juan de Grijalva, O.S.A., *Crónica de la orden de N. P. S. Agustín en las
provincias de la Nueva España* (Mexico, 1624), 218 pp.

[12] Gaspar de San Agustín, O.S.A., *Conquistas de las islas Philipinas* (Madrid, 1698), 544 pp.

[13] Casimiro Díaz, O.S.A., *Conquistas de las islas Filipinas* (Parte segunda;
Valladolid: Gaviria, 1890), 854 pp.

Osario Venerable,[14] written in 1780, containing brief biographical notices of notable Augustinians of these two centuries, as well as various statistical data of the Augustinian missions and several lists of corrections to the work of Gaspar de San Agustín. For general Augustinian biography Castro has been largely supplanted by the bio-bibliographical catalogue of Elviro J. Pérez,[15] while for Augustinian writers, the monumental work of Santiago Vela has superseded both these works.[16]

The Franciscans did least toward chronicling their mission activity in the Philippines, for not only do the principal chronicles not go beyond the end of the sixteenth century, but all concern themselves very largely with Japan rather than the Philippines. Ribadeneyra's account, however, is valuable for its information on early mission methods, written as it was by a contemporary participant.[17] A more extensive work, written in the seventeenth century, but published only in the nineteenth, is that of Santa Inés,[18] but San Antonio, writing in the eighteenth century and making use of Santa Inés, has treated the same period both with greater extension and generally greater competence.[19] For the

[14] Agustín María de Castro, O.S.A., *Misioneros agustinos en el Extremo Oriente, 1565–1780* (*Osario Venerable*), in "*Biblioteca 'Missionalia Hispanica,'*" Serie B, vol. VI, ed. by Manuel Merino, O.S.A. (Madrid: Consejo Superior de Investigaciones Científicas 1954), xl, 518 pp.

[15] Elviro J. Pérez, O.S.A., *Catálogo bio-bibliográfico de los religiosos agustinos de la provincia del Santísimo Nombre de Jesús de las Islas Filipinas* (Manila: Colegio de Sto. Tomás, 1901), xviii, 873 pp.

[16] Gregorio de Santiago Vela, O.S.A., *Ensayo de una biblioteca iberoamericana de la Orden de San Agustín* (7 vols.; Madrid: Imp. del Asilo de Huérfanos del S.C. de Jesús, 1913–1931). This work has been corrected and brought up to date in a series of articles entitled "Bibliografía misional agustiniana," by Isacio R. Rodríguez, O.S.A., appearing in *Archivo Agustiniano*, 1955–1958, and for the Philippines, in the work cited in note 36 below.

[17] Marcelo de Ribadeneyra, O.F.M., *Historia de las islas del archipiélago Filipino y reinos de la gran China, Tartaria, Cochinchina, Malaca, Siam, Cambodge y Japón*, edited by Juan R. de Legísima, O.F.M. (Madrid: Editorial Católica, 1947), lxxv, 652 pp.

[18] Francisco de Santa Inés, O.F.M., *Crónica de la provincia de San Gregorio Magno de religiosos descalzos de n. s. p. San Francisco en las islas Filipinas, China, Japón, etc.*, "Biblioteca Histórica Filipina," II–III (2 vols.; Manila: Chofre, 1892).

[19] Juan Francisco de San Antonio, O.F.M., *Chrónicas de la apostólica Provincia de San Gregorio de Religiosos Descalzos de N. S. P. San Fran-*

rest of Franciscan history there is only the account of Domingo Martínez,[20] which, unlike most other religious chronicles, limits itself almost completely to Franciscan history to the extent of becoming almost a series of biographies. Though not chronicles, the works of Huerta [21] and Gómez Platero [22] deserve mention here. The former supplies data—historical, statistical, and geographical —on the Franciscan parishes up to 1865, and is an invaluable source of information. The latter supplements the biographical sections of Huerta and brings them up to 1880.

The contemporary chronicle of the first generation of Jesuit missionaries is Chirino's *Relación,* informative on Filipino life as well as on mission methods.[23] The history of Colín [24] is much more detailed than Chirino, on whose unpublished notes it was partly based, and treats the events up to 1616. Though perhaps not of the same high quality as Colín as far as organization of its narrative, the continuation by Murillo Velarde, which brings the story up to 1716, is likewise a valuable source of information both on events and on mission methods.[25] For the Jesuit work among the Muslims of Mindanao and Jolo, the general history of that region by Combés [26] complements the accounts of Colín and Murillo Velarde.

The Dominicans were the most systematic in the chronicling of their mission work. Diego Aduarte narrated the Dominican efforts

cisco en las Islas Philipinas, China, Japón, etc. (3 vols.; Manila: 1738–1744). Portions in *BRPI,* XXVIII and XL.

[20] Domingo Martínez, O.F.M., *Compendio histórico de la apostólica Provincia de San Gregorio de Philipinas, de Religiosos menores Descalzos, de N. P. San Francisco* (Madrid, 1756), 342, 116, 248 pp.

[21] Felix de Huerta, O.F.M., *Estado geográfico, topográfico, estadístico, histórico-religioso de la Santa y Apostólica Provincia de S. Gregorio Magno en las Islas Filipinas* (Binondo, 1865), 713 pp.

[22] Eusebio Gómez Platero, O.F.M., *Catálogo biográfico de los religiosos franciscanos de la provincia de San Gregorio Magno de Filipinas* (Manila: Colegio de Santo Tomás, 1880), 813 pp.

[23] Pedro Chirino, S.J., *Relación de las islas Filipinas* (2nd ed.; Manila: Esteban Balbas, 1890), 275 pp.

[24] Francisco Colín, S.J., *Labor evangélica,* edited by Pablo Pastells, S.J., (3 vols.; Barcelona: Henrich, 1900–1902).

[25] Pedro Murillo Velarde, S.J., *Historia de la provincia de Philipinas de la Compañia de Jesús* (Manila, 1749), 419 pp.

[26] Francisco Combés, S.J., *Historia de Mindanao y Joló,* edited by W. E. Retana (Madrid, 1897), cxliv, 800 cols. The first edition is from 1667.

of the years up to 1636, principally in the difficult Cagayan Valley missions.[27] His narrative was continued by Balthasar de Santa Cruz,[28] though the latter's work is less rich in detail than Aduarte's. Vicente Salazar [29] brought the account up to the end of the seventeenth century, and Domingo Collantes narrated the years 1700–1765.[30] Juan Ferrando wrote a history combining his four predecessors' work, and continuing the story down to the year 1840.[31] Dominican biographies are to be found in the two works of Ocio y Viana.[32]

The last of the orders to begin mission work in the Philippines was that of the Discalced Augustinians or *Recoletos*. No chronicle of Recoleto work limited to the Philippines was published, but considerable space was given to the Philippine work in the four volumes of the general chronicle of the Recoletos, as follows:

[27] Diego Aduarte, O.P., *Historia de la Provincia del Santo Rosario de la Orden de Predicadores en Filipinas, Japón y China*, ed. by Manuel Ferrero, O.P. (2 vols.; Madrid: Consejo Superior de Investigaciones Científicas, 1962–1963). This work, originally published in 1640, was reprinted in 1693 with the work of Santa Cruz cited in note 28. Aduarte's history is translated, partly in synopsis, in *BRPI*, XXX–XXXII.

[28] Baltasar de Santa Cruz, O.P., *Historia de la provincia del Santo Rosario de Filipinas, Iapon y China de la sagrada Orden de Predicadores* (Tomo segundo; Zaragoza, 1693), 531 pp. Translation and synopsis in *BRPI*, XXXV and XXXVII.

[29] Vicente Salazar, O.P., *Historia de la Provincia de el Santissimo Rosario de Philipinas, China y Tunking, de el Sagrado Orden de Predicadores* (Tercera parte; Manila, 1742), 746 pp.

[30] Domingo Collantes, O.P., *Historia de la provincia del Santísimo Rosario de Filipinas, China y Tunquin, Orden de Predicadores* (Quarta parte; Manila, 1783), 659 pp.

[31] Juan Ferrando, O.P., *Historia de los pp. Dominicos en las Islas Filipinas y en sus misiones del Japon, China, Tung-kin y Formosa*, edited by Joaquín Fonseca, O.P. (6 vols.; Madrid, 1870–1872). The subtitle speaks of an appendix extending Ferrando's history from 1840 to the present, but at the end of the sixth volume Fonseca declares that it seems inopportune to treat contemporary events.

[32] Hilario María Ocio y Viana, O.P., *Reseña biográfica de los religiosos de la provincia del Santísimo Rosario de Filipinas desde su fundación hasta nuestros días* (2 vols.; Manila: Colegio de Santo Tomás, 1891). *Compendio de la Reseña biográfica de los religiosos de la provincia del Santísimo Rosario de Filipinas desde su fundación hasta nuestros días* (Manila: Colegio de Santo Tomás, 1895), 1240, lxviii, 167 pp. The two volume work, in spite of its title, goes only to the end of the seventeenth century. The second work gives a compendium of the two-volume work, and then completes it to 1895.

Andrés de San Nicolás (1606–1624); Luís de Jesús (1621–1650); Diego de Santa Theresa (1651–1660); Pedro de San Francisco de Assís (1661–1690).[33] Further information on the Recoletos, as well as on all ecclesiastical and secular history of the Philippines up to 1759 may be found in the extensive work of the Recoleto Juan de la Concepción, the only general synthetic work on the Philippines before the end of the nineteenth century.[34] For biographical sketches of individual Recoletos, there is the *Catálogo* of Sádaba, covering the entire Spanish period.[35]

All these chronicles contain much of the hagiographical, and all are more or less replete with miracle stories. Moreover, since the mission field in the Philippines was divided geographically for the most part among the five orders, the chronicles limit themselves to the work of the church in specific regions, though all deal to a certain extent with life and events in Manila and its environs. Since the orders were often involved in bitter rivalries, the accounts frequently present quite different versions, depending on the viewpoint represented. Finally, many of the chronicles, especially those dealing with the sixteenth and early seventeenth centuries, devote a large part of their attention, sometimes almost all of it, to the more spectacular events in the missions of Japan, China, and Tonkin, for which the Philippines tended to become merely a point of departure. In spite of these limitations, however, properly used they are still of great value for the understanding of these early centuries.

Modern studies of the religious orders are few, and even fewer are those which may be called critical synthetic works. A full-length monumental history of the Augustinians has been begun

---

[33] All of these volumes bear the title: *Historia general de los religiosos descalzos del orden de los ermitaños del gran padre, . . . San Agustín, de la congregación de España y de las Indias.* The places and dates of publication were, respectively: Madrid, 1664; Madrid, 1681; Barcelona, 1743; Zaragoza, 1756. The Philippine material has been translated or synopsized in *BRPI*, XXI, XXXVI, XLI.

[34] Juan de la Concepción, O.R.S.A., *Historia general de Philipinas* (14 vols.; Manila, 1788–1792).

[35] Francisco del Carmen Sádaba, O.R.S.A., *Catálogo de los Religiosos Agustinos Recoletos de la Provincia de San Nicolás de Tolentino de Filipinas* (Madrid: Imprenta del Asilo de Huérfanos del Sagrado Corazón de Jesús, 1906), 887 pp.

by Isacio R. Rodríguez,[36] which is planned to include five volumes of bibliography, followed by several of previously unpublished documents, an extensive historical synthesis, and finally a catalogue of unpublished documents. When finished, it should be a noteworthy contribution to scholarship on the Philippine church, particularly considering the wide extent of the Augustinians' mission territory, and the fact that they always outnumbered any other group of missionaries. At this writing, however, only the first four volumes of bibliography have appeared. For the meantime there is the synopsis written for intramural consumption by Bernardo Martínez.[37] Though without pretensions to being a scholarly work, it reproduces in full many unpublished documents. It is particularly valuable for the eighteenth and nineteenth centuries, the period after that covered by the chronicles, and contains much of interest for the latter period, not only for Augustinian, but for general church history as well.

For the Franciscans there is no single modern work, though a great deal has been published in the Franciscan *Archivo Ibero-Americano*, most notably by the indefatigable researcher, Lorenzo Pérez, O.F.M., some of whose contributions in the first three decades of this century are of book length.[38]

The history of the Jesuits from their return to the Philippines in 1859 to 1900 is chronicled in great detail, though without effort at synthesis, by Pablo Pastells, S.J.[39] The history of the Society of Jesus up to its expulsion in 1768 has recently appeared in an important study by Horacio de la Costa, S.J.,[40] a work of sound his-

[36] Isacio Rodríguez Rodríguez, O.S.A., *Historia de la Provincia Agustiniana del Smo. Nombre de Jesús de Filipinas* (Manila, 1965 ff.).

[37] Bernardo Martínez, O.S.A., *Apuntes históricos de la Provincia agustiniana del Santísimo Nombre de Jesús de Filipinas* (Madrid: Imprenta del Asilo de Huérfanos del Sagrado Corazón de Jesús, 1909), 551 pp.

[38] Published in Madrid, 1914 ff. The principle articles of Father Pérez are listed in Doris Varner Welsh (compiler), *A Catalogue of Printed Materials Relating to the Philippine Islands, 1519–1900, in the Newberry Library* (Chicago: Newberry Library, 1959), pp. 77–78. One series of these articles was published in book form: *Origen de las misiones franciscanos en el Extremo Oriente* (Madrid: López del Horno, 1916), 290 pp.

[39] Pablo Pastells, S.J., *Misión de la Compañía de Jesús de Filipinas en el siglo XIX; relación histórica* (3 vols.; Editorial Barcelonesa, 1916–1917).

[40] Horacio de la Costa, S.J., *The Jesuits in the Philippines, 1581–1768* (Cambridge, Mass.: Harvard University Press, 1961), xiii, 702 pp.

torical scholarship, based on extensive research, and containing much of value not only for Jesuit history, but for that of the church as a whole, and even for general Philippine history.

For the Dominicans there is a recent one-volume synopsis in Spanish, which, though written primarily for Dominican seminarians and not a work of critical scholarship, contains much information of value from unpublished documents of the Philippine Dominican archives.[41] For the Recoletos there is the synopsis of Ruíz de Santa Eulalia.[42] On the modern congregations in the Philippines, mention should be made of the somewhat popular synopsis of the first fifty years of the Vincentian Fathers and the Daughters of Charity in the Philippines, by Bruno Saiz, C.M.[43]

Special Topics of Church History

One of the most important works for the Philippine church as a whole, dealing principally with the sixteenth and seventeenth centuries, is Phelan's *The Hispanization of the Philippines*.[44] Though not without its limitations, and covering a broader field than church history, this pioneering work of ethno-history gives the best broad view of the impact of Catholicism on the Filipinos and the reciprocal Filipinization of Catholicism.

Staffed, as it was, almost exclusively by the members of the religious orders, and organized under the exceptional juridical regime obtained by the Spanish kings from the popes, the Philippine church was plagued with a series of jurisdictional disputes, in which bishops, often religious themselves, attempted to subject the orders to their jurisdiction, sometimes with the help of the state, sometimes in open conflict with it. The best brief treatment of this complex and controverted question is to be found in an essay by H. de la Costa in the present volume.[45] Another essay in

[41] Pablo Fernández, O.P., *Dominicos donde nace el sol* (Barcelona, 1958), 712 pp.

[42] Licinio Ruíz de Santa Eulalia, O.R.S.A., *Sinopsis histórica de la Provincia de San Nicolás de Tolentino* (2 vols.; Manila, 1925).

[43] [Bruno Saiz, C.M.], *Los Padres Paules y las Hijas de Caridad en Filipinas* (Manila: Santos y Bernal, 1912), vii, 435 pp.

[44] John Leddy Phelan, *The Hispanization of the Philippines* (Madison: University of Wisconsin Press, 1959), xi, 218 pp.

[45] Horacio de la Costa, S.J., "Episcopal Jurisdiction in the Philippines during the Spanish Regime," chapter 3 in this volume.

this volume by the same author does much to outline and explain, in a nonpolemic context, the Spanish failure to develop an adequate Filipino native clergy.[46] This failure, together with the traditional rivalry in the Philippines between the secular and the religious clergy, helps to explain in part the antifriar tendency with which nineteenth-century Filipino nationalism was born, and which became more and more dominant in the years before the revolution of 1896. The attack on the friars was spearheaded by the two nationalist novels of the leading Filipino patriot, José Rizal, the *Noli Me Tangere* (1887) and the *El Filibusterismo* (1891).[47] One of the more extended indictments, reasoned and moderate in tone, though scarcely dispassionate, by another leader of the nationalist movement, was the *La soberanía monacal* of Marcelo H. del Pilar, publisher under the pseudonym Mh. Pláridel.[48] The propaganda of the nationalist movement tended to emphasize the corruption, the wealth, and the oppressive political power of the four friar orders as the principal cause of the revolution, a view frequently echoed in the American regime which succeeded Spain in 1898. Two apologies by friars, Eladio Zamora, O.S.A.,[49] and Valentín Marín y Morales, O.P.,[50] both of them rather impassioned defenses, are nonetheless of value not only as a partial corrective to the antifriar charges, but also for their informative, if at times somewhat exaggerated and one-sided accounts of the contributions of the orders to Philippine life and culture. A more objective evaluation of the antifriar movement

[46] Horacio de la Costa, S.J., "The Development of the Native Clergy in the Philippines," chapter 4 in this volume.

[47] The two novels have been newly translated by León Ma. Guerrero as *The Lost Eden*, a new English translation of *Noli Me Tangere* (Bloomington: Indiana University Press, 1961), xviii, 407 pp.; and *The Subversive*, a new English translation of *El Filibusterismo* (Bloomington: Indiana University Press, 1962), xv, 299 pp.

[48] Originally published in 1888, the pamphlet recently received a new bilingual edition. See Marcelo H. del Pilar, *Monastic Supremacy in the Philippines*, translated by Encarnación Alzona (Quezon City: Philippine Historical Association, 1958), iv, 180 pp.

[49] Eladio Zamora, O.S.A., *Las corporaciones religiosas en Filipinas* (Valladolid: Martín, 1901), vi, 504 pp.

[50] Valentín Marín y Morales, O.P., *Ensayo de una síntesis de los trabajos realizados por las corporaciones religiosas españoles de Filipinas* (2 vols.; Manila: Imprenta de Santo Tomás, 1901).

may be found in an article of Vicente Pilapil,[51] while I have described the whole movement in its prerevolutionary phase and attempted to analyze the complex factors which went into it in my recent doctoral dissertation.[52]

The often confused and contradictory lists of bishops in the Philippines have been definitively clarified by the research of Domingo Abella in his *Bikol Annals,* and in a series of articles in *Philippine Studies* and elsewhere, effectively disproving the existence of any Filipino bishops during the Spanish regime.[53] Along the same line, Abella has provided a partial corrective in a recent article [54] to some exaggerations concerning the church's accomplishments in bringing higher education to Filipinos.[55] Education under the Spanish regime, however, was certainly one of the great glories of the church, and due almost exclusively to her, but its accurate history still remains to be written.

The Inquisition never played the role in the Philippines that it did in America, though on occasion it emerged into prominence in the affairs of Manila Spaniards. The only scholarly treatment is that of J. Toribio Medina.[56]

[51] Vicente R. Pilapil, "Nineteenth-Century Philippines and the Friar Problem," *The Americas,* XVIII (1961), 127–48.

[52] John N. Schumacher, S.J., *The Filipino Nationalists' Propaganda Campaign in Spain, 1880–1895* (Ph.D. dissertation, Georgetown University, Washington, D.C., 1965, xiii, 696 pp.; available from University Microfilms, Ann Arbor, Michigan).

[53] Domingo Abella, *Bikol Annals* (Manila, 1954), xiv, 384, vi pp. For dioceses other than Cáceres, his principal articles are: "Episcopal Succession in the Philippines," *Philippine Studies,* VII (1959), 435–47; "The Succession of Bishops of Cebu," *ibid.,* VIII (1960), 535–43; "The Bishops of Nueva Segobia," *ibid.,* X (1962), 577–85; "The Bishops of Cáceres and Jaro," *ibid.,* XI (1963), 548–56; "Episcopal Succession in the Philippines During the Spanish Regime," *The Beginnings of Christianity in the Philippines* (Manila: Philippines Historical Committee, 1965), pp. 201–24.

[54] Domingo Abella, "State of Higher Education in the Philippines to 1863—A Historical Reappraisal," *Philippine Historical Review,* I (1965), 1–46.

[55] Evergisto Bazaco, O.P., *History of Education in the Philippines: Spanish Period—1565–1898* (2nd ed.; Manila: University of Santo Tomás Press, 1953), xiv, 423 pp. See also Encarnación Alzona, *A History of Education in the Philippines, 1565–1930* (Manila: University of the Philippines Press, 1932), xi, 390 pp.

[56] José Toribio Medina, *El tribunal del Santo Oficio de la Inquisición en las Islas Filipinas* (Santiago de Chile, 1899), 190 pp.

Considerable interest has been aroused in recent years in the religious art and the church architecture of the Spanish period. The principal work on religious art has been done by Fernando Zóbel de Ayala in his book *Philippine Religious Imagery*.[57] The quarterly review *Philippine Studies* has carried important articles by Benito F. Legarda, Jr.,[58] and by Richard Ahlborn[59] on Philippine church architecture, all copiously illustrated. There are likewise several chapters devoted to church architecture in María Lourdes Díaz-Trechuelo's study of Spanish architecture in the Philippines.[60]

The history of Catholicism in the twentieth century is still unwritten, even in imperfect form. One of the few works which give any extended treatment of the church at all is Zwierlein's book *Theodore Roosevelt and Catholics*.[61] Some two-thirds of the book is devoted to the problems the first American bishops in the Philippines faced in the opening years of the twentieth century. In spite of its unsystematic character and extraneous subject, the book has considerable value for the large number of documents reproduced in whole or in part from Philippine diocesan archives, and from the letters of the bishops involved, particularly Bishop Augustine Hendricks.

Among the scholarly reviews which more frequently publish articles concerning Philippine church history are *Missionalia Hispanica*,[62] *Archivo Ibero-Americano* (published by the Franciscans),[63] and *Archivo Agustiniano* (by the Augustinians).[64] In

---

[57] Fernando Zóbel de Ayala, *Philippine Religious Imagery* (Quezon City: Ateneo de Manila University, 1963), 154 pp. This is a revision and extension of his article "Philippine Colonial Sculpture," *Philippine Studies*, VI (1958), 249–94. Cf. Galo B. Ocampo, *The Religious Element in Philippine Art* (Manila: University of Santo Tomás, [1966]), 130 pp.

[58] Benito Fernández Legarda, "Colonial Churches of Ilocos," *Philippine Studies*, VIII (1960), 121–58.

[59] Richard Ahlborn, "The Spanish Churches of Central Luzon," *ibid.*, VIII (1960), 802–13; XI (1963), 283–300.

[60] María Lourdes Díaz-Trechuelo Spínola, *Arquitectura española en Filipinas, 1565–1800* (Sevilla: Escuela de Estudios Hispano-Americanos, 1959), 562 pp.

[61] Frederick J. Zwierlein, *Theodore Roosevelt and Catholics, 1882–1919* (St. Louis: The Rev. Victor T. Suren, 1956), xii, 392 pp.

[62] Madrid, 1944 ff.   [63] Madrid, 1914 ff.   [64] Valladolid, 1914 ff.

the Philippines the principal one is *Philippine Studies*.[65] To commemorate the fourth centenary of the Christianization of the Philippines, the *Boletin Eclesiástico de Filipinas* published (in English) an issue devoted to various aspects of the evangelization of the Philippines. Though the articles are uneven in quality, some of them contain information not easily available elsewhere.[66]

Archives and Libraries

Extensive deposits of archival material for church history exist, in many cases almost untouched as yet. As might be expected from the close interrelationship of church and state, the Archivo General de Indias in Seville contains an enormous amount of material dealing with church history, either directly or indirectly, for the entire Spanish period up to about 1836. With the abolition of the Consejo de Indias, after a short period of experimentation with various ministries, the *Ministerio de Ultramar* handled Spain's colonial affairs till 1898. The archives of this Ministry are now in the Sección de Ultramar of the Archivo Histórico Nacional in Madrid. The principal category under which ecclesiastical affairs are to be found is that of "Gracia y Justicia," where, unfortunately, they are indiscriminately mixed with judicial documents, and no catalogues or inventories exist.[67]

The Archivo General de la Nación in Mexico contains much Philippine material, which, however, seems generally to be duplicated in Seville and Manila. The records of the Inquisition, however, would probably be most valuable there, since, unlike general civil and ecclesiastical government, the Inquisition in the Philippines remained dependent on Mexico.

[65] Manila, 1953 ff. See also *Philippiniana Sacra* (1966 ff.), published three times a year by University of Santo Tomás, Manila.

[66] Manila, XXXIX, no. 435 (Jan.–Feb., 1965), 352 pp.

[67] For a description of the Archivo de Indias and the Archivo Historico Nacional, see the extremely useful article of Ernest J. Burrus, S.J., "An Introduction to Bibliographical Tools in Spanish Archives and Manuscript Collections Relating to Hispanic America," *Hispanic-American Historical Review*, XXXV (1955), 444–83. Reference is here given to more detailed guides and catalogues of these archives. For Seville, specifically regarding the Philippines, see *BRPI*, LIII, 15–29.

More important than any of these, except perhaps Seville, are the archives of the religious orders. The Colegio de PP. Agustinos in Valladolid contains not only the archives of the Philippine Augustinians but likewise the extraordinarily rich Navarro collection of books on the Philippines, containing many titles not to be found elsewhere.[68] The archive of the Franciscans is found in the Colegio de PP. Franciscanos in Pastrana, Guadalajara, Spain, and though considerable use has been made of it in articles published in the *Archivo Ibero-Americano,* much of it is still unexploited. The Dominican archive, likewise very extensive, and relatively unexploited, still remains in the Philippines in the Convento de Santo Domingo, Quezon City. The Jesuit archives have been scattered to more than one place as a result of their expulsion from the Philippines in 1768. An important part of these pre-1768 documents is to be found in the "'Papeles de Jesuítas" in the Real Academia de Historia in Madrid.[69] A complement of these is in the section "Clero regular y secular" in the Archivo Histórico Nacional.[70] A certain amount of earlier Jesuit material, together with the documentation of the nineteenth and early twentieth century, will be found in the Archivo de la Provincia de Tarragona de la Compañía de Jesús in the Colegio de San Francisco de Borja in San Cugat del Vallés, Barcelona. Also in this archive is the Pastells collection of transcripts from the Archivo de Indias and elsewhere, which, though containing documents on all phases of Philippine history, is heavily ecclesiastical.[71]

The Roman archives contain less than might be expected on the church in the Philippines. For not only was direct communication with the Holy See generally prohibited under the regime of the patronato, though often carried on clandestinely, but some of the orders were governed from Spain in almost complete independence of their Roman superiors during much of these three

---

[68] There are plans to publish much of the archival material, as well as the catalogue of the books.

[69] For further descriptions, see *BRPI,* LIII, 30–31; Burrus, *op. cit.,* p. 471.

[70] Burrus, *op. cit.,* p. 463.

[71] For a description of the Pastells collection and its origin, see Francisco Mateos, S.J., "La Colección Pastells de documentos sobre América y Filipinas," *Revista de Indias,* VIII (1947), 7–52.

centuries.[72] The Jesuits, however, have extensive material in the Archivum Romanum Societatis Iesu, which has been microfilmed for the Pius XII Library at St. Louis University.[73]

In the United States the important manuscript collection for Philippine church history is that of the Newberry Library in Chicago, though much of this has been published in translation in Blair and Robertson.[74] The other collection of importance is the already-mentioned microfilm collection of St. Louis University, containing Jesuit documents both from Rome and from San Cugat del Vallés.

In the Philippines, besides the important Dominican archives at the Convento de Santo Domingo and in the University of Santo Tomás, there is the Philippine National Archives. Until recently badly housed and uncatalogued,[75] it has now been transferred to the National Library, where its organization and cataloguing has begun. The Ateneo de Manila University also possesses a large microfilm collection of documents, including duplicates of the St. Louis University Philippine materials, and a good deal of the more important manuscript and printed works from Spain and the United States, particularly on the Jesuits.

The most important collections of books on the Philippine church are those of the Biblioteca Nacional in Madrid, and of the Augustinians in Valladolid; the British Museum; and, in the United States, the Newberry Library,[76] the New York Public Li-

[72] For information on the various Roman and other Italian archives see Ernest J. Burrus, S.J., "Research Opportunities in Italian Archives and Manuscript Collections for Students of Hispanic American History," *Hispanic-American Historical Review*, XXXIX (1959), 428–63, especially 430–44.

[73] Briefly described in Phelan, *op. cit.*, pp. 203–204.

[74] See Paul S. Lietz, *Calendar of Philippine Documents in the Ayer Collection of the Newberry Library* (Chicago: The Newberry Library, 1956), xvi, 259 pp.

[75] A brief survey of the conditions and contents by Edgar B. Wickberg, "Spanish Records in the Philippine National Archives," *Hispanic-American Historical Review*, XXXV (1955), 77–89.

[76] Doris Varner Welsh, *A Catalogue of Printed Materials Relating to the Philippine Islands, 1519–1900, in the Newberry Library* (Chicago: The Newberry Library, 1959), viii, 179 pp. Further books and manuscripts have been added to the Newberry collections since the publication of this book and that of Lietz in note 74.

brary, and the Library of Congress.[77] Scarcely any collection in the Philippines, except that of the University of Santo Tomás, can compare with these great collections abroad, especially since the destruction of most of the Philippine National Library during the Second World War.

II

The Philippine Independent Church

The Philippines Calling by Louis C. Cornish contributes toward an understanding, in part, of the position of the Philippine Independent Church just prior to World War II.[78] Dr. Cornish, who had been president of the American Unitarian Association and was then president of the International Association for Liberal Christianity, visited the Philippines at the invitation of *Obispo Maximo* Gregorio Aglipay, and was made an honorary president of the Philippine Independent Church. In this book, Dr. Cornish reports on his visit and on the religious situation in the Philippines, especially the background and beliefs of the Philippine Independent Church, as he understood them and as they were related to the Unitarian movement in other parts of the world.

In the years following the war, there was considerable research and writing on the history of the Philippine Independent Church as it prepared to enter into a concordat of full communion with the Protestant Episcopal Church in the United States in 1961. *Struggle for Freedom* is a highly favorable study of the "History of the Philippine Independent Church" by Lewis Bliss Whittemore, a bishop of the Protestant Episcopal Church, that is marred somewhat by careless errors in names, dates, and certain factual accounts.[79] *Religious Revolution in the Philippines* is a highly

---

[77] A. P. C. Griffin, *A List of Books (with References to Periodicals) in the Library of Congress* (Washington, D.C.: U.S. Government Printing Office, 1903), xv, 397 pp. Of course, the collection has grown considerably since 1903.

[78] Philadelphia: Dorrance and Co., 1942, 313 pp.

[79] Greenwich, Conn.: Seabury Press; and London: S.P.C.K., 1961, xi, 228 pp. See the critical review of Whittemore's book by Achútegui and

critical study of "The Life and Church of Gregorio Aglipay: 1860–1960" by two Jesuit scholars, Pedro S. de Achútegui and Miguel A. Bernad, who do not conceal their prejudice against Aglipay and his church in their interpretation of the records.[80] Isacio R. Rodríguez, a Spanish Augustinian, has also published a critical two-volume study, *Gregorio Aglipay y los Orígenes de la Iglesia Filipina Independiente* (*1895–1917*), of which the second volume contains 371 pages of documents, with 28 pages of indices and cross references.[81] The Ph.D. dissertation by Sister Mary Dorita Clifford, B.V.M. on "Aglipayanism as a Political Movement," for Saint Louis University (Missouri), 1960, contains a wealth of research material and an exceedingly valuable bibliography.[82] *The Christian Register* is a monthly magazine published by the Philippine Independent Church.[83] The archives of the church are located in the library at Saint Andrew's Theological Seminary in Quezon City.

Bernad in *Philippine Studies*, X, 4 (1962), 684–705, and in Vol. II of their *Religious Revolution in the Philippines*, pp. 424–31.

[80] Three vols.; Manila: Ateneo de Manila, 1960–1969 (Vol. I, 2nd ed. rev., 1961, xiv, 588 pp.; Vol. II, 2nd ed. rev., 1968, xiv, 502 pp.; Vol. III, Documentary appendix, 1969). See the critical comment on the historical method of Achútegui and Bernad by William Henry Scott, "The Proper Use of Documents," *Philippine Studies*, XI, 2 (1963), 328–35; and "Reply to Mr. Scott" by Achútegui and Bernad, *ibid.*, pp. 335–41. See also the important critical review of Vol. II by Peter G. Gowing, "An Anti-Independiente Tract," *Silliman Journal*, XV, 2 (1968), 304–308.

[81] Two vols.; Madrid: Consejo Superior de Investigaciones Científicas. Departamento de Misionología Española, 1960 (Vol. I, xxxii, 597 pp.; Vol. II, 399 pp.).

[82] Ann Arbor, Michigan: University Microfilms, 1960, vii, 585 pp. See also two M.A. theses dealing with the P.I.C., both done at University of the Philippines, which have been published and are frequently cited, though they are less thorough and scholarly than some later studies (Juan A. Rivera, "The Aglipayan Movement" [University of the Philippines, 1932], *The Philippine Social Science Review* [Manila], IX, 4 [1937], 301–28, and X, 1 [1938], 9–34; and Francis H. Wise, "The History of the Philippine Independent Church" [University of the Philippines, 1955], mimeographed in 1965 by Silliman University College of Theology, St. Andrew's Theological Seminary, and Union Theological Seminary, 273 pp.). The Rivera thesis is especially significant because it was done before World War II by an *Indepentiente* who actually interviewed Aglipay.

[83] Philippine Independent Church, 1327 Calle Alfredo, Sta. Cruz, Manila. Cf. *Concordat*, published quarterly by the Joint Council of the Episcopal Church and the Philippine Independent Church (P.O. Box 3167, Manila).

The Protestant Churches

Islands Under the Cross by Peter G. Gowing is a comprehensive and critical study, including a lengthy bibliography, of the whole period of Philippine church history, from the pen of a reliable Protestant scholar.[84] Another bibliographical source is the Philippines section in *Christianity in Southeast Asia: A Bibliographical Guide*, edited by Gerald H. Anderson.[85]

From the period of Protestant beginnings in the Philippines, the two most important books are *The New Era in the Philippines* by Arthur Judson Brown,[86] a Presbyterian missions executive, and *The Philippines and the Far East* by Homer C. Stuntz, a Methodist missionary in Manila.[87] Brown's book was written in New York after a visit to the Philippines and is generally more reliable than that by Stuntz which was written "on the scene." *Protestantism in the Philippines: Its Relation to the State, to the Roman Catholic Church, and to the People* was a published sermon that had been preached in Manila on Sunday, December 21, 1902, by the Rev. George F. Pentecost, in which he attempted to explain the aim and purpose of Protestant missions in the Philippines.[88] Henry Otis Dwight, the recording secretary of the Amer-

[84] Manila: National Council of Churches in the Philippines, 1967, xvi, 286 pp.; rev. ed., Grand Rapids: William B. Eerdmans Publishing Co., 1969.

[85] New York: Missionary Research Library; and New Haven: Yale Southeast Asia Studies, 1966, pp. 51–59. See also "Missionary Readings on the Philippines: A Guide" by the same writer in the *Occasional Bulletin* from the Missionary Research Library (New York), XV, 7–8 (1964), 12 pp.; revised and reprinted in *Silliman Journal*, XII, 2 (1965), 211–27.

[86] New York: Fleming H. Revell, Co., 1903, 314 pp. See John Marvin Dean, *The Cross of Christ in Bolo-Land* (New York: Fleming H. Revell Co., 1902), 233 pp., for another account of Protestant beginnings, with special reference to Y.M.C.A. work.

[87] Cincinnati: Jennings and Pye, 1904, 514 pp. An earlier book, *Old Glory and the Gospel in the Philippines* by Alice Byran Condict, M.D. (New York: Fleming H. Revell Co., 1902), 124 pp., was more general in its observations and of value primarily only for some comments in the prefatory note by Methodist Bishop Frank W. Warne, and the author's discussion about the formation of the Evangelical Union in 1901. One Catholic scholar has commented on Condict's book, "Evidently separation of church-state applied to the Roman Catholic Church only, for this author, who writes as if Protestantism were the religion of America" (Clifford dissertation, *op. cit.*, p. 558).

[88] Manila: American Bible Society, 1903, 22 pp.

ican Bible Society, recounted—with strong tones of anti-Roman Catholic sentiment—the beginnings of the Bible Society work, in his pamphlet of 1916, *Light After Dark Centuries in the Philippines*.[89]

One of the most frequently quoted Protestant studies of the first twenty-five years of missionary work is *The People of the Philippines* by Frank C. Laubach.[90] Dr. Laubach, who started his world-famous career as a missionary in the Philippines, was not primarily a historian and this book tends to be rather homiletical, but it is still a valuable survey, in part, of Philippine religion. *Religious Education in the Philippines* by Archie Lowell Ryan contains some material on the general history of Protestant missionary work in the Philippines as well as the story of this particular movement with which the author was associated.[91] *Evangelical Christianity in the Philippines* by Camilo Osias and Avelina Lorenzana, which was published in 1931, represents one of the first efforts by Filipinos to write a substantial account of Protestant work.[92] *The Filipino Church* by Walter N. Roberts is "The Story of the Development of an Indigenous Evangelical Church in the Philippine Islands as Revealed in the Work of 'The Church of the United Brethren in Christ,'" from 1901 to 1936.[93] Dr. James B. Rodgers was the first regularly appointed Protestant missionary in the Philippines and his book *Forty Years in the Philippines*, which is notable for its irenic spirit, is one of the most important references for the early period of Protestant work.[94] *From Carabao to Clipper* by Dr. and Mrs. E. K. Higdon, distinguished missionaries from the Disciples of

[89] New York: American Bible Society, 1916, 19 pp.

[90] New York: George H. Doran Co., 1925, 515 pp.

[91] Manila: Methodist Publishing House for The Philippine Council of Religious Education, 1930, 205 pp.

[92] Dayton, Ohio: United Brethren Publishing House, 1931, xx, 240 pp. For an interesting and important contribution to the study of Protestant beginnings by a Filipino scholar, see: T. Valentino Sitoy, Jr., "An Abortive Spanish Protestant Mission in the Philippines," *Silliman Journal*, XV, 2 (1968), 243–80.

[93] Dayton, Ohio: Foreign Missionary Society . . . United Brethren in Christ, 1936, x, 158 pp.

[94] New York: Board of Foreign Missions of the Presbyterian Church in the U.S.A., 1940, viii, 205 pp. See also Rodgers earlier report, *Twenty Years of Presbyterian Work in the Philippines* (Supplement to the *Philippine Presbyterian*, 1919).

Christ, was written just prior to World War II and presents a
popular but reliable report on the progress and problems of evangelical Christianity during the first forty years.[95]

Popular studies of denominational missions would include:
Isles of Opportunity by Lee Donald Warren,[96] an early book on
Seventh-Day Adventist work; *Philippine Kaleidoscope* by Vincent
H. Gowen,[97] an illustrated introduction to the mission of the
Protestant Episcopal Church on the eve of World War II; *Mis-
sion to the Philippines* by Joseph S. Pitts [98] for the Church of the
Nazarene; *The Story of Methodism in the Philippines* by Richard
L. Deats,[99] which covers the period from 1899 to 1963 in ad-
mirable fashion; *Beyond Cotabato* by Curran L. Spottswood,[100]
a popular account of the personal experiences of Methodism's
"Flying Missionary" in the Philippines after World War II; and
That They May Be One by Enrique C. Sobrepeña,[101] which is a
brief account of the united church movement which led to the
formation of the United Church of Christ in the Philippines in
1948. *Multiplying Churches in the Philippines* by Donald A. Mc-
Gavran [102] is a study of church growth and evangelistic strategy
in the United Church of Christ. *The Book of Common Worship* [103] and *The Book of Government: Constitution and By-
Laws* [104] of the United Church of Christ are essential documents

[95] New York: Friendship Press, 1941, 120 pp. *Fifty Years of Attack and
Controversy* by Stephen J. Corey (St. Louis: Christian Board of Publication
for The Committee on Publication of the Corey Manuscript, 1953), pp. 85–
126, discusses with documentary details the controversy and split within the
Disciples of Christ mission in the Philippines in the period 1922–1926, in
which Higdon was a figure.

[96] Washington, D.C.: Review and Herald Publishing Association, 1928,
224 pp.

[97] New York: National Council, Protestant Episcopal Church (1939), 72
pp. Cf. Constance White Wentzel, *A Half Century in the Philippines* (New
York: National Council, Protestant Episcopal Church, 1952), 64 pp.

[98] Kansas City, Missouri: Beacon Hill Press, 1956, 127 pp.

[99] Manila: Published for Union Theological Seminary by the National
Council of Churches in the Philippines, 1964, xi, 129 pp.

[100] Westwood, N.J.: Fleming H. Revell Co., 1961, 256 pp.

[101] 2nd ed., Manila: United Church of Christ in the Philippines, 1964, vii,
177 pp.

[102] Manila: United Church of Christ in the Philippines, 1958, 145 pp.

[103] Quezon City: United Church of Christ in the Philippines, 1962, vi,
186 pp.

[104] Quezon City: United Church of Christ in the Philippines, n.d., 72 pp.

for understanding the faith and order of the largest Protestant denomination in the Philippines.

Three books of sermons by Filipino preachers represent the mind and spirit of contemporary evangelical preaching: *Rebuilding Our Broken Faith* by Cirilo A. Rigos,[105] *Call to Moral Renewal* by Enrique C. Sobrepeña,[106] and the collection of *Selected Philippine Sermons.*[107]

Those who have a special interest in ministerial education should see the comprehensive *Survey Report on Theological Education in the Philippines* by Walter N. Roberts and others, which includes a detailed study of five seminaries and six Bible and deaconess training colleges, in addition to a wealth of other valuable information.[108] *The Evangelical Ministry in the Philippines and Its Future* by Albert J. Sanders discusses the problems and prospects that are peculiar in some measure to the ministry in the Philippines; the author was a long-term Presbyterian missionary in the Philippines and formerly president of Union Theological Seminary in Manila.[109]

Nationalism and Christianity in the Philippines by Richard L. Deats is a scholarly study of the response to nationalism by the Roman Catholic Church, the Philippine Independent Church, the Methodist Church, and the United Church of Christ in the Philippines.[110] *The Religious Thought of José Rizal: Its Context and Theological Significance* is a thorough study by Eugene A. Hessel of the writings of the national hero.[111] *Philippine Social Issues*

[105] Manila: Cosmopolitan Church, 1964, xiv, 272 pp.

[106] Manila: United Church of Christ in the Philippines, 1963; 2nd ed., 1964, vii, 83 pp. Cf. an earlier volume of sermons by the same writer, *A New Emphasis in Religion* (Manila: The United Church of Manila, 1925), xii, 114 pp.

[107] Manila: Published for Union Theological Seminary by the National Council of Churches in the Philippines, 1967, vi, 110 pp.

[108] Mimeographed; Quezon City: Philippine Federation of Christian Churches, 1962, vi, 207 pp.

[109] Manila: Published for Union Theological Seminary by the National Council of Churches in the Philippines, 1964, 70 pp.

[110] Dallas: Southern Methodist University Press, 1967, ix, 207 pp. For additional insight into nationalism and religion in the Philippines, see *Cults Honoring Rizal* by Marcelino A. Foronda, Jr. (Manila, 1960), 98 pp.

[111] Manila: Philippine Education Co., 1961, xii, 289 pp. A major review of Hessel's book by John N. Schumacher, S.J., appeared in *Philippine Studies*, XIII, 3 (1965), 707–21.

from a Christian Perspective is a Protestant symposium edited by Richard P. Poethig.[112]

The following journals have devoted whole issues to special articles and reviews dealing with Christianity in the Philippines, with emphasis on the Protestant churches and the ecumenical situation: *The South East Asia Journal of Theology* (Singapore) for July, 1962, and October, 1967; *Evangelische Missions-Zeitschrift* (Hamburg) for May, 1964; and *Silliman Journal* (Dumaguete City) for April–June, 1965.

The *1962–1963 Philippines Christian Yearbook*, edited by Benjamin I. Guansing, includes a listing of Protestant denominations, missionaries, Filipino pastors, church-related institutions, and several interpretative articles.[113] There are also *The National Directory of the Philippine Independent Church*,[114] and the *UCCP Yearbook*.[115] *Churches and Sects in the Philippines* by Douglas J. Elwood is the most comprehensive descriptive study of contemporary religious group movements that has been published.[116]

A selection of the journals published under Protestant auspices would include the *Silliman Journal*,[117] *Church and Community*, published by the United Church of Christ,[118] *The Philippine Chronicle* from the Philippine Episcopal Church,[119] and *The Philippine Lutheran*.[120]

[112] Manila: United Church of Christ in the Philippines, 1963, 222 pp.

[113] Manila: Union Theological Seminary, 1962, xvi, 161 pp. See also the *Philippine Missionary Directory for 1967–1968* (Manila: Philippine Crusades, 1967), 112 pp., for a listing of the names and addresses of 1,251 Protestant missionaries and 57 Protestant mission agencies working in the Philippines.

[114] Manila: The National Directory Committee of the Philippine Independent Church, 1963, vi, 130 pp.

[115] Manila: United Church of Christ in the Philippines, 1964, 64 pp., appendices. See also the annual reports of the Philippine Episcopal Church (Quezon City), and the yearly *Journals* of the five annual conferences of The United Methodist Church in the Philippines (Manila: United Methodist Church Headquarters).

[116] Dumaguete City: Silliman University, 1968, xi, 213 pp. See the critical "Review Article" by P. S. de Achútegui, S.J., in *Philippine Studies*, XVI, 3 (1968), 577–86.

[117] Dumaguete City: Silliman University (quarterly).

[118] Quezon City: United Church of Christ in the Philippines (bimonthly).

[119] Manila: Philippine Episcopal Church (bimonthly).

[120] Manila: Lutheran Philippine Mission (quarterly).

The two best Protestant libraries for the study of Philippine church history are the Missionary Research Library at Union Theological Seminary in New York City, and the Day Missions Collection at Yale Divinity School Library in New Haven, Connecticut. Several important archives for Protestant missionary work are located in New York City: the United Presbyterian Mission Library and the library of the Board of Missions of the United Methodist Church are in the Interchurch Center at 475 Riverside Drive; the Y.M.C.A. Historical Library is at 291 Broadway; and the American Bible Society Library is at Broadway and 61st Street. Other archives are to be found in the headquarters of the American Baptist Convention at Valley Forge, Pennsylvania; in the Harvard College Library and the Andover-Harvard Library in Cambridge, Massachusetts, for the archives of the American Board of Commissioners for Foreign Missions of the former Congregational Churches (now the United Church of Christ in the U.S.A.); in the library of the United Christian Missionary Society in Indianapolis, and the Disciples of Christ Historical Society in Nashville, Tennessee; at Episcopal Theological Seminary of the Southwest in Austin, Texas, for Episcopal Church mission archives; and in the Manuscript Division of the Library of Congress in Washington, D.C. for Bishop Charles H. Brent's Papers.

The Iglesia ni Cristo

The *Iglesia ni Cristo* represents a unique and significant movement on the Philippine religious scene, about which there is relatively little literature of substance. One of the earliest studies of importance was *Iglesia ni Kristo: A Study,* the M.A. thesis by Julita Reyes-Sta. Romana that was published in the *Journal of East Asiatic Studies* (University of Manila).[121] *A Historico-Critical Study on the Iglesia ni Kristo* by Manuel P. Alonzo, Jr., is the effort of a Roman Catholic priest to analyze, evaluate, and refute the teachings of the *Iglesia,* from the standpoint of orthodox

---

[121] IV, 3 (1955), 329–437. Includes extensive bibliography, hymns, and illustrative documents such as the Articles of Incorporation. See the same author's "Membership and Norm of Discipline in the *Iglesia ni Kristo,*" *Philippine Sociological Review,* III, 1 (1955), 4–14.

Catholic theology.[122] Alonzo's book also contains six pages of valuable bibliography. Joseph J. Kavanagh, S.J., published several critical articles on the *Iglesia* in *Philippine Studies,* including one that made a careful study of articles appearing from 1951 to 1961 in *Pasugo,* the official journal of the *Iglesia.*[123] *A Protestant View of the Iglesia ni Cristo* by Albert J. Sanders provides an excellent summary of the movement's history and teaching, as well as a critical appraisal.[124] In 1969 an official booklet, *55th Anniversary of the Iglesia ni Cristo, 1914–1969,* appeared in attractive format with informative articles on the history, missions, social outreach, radio stations, voting power of the *Iglesia,* and a directory of church officials.[125]

[122] Manila: U.S.T. Press, operated by Novel Publishing Co., 1959, 102 pp.

[123] "The Iglesia ni Cristo," *Philippine Studies,* III, 1 (1955), 19–42; "The Stars That Fall—And Mr. Manalo," *ibid.,* III, 3 (1955), 289–96; "The Voice of the Iglesia ni Cristo: 1951–1961," *ibid.,* IX, 4 (1961), 651–65.

[124] Quezon City: Philippine Federation of Christian Churches, 1962, 77 pp.

[125] Manila: Iglesia ni Cristo, 1969, 178 pp.

Contributors

Gerald H. Anderson, Professor of Church History and Ecumenics, Union Theological Seminary, Philippines.

J. Gayo Aragón, O.P., Provincial, Dominican Province of the Most Holy Rosary of the Philippines.

H. Ellsworth Chandlee, Professor of Liturgics, Saint Andrew's Theological Seminary, Quezon City.

Sister Mary Dorita Clifford, B.V.M., Assistant Professor and Chairman of the Department of History, Clarke College, Dubuque, Iowa.

Horacio de la Costa, S.J., Provincial, The Philippine Province of the Society of Jesus.

James S. Cummins, Reader in Spanish and Head of the Department of Hispanic Studies, University College, London.

Richard L. Deats, Professor of Social Ethics, Union Theological Seminary, Philippines.

Douglas J. Elwood, Professor of Systematic Theology, The Divinity School, Silliman University, Dumaguete City.

Peter G. Gowing, Professor of Christian History and World Religions, The Divinity School, Silliman University, Dumaguete City.

León Ma. Guerrero, Ambassador of the Philippines to the Court of St. James (1954–1962), to Madrid (1962–1966), and to New Delhi (1966–   ).

Eugene A. Hessel, Professor of New Testament, Union Theological Seminary, Philippines.

Cesar Adib Majul, Dean, College of Arts and Sciences, University of the Philippines.

Conrad Myrick, Professor of History, Saint Andrew's Theological Seminary, and Dean, Cathedral Church of St. Mary and St. John, Quezon City.

Stephen Neill, sometime Professor of Missions and Ecumenical Theology, University of Hamburg, Germany; formerly Anglican Bishop of Tinnevelly, India.

413

John Leddy Phelan, Professor of History, University of Wisconsin, Madison.

Albert J. Sanders, Presbyterian missionary in the Philippines over a period of thirty-seven years; President of Union Theological Seminary, Philippines, 1946–1954; presently on assignment in the United States as consultant for theological education overseas.

John N. Schumacher, S.J., Associate Professor of Church History, Loyola House of Studies, Ateneo de Manila University.

William Henry Scott, Professor of History, Trinity College of Quezon City.

Index